Red Ink

A volume in the SUNY series, Native Traces

Gerald Vizenor and Deborah L. Madsen, editors

Red Ink

Native Americans Picking Up the Pen in the Colonial Period

Drew Lopenzina

SUNY PRESS

Certain portions of chapter five appeared in a slightly altered form in *The American Quarterly*, vol. 58, num. 4, Dec. 2006 issue.

Published by State University of New York Press, Albany

Printed in the United States of America

For information, contact State University of New York Press, Albany, NY
www.sunypress.edu

Production by Diane Ganeles
Marketing by Anne M. Valentine

Library of Congress Cataloging-in-Publication Data

Lopenzina, Drew.
Red ink : native Americans picking up the pen in the colonial period / Drew Lopenzina.
p. cm. — (Native traces)
Includes bibliographical references and index.
ISBN 978-1-4384-3979-2 (hardcover : alk. paper)
ISBN 978-1-4384-3978-5 (pbk. : alk. paper)
1. American literature—Indian authors—History and criticism. 2. American literature—Colonial period, ca. 1600–1775—History and criticism. 3. Indians in literature. 4. Indians of North America—Intellectual life. I. Title.

PS153.I52L67 2012
810.9'897—dc22 2011009763

10 9 8 7 6 5 4 3 2 1

Contents

Illustrations

Preface

This work takes for its title *Red Ink*, which implies not only the written literary output of Native Americans in the colonial period, but the great difficulties of accessing a literature so over-inscribed by colonial norms and expectations—a literature that has been compulsively "corrected" with the red ink of the colonial educator, novelist, historian, moviemaker—in short, the ubiquitous productions of a dominant culture. *Red Ink* also invokes the bloody backdrop upon which such a literature came into being, the often violent tensions of "contact" and the processes of cultural containment that are endlessly reinforced, resisted, internalized, and contested in the archival remnants of such encounters. This is a work that centers upon the nature of power, how it constructs its own provisional realities through the superstructure of master narratives, and how Native American writers have historically endeavored to reassert their own identities in the face of such power, maintaining ligaments of cultural narratives and belief systems that work to subtly subvert or defy imposed narratives of dominance.

My focus here is on the period known as "colonial," a time when Native peoples are not presumed to be engaging in literary endeavors. Part of what I want to delineate is how those early Native writers whose works do, in fact, appear in the colonial archive are not tacitly turning their backs on traditional lifeways, as might often appear to be the case, but are actually negotiating a crucial set of tools and circumstances upon which survival and cultural continuance hinges. In most cases, however, their stories and the historical possibilities made available through their lives and works have remained untold or inadequately examined by the forces that cobble together the dominant narratives of history and literature in this country. If we begin to create a narrative space for these stories to breathe and grow, however, it also becomes possible to imagine new possibilities branching out from such roots, different understandings and modes of interacting with the past and the present that begin to form the materials for a narrative of what Anishinaabe poet and critic Gerald Vizenor refers to as *survivance*.

One realization I carry away from this effort is just how powerful a role narrative plays in our lives. That may appear to be an overly generalized statement, and yet it seems we are held in near absolute thrall by the cultural narratives to which we come of age, regardless of whether these narratives support and strengthen us as a people, or ruthlessly knock us down and fragment us. When events do not conform to the master narratives informing our lives, we are psychologically skilled at collectively ignoring or devaluing the resistant elements. I imagine that all cultures are equally susceptible to the sort of suggestibility of which I speak. But the disadvantage colonized cultures face in a world that strains under a largely white hegemonic power structure is that a significant number of peoples have found their own cultural narratives devalued, ignored, or systematically repressed. Often they are forced to live in the shadows of master narratives that brutally denigrate their own lives and identities. Few suspect how difficult it is to push against such narrative currents or how dangerous it is to switch horses in midstream, so to speak.

The point here is not necessarily to affix blame, but ultimately it is the regime in power that must answer for its policies, mistakes, ideologies, and abuses. If I find myself being somewhat more reflexively critical of Euro-American epistemologies than of Native epistemologies in this work, this results from the fact that I live in a moment largely constructed by the force and will of long-maintained Western values, and I feel the world would benefit from a healthy reexamination of how those values have become locked in place and where they have ultimately failed us. So much of Native tradition has been held in a colonial lockbox, unable to breathe or fully express itself on a world stage because of the illusion of totality that is conjured up in written histories. One small way that I can contribute to breaking down the psychological hegemony of white Euro-American-Western culture is to bear witness to what emerges when we begin to carefully disentangle Native voices of the past from the sophisticated historical containments in which they have been held right through to the present.

This has proven an exciting project for me, and one that has kept me riding a fast-moving and ever-expanding learning curve throughout. *Red Ink* was written against the backdrop of America's decade-long wars with Iraq and Afghanistan, and the provocatively nondescript "War on Terror"—a designation prescribing that such war might be waged unto perpetuity. Regardless of how this current moment in history resolves itself, the fears, the willful ignorance, the forces of exploitation that fan its fires are familiar to students of literature and history. An entire people are at once demonized and trivialized in response to the acts of a few, so that the only response seems to be a benevolent, if forceful, intervention. Just as it once seemed important for Christians to impose their system of belief upon foreign cultures—violently if need be—it now appears an imperative to "advance democracy" into regions that are deemed incapable of organizing their own peaceful existence. All the while the aggressors turn a blind eye to their historical role in contributing to the instability of these regions, and downplay the vital economic resources that fall within their grasp as a result of assuming authority over a conquered people. Replace oil with wampum, and we find ourselves in the Pequot War of 1636–1637 all over again.

These are age-old tactics, and no one practices them with more ruthless efficiency than the enlightened West. So *do* read this as an indictment of all those who put in motion such cynical forces, regardless of their cultural orientation or stated intentions. But also consider that when I frequently employ the pronoun "we," I do so from a personal conviction that, regardless of differing belief systems or the cultural narratives that shape and define us, there is not all that much differentiating us as human beings on this planet. Our culturally informed belief systems are in some ways mere window dressing in comparison to everything that unites us as a species, and rather than constantly emphasizing our differences or the inability to determine or construct meaning, this work makes a bid for ethical commitments based upon listening and witnessing, upon sounding out the right words and putting them in motion to heal old historical wounds, upon the conviction that language itself is a form of commitment. It is a modest attempt to wipe the tears from the eyes, the dirt from the ears, and to remove the obstructions from the throat to achieve what is known amongst certain indigenous nations of the Northeast as "Gaiwiio," or good mind.

In this effort, it is important for me not to forget some of the people who assisted me, or contributed to this work in significant ways along the journey. First of all I thank my wife and children, who supported and encouraged me through many long hours, days, months, and years of work. There is a tendency to underestimate the sheer commitment in time a project like this demands, and nobody felt those demands, the false starts and finishes, more acutely than my immediate family, who nevertheless helped carry me through to the end. I can honestly say that I could not have accomplished any of this without you. I am greatly indebted to my professors and mentors at the University of New Hampshire, in particular, to Siobhan Senier, who nudged me in all the right directions when I embarked upon this effort, but also to Brigitte Bailey and John Ernest, who were always incredibly generous with their time and advice during the early stages of this book. All of you helped to instill the discipline and appreciation for the finer points of critical discourse that steered me toward my first publications and afforded me the intellectual tools to pursue this project. Heartfelt thanks must go out to Gerald Vizenor, who graciously extended himself when he didn't have to in order to launch this project, and to Deborah Madsen for her astute editorial advice and encouragement. Also thanks go out to Lisa Brooks and Rae Gould for insight and research advice at critical moments, as well as David Watters, Cynthia Van Zandt, Lee Bebout, and Greg Guthrie who all, at one phase or another, read portions of this work and offered helpful commentary. I would like to express my gratitude to Keith Botelho for long discussions over coffee and renegade Ping-Pong matches in the UNH rec room, for offering an extra pair of eyes on the manuscript, and for being the kind of colleague who challenges as well as inspires. Thanks to my old and dear friend Terry Stigers, who brought a distinctive level of detail to the maps he designed for this book. I would like to express appreciation to the librarians and staff at the various archives where I worked, but in particular the Massachusetts Archives, the Connecticut Historical Society, the Rauner Special Collections, and the Stockbridge Town Library. Thanks must also go out to James Peltz, Michael Rinella, Diane Ganeles, and everyone else at SUNY Press for taking this project on and bringing it to fruition. I would like to express appreciation to Greg Brennan for remaining endlessly interested and Pete Lopenzina for hosting evening volleyball tournaments after long days at the computer. My students deserve credit and thanks for keeping me grounded in what really matters. How can I properly express the gratitude I feel toward Betty Morrison whose faith and encouragement never failed to surprise me and buoy my spirits while writing this book? Although it saddens me that she will not see the final product, she never once entertained a doubt that it would finally get here. And I also cannot forget to thank my mother and father, who offered patience, love, and support whenever needed for this project and all my others, for modeling extraordinary values that have carried with me over the years, and for occasionally providing a quiet place to write.

Abbreviations

AN — Second Autobiographical Narrative, Samson Occom, Second Draft, September 17, 1768. The original draft is located in the Rauner Special Collections at Dartmouth College.

CHS — Occom Papers at the Connecticut Historical Society.

CMHS — *Collections of the Massachusetts Historical Society.*

ET — *The Eliot Tracts*, ed. Michael P. Clark (Westport, CT: Praeger Press, 2003).

JR — *Jesuit Relations and Allied Documents: Travels and Explorations of the Jesuit Missionaries in New France, 1610–1791*, ed. Reuben Gold Thwaites, trans. Finlow Alexander, Percy Favor Bicknell, William Frederic Giese, Crawford Lindsay, and William Price (New York: Pageant Book Company, 1959).

MA — Massachusetts State Archives.

OP — Occom Papers at Rauner Special Collections at Dartmouth College.

PL — Pittsfield Library Special Collections.

RCNP — *Records of the Colony of New Plymouth*, ed. David Pulsifer (Boston: Press of William White, 1861).

RMBC — *Records of the Governor and Company of the Massachusetts Bay Colony in New England* (Boston: Press of William White, 1854).

SC — Sergeant Collection at the Stockbridge Town Library.

SISC — Stockbridge Indian Study Collection at the Stockbridge Town Library.

Introduction

Survival Writing

Contesting the "Pen and Ink Work" of Colonialism

> The United States insulates itself within an amnesia that doesn't acknowledge that kind of history. The victors (discoverers, settlers, real estate developers, government leaders, etc.) can afford that, it seems, as long as they maintain control and feel they don't have to face the truth. But Indians? What choice do we have?
>
> —Simon Ortiz, *From Sand Creek*

> But spring is floating / to the canyon rim; / needles burst yellow / And the stories have built a new house.
>
> —Wendy Rose, "Story Keeper," *Halfbreed Chronicles and Other Poems*

William Apess: Nineteenth-Century Postindian Warrior

In 1829 William Apess, a member of the Pequot tribe of Indians by birth and an itinerant Methodist minister by trade, offered a poignant articulation concerning the power and influence of writing and how it had, in effect, shaped the consciousness of nineteenth-century Americans in a manner detrimental to Natives. He wrote in his autobiographical *A Son of the Forest*, that

> The Indian character . . . has been greatly misrepresented. Justice has not and, I may add, justice cannot be fully done to them by the historian. My people have had no press to record their sufferings or to make known their grievances; on this account many a tale of blood and woe has never been known to the public. And during the wars between the natives and the whites, the latter could, through the medium of the newspaper press, circulate extensively every exaggerated account of "Indian cruelty," while the poor natives had no means of gaining the public ear.[1]

Apess was amongst the earliest of Native Americans to commit a chronologically organized idea of his life to pen and ink. In 1829 he published his autobiography, which spoke of his maturation from an abused and discarded child of Pequot stock to a practitioner of the Christian faith who used his considerable energy, talent, and wit to spread a syncretic brand of spirituality amongst the economically marginalized and struggling indigenous populations of New England.[2] Like a handful of other Native figures of his era who, against considerable cultural and institutional odds, made their way into the realm of print discourse, Apess seemed to have found in Christian evangelism a strategy for survival as well as a venue for doing good amongst his people.

While Apess' Christianity appears to have been perfectly sincere, it is also true that the conventions of his time hardly allowed for him to publicly express his identity in any other manner. As a result, for many generations his life story (and the stories of most writing Indians of this era) was more or less understood as a Christian conversion narrative exemplifying the mandated trajectory of colonial hegemony in which the savage child of the forest willingly takes on the presumably more civilized conduct and beliefs of Western tradition in an effort to lift himself up from the ruins of his race. This narrative was (and is) a form of containment. As long as Apess' story could be fitted within such a crucial dominant paradigm it remained possible to overlook the many instances of resistance and defiance that surface, at times none too subtly, in his body of work.

Apess was not in a complete rhetorical wilderness however. Some sixty years prior to Apess' autobiography, the Mohegan preacher Samson Occom had expressed his own concerns about being misrepresented by colonial powers. In 1768, he opened up a short narrative of his life with these words: "Having Seen and heard Several Representations . . . made by Some gentlemen in America, Concerning me, and finding many gross Mistakes in their Account,—I thought it my Duty to give a Short, Plain and Honest Account of myself, that those who may hereafter see it, may know the truth."[3] Like Apess, Occom apprehended the utility of constructing and circulating his own narrative in print to contest the many false suppositions concerning Indian identity that preceded him wherever he traveled.

That their works appeared in print at all was testament to the fact that both Apess and Occom had mastered certain conventions of speech and sentiment that rendered their messages palatable to colonial audiences. Both were professors of the Christian faith and both reflexively resorted to derogatory, but ubiquitous, terms like "my poor brethren" or "the sons and daughters of the forest" when referring in print to their fellow Indians. Such language, however demeaning or culturally biased toward colonial perspectives, had a proven track record of gaining the ears of its intended white audience. Almost invariably, however, these practitioners of red ink (the first Native writers to emerge in print), despite having taken the measure of the discursive expectations of their day, became controversial and conflicted figures in their time. While their publicized works were upheld as exemplary models of missionary successes in bringing to light a people who, according to many a colonial observer, had heretofore "sate in hellish darknesse," Native writers found themselves at perpetual cross purposes with colonial/evangelical concerns.[4] This often led to public denunciations or loss of stature in colonized space, as with Apess who found himself the target of concerted assaults by the press when he attempted to use his traveling pulpit and the power of the pen to argue for the sovereign land rights of the Mashpee Indians of Cape Cod in 1833. The local newspapers labeled Apess an embezzler, agitator, and one whose sermons were "injudicious and somewhat offensive."[5] While praised and ordained upon the basis of his early conversion rhetoric, once Apess turned his attention to causes more sympathetic to Native concerns, he was reviled by an evangelical community more interested in Indian subordination than congregation.

The events and stories that shaped Apess' life drew him to the aforementioned conclusion that "justice has not, and I may add, justice cannot be done to them [the Indians] by the historian." History, as Apess saw it, was a closed book that had already inscribed its entries in indelible ink, having so convincingly cast the Indian in the role of "blood-thirsty savage," "child of the forest," and enemy of "civilization," that few could see around the offered representations or were capable of considering the Native of America a creation on equal footing with good, white, Christian folk. The functions of history-keeping remained, in fact, the central problematic of Apess' career as a writer, and I presume, as a preacher. He apprehended how print discourse had stamped a lasting impression upon the cognitive processes of the colonist, in which the Indian was "greatly misrepresented." Lacking presses, newspapers, or any other means of disseminating information to the public, the Indian seemingly had no tools to counteract the powerfully enduring narratives manifested in colonial writing or to relate the "many a tale of blood and woe [that] has never been [made] known to the public." If the historian could not do the Indian justice, then who would?

Apess' perception of this question and his nuanced response in his autobiography and other works make him, in my estimation, one of our earliest models of what Anishinaabe author and critic Gerald Vizenor calls the "postindian warrior." If the record of the colonist elaborately constructed and maintained a manufactured image of Indianess (a process that Vizenor refers to as "manifest manners"), Apess took it upon himself to gather up the loose makings of memory, experience, and impression, and fashion them into a construct by which he could begin to counter colonial representations with new and radical expressions of Native identity.[6] "My image is of God," he noted in his 1836 *Eulogy on King Philip*. "I am not a beast."[7]

Apess saw that, where one might hope to find posted a rich historical record of Native engagements and observances in the time of contact, we find instead a counter presence, a canard, a complex fiction of Indian identity that, in various ways, fulfilled a multifaceted colonial agenda. Sometimes, as in the story of the "Pilgrim fathers" arriving on these shores, that representation was of the helpful Indian, usually acting in isolation of other members of his race, who taught the settlers how to plant in a strange climate and survive the harsh New England winters. These Natives were presumably drawn in by the innate superiority of European culture and religion, and many were reported to have converted over to this new form of spirituality (usually on their death beds, where there was little chance for circumstances to test the veracity of such claims). More often, however, the Native was seen as the irredeemable "beast" or savage, so vile and treacherous that he needed to be wholly exterminated from the face of the earth both physically and psychologically.[8] These contrasting Native figures are largely irreconcilable to the American consciousness, occupying the same space at once in an image that flits back and forth with the light as in a child's refractor toy. But in either case, these figures represent a glaring absence of indigenous thought, belief, community, practice, and presence.

These enduring colonial representations are usefully acknowledged by Vizenor to be "the simulations of dominance," reflecting the "absence of the tribal real" over "the ruins of tribal representation."[9] In back of Vizenor's assertion is the apprehension that representation can never make claims to authenticate reality. History itself is an acknowledged construction that simply furthers the biases of its scribes and compilers. It cannot transcend its own medium as representation. In his work *Manifest Manners*, Vizenor draws upon the example of Rene Magritte's painting of a pipe that bears the inscription "Ceci n'est pas une pipe." Likewise, he views Andy Warhol's silkscreen of Indian activist Russell Means and concludes, "this is not an indian."[10] By extension, one can trace the entire colonial record of contact with Natives and ask, what of Native identity is legitimately being portrayed? Vizenor writes,

> The Indian was an occidental invention that became a bankable simulation . . . The postindian is the absence of the convention . . . the critical distinction is that postindian warriors create a new tribal presence in stories. The simulations of manifest manners are dominance, the scriptures of civilization in paradise. The counteractions of postindian warriors are the simulations of survivance.[11]

In other words, colonial representations of Native identity, solidified and passed down through the historical archive, create a fictive presence around which colonial aggression and acquisition have been carelessly, and often ruthlessly, justified. These fictive presences have cast their shadow over the work of Native writers in the colonial period, who, while struggling to effect positive change in their respective communities, were ultimately cast as apostates to Native identity. If Apess was a postindian warrior, it is because he labored in his written works to counteract such representations and place something substantive and complex in their stead that took into account indigenous memories and epistemologies mixed with a liberal sprinkling of historical irony. As such, William Apess was a practitioner of *survivance*.

It remains certain, however, that when Americans reflect back upon their early days of nation formation, their imagination rarely settles upon the Native who, with pen in hand, forged intellectual arguments for Native rights, Native sovereignty, and peaceful coexistence on the land. The silence Apess apprehended concerning the legitimacy of Native experience was rendered as an absolute absence in the colonial archive, a stricken signifier, or what I refer to in this work as the repeated acts of colonial *unwitnessing*. Native writers of the colonial period and beyond were under the constant imposition of having to forge an idiom that recognized the tightly constrained discursive parameters permitted them by print culture, while simultaneously reconstructing a positive Native presence from within those constraints and holding it out for colonial audiences to acknowledge. The result of such efforts was an at times conflicted, always embedded literature that has been regarded more for its implied cultural concessions to colonial pieties than for its heroic acts of Native advocacy, invention, and resistance.

Apess, from his nineteenth-century perspective, would have had little insight, given the scarce resources at his disposal, into the efforts of the many Natives who preceded him, employing the tools of European literacy in an attempt to benefit Native lives and political standing in an earlier period of contact and colonization. In fact, there remains even today a paucity of information dealing directly with this subject. While Apess was correct in noting how those powerful tools of empire, the pen and the press, remained the bulwark of colonialism, still, others had stood before him, making similar claims and protests, marshaling many like forces of compromise and resistance, and endeavoring to leave some kind of lasting impression not only of the individual self, but of sustained Native presence in a newly colonized world. Perhaps Apess had apprehended bits and pieces of this written legacy, and I am inclined to believe that he hoped to place himself somewhere within that still elusive, amorphous tradition that included such figures as Samson Occom, Hendrick Aupaumut, Joseph Johnson, James Printer, Caleb Cheeshateaumauk, Thomas Waban, and others. Natives had, in fact, been picking up the pen in America for nearly two hundred years prior to Apess' literary interventions in the early nineteenth century. As will be made apparent, many of these individuals were closely associated with the leadership and community structures of their people and played an integral role in strategizing and negotiating tribal standings. They remain, for the most part, fondly recalled by the local indigenous groups they served as they helped to effect substantial accomplishments and lasting gains for their respective communities in their time. They had bartered for their indigenous rights, inscribed the decisions and decrees of their councils, negotiated land transactions, penetrated Harvard College and other colonial institutions of higher learning, and labored to become brokers for their often embattled communities. Some there were who actually held their hand upon the very lever of the press that Apess claimed had been historically denied them. But their efforts have rarely been noted or offered up as a body of work that might be considered to have the substance that adheres to what we in the business refer to as a "literary tradition." Each Native writer of this period has been traditionally regarded as a figure standing in isolation, an exception, or a genius of unusual talents who, by mastering European literacy, had in effect embraced colonial norms and turned his or her back upon Native peoples and traditions. Rarely if ever has anyone attempted to place these writers in a continuum of influence and tradition that values their contribution to the persistence of Native lifeways in colonial times. The project of *Red Ink* is to acknowledge and define such a contribution and to examine the manner in which a reinvigorated methodology for processing the works and lives of these Native writers must inevitably recalibrate our understanding of the colonial period and the dynamics of contact. While Western modes of literacy were introduced with a very specific set of colonial intentions, they were most often appropriated and mastered by Natives for quite different reasons. *Red Ink* is an extended effort to comprehend and delineate the motives of these individuals, their writings, and the unacknowledged indigenous epistemologies they served.

Unwitnessing: Cultural Amnesia and the Art of Continuance

To the European adventurer, explorer, or settler of the sixteenth, seventeenth and eighteenth centuries, the indigenous peoples of America had no real culture of which to speak. A people without writing were regarded as a people without the means of organizing themselves under any sort of defined spiritual, legal, or historical principles. As such, their claims to sovereignty, land entitlement, or even the most basic human right to exist became suspect in the eye of the dominant culture and remains so to this day. Historian

Douglas Edward Leach noted in his influential 1958 *Flintlock and Tomahawk*, that "The New England Indians were a primitive people occupying a much lower level of civilization than that of the English settlers who moved in upon them during the seventeenth century."[12] This leads him to infer that "government and law, like religion, seem to have been no more than vague concepts amongst these Indians."[13] Leach was merely echoing a long line of assumptions that had been sustained and promoted by the manifest manners of the colonial archive from the very first moments of cultural contact.

Columbus, upon reaching the West Indies in his first voyage in 1492, persistently remarked how the islanders he met "would easily be made Christians, for they appeared to me to have no religion."[14] Amerigo Vespucci wrote back from his travels in 1498 that "amongst those people we did not learn that they had any law, nor can they be called Moors nor Jews, and they are worse than pagans, because we never saw them offer any sacrifice."[15] In the earliest document brought back from New England's first settlement in Plymouth, Massachusetts, one commentator noted how the Natives are "few and doe but run over the grasse, as doe also the Foxes and wildebeests: they are not industrious, neither have art, science, skill or faculties to use either the land or the commodities of it."[16] From the very first recorded meetings, then, Europeans saw Native culture as a blank slate upon which they could (and must) superimpose their own belief systems.

The sense that the indigenous peoples of America were scattered and unformed, lacking the most basic ligaments of community, artistic expression, and belief, was patently false, and is quite often belied by the very commentators who made such assertions. For instance, during his second voyage, Columbus noted that "each of the many kings in Hispaniola and the other islands and on the mainland has his special house apart from the village . . . Here there is no other activity except the service of the *cemies* [religious idols carved from wood] and the Indians perform certain prayers and ceremonies here as we do in church."[17] While Columbus continues to describe these and other ceremonies at some length, the whole passage is prefaced with the claim, "I have not been able to discover any idolatry or other religious belief amongst them."[18] Fray Ramon Pané, who was sent by Columbus to study and, if possible, convert the Tainos in 1494, offered an even more detailed account of their cultural lives, observing,

> they have their laws gathered in ancient songs, by which they govern themselves, as do the Moors by their scripture. And when they wish to sing their songs, they play a certain instrument that is called mayohabao, which is made of wood, hollow, strong, and very thin, the length of an arm and half in width. The part that is played is made in the shape of a blacksmith's tongs, and the

> other part resembles a mace so that it looks like a long-necked squash. And they play this instrument, which has a voice so loud that it can be heard from a distance of a league and a half. To its sound they sing their songs, which they learn by heart, and the principal men play it; they learn to play it as children and to sing with it, according to their custom.[19]

These passages and countless others make it abundantly clear that indigenous life was highly codified, deeply spiritual, and held together by the same kinds of sustaining rituals, based in organically conceived, communally acknowledged narrative constructs, as were the orders of European belief.

The early English settlers of the American northeast in the seventeenth-century also came into contact with organized communities, that however different from European models, were nevertheless easily recognizable to them as villages replete with laws, customs, and cultivated fields for sustenance. It was the bounty of these villages that sustained the Puritans in the first years at Plymouth. While we often think of the Pilgrims as having learned, with the help of Squanto, to provide for themselves, they in fact traded vigorously with the local Native villages. Edward Winslow notes how, in one 1622 excursion, the settlers purchased "eight hogsheads of corn and beans" at Manamoycke and "eight or ten hogsheads" more at Mattachiest.[20] The Pilgrims survived on these Native surplus stores, and yet, as noted earlier, Winslow was still capable of asserting of these locals that "they are not industrious, neither have art, science, skill or faculties to use either the land or the commodities of it." What European explorers witnessed on the one hand, they *unwitnessed* with the other.

As Roy Harvey Pearce has observed, colonists came to define *civilization* itself as the counterpart to *savagism*, which was the term most often used to evoke (or revoke) Native civilization. In fact, according to the sixteenth-century Spanish monk Bartolomé de las Casas, the very term "barbarian" was commonly understood to denote "those who do not have a written language that corresponds to the spoken one."[21] In effect, as European culture began to violently plant itself on these American shores, it subsequently suffered a crisis of identity that could only fully define itself in contrast to what it supposed it was not. The way to maintain such a dichotomy was by categorically refusing to acknowledge the cultural validity, even the essential humanity, of that which was being culturally eliminated. For, if indigenous culture proved all too human, all too civilized, the violence of removing it from view would provoke an axial shift, all at once illegitimating the presumed superiority of European culture.[22]

Writing itself becomes the essential cultural marker of Western superiority. A people who write are a people whose traditions and laws are preserved and passed on coherently from one generation to the next. And at the foundation of all Western writing was the book, the Bible, the word of God, beamed from the mind of God himself to the pens of the prophets. While Western epistemologies were seen as fixed, set in stone so to speak, Native systems of thought and belief appeared prone to corruption, fantasy, and invention. And so it was recorded by every European commentator who visited these shores. As long as Native responses to such frameworks of thought remained tightly sealed in the colonial lock box of archival containment and representation serving the agenda of colonial discourses, it was difficult for any resistant understanding of these encounters to materialize. The authority invested in such claims, supported as they are by centuries of colonial reportage, continue to weigh heavily on the consciousness of the twenty-first century.

It is my contention that, by summarily *unwitnessing* Native civilization and refusing to acknowledge the ligaments of community and belief upon which Native lives were structured, the colonists behaved much like trauma patients who have "blocked out" certain memories of the past in order to cope in the present. The result is that narratives sustaining to Native life in colonial times were effectively papered over by the dominant discourse disseminated in print. While Natives who entered into the realm of print discourse in the colonial period were not always, in their views and stances, in lock step with one another or necessarily representative of all indigenous culture at the time, they nevertheless contributed to an emerging body of Native intellectual tradition that dynamically engaged the settler culture and stamped their own presence upon a period that, in response, has collaborated to deny their historical relevance.

Unwitnessing is not simply the conscious act of turning a blind eye. Nor is it the result, necessarily, of ignorance or an utter failure of imagination. *Unwitnessing* is the largely passive decision to maintain a particular narrative structure by keeping undesirable aspects of cultural memory repressed or inactive. For European explorers and settlers of the colonial period these undesirable aspects of memory consisted of repeated acts of denigration and violence toward Native peoples, which stood in sharp relief to the rhetoric of uplift driving so much of the colonial endeavor. The Puritans of New England, in particular, were heavily invested in "convincing the heathen of their evil ways, and converting them to the true knowledge and worship of the living God, and so consequently the salvation of their souls."[23] In the charters of all the English companies that first settled America were prominently placed provisions for improving the lives of the "savages." Their unrealistic expectation was that Native peoples would quickly acknowledge the superiority of European belief systems and seamlessly assimilate themselves into the rank and file, ceding land and culture along the way. The resulting rift between rhetoric and deed was not simply an embarrassing contradiction. It was, in my estimation, a trauma operating on a culture-wide level, driving colonists to spontaneously distort and amend their collective memory. This distortion inevitably manifests itself in the archival representation of the acts in question, in which undesirable knowledge is at once noted and then immediately stricken out, or unwitnessed. As with all significant trauma narratives, these representations bear the burden of knowing and not knowing, seeing and not seeing all at once.[24]

As I will demonstrate, the process of unwitnessing can be seen in effect almost every time a European observer commented upon the lives and cultures of America's indigenous peoples. Colonial reporters would offer detailed observations about Native customs, traditions, and spiritual practices before concluding that these very same qualities were, in fact, nonexistent in indigenous life. In every case what was physically observed gave way to a more persuasive ideological noesis in which the colonists might see themselves as bringing Christian belief and civilization to a people who suffered for the want of such niceties as law, culture, religion, and, most importantly, writing. In other words, to maintain the ideological framework of the colonial endeavor the evidence of the senses had to be rhetorically undone. Once having denied the existence of Native culture it was a relatively small step to deny or suppress the presence of the Indian himself, leading to the unwitnessing of entire Native communities referred to in modern parlance as the trope of the vanishing race.

To properly understand the paradoxical functions of unwitnessing, one must first appreciate the significance of narrative, strictly speaking, in the cultural lives of all peoples. When Greek/Cherokee novelist and essayist Thomas King asserts, "the truth about stories is that that's all we are," he is acknowledging the important, even indispensable, role narrative plays in the formation of cultural identity.[25] If one's cultural narrative is disrupted by violent events or policies, the core of selfhood is disrupted as well. Psychologist and trauma scholar Judith Herman writes about the manner in which trauma, as clinically understood, is also in essence the disruption of narrative. She notes that traumatic memories "are not encoded like the ordinary memories of adults in a verbal, linear narrative that is assimilated into an ongoing life story," but rather it is as if "time stops at the moment of trauma."[26] The person or group of people who suffer from this effect have lost the ability to enfold the moment of rupture at the heart of the trauma into a linear narrative structure. Even the verbal or oral structure of the memory is inhibited. The narrative of the trauma sufferers becomes static. Such a trauma defines the colonial encounter and informs the history that has resulted from it. The dominant society manifests this trauma by exhibiting historical or cultural amnesia, a willful forgetting of their complicity in acts of violence by which they claimed an "emptie" land for themselves. By forging a narrative in which Native community did not exist or was "static" and incapable of moving forward, the dominant culture solidified a paradigm that insinuated itself into every aspect of its historical and literary narratives.

In Native American studies the concept of "continuance" offers the rhetorical materials of healing traumatic rupture or unwitnessing. Continuance might be viewed as the assertion of a political and cultural consciousness that works to restore Native traditions and histories to a linear narrative structure after centuries of colonial disruption. Rather than regarding the moment of contact with Europeans as the locus of an irrevocable epistemological split or fragmentation, Native scholars like Robert Warrior, Jace Weaver, Lisa Brooks, and Craig Womack have succeeded in recent years in focusing instead on the unbroken materials of culture, tradition, and history that can be made a part of a continuing narrative of Native presence on the North American continent both before and after contact. Osage scholar Robert Warrior refers to this renewed focus as exercising "intellectual sovereignty," and his articulation of this concept has helped carve out a wider trail for those interested in honoring the "intellectual traditions" forged by earlier Native thinkers and writers. Rather than regarding Native American civil rights movements as a modern phenomenon spontaneously generated from within the cultural milieu of the sixties and furthered by the subsequent "Native literary renaissance" of the seventies and eighties, Warrior maintains that the roots of rhetorical resistance sink much deeper. He suggests that Native writers and scholars of the past faced similar situations and that

> when we take that tradition seriously . . . we empower our work . . . Far from engaging in some new and novel practice that belongs necessarily to the process of assimilating and enculturating non-Native values, we are doing something that Natives have done for hundreds of years—something that can be and has been an important part of resistance to assimilation and survival.[27]

Declaring intellectual sovereignty is a process of cultural affirmation in the current moment, but it is also necessarily a historical process and one that more often than not finds itself in contention with the institutional memory of the dominant culture. For instance, as indigenous nations search for ways, both within their own communities and within the legal frameworks of American jurisdiction, to solidify their political and historical presence, the United States refuses to officially remember the particulars of treaties or to even recognize the existence of entire nations despite the unambiguous manner in which these entities appear in archival sources. An excellent example of this, as the ensuing chapters will demonstrate, is the case of the Nipmuc of New England who, despite being referenced in the earliest colonial records and maintaining a continuous land base from colonial times to the present, remain federally unrecognized (unwitnessed) as a tribal entity. In the eyes of the federal government, the Nipmuc do not exist.

One might conclude that such results are part of an inevitable power dynamic, and that the victors of a particular encounter have always retained the privilege of writing and defining history. As I hope to demonstrate however, the process at work is more complicated than this. In fact, those who do return to the written archives to construct historical narratives are often tarred with the dubious label of "revisionist," as though *they* are the ones in fact altering the historical record. This is largely a consequence of the manner in which the settler culture has so meticulously forgotten the materials, in effect the history, it has itself recorded but subsequently repressed. The inherent violence of unwitnessing destabilizes the historical process, legitimating violence and oppression by relying on intrinsically ahistorical narrative frameworks. The maintenance of such frameworks is ultimately detrimental to the psychic and material life of a community, locking it into cycles of irreparable violence to itself and others. As Judith Herman makes clear, it takes more than the recovery of a particular historical narrative to heal this affliction. She observes that advances only occur when they are supported by political movements powerful enough to legitimate alliances between groups, and

> to counteract the ordinary social processes of silencing and denial. In the absence of strong political movements for human rights, the active process of bearing witness inevitably gives way to the active process of forgetting. Repression, dissociation, and denial are phenomena of social as well as individual consciousness.[28]

Shamefully violent historical events, policies, and decisions may acquire an archival presence—the Pequot massacre, Sand Creek, Wounded Knee, Rosewood, My Lai, Abu Ghraib—but even when such occurrences are repeatedly addressed and articulated by those who feel afflicted by them, they have a tendency to recede back into the peripheries of acceptable knowledge, unable to permanently lodge themselves in the general consciousness. This speaks to the political resiliency of the narratives that have been used to paper over traumatic knowledge. Nevertheless, traumatic knowledge, or what Vizenor sometimes refers to as the "tragic wisdom" of those who must continue to bear these disrupted memories, does not go away. It surfaces and resurfaces throughout time, bleeding through the protective layers of colonial coating like thick red ink.[29] In ways with which we have yet to adequately come to terms, it is the colonizing culture in the Americas that suffers irreparable traumatic lapses, while it becomes incumbent upon the indigenous cultures to practice acts of what Vizenor thinks of as *survivance*, or the furtherance of indigenous narrative structures that work to "mediate and undermine the literature of dominance."[30]

The attempt to reenvision narratives of Native presence in the colonial period so that they reflect continuity and survivance rather than inevitable fragmentation and loss of culture is a viable method for confronting the trauma that still actively disrupts America's intellectual engagement with its past. To achieve this, however, we must cultivate new strategies of engaging with the archival materials at hand. The disruptive force of cultural contact was not such that all traces of prior indigenous understanding and practice simply crumpled upon impact. Native writers of the colonial period were inevitably drawing from the discourse communities with which they were most familiar when Native space and colonial space overlapped. Native writers more often than not mastered alphabetic literacy for the purposes of assisting those communities in their interactions with the colonists. As such, many of the works I examine here fall securely under the rubric of what Jace Weaver has called "communitist" or literature that demonstrates "a proactive commitment to Native community."[31] If this simple but vital notion has often been overlooked by commentators and critics, it is largely because history failed to thoroughly examine from a Native-centered perspective the intellectual traditions that powered such a discourse.

Containment and Engagement: Unpacking History in the Longhouse of the Archive

It is often assumed that Native groups resisted the introduction of what, for the purposes of clarity, I refer to here as "alphabetic writing."[32] This skill, however, was actively sought out and incorporated into existing Native systems of encoding information, just as a host of other European tools, trade goods, and practices were appreciated and folded into traditional routines. The reasons for doing so were complex and varied, but predominately centered upon combating the effects of colonialism by improving negotiating positions in treaties, land sales, and other cultural transactions. If it is assumed that with the introduction of writing came an uncritical assimilation into Christian norms, a May 19, 1774 letter from the "Farmington" Indians to Governor Trumbull of the Connecticut Colony demonstrates the complexity of Native motives. The letter reads:

> Most of us have . . . in some measure become acquainted with, and formed some General Ideas of the English Custom and

> Manners, and many of said Tribe have been instructed in Reading and writing in English, and have at Considerable expense in attaining the same, and furnishing our Selves with Bibles and some other Books in English, for our further Instruction though poorly able to bear the Expense thereof. And we being desirous to make further proficiency in English Literature, and especially to be acquainted with the Statute Laws of this Colony, which appears to us highly Necessary, since our English Fathers inform us that we are Considered by them as being Subject to the Laws and Civil Regulations of this Colony, and many of said Statutes being made with a Special view for the Government and regulation of the Indians . . . do therefore pray your Honors to give us a Colony Law Book.[33]

The Farmington Indians may have had to pay lip service to Christianity in order to gain the education in alphabetic literacy they sought, but of more concern to them were the "Statute Laws of this Colony" that directly and adversely affected their livelihoods despite their lack of representation in devising such laws. Having come within a ring of colonial containment, they sought to master the forms by which they were being subjugated in order to better protect and preserve their own status as an individual people.

The ways that Natives engaged with Western literacy cannot, in the end, be read as an unqualified success story, nor is it my objective to make it one. The price Native communities have been forced to pay so that Europeans could transplant themselves on this soil is by every measure too high. By investigating the textual endeavors of Natives in this period, however, and the underlying motives for such endeavors, we can harvest the narrative materials that lead to a more cohesive understanding of both Native and colonial life. As Native communities became increasingly more disenfranchised, marginalized, and therefore "invisible" in the seventeenth and eighteenth centuries, it became imperative for Natives to further engage with the dominant culture and insist upon a political presence within this nation's borders. On some occasions such an insistence was pursued through retaliation and open warfare. But a battle was also being waged on the textual front, an effort to either secure the rights of Native communities or to influence the overall conversation concerning indigenous rights and historical grievances.

Through an engagement with European literary practices, many Native communities, and particularly the Algonquian communities I focus on here, were able to sustain a period of stability and keep alive traditional modes of existence that were otherwise threatened by forced fragmentation and the transformed physical reality of the colonized world. What began as a series of pragmatic engagements to achieve quite local ends became an increasingly more innovative and energetic process by which embattled, decimated communities seized the opportunity to come together in a revitalized Native space. This process also became the means of challenging the dominant culture's ability to construct and control Native identity from both within and without the very site of power, the house of the archive, from which such a construction is generated.

It remains problematic, therefore, that the first steps that Natives took toward reading and writing are often thought of as the first steps taken away from traditional Native culture and Native community. Laguna Pueblo author Leslie Marmon Silko notes that "amongst the Pueblo people, a written speech or statement is highly suspect because the true feelings of the speaker remain hidden as she reads words that are detached from the occasion and the audience."[34] Such sentiments are as old as Socrates, but a distrust of writing also stems from the very real awareness that Native communities were misled time and time again in land sales and treaty documents with colonial powers, the contents of which often differed greatly from the details of the orally communicated agreements through which they were negotiated. A telling example of this can be found in the transcription of the 1744 treaty at Lancaster, Pennsylvania when the Seneca orator Canassatego pointed out to the assembled delegates that his people had been constantly deceived in such negotiations. He claims, "we are now straitened, and sometimes in want of Deer, and liable to many other Inconveniences since the English came amongst us, and particularly from that Pen and Ink Work that is going on at the Table (pointing to the secretary)."[35] Canassatego's explicit distrust of "pen and ink work," while justified in every way, provoked many Native individuals and communities at the time to seek to master its properties rather than shun them.

But the sense of tension between American Indians and the written word clearly persists. In well-meaning high school and college curricula it is taught that Native Americans first encountered the letter through nineteenth-century institutionalized boarding schools. Native children were brought far from their homes to reside in these schools and were forced to cut their hair, abandon their traditional dress, and forbidden to speak their own languages. Carlisle School founder Richard Henry Pratt's often invoked dictum, "kill the Indian and save the man," offers a helpful summation of the cultural violence done by these institutions, whatever the intentions of some of the well-meaning people (including Natives) who signed on to such endeavors. Countless children died in these institutionalized incubators of germs and disease. Many others came home and faced difficulties reintegrating themselves into their own families and communities after having been so forcefully purged of their cultural underpinnings. But these schools also became a launching pad for the careers of prominent nineteenth-century

Indian writers, activists, and intellectuals like Charles Eastman, Zitkala-Sa, Charles Montezuma, and Luther Standing Bear, all of whom had ultimately conflicted feelings about their schooling and wrote eloquently of their experiences.[36]

These are all important remembrances, and they have been brought into our educational discourse, in part, to repair a historical trauma. But they also help to reinforce the impression that Native Americans were ultimately resistant to the technology of writing or that writing was a tool that did more harm than good for a people grounded in oral traditions. As Peter Nabokov notes in his investigation of oral noetics, *A Forest of Time*, the "symbols of writing and the Book became such diagnostics for the invasive society, and of its ominous, depersonalized efficiency, as to insinuate themselves into their [indigenous peoples'] most ahistorical genres."[37] Writing and the Book are repeatedly held up as the distinctive markers of the civilization being imposed by Euro-Americans and vehemently rejected by Natives. And, as Nabokov suggests, even attempts to recuperate "ahistorical," or oral, traditions are considered to be contaminated by their emergence into the realm of written records and accounts. In effect, once a discursive tradition is communicated in alphabetic writing, it is thought to have entered into what French theorist Jacques Derrida refers to as the "house of the archive," or "the residence of the superior magistrates, the archons, those who commanded."[38] Having entered into such a space is, at least according to many theorists, like entering into the "Roach Motels" advertised some years ago on television with the understanding that once you "check in" you can never "check out." Narrative then falls under the interpretive jurisdiction of those who control its production. I will refer to this "house of the archive," which is the house of hegemonic control and containment, throughout this work.

The house of the archive is engendered by a cultural impulse, or instinct, that necessitates the construction of an external house of memory, a domicile where memory is officially stored and inevitably molded into the shape of the desire of those who determine to house such memories. But the archive, as it is manifested in the domain of Western influence, also manages to hide from itself its authoritative, or patriarchic, agenda. As Derrida elucidates, the word itself, *archive*, shelters its own roots. Within its linguistic coding resides the Greek *arkheion*, which means "house or domicile," and *arkhe*, which means both "government" and "to rule," suggesting that the archive is both the location of power and the will to power. But the contemporary usage of the word "archive" typically suggests something more passive, a purely neutral information bank, completely unwitnessing its lineage to power. This is called up, as well as partially forgotten, in the notion of the "ark of the covenant," the lost archive that remains, nonetheless, the source of authority for Judeo-Christian culture. As Derrida notes, "it contains the stone tablets, but *arca* [in Latin] is also the cupboard, the coffin, the prison cell, or the cistern, the reservoir" that holds and concretizes law from its lost or displaced center.[39]

The idea that the archive seems to shelter both memory and forgetfulness is useful for a number of reasons. The presumably neutral archive brought under our interpretive historical lens contains deposits of both colonial and indigenous memory. But because what has been housed there is catalogued and maintained by the authorizers of a particularly monologic set of skills and beliefs, the materials that have been preserved, under house arrest so to speak, work in the service, both advertently and inadvertently, of that authority or system of laws. Native civilization and title to the land may seem to rhetorically vanish within the jurisdiction of this archive, but such presences also had to be inscribed before they could be elided. Thus the archive maintains a substratum of suppressed memory. As Derrida notes, "if one is under the impression that it is possible not to take this into account, forgetting it, effacing it, crossing it out, or objecting to it, one has already confirmed, we could say even countersigned (thus archived), a 'repression' or a 'suppression.'"[40]

That which is archived works inexorably toward the production of a deliberate field of knowledge. It constructs thought and tradition in accordance with the powers of the house of the archive. Whatever works in resistance to that field of knowledge, thought, and power is not necessarily erased, but stricken out or decontextualized. As such, the house of the archive is a source of power and containment. And yet I remain somewhat skeptical of its totalizing nature as expressed by Derrida and others, and tend to view it as yet one more gesture toward colonial appropriation. There remain bodies of thought and knowledge that, even as they interact with the archival house of power, draw their narrative cohesion from beyond its purview and are a part of what anthropologist James C. Scott refers to as the "hidden transcript," or the vestiges of cultural narrative that escape the notice of the "archons" or keepers of the archive.[41] According to Scott, in *Domination and the Arts of Resistance*, "every subordinate group creates, out of its ordeal, a 'hidden transcript' that represents a critique of power spoken behind the back of the dominant."[42] This critique, far from being an ineffectual venting of frustration or acting out of resistant fantasies, forms the parameters of resistance that define the privileges even the most oppressed populations negotiate for themselves on a daily basis from within the realms of power. Scott acknowledges the inherent problems of delving into the archive, which is "consecrated to the official 'public transcript,'" as a means of interpreting so-called marginalized cultures and their forms of resistance. He correctly observes that resistance within the archive is always "mediated by the interpretation of dominant elites." But he also perceives the strategies that resistant groups employ to subvert such mediation.

One way in which subordinate groups cover their tracks is by *appearing* to contribute to the authorized transcript. The result of this is that resistance is always present and always masked. Scott concludes that, for the sake of the official transcript, a resistant slave will always strike the appearance of the model slave, a poacher will always present the face of the peaceful respecter of property, a tax cheat will always file a form that looks proper on the books, and so forth. "The social evidence will almost always represent a confirmation of the status quo in hegemonic terms."[43] By the same token, a Native who lives according to her/his traditional beliefs within a colonized space will most likely wear the mantle of Christian conversion. Resistance may be fully anticipated and even assumed, but historically speaking, it remains difficult to pinpoint its locus unless it erupts in outright rebellion. While Scott, in his analysis, does not deal explicitly with Native American cultures, he notes how oral traditions, in particular, "due simply to their means of transmission, offer a kind of seclusion, control, and even anonymity that make them ideal vehicles for cultural resistance."[44]

Can there not stand alongside the house of the archive interpretive frameworks that do not fall under its domain? Perhaps a *longhouse* of the archive, with roots in Native epistemologies? In Algonquian culture, of course, the longhouse, or big house as it is sometimes called, is the central location of ceremony and spirituality, a structure whose form and design embraces "the celestial universe . . . in terms of time and space," offering an architecture of meaning and experience that eludes Western structures of knowledge.[45] It is a space of vision and memory, narrative and tradition that is altogether too tangible and rich to be consigned to the margins of experience or interpretive suzerainty.

Even granting the possibility of an independent, sovereign archive, however, we must remain keenly aware of just how much historical interpretation is driven by European standards of perception and European agendas organized around the principle and authority of the written word. Luther Standing Bear, who was amongst the first class of Native Americans to attend the Indian Boarding School at Carlisle, Pennsylvania in 1879, wryly noted of the "white man,"

> his law was a written law; his divine Decalogue reposed in a book. And what better proof that his advent into this country and his subsequent acts were the result of divine will! He brought the Word! There ensued a blind worship of written history, of books, of the written word, that has denuded the spoken word of its power and sacredness [my text reads "scaredness," but I

> trust that this, too, might be thought of as a culturally driven editorial slippage]. The written word became established as a criterion of the superior man—a symbol of emotional fineness. The man who could write his name on a piece of paper, whether or not he possessed the spiritual fineness to honor those words in speech, was by some miraculous formula a more highly developed and sensitized person than the one who had never had a pen in hand, but whose spoken word was inviolable and whose sense of honor and truth was paramount.[46]

We should not regard it as ironic that Standing Bear himself was leveling this indictment in writing. He is not *against* writing as a technology. He is merely cognizant of the bogus hierarchy that has been established and maintained—the fact that "with false reasoning was the quality of human character measured by man's ability to make with an implement a mark upon paper."[47]

For those of us who would like to engage in a historical/literary discourse of the Americas that takes into account Native American viewpoints, the project becomes one of locating Native texts and traditions and placing them within a context that is neither entirely separate from, nor beholden to, Western literary traditions or archival jurisdiction. Native American literacy has a life and mind all its own and its roots sink deeper than even our latest academic forays into gaze-shifting, or a more inclusive canonical framework, might suggest. As Womack has asserted, a Native American literary criticism should "emphasize unique Native worldviews and political realities, search for differences as often as similarities, and attempt to find Native literature's place in Indian country, rather than Native literature's place in the canon."[48]

This certainly applies to Native-produced texts during the colonial period. Abenaki historian Lisa Brooks explains how the most common forms that Native writing took in the eighteenth and nineteenth centuries reflect earlier Native traditions. She points here to *awikhigans*, or hieroglyphic symbols written on trees and birch bark to recount the results of hunting or military expeditions, and wampum, the small shells strung together in patterns, which according to Iroquois tradition, bound "words to deeds." In other words, she views Native forays into the textual world of Europeans as an extension of their own non-alphabetic modes of encoding history and culture. Brooks notes that "transformations occurred when the European system of writing entered Native space. Birch bark messages became letters and petitions, wampum records became treaties, journey pictographs became written 'journals.'" Brooks maintains that the "texts that emerged from within the Native space of the northeast represent a uniquely indigenous literary tradition."[49]

This tradition needs to be comprehended more fully before one can enter into a useful discussion on how Native Americans appropriated the skills of alphabetic literacy, and in my first chapter I spend some time thinking about how pre-Columbian systems of Native writing functioned within a primarily oral culture. I have personally seen belts of wampum, looked at Sioux Winter Counts, even walked through Petroglyph National Forest in Albuquerque, New Mexico, and yet it still came as something of an epiphany to me when I began this project that American Indians had their own recorded systems of transmitting information prior to European colonization. Perhaps I had read at some point that the Mayans had developed systems of writing, and kept libraries full of books before Cortez appeared and razed it all to the ground. I had heard, in some vague context, of the Quiche Mayan *Popol-Vuh* and the *Walam Olum* of the Lenape. But even this information somehow evaded my overall sense of Native *civilization* or remained stubbornly isolate from a more persistent cultural narrative that I was familiar with inhabiting, in which Native culture was an *oral* culture and therefore didn't have, or even understand, the concept of writing. I had witnessed these practices and then conveniently *unwitnessed* them to maintain the integrity of Western nationalist paradigms. Useful for me, then, is not only the manner in which Brooks introduces a counternarrative about Native writing, but also how she sees this narrative originating from what she refers to as "Native space."

Native space, as Brooks conceives it, is a site both conceptual and geographical. It consists of the cognitive space that arises from "a network of relations: the marriages and relationships that connected people and the places they inhabited," but it is also the physical space of villages and "waterways containing many different groups of people as well as animal, plant, and rock beings that was sustained through the constant transformative 'being' of its inhabitants."[50] Ultimately, I feel it is a narrative space that exists within a chain of stories and traditions that are passed from generation to generation and remain deeply rooted to a relationship with a particular geographical environment.

When Europeans arrived on these shores, they too entered into this Native space, which Brooks metaphorically equates with "the Common Pot," where "sharing space meant sharing resources" and where the actions of all its inhabitants "affected the whole."[51] Part of the colonial project of acquisition and containment, however, was to transform Native space into colonial space, and this too occurs, in many ways, on a textual or conceptual plane. As Mary Louise Pratt points out in her influential treatise on colonial travel narratives, *Imperial Eyes*, from the very first moments of encounter the colonist regarded both land and inhabitants as resources to be contained, collected, and sold on the open market. Much of how we understand these contacts is defined by the textual productions that flow from colonized space and the appropriations of the "seeing man," or "he whose imperial eyes passively look out and possess."[52]

In the minds of America's colonizers this space was in some cases regarded as an uncultivated paradise, or in the words of the English trader Thomas Morton, a virgin land "longing to be sped."[53] In the first batch of letters to come out of the new settlement in Plymouth, often referred to as *Mourt's Relation*, one commentator would write about the necessity of converting the Natives, observing "to us they cannot come, our land is full—to them we may goe; their land is emptie."[54] The notion that a land populated by some ten to twelve million indigenous people was somehow "emptie" was a powerful and compelling justification for settlement and expansion.[55] In all these instances it is the colonists who are the actors, the redeemers, and the definers of space. But we should labor to give equal credence to Brooks' interpretation, wherein it is the colonists entering upon Native space—not a desert wilderness, but a space of cooperation and interdependence, a sustaining space of villages and larger kinship networks that has been proven the most agriculturally productive in the history of the world. And it is a narrative space, too, whose stories can still be told and heard and enfolded into codes of conduct and belief.

If colonial paradigms were generally geared toward the containment of space and knowledge, Native epistemologies seemed to favor a kind of engagement with the experiential world. As such, Natives did not immediately tune out the introduction of Christian rhetoric into their worlds. In many cases they attempted to incorporate it into the body of useful knowledge that was already inherent in their belief systems and practices. Unlike Europeans, their cognitive presence in the world was not anchored in doctrine or exclusivity. Something similar might be construed from Native traditions of signification, as opposed to the European custom of alphabetic literacy with which most of us are more familiar. Wampum, *awikhigans*, birch bark writing, *quippo*, memory sticks, winter counts are all forms of Native inscription that encourage engagement with spiritual and intellectual traditions. They do not contain knowledge so much as interact with it. While the alphabetic tradition was bent upon imposing monologic responses to one's encounter with the world, Native modes of representation could accommodate varied interpretations and impressions of reality. Such a worldview was disorderly and threatening to most European minds. Colonists were not capable of locating any kind of pattern or consistency within it, particularly as it failed to conform to their own textualized traditions and belief systems that they believed to be set in stone. As a result they rejected the authority and viability of such communicative forms and, by extension, either denounced or denied the presence of Native religion, law, and civilization.

"I Would Take These Shell Strings in My Hand and Console Them": Clearing Historical Unresolved Grief

If the colonists who came to settle America fell prey to repeated acts of unwitnessing in their historical recollections, Native epistemologies offered an alternative to ordering experience and the ever competing narratives that often destabilize our engagement with the open world. Some very basic acknowledgment and comprehension of such epistemologies offers a key to better understanding the colonial dynamic and how Natives attempted to survive it. The Iroquois, or Haudenosaunee, have a ritual called the condolence ceremony, which was traditionally put into motion whenever the various nations, whether "white" or "red," came together in council or mourning. The ceremony codified the assumption that two parties would have contesting versions of reality, differing accounts of significant events, and personal grievances that might bar the way to reconciliation or constructive deliberation. As Lisa Brooks states, "they understood that before peacemaking could begin, nations had to acknowledge and clear each other's grief."[56] The condolence ritual (reductively referred to in white man's parlance as "passing around the peace-pipe" or "burying the hatchet") failed to signify for European adventurers, who recognized the ceremonial gravity of the event but merely went through the motions it demanded of them in order to humor their "red children." The ceremony asked that when two parties come together they engage in a mutual process of wiping the smoke from the eyes, the dirt from the ears, and the obstructions from the throat. These rituals, if followed precisely, would lead to a requickening, or revitalization that enabled physical or psychological healing. Drawn from the foundational Deganawidah myth, the process was central to the success of Hiawatha in bringing peace to the warring clans and establishing the Longhouse of the Five Nations of the Iroquois in the time before Europeans arrived on the continent.

Europeans, taking hold of this narrative in the nineteenth century, refashioned it to suit their own rhetorical purposes. As the culture hero Hiawatha tells his people in Longfellow's iconic poem, "I am going, O my people, / On a long and distant journey . . . But my guests [the blackrobes] I leave behind me; / Listen to their words of wisdom, / Listen to the truth they tell you, / For the Master of Life has sent them / From the land of light and morning."[57] In this version, the epic figure of Hiawatha is reduced to the role of mere placeholder, taking his leave once the Jesuits arrive on the scene with their superior "truths." Longfellow's poem conveniently unwitnessed the poignant and layered belief systems, both political and spiritual, underlying the Haudenosaunee narrative.

The condolence ritual marks a deliberate and psychologically profound attempt to coax reconciliation from the chaos of war and to alleviate the endless cycles of violence and grief by establishing *Gaiwiio*, or "Good Mind."[58] This ritual, historically, was also the source of wampum exchange, which originated not as a bartering system or currency as Europeans interpreted it, but as a symbolic representation that gave force and presence to the spoken words of the ceremony. The culture hero commonly known as Hiawatha is said to have created the wampum, stringing shells onto braided lengths of lake rushes and repeating the words, "this I would do if I found anyone burdened with grief even as I am. I would console them for they would be covered with night and wrapped in darkness. This would I lift with words of condolence and these strands of beads would become words with which I would address them."[59] The exchange of wampum was then used in the ceremony by which the warring tribes of the Northeast became reconciled, creating a ritualized space for aggrieved parties to tell their tales. In a sense, wampum, which has taken on a very different meaning in the cultural relationship European adventurers have had with it, was the original trauma literature of the Haudenosaunee, or Longhouse People. It is a literature meant to both express and displace grief. The condolence ceremony, acknowledging that "all around you are hostile agencies which are each thinking, 'I will frustrate their purpose,'" was an attempt at healing cultural discord, lifting the veil of traumatic grief that cultures invariably experience, particularly in time of war, establishing consensual agreements, and restoring the "good mind."[60]

Abenaki ethnographer Fred Wiseman notes that "condolence is based on the theory that the emotions must be addressed before politics."[61] To create a community of listeners is the goal of the condolence ceremony—to restore a new sense of what's right, or *Gaiwiio*, through the ritualized clearing of grief and the airing out of grievances. But the wampum was also used, by the Haudenosaunee and others, as a means of recording history, making of these historical records the locus of peace, healing, and intercultural well-being. In my mind, this is something that all responsible literature and all responsible criticism might reasonably aspire toward—to create a space where grief may be cleared and competing narratives lifted up from the fog of discursive containments. I take this as a model for my work, believing that the text itself may serve as a space where competing narratives may come together, each side given voice, and a collective understanding nurtured. By wiping the tears from the eyes, the dirt from the ears, and clearing the obstructions from the throat, perhaps the violent processes of historical unwitnessing may be undone. For too long, the colonial historian has held this space of narrative offering exclusively to him or herself. This sense of history has infiltrated the understanding of generations and become the lynchpin by which America affirms its place in the world as a beneficent force for freedom and tolerance. By respecting emotions before politics, we take into account the visceral attachment that cultures have to their sustaining narratives, the legitimate and illegitimate concerns, and acknowledge the scars that have formed over the ruptures in those narratives. The result is not simply an attempt at cultural objectivity, but the attempt to hold two competing thoughts in one's mind at the same time and address them simultaneously.

My own concern here, then, is not with the victimization of Native peoples, so much as with how cultures experience a psychogenic amnesia in their attempts to block out the disturbing, threatening, and undesirable narratives of others. The act of addressing this cultural amnesia and healing its ruptures is always a sociopolitical as well as historical/literary one. Herman maintains that

> denial, repression, and dissociation operate on a social as well as an individual level . . . like traumatized people, we have been cut off from the knowledge of our past. Like traumatized people, we need to understand the past in order to reclaim the present and the future. Therefore, an understanding of psychological trauma begins with rediscovering history.[62]

This act of rediscovery must, by necessity, involve making a space for the narrative that has been elided, must make a space for the narrator of alterity, the voice that threatens, challenges, recovers. For Native American communities, having survived centuries of war, poverty, and pestilence as a direct result of colonization, it is not simply a matter of discovering their own histories (which are, in fact, fairly well realized in certain settings), so much as realizing strategies to make such histories available to a settler culture that has conveniently forgotten its own complicity in bringing about these outcomes. Sometimes it is a matter of taking the narratives that exist and freeing them from their sites of archival containment, allowing them to speak in a new contextualized setting, or a "new house" as Hopi poet Wendy Rose calls it in my epigraph to this introduction.

Red Ink attempts to contribute to the opening up of such a space. Chapter 1 begins by looking at the phenomenon of "Contact," the early meetings of Natives with Spanish, French, and English colonizers, and focuses on the scene of writing itself. European observers were invested in declaiming the validity of Native civilization, their narratives tending to obfuscate or dislocate evidence of the complexity and richness of indigenous traditions. Through colonial commentaries by Columbus, the French Jesuit Paul Le Jeune, and the Puritan exile Roger Williams, one begins to see how colonizers engaged in deliberate acts of unwitnessing in order to justify their violent excesses. "Writing" itself comes to be seen as the dominant marker distinguishing between civilized and savage, but to maintain this dichotomy, European explorers have to unwitness Native models of signification such as hieroglyphs, birch bark writing, rock drawings, and wampum. As European modes of writing enter Native space they become, according to Roger Williams, *Wussuckwheke* or painted letters. Early English efforts at bringing literacy (i.e., Christianity) to the Indians converge upon a Pequot named Wequash, who is offered up as either an early missionary success or a conflicted and traumatized survivor of colonial massacre, depending on whose version you believe. I demonstrate how efforts to contain and control the events of the 1636–1637 Pequot War become inseparable from the program of "educating" and spreading the gospel to the Natives. The result, however, is the unwitnessing of the Pequot themselves, as the colonists strike the very name from their record books.

Chapter 2 follows the curious progress of the first printing press through colonial New England in the 1600s as it becomes not only the voice of Puritan hegemony, but the premier tool in the endeavor to assimilate the local Natives. In fact, the printing press becomes so entangled in the cultural encounter between Europeans and Natives that it spends its formative years housed in the building of the Indian College at Harvard, where it is maintained by a Nipmuc "printer's devil" named James Printer and a large portion of its output, including the first "Eliot Bible," is written in the Algonquian language. Harvard itself is founded with the understanding that one of its major functions will be to educate the "poor Indians." In this chapter I follow the lives of three writing Natives, Thomas Waban, James Printer, and Caleb Cheeshateaumauk, whose fates become closely entwined with Native education and the press. Following their engagements through *The Eliot Tracts*, Daniel Gookin's *Historical Collections*, and other texts and fragments of the period, I locate their contributions and their influences, noticing how, in significant ways, the first printed matter in colonial New England was printed in red ink.

Chapter 3 focuses on the disputes and grievances that led up to King Philip's War, concentrating on the manner by which the Wampanoag, in particular, attempted to preserve their rights and social integrity through textual processes. Both Philip and his equally renowned father Massasoit had presided over the drawing up of land deeds and treaties. The language of these documents (alongside other writings in the Algonquian language) often reveals tensions and determinations that ultimately resolved in open warfare. Standing in bold contrast to such revealed tensions are the encounters described in John Eliot's *Indian Dialogues* in which the political presence of the living Philip was replaced by a fictionalized figure who eagerly attests to the superiority of Christianity as a religion and offers no political resistance to the idea of total assimilation. The very Philip who appears to congenially capitulate to European norms in *Indian Dialogues* will, in later texts, become the polar opposite—a figure whose arbitrary warlike behavior exemplified savage qualities and necessitated the complete eradication of Native presence in New England. In either case, the literary Philip is a vessel through which colonial agendas and wish fulfillment are affected while the historical Philip flounders in a sea of misrepresentation.

Chapter 4 focuses on the early career of Samson Occom, an eighteenth-century Mohegan and the first American Indian to leave behind an extensive legacy of publications, journals, sermons, and letters. While it may be tempting to view Occom, an ordained and deeply committed Presbyterian minister, as one who has fully assimilated himself into a system of European thought and tradition, I will demonstrate the numerous ways in which Occom's communitist commitment to his own traditions and people are expressed and kept alive, not only within his published writings, but through his private life and actions. Many of these actions occur "beneath the wave" of colonial surveillance, but can be reinterpreted by better comprehending Native perspectives and agendas of the period. Colonists may have sought to eradicate Native presence in the wake of King Philip's War, but Native communities hung on and struggled to maintain themselves. Paying particular attention to his journals and his 1768 "A Short Narrative of My Life," I demonstrate how Occom, and others associated with his movement, carried on the struggle for tribal autonomy, following in the tradition of Waban, Printer, and Cheeshateaumauk, by becoming a cultural intermediary looking for inventive ways to keep his community of Mohegan intact.

Chapter 5 details the formation of a community of both Mohican and English settlers in Stockbridge, Massachusetts in 1734. Begun as a kind of social experiment in mutual habitation and governance, this scheme quickly congealed around the paradigm of colonial containment and control. The Mohican in Stockbridge hoped to attain literacy to protect their endangered lands and traditions. Ultimately the tool of literacy enabled their survivance in unexpected ways. This chapter also transitions from Samson Occom's life to the life of his son-in-law, Joseph Johnson. In Johnson's journals and letters we discover the voice of an often-conflicted Mohegan youth whose personal crisis of identity is, in many ways, the crisis of his people. Both the Mohegan and the Mohican are caught up in a cultural moment that will soon become defined by the likes of James Fenimore Cooper, Catherine Maria Sedgwick, Lydia Maria Child, and other nineteenth-century American writers. But Johnson emerges as a charismatic and influential force in the lives of New England Natives, clearing the path for the unforced removal of his people to the newly conceived town of Brothertown, on Oneida territory in Upstate New York. Johnson virtually writes Brothertown into being in a tireless string of letters to government agents, fellow Mohegan, patrons, preachers, teachers, and missionaries. He must negotiate with other Indian nations and master the customs of oratory as well as print discourse in his dizzying campaign to create a new homeland for his people. The newly created settlements of Brothertown and New Stockbridge are forged side by side in the very epicenter of America's emerging fictionalized frontier.

While this project restricts its focus to the era known as the colonial period, I conclude with an extended glance at Brothertown and New Stockbridge in the 1780s and an articulation of the hopes and dreams invested in this newly established Native space. Ultimately, my objective is not to coerce optimistic readings out of seemingly unresponsive texts, but to retrace complex paths of shared history, and to tease back into view the neglected, often intentionally elided, narratives that carry within their structural essences the materials, the bright and serviceable filaments, of a narrative of continuance and survivance. Furthermore, it is my hope that by paying special attention to the dynamics of contact, of cultures coming into one another's spheres of influence, we may gain a template for comprehending the dynamics of contemporary power struggles in a way that might lend itself to the nurturing of positive, peaceful resolutions, not just between Nominal Americans and Native Americans, but for all nations.

The Puritans who came to settle in North America in the early seventeenth century saw themselves as God's singularly chosen people, come to a land that God had promised to them in a sacred covenant. They never believed anything but that the people already occupying these lands were simply placeholders, misled there by the devil and awaiting spiritual salvation at the hands of the Puritans themselves. As such, the company seal for their campaign pictured a Native, his private parts covered with leaves like some lesser, latter-day Adam, waving them forward with the words "Come Over and Help Us" streaming from his lips (see figure I.1). And come they did. And they kept on coming. Theirs was a benevolent endeavor, or so they believed, sanctioned by higher powers even in their bloodiest usurpations. But Natives, as an occupied people, saw such events in a different light, and as Apess noted, if anyone were presumptuous enough to take such liberties in present times, "it would be called an insult, and every white man would be called to go out and act the part of a patriot, to defend their countries rights; and if every intruder were butchered, it would be sung upon every hilltop in the Union that victory and patriotism was the order of the day."[63] But, as Apess added, "when a few red children attempt to defend their rights, they are condemned as savages."[64]

Apess concluded his 1636 *Eulogy on King Philip*, stating, "we have not to answer for our fathers' crimes; neither shall we do right to charge them to one another. We can only regret it, and flee from it; and henceforth let peace and righteousness be written upon our hearts and hands forever, is the wish of a poor Indian."[65] Ultimately Native writers engaged with literacy in the colonial period in an effort to enter into conversation with the colonizing agent and to address the ongoing traumatic elisions of white writing or history-making. If the history of the colonizers failed to do justice to Native peoples of America, perhaps there was another history, one written on the hearts and hands of those who lived it, that might survive to stand apart or across from the colonial version. An intervention of sorts was needed. Expressing the nature of this intervention, Apess informs us that his reason for bringing such Native "beings" before the public is so that they "shall live forever in the memory of the world" and if possible "melt the prejudice that exists in the hearts of those who are in the possession of his soil."[66] Some 170 years later, this remains a worthy endeavor.

Ceci n'est pas une Indian

Figure I.1. Seal of the Massachusetts Bay Colony. Courtesy of Massachusetts Archives.

1

Wussuckwheke, or the Painted Letter

Glimpses of Native Signification Acknowledged and Unwitnessed (1492–1643)

Wussuckwheke: A letter which they so call from *Wussuckwhommin*, to paint; for having no letters, their painting comes nearest.

—Roger Williams, *A Key into the Language of America*

The advent of Native written literature did not, in any way, mark the passing of Native oral literature. In fact, they occupy the same space, the same time. And, if you know where to stand, you can hear the two of them talking to each other.

—Thomas King, *The Truth About Stories*

Eden as Ground Zero: Oral Engagements and Western Epistemologies of Containment

In an indigenous creation account often referred to as the "earth-diver" narrative, a number of animals agree to dive into the water one by one in search of mud that they might carry back to the surface in order to create land upon which humans, animals, and plants can live.[1] As Arthur Parker, an early twentieth-century Seneca historian and ethnographer, tells it, Sky-Woman, or Iagen'`tci, was pushed through a hole in the clouds left by the uprooting of the celestial tree and plummeted toward earth. As she fell, the creatures of the watery world below collaborated to cushion her fall. The duck-creatures received her "on their interknit wings," and the great turtle from the underworld arose to "make his broad back a resting-place." Having secured a safe haven for the woman to land, there remained, however, a need for soil so things might grow. Therefore the creatures dove "to the bottom of the water seeking to find earth to plant upon the turtle's back."

In Parker's version, first the duck descended, then the pickerel. Each creature that went down into the watery depths failed in its attempt to find earth until, at last, the unassuming muskrat succeeded in touching bottom with its nose. This proved sufficient, for he was able to make his way back to the surface and smear the collected mud "upon the [turtle's] shell and the earth immediately grew," providing a home for Sky-Woman and her ancestors.[2]

The story of the "earth-diver," overheard and recorded by many a colonial observer, was often equated with the biblical tale of the flood. In 1634 the French Jesuit Paul Le Jeune had a version recounted to him by the Montagnais to which he responded, "you see they have some traditions of the deluge, although mingled with fables."[3] For Le Jeune and his fellow Jesuits such tales were not to be credited, or were regarded as gross corruptions of the "true" biblical version. Le Jeune felt that the Native story had indeed sprung from the tradition of Noah and the arc, but "that the first ones who came to their country did not know how to read and write, and that was the reason their children remained in ignorance."[4] The lack of writing amongst the Native peoples of America was, for the colonist, a vital referent to their overall barbarity. As a result of this absence, there could be no possibility of keeping records, preserving history, or maintaining the integrity of spiritual narratives. It was generally perceived that a people without writing were a people without law, without culture, without religion.

In 1636 Le Jeune's contemporary and colleague Father Brebeuf recounted a similar version of the earth-diver tale told to him by the Huron. In this story, a sky woman, known to the Huron as Ataentsic, had gone to a certain tree to attain a healing "fruit" for her husband. Having split the tree with her "axe," she immediately fell into the hole there created and found herself plummeting down into the world below. As in Le Jeune's version, the animals expressed concern for the falling woman and consulted with her about what to do in this crisis. The result of their cooperative effort was that the sky woman "fell very gently on this Island," and made of it her home, shortly thereafter giving birth to a daughter who in turn gave birth to feuding twins. Brebeuf saw in this tale "some relation to the case of Adam," but he quickly concludes that "falsehood makes up the greater part of it." Ask how the daughter became pregnant, he scoffed, "and you puzzle them very much." Although decidedly untroubled by similar inconsistencies at the center of his own culture's spiritual narratives, Brebeuf summarily dismissed the Huron version of the world's origins. He observes that, although "there are some indications that they had formerly some more than natural knowledge of the true God, as may be remarked in some particulars of their fables," they had nevertheless "lost the thought of him and have become worse than beasts in his sight."[5] Brebeuf was echoing Le Jeune's belief that the indigenous peoples of New France had strayed over time from the "original" version of the biblical narratives, and as such, had been reduced to a culture without civic structure or proper spirituality. He maintained that the Huron "have hardly any virtue or Religion, or any learning or government," and thus "no simple words suitable to express what is connected with these." Lacking such concepts, he claims, "we are at a loss in explaining to them many important matters."[6]

Of course, it is well worth noting that Europeans journeying to America in the early days of colonization were busy teasing out a creation story of their own—a "New World" creation story that continues to pass down from generation to generation in which the Natives of America were a simple people who left no durable trace on the world, unknowledgeable as they were of the rudimentary elements of civilization. It was left to the colonizers to play the role of the American Adam, breathing new life into a waste of wilderness.[7] Nevertheless, one wonders what the French Jesuits imagined as they first listened to these Native tales, how far they allowed themselves to wander into the narrative worlds there unfolding, and if the cognitive circumferences elaborated by such voicings were met with either fear, disgust, or fascination. Did the materials of unfamiliar narratives, conjoined with the day-to-day practices of the Natives that the Jesuits so scrupulously observed and to a degree participated in, begin to pattern new constellations of meaning for them? As the vast exterior of the American continent shrank down to the flickering circle of light illuminated by a winter campfire and the single voice of the storyteller, did the foundations of knowledge begin to groan and admit of other possibilities? Or were these men forced to quickly shut their minds to the world engendered by such visions, fixed like pins to their own epistemological cartographies? Whichever the case, it was a given of colonial literature that their *recorded* responses remained resolute. The Jesuits' allegiance to the scriptural order of beginnings recounted in Genesis forced them to regard all variations as either "gross fables" or corruptions of scriptural truth. As one Jesuit remarked, "it is wearisome to recount the tales which they [the Natives] invent concerning the creation of the world." The "author" of such abominable notions could only be Satan, "the enemy of the human race" himself, whose book needed to be stamped out before it could be further spread.[8]

Creation stories are, of course, creations themselves, with the potential at each telling (and consequently, with each listening) to imagine the world anew. As Gerald Vizenor reminds us, in the oral tradition "the tribal creation takes place at the time of the telling," and "the teller of stories is an artist, a person of wit and imagination, who relumes the diverse memories of the visual past into the experiences and metaphors of the present."[9] It is not the written translations that are of significance so much as the telling itself. There is a participatory aspect in our engagement with beginnings, a sense of wonder and, perhaps, trepidation in both knowing and not knowing how the finished version will breathe life into the world anew. And it is within these tensions of knowing and not knowing that the materials of the world await us.

As it turns out, Native American stories of how the earth was constituted from its watery beginnings retain a reach and currency far beyond the narrow interpretations inscribed by seventeenth-century Jesuits in New France. Like the foundational narratives of other cultures, the earth-diver narrative establishes a set of relations between a people and the world they inhabit, articulating the spiritual as well as material contours of belief and practice that give shape and meaning to the organizational structures of day-to-day life. In the earth-diver narrative, Sky-Woman not only collaborates in the creation of this sphere, suggesting a spirit of cooperation with the earth's nonhuman entities, but she is responsible for bringing with her from the upper world the necessary materials for life such as corn, squash, beans, and tobacco. She carries with her certain roots and seeds from the celestial tree that will make life livable on earth and the fruit of these seeds will ultimately form the center pole of existence in the longhouse, which is at once a shelter and a metaphor for the land itself. Each telling of the story, regardless of its variations, presumably emphasized these ongoing relationships. European observers, however, were largely indifferent to the intimate ties connecting the spiritual and material elements of indigenous belief. They could only regard such stories as mere vestiges of the immutable tenets of scripture. Upon their interpretations and retellings of the narrative they infused their own particular understanding of creation with its gender-based hierarchies and strict dichotomies of good and evil.[10]

The fact that European adventurers had more than just a passing interest in the Native creation stories they heard, however, is made evident by the ubiquity with which they reported the various versions recounted to them. They sensed in these tales not only something exotic and new, but the traces of a common ancestry, and they labored to make these traces fit into their own sense of the world's beginnings. The English settler and royalist Thomas Morton noted in his 1637 promotional tract *New English Canaan* that,

> although these Salvages are found to be without Religion, Law, and King . . . yet are they not altogether without the knowledge of God (historically); for they have it amongst them by tradition that God made one man and one woman, and bad them live together and get children . . . and that their posterity was full of evill, and made God so angry that hee let in the Sea upon them, and drowned the greatest part of them.[11]

Morton, of course, is careful to make the distinction here between "history" (in parentheses) and "tradition." If Natives knew something of the actual history of the earth's beginnings, it was a faded and impartial knowledge maintained merely by the loosely knit structures of oral "tradition." The English observer John Josselyn, in his 1674 *Account of Two Voyages to New-England*, also records that the Natives in his region "do hint at Noah's Floud, as may be conceived by a story they have received from Father to Son." In this account, one *Powaw* anticipated the deluge and fled to the White Mountains when the flood came, taking with him a hare, which he then set loose to discover if the waters had yet receded, much as Noah lets loose the dove for similar purposes. Again we see how such stories "hint" at the real truth, but Josselyn is careful to note in the same breath that "their Theologie is not much . . . [and] their learning is very little or none."[12]

These later stories recounted by Morton and Josselyn must be understood to relate not just to the creation of the world, but to a second incident that mirrors or integrates with the Sky-Woman story in important ways. Anishinaabe author Basil Johnston observes how it is during this second watery epoch that the culture hero Nana'b'oozoo remembers the story of Sky-Woman and so enlists the animals in helping him to repeat the process of restoring the land. One by one the animals dive. Sometimes it is the muskrat who succeeds in scoring the mud. In other versions it is the fox, the beaver, the loon, or the otter. Either way, earthly balance is achieved precisely because Nana'b'oozoo calls upon and respects tradition, remembering the stories of elders and enlisting their wisdom in a new act of creation. If European colonists saw such tales as childish, according to Johnston they reflect how "from the beginning, men and women of all races and nations have borne out the reality of their dependence upon plants and animals represented in the Anishinaube story of the great flood."[13] Johnston attributes to such cultural narratives an "expression of thanksgiving" that portrayed not only "gratitude but an admission of . . . dependence on the goodwill of the manitous."[14]

The stories, in a sense, are fluid and infinitely adaptable, but at the heart of the spirituality they communicate rests a notion of balance that one maintains with the universe as a whole, bringing the past and present together in the materials of the story itself. Vizenor speaks of a "trickster hermeneutics" in relation to such tales. He writes, "in the oral tradition, the mythic origins of tribal people are creative expressions, original eruptions in time, not a mere recitation or a recorded narrative in grammatical time."[15] He notes that "tricksters are the translation of creation; the trickster creates the tribe in stories, and pronounces the moment of remembrance as the trace of liberation. The animals laughed, birds cried, and there were worried hearts over the everlasting humor that would liberate the human mind in trickster stories."[16] While in the Christian story of the flood animals are rounded up in an ark and kept in a sort of floating zoo, reinforcing man's absolute dominion over the beasts of the field, the Native stories emphasize an ongoing partnership with the natural world, a relationship of reciprocity that is threaded into the daily structure of Native lives.

Ethnographers of the past made the mistake of conflating various Native cosmologies, interchanging the names of their respective culture heroes and homogenizing the particulars of their religious practice and belief.[17] While not wishing to perpetuate such errors here, it nevertheless might be said that these Native stories, in their cooperative dynamic and their ability to adapt to changing circumstances and competing narratives, are at least in part indicative of *Gaiwiio*, or Good Mind, which is personified by the grandson of Sky-Woman in the Seneca version of the tale.[18] Good Mind or, more accurately in the Haudenosaunee language, "Smooth Mind," is responsible for creating all the good things on earth and maintaining balance with all its natural forces (he collaborates in this effort with his twin brother "Wrinkled" mind, making of the natural world a combination of positive and disruptive features). While there remain tensions between these two forces resulting in epic sequences of cosmic consequence, their relationship nevertheless defies simple binaries of good versus evil and suggests an ongoing spirit of engagement and cooperation.[19]

Doubtless such a paradigm is in danger of presenting itself as a species of new-age reductionism, or an essentialist notion that romanticizes a Native relationship with the natural world, having more to do with contemporary wishes of an anthropomorphized "Mother Earth" than any verifiable Native epistemology. One immediately thinks of Disney's *Pocahontas* cartoon, in which the overly developed ten-year-old is depicted as cavorting with raccoons, hummingbirds, and talking willow trees while the crushing realities of colonialism vanish behind a façade of interracial romance.[20] The more recent blockbuster movie *Avatar* also flirts blatantly with hyper-idealized tropes of indigenous connectivity with natural forces. However John Heckewelder, who spent a number of years living amongst the Delaware, or Lenape, offered an assessment as a result of his eighteenth-century mission that gets closer to the manner in which such beliefs were threaded into daily life. He comments in his *History, Manners, and Customs of the Indian Nations* that the Delaware, according to their traditions, are

> only the first among equals, the legitimate hereditary sovereigns of the whole animated race, of which they consider themselves a constituent part. Hence in their languages, these inflections of their nouns which we call *genders*, are not, as with us, descriptive of the *masculine* and *feminine* species, but of the *animate* and

> *inanimate* kinds. Indeed they go so far as to include trees, and plants within the first of these descriptions. All animated nature, in whatever degree, is in their eyes a great whole, from which they have not yet ventured to separate themselves.[21]

Heckewelder, unsurprisingly, categorizes this knowledge within a hierarchy of relations in which Natives have yet to fully "separate themselves" from the beasts. We need not be so derisive, however, in considering the cultural implications of such practices. The better part of indigenous religion, lore, and tradition speaks of an intimate relationship with the earth that transcends a simple equation of reliance and subsistence but is, in fact, embedded in the language.[22]

Such an articulation of experience stands in stark contrast to the religion of the European colonizers of North America who, as Vine Deloria Jr. has noted, tended to view the world as "a vale of tears filled with unexplained human tragedies. Animals are definitely placed beneath humans in the hierarchy of things and religious ceremonies seek to purge nature from participation in the rituals . . . In many ways the human body is seen as evil."[23] Richard Slotkin, too, comments upon the fundamental difference in the manner in which Europeans and Native peoples narrate their engagement with the natural world, noticing that while Christian myth deplores its entry into the world as a tragic fall from a gracious, satisfyingly womblike condition, the Indian myth rejoices in "the discovery and in the movement of the world." Slotkin notes that "the exile of Adam and Eve results from their disobedience to their transcendent father . . . [whereas] for the Indian it is virtue that leads man into the world."[24] The French Jesuit Brebeuf seems to acknowledge this when, in reflecting upon the Huron creation story, he refers to Sky-Woman's fall from the clouds as "being more favorable than she had supposed." He apprehends a kinder system at work in this "gentle" entry into the "real" world, but rather than meditate upon the positive implications of such a beginning, he reimposes Christian orthodoxy, concluding that "barbarism, ignorance, poverty, and misery which render the life of these Savages more deplorable than death, are a continual reminder to us to mourn Adam's fall, and to submit ourselves entirely to him who still chastises disobedience in his children, in so remarkable a way."[25]

Do such diametrically opposed systems of representing the human condition and the means of disseminating them have real consequences in the development and organization of culture, the psychological well-being of a people, and the practical effect of a people upon their environment and upon history? Biblical scholar Elaine Pagels suggests that the archaic story of Adam and Eve "wields an extraordinary influence upon Western culture," and for Christians and Jews it becomes the primary means "for revealing and defending basic attitudes and values."[26] What is striking about the Old Testament creation story of Adam and Eve is not only how it establishes an oppositional relationship between man and the natural world, but as Slotkin points out, the imposed exile embedded within the narrative. Paradise, a place where balance between the human and natural world is a given and individuals can speak directly to their gods and the animals, cannot be regained save through death. The working assumption is that humanity, as a consequence of sin, is barred from reentry into this garden and the prelapsarian state it represents. Eden engenders in us a sense of alienation and nostalgia, positing a former period of innocence and peace in human affairs suggestive of the condition of Rousseau's "natural man" (i.e., the noble savage).[27] As Greek/Cherokee author Thomas King observes, "in Genesis, we begin with a perfect world, but after the Fall, while we gain knowledge, we lose the harmony and safety of the Garden and are forced into a chaotic world of harsh landscapes and dangerous shadows."[28] Genesis, as story, contributes to Western culture's persistent sense of existential crisis, as it asks us to mourn a former state of human relations that is always beyond recovery, always hopelessly displaced by the present.

Another consideration, however, is that the Genesis narrative itself is specifically constructed to protect its practitioners from the uncomfortable truths contained in that garden abode. Eden is not a desirable place to return to, so much as a patch of mental real estate from which Western culture has gone to extraordinary labors to remove itself, setting seraphim with burning swords outside the gate and geographically displacing its location so that it is not to be discovered within the physical realm as we know it. While Native peoples of America will often point directly to their places of origin as part of their culturally incorporated landscape, Christians have physically and spiritually displaced themselves from their center of creation. Eden is a space of genesis and trauma, a gated enclosure meant to contain inconvenient knowledge (in particular the tree of knowledge). One can never return to this place but only encounter written representations of it. It is cognitive ground zero, surrounded by yellow tape, indigenous to all, inhabited by none. In a sense, the Genesis story recounts Western culture's first narrative of forced removal.

But Genesis, as text, contains even more. It contains the possibility of conflicting accounts or versions of the same tale. It combines various oral narratives of Judeo origin and in masterfully persuasive language welds them into a monologic containment, as though they had never been anything other than one coherent tale, the product and creation of the single unerring voice of God.[29] The house of the archive actively represses acknowledgment of the multiple strands of narrative that undoubtedly inform this tale. By establishing an orthodox version of creation, Genesis ensures its irrevocable nature—there is no other way to tell it so that things might work out differently. Humans are wedded, through the power of tradition, to its tragic outcome, endlessly rehearsing its unfortunate occurrence yet unable to alter it from within. There is nothing contemporary man can do to change what Saint Augustine regarded as our "diseased" relationship with the creator or atone for the sins of ancestral parents.[30] While Genesis may not be the last word on creation, it does suggest a kind of beginning of *writing* as orthodox containment or a closed book wherein the written Word itself is of endlessly greater significance than the rich metaphorical elements clearly at work within this network of stories. Eden is not a state to which we long to return. It is the place we have purposefully inscribed to avoid a traumatizing notion. Like the Deganawidah legend of the Iroquois, the book of Genesis is one of our earliest trauma narratives (what else can the loss of paradise, the loss of God's most intimate presence, be but traumatic?), but unlike the Iroquois narrative it does not propose a strategy, beyond additional sweat and labor, for engaging with troubling or conflicting truths in this lifetime. It merely offers comfort in the hope that our diseased state will be repaired in the next life.

The act of engaging with the postlapsarian world of Genesis becomes, in Mary Louise Pratt's estimation, a classificatory one. According to Pratt, European adventurers, following the example of the biblical Adam, took on the task of "locating every species on the planet, extracting it from its particular, arbitrary surroundings (the chaos), and placing it in its appropriate spot in the system (the order—book, collection, or garden) with its new written, secular European name."[31] In an effort to reimpose order on chaos, "one by one the planet's life forms were to be drawn out of the tangled threads of their life surroundings and rewoven into European-based patterns of global unity and order."[32] This impulse, the act of restoring order through compulsive categorization, is perhaps in accordance with the attempt to keep chaos, or troubling knowledge, at bay. Western culture constructs order around the possibility of the textual containment held out by the book of Genesis, continuing to operate along the elaborately maintained lines of space, gender, and race established within its narrative confines. These hierarchies, or the lack thereof in Native stories, are reflected in the laws and governments of these two civilizations. The materials of their respective stories seep deeply into the cognitive processes and culminate in the manners in which two worlds are conceived and engaged.

We must accept, however, that containment of the garden is never perfect and its leaks, regarded as Satanic infiltrations and influences, must be diligently policed. Therefore, when the so-called New World was officially located by European powers in 1492 and loosely equated with paradise, the notion had already been culturally internalized that Satan ran free within its boundaries (*Et in Arcadia Ego*) and what was needed were aggressive acts of containment of both a rhetorical and physical nature to put the devil back in his box. One of the most powerful weapons by which Europeans hoped to accomplish this task was alphabetic writing, or more specifically, the book, which was to be the primary tool of *unwitnessing* in the colonial endeavor. The Christian book was one that erased even as it espoused, a tool that sought to draw tight circles around contradictory belief and practice and position armed seraphim at the entryways to such cognitive tabernacles.

Walter Mignolo observes that in the period of Spanish colonization the human book had "two functions: to know the creator of the universe by reading His Book and, at the same time, to censure every human expression in which the Devil manifests itself by dictating false books."[33] Such a philosophy could tolerate only *one* version of events, *one* cosmology, *one* set of spiritual beliefs and was in absolute antipathy to oral belief systems which did not depend upon a closed finite reading of a particular narrative. The American Indian worldview, however, seemed capable of accommodating competing ideologies. Vizenor notes how in tribal creation stories "the variations are the work of imagination, not disagreement. [The Native storyteller] is an artist, not a scrivener; he does not recount a standardized historical narrative for the pleasure of culture cultists and methodologists."[34] If Christian explorers were wedded to their totalizing ideology of one God, one creation, one religion, Native epistemologies seem not to have demanded such uniformity of belief, did not demand the illusion of absolute closure that print discourse imposes on perception.

As the orator Gachradodow of the Iroquois spoke during the 1744 treaty hearings in Lancaster, Pennsylvania, "the World . . . was made on the other Side of the Great Water different from what it is on this Side, as may be known from the different colours of our Skin, and of our Flesh, and that which you call Justice may not be so among us."[35] Gachradodow does not condemn European epistemologies or demand adherence to his own views, but rather posits the existence of separately conceived worlds allowing for variant modes of thought and belief to simultaneously exist. His hope, however, is that the two parties can come to a mutual understanding by hearing out one another's narratives. Although Native peoples did have their own systems of signifiers, symbols or hieroglyphs capable of transmitting information over distances prior to European contact, the purpose of these symbols was not, as we will see, to cordon off spiritual or intellectual enquiry. They served instead to offer interpretations of events that could be told in a different manner by different interpreters and were not necessarily in need of absolute (authorized) versions to retain cultural validity. While Native mysteries were preserved and rehearsed, they nevertheless issued from an open space of human breath and possibility.

The imposition of Christian orthodoxy on Native communities was regarded as a benevolent act by the colonists, even when it required the utmost violence to effect. It was the rhetorical lock, stock, and barrel of colonial conquest, the altruistic impulse by which cultures perceived to have been seated in darkness were given the once-in-a-lifetime opportunity of embracing Christian light and community. As the Royal Patent of the first settlers in Virginia affirmed, the chief end of the colony was the "propagating of Christian religion to such people as yet live in darkness and miserable ignorance of the true knowledge and worship of God, and may in time bring the infidels and savages living in those parts to human civility and to a settled and quiet government."[36] And since the heart of the Christian religion resided in the "word" of God, the scene of contact in American colonization was also the *scene of writing*. The assimilation of Natives into, not just Christianity, but alphabetic literacy lay at the very forefront of European evangelistic endeavors and, as I will demonstrate, had lasting effects on the laws, institutions, and human communities that constitute our present reality.

Writing is the scene of appropriation, anxiety, and, importantly, self-preservation in the face of perceived threats to one's identity. As words and letters were making their way into Native space, American Indians in most instances attempted to appropriate this tool of the Europeans in a pragmatic attempt to preserve and further what they could of the integrity of their own cultural structures, not to replace them. Natives were not only responding to the tool of writing throughout each successive wave of colonization, they were engaging with it, bringing their own repressed practices in relation with both its political and cultural potentialities. Hardly recognized in the prevailing literature, however, is the idea that Native correspondents left any kind of record of these ultimately violent interactions, or that indigenous peoples had any sort of substantial literatures of their own when all this got under way. In this chapter I examine how the archive begins to make available the traces of Native inscription that circulated in the midst of colonization. It is precisely at the moment that the colonizer attempts to unwitness Native culture, that Native culture, Native writing, and Native civilization appears, however briefly, on the periphery of colonial vision. By surveying accounts of Spanish, French, and English adventurers in the earliest moments of contact, one can locate these traces of tribal presence in acts of physical and cognitive annihilation.

The Spanish conquistadors practiced unwitnessing by attempting to destroy every aspect of Native civilization that affronted them. Early French explorers and missionaries of New France labored to elide Native writing by averting their gaze from what they considered to be a "grotesque," devilish script. Indigenous inscription in the English colonies, when acknowledged at all, was conceptualized as the remnant of a former great civilization that had found its way here in biblical times, and had, through the loss of writing, forgotten its roots in Western systems of knowledge. Native civilization, a type of forbidden knowledge, is displaced into a mythological Edenic realm where it cannot be recovered or penetrate the psyche of the settler. For to accept that Natives were accurate repositories of their own histories and origins would be to acknowledge them as legitimate civilizations and by extension, delegitimize the entire basis for colonial expansion. The figure of the Native that endures this framework—the textualized Native as will be presented in this chapter most specifically in the person of the Pequot convert Wequash—is but a cipher for English ambitions and agendas, the epitome of what Vizenor calls the "simulations of dominance." Therefore, prior to focusing solely on the written texts of Natives in the colonial period, it is necessary to comprehend the dynamic by which alphabetic literacy is introduced and Native literature is elided.

The very first texts to come out of the new colonial world, such as Columbus' journals, Bernal Diaz's history of *The Conquest of New Spain*, the early *Jesuit Relations*, *New England's First Fruits*, and Roger Williams' *Key to the Language of America*, are largely concerned with representing Natives and, in some measure, controlling the discourse by which the rest of the Western world will view their subjugation. Although resistant Natives were not immediately able to "write back" against the grain of Western history, residing behind the offered one-dimensional representations were politically engaged figures who inscribed their own presence in the historical moment in ways that defy and transcend European containments.

"It was simply their word that brought it forth": Unwitnessing the Materials of Civilization in New Spain

The very first mention of Native American inscription in the European historical archive appears on the periphery of Columbus' commentary in his first journal, a sort of sideways glance that never comes fully into focus. On his fifth day of having made landfall in the West Indies, Columbus walked the island he (re)named "Fernandina," admiring the tall trees that reminded him of Andalusia in May and the people he called Indians, whom he found to be "naked" and willing to offer "whatever they possessed" to the visitors. It is here that his crew encountered a "man who wore in his nose a piece of gold about half the size of a castellano on which they saw letters."[37] It is perhaps all too fitting that letters and gold are bonded to the same material object in this first sighting. The historian Howard Zinn noticed how, in the first two weeks of Columbus' journal entries upon reaching the West Indies, "there is one word that recurs seventy-five times: Gold."[38] Conversely, the reference to Indian "letters" appears only this once. Columbus is angered by the fact that his men, despite the alleged willingness of the Natives to give away their every possession in exchange for trifles, had not bartered for this particular specimen "and given as much as they [the Natives] asked."[39] He immediately assumes that the "coin" with its inscription must come from some other, more civilized, country and that he might be able to determine something about his proximity to the Asian mainland through this curiosity. But, as his men cryptically respond, "they did not dare to bargain for it."[40] This is not only the first sign of Native writing recorded by Europeans in the American continent, but it is an early indicator that not all was transpiring as swimmingly as Columbus' journals generally suggest. What could not be "dared" amongst so "tractable" a people willing to offer up all possessions? Perhaps his predilection toward welcoming Natives on his boat and then keeping them there against their will had provoked tensions of which Columbus had nothing to say at the moment. As near as Columbus could tell, the Natives of these islands "would easily be made Christians, for they appeared to have no religion. God willing, when I make my departure I will bring half a dozen of them back to their Majesties, so that they can learn to speak."[41] The incident of the lettered gold piece passes, however, without further comment.

Some twenty-nine years after Columbus' landfall in the Americas, Bernal Diaz, a foot soldier in the armies of Cortes, would bear witness to that army's first forays on the Mexican mainland. Early in his adventures, he tells how the Natives they encountered

> led us to some very strange buildings of fine masonry which were, the prayer-houses of their idols, the walls of which were painted with the great serpents and evil-looking gods. In the middle was something like an altar, covered with clotted blood, and on the other side of the idols were symbols like crosses, and all were colored. We stood astonished, never having heard of such things before.

This refrain, of things never before heard of, would be repeated as he and Cortes' men arrived at the capital city of Tenochtitlan (today, Mexico City) in 1521 and viewed "these great towns and cues and buildings rising from the water, all made of stone . . . like an enchanted vision from the tale of Amadis. Indeed some of our soldiers asked whether it was not all a dream . . . I do not know how to describe this first glimpse of things never heard of, seen or dreamed before."[42] Such first glimpses of "evil" runes, pagan crosses, enchanted architecture, the wondrous materials of things seen and not seen, were extremely telling. Diaz had no cultural reference in which to place such visions. He was more comfortable viewing them as dream than as reality, even if, in his own estimation, such things as this were "never heard of, seen or dreamed before." He finally resorts to a literary reference, the story of Amadis, to somehow encompass it all. Diaz, expecting to encounter the naked savages promised by Columbus' accounts, instead found himself confronted with the materials of what he clearly recognized as civilization. But the processes of containment, by which such first reactions would be subdued and reordered, were quick to assert themselves.

Diaz notes that when Cortes first introduced to the Aztecs his cross and an image of the Virgin Mary during this initial visit to Tenochtitlan, the ruler of the great metropolis, Motecuhzoma, attempted to place the offered symbols of Christianity alongside his own idols of worship. Cortes recoiled at such a gesture of accommodation. He ultimately sought to replace every material aspect of Aztec religion, including their books or codices, with a Christian counterpart. While Motecuhzoma was able to tolerate the symbolic coexistence of two spiritual universes, Cortes viewed this as the ultimate degradation of his principles, responding "these idols of yours are not gods but evil things, the proper name for which is devils." He suggested instead that they place a cross over the entire temple and create a separate room for the "image of Our Lady . . . and then you will see by the fear that your idols have of her, how grievously they have deceived you."[43]

Ultimately Motecuhzoma, himself, represented an affront to Spanish hegemony, and just as the Aztec symbols were soon replaced by Christian symbols, so did it come about that the Aztec ruling families were violently displaced by Cortes and his descendants. The end result was that, the exchange rate was dreadfully high. For Natives to become a witness to the Christian god, they had to, in fact, undergo a violent unwitnessing in which their songs, their books, their relics, their corporeal bodies, and presumably even their souls, were brought under containment by the superimposition of Christian forms. Jose de Acosta, compiling his *Natural and Moral History of the Indes* in 1590, recalled that within the libraries of the Aztecs one might find books,

> either bound or folded, in which the wisest Indians kept the distribution of time, and knowledge of plants and animals and other things pertaining to nature, as well as their ancient customs . . . [but] a missionary there thought that all of it must be a witches' spell and magic art and insisted that they be burned, and indeed those books were burned, which was regretted afterward not only by the Indians but by curious Spaniards who desired to know the secrets of that land.[44]

The very existence of these markers of Native belief, spirituality, learning, and history could not be tolerated by the Spaniards. The burning of these books has been poignantly characterized by Thomas King as an occurrence as "devastating as Julius Caesar's destruction of the library at Alexandria."[45]

The pre-Columbian texts of the Aztecs, Mayans, and other Meso-American cultures did not consist of a system of strictly phonetic characters organized into signifiers and designed to independently convey information to anyone who happened to be instructed in the deciphering of their values. The word "word" was nonexistent in the pre-Columbian Náhuatl language.[46] Mignolo notes that "in all Mayan languages there is no linguistic or semantic differentiation among the words for painting, drawing, and writing."[47] *Tlacuiloliztli* was the Náhuatl expression for both writing and painting.[48] The figures in sacred texts such as the *Popul Vuh* or the *Chilam Balam* do not dictate verbatim words, sentences, and paragraphs, but rather convey a series of associations for those who have been ordained in the corresponding mysteries—they comprise a particular blueprint around which the orator must construct narrative presence (see figure 1.1).[49] As expressed in the alphabetic translation of the *Popul Vuh*, "it was simply their word that brought it forth."[50]

Figure 1.1. Aztec tribute roll.

As such, these documents cannot be directly equated with the textualized inscriptions of Western culture. The *Popul Vuh* is meant to be enacted as much as read, so that the decrees and actions of the gods are rehearsed and held in the hearts of those who participate in the ceremony. As the scribes who compiled the surviving alphabetic text pointed out, "it takes a long performance and account to complete the lighting of all the 'sky-earth.'"[51] Such a performance is not regarded as a nostalgic recollection of the world's creation, but a rekindling of the forces that bring light into being and allow it to so remain (perhaps a Christian comparison might be noticed in the manner in which Catholics experience the body and blood of Christ reconstituting itself in the Eucharist). Dennis Tedlock notes in the introduction to his English translation of the *Popul Vuh* that "if a divinatory reading or pondering was a way of recovering the depth of vision enjoyed by the first four humans, a long performance, in which readers may well have covered every major subject in the entire book, was a way of recovering the full cosmic sweep of that vision."[52] The figures, or logographs, that occupied the codex were to form a path that a priest, trained in the mysteries, would follow in his reenactment of the ceremony. Those who knew the paths were held in highest regard. The book makers, or history keepers, were known as "the ones who continually carry us, they guide us, they cause the path to speak to us. They are the ones who put us in order."[53] The production of such writings was more aligned with the cognitive processes of an oral culture than one steeped in Western writing. Elizabeth Hill Boone suggests that "images in Aztec pictorial histories were fashioned as signal references to an oral story . . . Varied events in the histories are reduced to their epitome, their most essential and distilled visual form."[54] If pre-Columbian systems differed from Western European notions of writing, they nevertheless comprised reflective and fluid means of recording and imparting culture.

While Columbus and Diaz offer us a sense of how Europeans first responded to Native text and inscription, Fray Toribio Motolinia offers a glimpse into the Native's initial encounter with alphabetic literacy. Motolinia was amongst the first group of twelve Franciscans to travel to New Spain in 1524, and in his book *History of the Indians of New Spain*, he reports on the degradations of the slave trade that had quickly blossomed in the newly colonized territory under Cortes. The Indian slaves were employed in every facet of labor, but most specifically in the massive dismantling and reconstruction of Tenochtitlan, or Mexico City. Motolinia writes of the Spanish that

> so great was their haste, in some years, to make slaves that from all parts of Mexico they brought in great herds of them [indigenous peoples], like flocks of sheep, in order to brand them. They were not content with those among the Indians

> are called slaves (for, although according to cruel and barbarous law some may be slaves, in actual truth almost no one is), but hurried the Indians so to produce slaves as tribute—so many every eighty days—that having exhausted the supply of real slaves, they brought their children and their *macehuales* (who are of a low social class, like farmer vassals) and all whom they could get together, and brought them in, terrifying them into saying they were slaves. The fact that no careful investigation was made and that the branding was cheap produced so many marks on their faces, in addition to the royal brand, that they had their faces covered with letters, for they bore the marks of all who had bought and sold them.[55]

Columbus and Cortes did not come with Bibles in hand to teach the Natives the word of God. The printing press itself was only some fifty years old at the time of Columbus' arrival in the West Indies, and bound and printed texts were not yet in wide circulation. The Spanish conquistadors relied more heavily on symbols, the cross itself, and images of the Virgin Mary, and these symbols were wielded as an expression of their power and dominance. But the Natives of New Spain were indoctrinated into alphabetic literacy by having it burned into their very flesh, an inscription of their condition of servitude that could not be erased, even as ownership changed hands and new inscriptions were added on top of the old making a palimpsest of Native flesh. The European letter manifested itself as trauma. The marks of alphabetic literacy, seared on the skin, must have appeared as a sign of contagion, a virulent reinscribing of identity transcendent of the mere scars on the surface.

The Franciscans established the Royal College of Santa Cruz in 1536, where they instructed Natives in alphabetic literacy, focusing on Latin and Náhuatl as the primary languages. The college, which drew its students from the primary schools that were already up and running by then, was said to have housed up to seventy students at its peak, all of whom were capable in their letters.[56] It had been determined early on that the only efficient means of converting the Native population was through learning their language, and friars like Motolinia and a handful of others were able to acquire it quickly enough to become writing instructors. One such friar, Bernardino de Sahagun, scorned other missionary efforts that failed to adopt this practice, claiming their lack of effectiveness was rooted in their unwillingness to learn the Native culture. He, on the other hand, seemed to have mastered the language and knew more of Náhuatl religious rites than probably any other nonindigenous man in the region. His method of acquiring such knowledge was to gather village elders in various towns to paint versions, not only of their historical and religious narratives, but of their own eyewitness accounts of the Spanish invasion and the fall of Tenochtitlan. He would then have his students trained in writing the Náhuatl language transcribe these accounts in letters which Sahagun himself would then translate in Spanish. This meticulous, fortuitously ethical process, requiring over thirty years to complete, resulted in what is now known as the *Florentine Codex*, a mix of Mexican figure painting, Náhuatl writing, and Spanish translation.

Sahagun took an extraordinary amount of pride in this accomplishment, stating, "I, Fray Bernardino de Sahagun . . . wrote twelve Books of the *divine*, or rather *idolatrous*, human and natural things of New Spain [italics mine]."[57] His seeming confusion over whether the contents of his books were "divine" or "idolatrous" in some manner reflects the intense level of his own engagement with these texts. Rather than efface his original thought, he allows both the "error" and the "correction" to stand, and in some ways this speaks toward the nature of the project as a whole which is bizarrely one of erasure and preservation. Sahagun was the first to admit that "it was necessary to destroy all adulterous things." But this notion is somehow tinged with regret, as he notes the effects of this violent cultural displacement. He writes, "they and all their possessions were trampled underfoot and destroyed that no vestige remained of what they were before. Thus they are considered as barbarians, as a people at the lowest level of perfection, when in reality . . . in matters of good conduct they surpass many other nations."[58]

It seems that Sahagun's students were able to quickly acquire the skills of European literacy. The transition was probably made less difficult by the fact that these students, "the sons of native rulers and native nobility," were already accustomed to the disciplines of the scribe.[59] They were familiar with books, study, and reading, and did not have to significantly alter such known routines in order to appropriate this new form of literacy. Miguel Leon-Portilla observes that

> for over a hundred years before the Conquest education in Tenochtitlan was compulsory for all male children. They . . . studied the tribe's history and traditions, and memorized the sacred hymns and other texts. So much emphasis was placed on accurate memorization that after the Conquest it was possible to record many poems and traditions that would otherwise have been lost forever.[60]

While the Spanish were engaged in destroying every vestige of Native culture, dismantling the very architecture of Native lives and rebuilding a new empire with the materials of the old, these students were managing to reinscribe their endangered culture in new forms.

In a similar fashion, the Quiché who wrote the alphabetic *Popul Vuh* (in roughly the same period that Sahagun was compiling the materials of the *Florentine Codex*), were able to transcribe their sacred narrative for historical purposes, though "in Christendom now," as the text carefully proclaims. Tedlock posits that "if the missionaries wanted them to write translations of Christian prayers, sermons, and catechisms into Mayan languages . . . very little time passed before some Mayans found political and religious applications for alphabetic writing that suited their own purposes." As for the original book and ancient writings of the Quiché, we are told, "the one who reads and assesses it has a hidden identity." The voice of the one who reads and assesses must remain part of the hidden transcript until that time when the books can be brought into the light again and the voice unleashed. In such a way might the world be created once more, for, as the alphabetic *Popul Vuh* states, "it was simply their word that brought it forth."[61]

The Franciscan College of Santa Cruz lasted for some forty years before finally succumbing to disease and entropy. Sahagun wrote, "the plague that occurred thirty-one years ago gave the college a great blow, and this plague, of this year of 1576, has not given it a lesser one, for there is hardly anyone still in the college. Dead and sick, almost all are gone."[62] Sahagun himself nearly succumbed to the sickness, but he recovered and his health prevailed for the next decade. The codex he painstakingly compiled, however, was confiscated by Spanish authorities in response to a 1577 royal decree forbidding anyone to write "concerning the superstitions and way of life these Indians had."[63] The text was taken from Sahagun and brought back to Spain where it was fortuitously preserved by an apparent accident of filing. As for the state of Christianity in the colonies, Sahagun confessed, "the Catholic faith has very shallow roots, and with much labor little fruit is produced, and from little cause that which is cultivated withers."[64] Fray Motolinia wrote optimistically of single priests, through the Requiermento, baptizing "four, five, six thousand" Indians in a day.[65] Sahagun wrote of overseeing the burial of "more than ten thousand bodies."[66] Somewhere amid these competing narratives of death and rebirth through conversion, the indigenous people were busy surviving and keeping their own narratives alive through memory, trickery, resistance, and writing.

Blackrobes and Birch Bark: Jesuits Encountering Native Writing in New France

If the book, as material object, did not figure largely in the reports that traveled out of New Spain, colonial recorders of New France offered a large number of accounts in which the indigenous man first encountered alphabetic writing. Such accounts were of special interest to the colonist because they presented an opportunity to display what were felt to be the superior qualities of their culture. It was the book, more than guns, cook pots, and other trade goods that best represented the civilization colonists were exporting to this world. The French Jesuit Le Jeune would claim of the Huron in his 1635 *Relation* that "above all," they admired European "writing, for they could not conceive how, what one of us, being in the village, had said to them, and put down at the same time in writing, another, who meanwhile was in a house far away, could say readily on seeing the writing. I believe they have made a hundred trials of it."[67]

Ethno-historian James Axtell, in his book *After Columbus*, posits that "the ability to read and write was awe-inspiring to the Indians largely because it duplicated a spiritual feat that only the greatest shamans could perform, namely, that of reading the mind."[68] In a sense, European explorers tried to position themselves as the more powerful shamans, introducing their technologies in a manner designed to trump the spiritual leaders of Native communities in scenes reminiscent of Moses taking on the magicians of the court of Ramses II. The desired outcome of these confrontations was to demonstrate how the European God was indeed more powerful, or, in effect, the *one true* God.

Axtell provides a number of examples in which writing is perceived to have talismanic power during early cultural encounters, particularly amongst the Jesuit priests who established missions in New France. One telling incident, taken from the *Jesuit Relations*, occurs during a smallpox epidemic amongst the Hurons in the winter of 1640. As Axtell relates, "fear and despair swept through the cabins" and "stubborn traditionalists reported dreams in which the Jesuits unfolded 'certain books' on the shore of Lake Huron, 'whence issued sparks of fire which spread everywhere, and no doubt caused this pestilential disease.'"[69] In this passage it can be seen that writing is equated with both disease and fire. It is something that spreads and consumes, and once let loose it cannot be reined in. It leaves a path of death and destruction in its wake. Many early tales of a North American Native engagement with writing take a certain pleasure in portraying how the "simple" Natives were duped by their unfamiliarity with the notion of "paper that could speake" or frightened by its seemingly magical properties.[70] As Roger Williams noted, when confronted with books and letters the Narrangansett would exclaim "Manittowock They are Gods."[71] Of course such early anecdotes when combined had the desired effect of infantilizing a Native response to writing.[72] A closer look at the *Relations* of the French Jesuits complicates this view, however, rendering uncertain the power of writing to amaze.

The country of the various nations of Micmac, Abenaki, Passamaquoddy, Iroquois, Montagnais, Ottawa, Huron, and others visited by the Jesuits in the early seventeenth century was called *Canada*, an Iroquoian word that the explorer Jacques Cartier understood to mean "this is our village."[73] Prior to the arrival of the French on Canadian shores, the indigenous peoples who occupied these lands lived in small well-spaced villages, occasionally fortified by wooden palisades erected in a circle around their dwellings, other times more openly spaced along the river valleys with crops of beans, squash, and corn growing in the fields beyond. Many village populations would break into smaller bands, moving deep into the woodlands to hunt and forage through the winter. Most would move again toward water during the seasons when certain fish migrations were anticipated. Fields and woodlands were regularly cleared by fire to make room for planting and to accommodate hunting practices. Families were matrilineal, tracing their lineage through the female side of the family rather than the male. The larger network of villages was bound together not through nationalistic or tribal affiliations, but through kinship, shared traditions, and a system of clans represented by specified animal totems, their significance deeply integrated into the spiritual and literary narratives of the overall community. Different villages, as well as different nations, would trade amongst one another, intermarry, and occasionally fight wars, although, as Father Brebeuf noted, "they never undertake war without reason."[74] According to Richard White, "socially and politically this was a village world," and these villages were held together, as always, by ties of kinship, tradition, and shared narratives that often transcended common contemporary designations of Indian nationhood.[75]

The Jesuits first arrived in New France in 1611, following a decree given by King Henry IV, who, "more solicitous for religion than for commerce, resolved, in the year 1608, to introduce Christian rites into this part of the New World."[76] Early efforts at establishing missions all failed, however, despite Father Baird's 1611 letter asserting that certain missionaries had "baptized about one hundred savages."[77] Baird was surprised to learn upon closer inspection that of these new converts hardly a one knew his own baptismal name, and mostly all kept more than one wife.[78] This was all proof enough to the early Jesuits that instruction must precede baptism, and both Baird and Enemond Masse agreed that learning the language of the Micmacs would be the key to their success. They went so far as to propose the composition of a "Canadian catechism," but for various reasons their efforts were thwarted and these early missionary efforts were broken up by internal opposition and conflicts with the English.[79] A permanent missionary effort would not be established until Paul Le Jeune arrived in New France in 1632 and was placed at the head of the Jesuit missionary efforts there.[80] Le Jeune, in his yearly reports back to the home office in France, labored tirelessly and imaginatively to recreate his encounters with the indigenous people, repeatedly offering a sense of cultural one-upmanship between himself and the Natives with whom he came in contact. But he repeatedly returned to the book as the absolute marker of his and his culture's inherent superiority. One early assessment of the Native response to his tutorials appears in the 1633 *Relations* where Le Jeune writes, "when I told them we had a book which contained the words and teachings of God, they were very anxious to know how we could have gotten this book—some of them believing that it had been let down from the Sky at the end of a rope, and that we had found it thus suspended in the air. This simplicity made me laugh."[81] The Jesuit never pauses for a moment to think that maybe the individuals of whom he speaks are, themselves, having a good laugh at his simplicity. Clearly Le Jeune has constructed the scene otherwise, but it should not strain credulity to believe that it is, in fact, Le Jeune who is reading the scene incorrectly. His own frustration is made apparent in the very next paragraph in which he bemoans, "if these barbarians would only display some curiosity to know things . . . but they are as cold as marble, and are so imbued with this indifference that you would say they are *surprised at nothing* [italics mine]."[82] In effect, the author, in a moment of excess representation, contradicts his earlier statement of laughable Native "simplicity" by betraying the suspicion that his audience is not quite so dumbstruck as he originally implied. They remain perfectly impassive to his demonstrations and are, more than likely, ridiculing his presumed connection with divine inscription when they invoke the image of a book being lowered down from the heavens on a rope. Only the Jesuit himself refuses to get the joke, but he nevertheless concedes that his discourse has failed to elicit the intended response. Le Jeune fumes that in Canada, instead of being considered "a great master and great Theologian as in France, you must reckon on being here a humble Scholar, and then, Good God! With what masters!—women, little children, and all the Savages,—and exposed to their laughter."[83]

Despite having to face constant ridicule, Le Jeune's reports, and the accounts of the Jesuits in general, might be regarded as admirable in the sense that they remain remarkably willing to engage the Natives of Canada in dialogue and they are tireless in their efforts at recording such accounts, however culturally biased their recollections. In one dialogue offered by Le Jeune, we hear how he and a Huron man sat up one night discussing their peoples' differing versions of the ancient flood. As Le Jeune supposes, "they had indeed preserved the account of this deluge, but through a long succession of years they had enveloped this truth in a thousand fables." The French on the other hand "could not be mistaken about this event, having the same belief as our ancestors, since we see their books." Le Jeune argues for the contiguous infallibility of his version by stating, "God sent men whom we call prophets, because they learn the truths of God and teach them to men."[84] The virtue of these "truths" is that they have traveled from the mind of God directly to the pens of these prophets, so that what they recorded was God's own will and testament. It was the lack of writing then, and particularly God's writing, that had led the Huron to their misconceptions. As the races of man were scattered in the wake of the flood, some were able to retain the original stories through the dissemination of texts, while others, like the Natives of Canada, only maintained versions of the tale that became corrupted over time through the repetition of oral narratives.

Most remarkable about this encounter, however, is the fact that the Huron man, after listening politely to Le Jeune's entire conversation without ever once offering objection or contradiction, is said to have picked up a "pencil" and begun marking on the ground an entire recreation of the history the Jesuit has just unfolded.

> "Here is he who made all," said he [the Huron]; "He [God] begins in this place to create Angels and the world; there he created the first man and first Woman; see how the race of men, increasing, divides and offends God; Here is the deluge, here are the prophets,"—in short he came up to our own time; then rising, he began to laugh; "I am not surprised at our being tired," said he, "for we have made a long journey."[85]

Although the intended point of the passage may be that without the knowledge of writing Native belief had lapsed into error, through a certain excess of representation the Jesuit priest opens to us the manner in which the Huron was also, in fact, writing history. The specific figures of his interpretive sketch remain hidden from us, their inscription in the dirt suggesting their impermanence. Perhaps for Le Jeune they remain unreadable, an inscription founded in error, and in a sense he has already censured them, wiped them out for us as effectively as if he had swiped his boot across the Huron's drawings. Nevertheless the scene suggests that the Huron man, at least, had perceived the agenda in back of Le Jeune's discourse. Without openly contradicting the Jesuit's assertions he modeled the way in which his own people kept traditions intact, positing narrative itself as a kind of journey, a path that one inhabits, employing figures like stepping stones to retrace the important stops along the way.[86]

It is doubtful whether Le Jeune was receptive to such an example or if he even realized it was being offered. But once again one senses his frustration with the encounter as he concludes, "it is not thus that one should begin to instruct the nonbeliever; for, since all these things are historical, the mind which has no knowledge of him who has revealed to us these truths remains free to believe or not believe."[87] For Le Jeune such freedom was intolerable. Even "historical" details had no implicit integrity if not bound to the bedrock "knowledge" of biblical "truths." The issue remained fixed on a simple binary of truth and error. His system of thought was virtually incapable of accommodating that which did not conform to his own idea of truth, and he was engaged in an endless task of, if not quite erasing such errors, then containing them, using his written accounts to force experience into some form of compliance with his desires. An undesired effect, however, is that the Huron man may be regarded as more a creature of genius than the Jesuit, as he seems able to hold two opposing systems of thought in his mind at the same time.

In a letter to his superior in France, dated 1637, Le Jeune offered a surprising metaphor as he contrasted the comfort and encouragement he received from his homeland with the entrenched resistance he now faced in New France. He wrote, "I learned through a great many letters that people of high rank and most signal virtue were contending for us in heaven and upon earth; and it was made evident to me, on a bit of bark or paper, that the demons were let loose and were powerfully opposing our plans."[88] Interestingly, the passage implies that Le Jeune was conscious of two modes of writing, a European writing of letters as well as an indigenous writing on birch bark, one writing aligned with heavenly forces, one aligned with the forces of Satan, each working in seeming opposition to the other.

Birch bark writing was a common practice amongst the indigenous peoples of the Northeast, who utilized a recognized store of symbols with slight variations (similar in some respects to the better-known "winter counts" of the Sioux), to suggest concepts and events both historical and contemporary. The most studied examples of this can be found amongst the Anishinaabe who continue to hold in their possession sacred birch bark scrolls that recount their cosmology, their migrations as a people, and the creation of the Midawewin or Mide Lodge.[89] The mixed-blood Ojibwe historian William Warren, who described himself as "a person in language, thoughts, beliefs, and blood, partly an Indian," noted in 1853 that

> they fully believe, and it forms part of their religion, that the world has once been covered by a deluge, and that we are now living on what they term "new earth." This idea is fully accounted for by their vague traditions; and in their Me-da-we-win or Religion, hieroglyphics are used to denote this second earth.[90]

When Warren uses the term "vague" to describe these traditions, he is unconsciously subscribing to a separate tradition founded in the Western epistemologies to which he has been reared despite his Anishinaabe ancestry. The traditions in question are "vague" only from a Western perspective because they have never been fully acknowledged or granted cultural authority by the keepers of the Western archive. From the very start of

Western history-keeping, in fact, Native spiritualities and the various means of preserving narrative have been scorned, denigrated, and unwitnessed as though they simply don't exist.

It is evident, however, that the nations encountered by the Jesuits in the first half of the seventeenth century, who had economic, cultural, and linguistic ties to the Anishinaabe, had similar methods of recording history and spiritual practices. Father Brebeuf notes in 1636 how at the burial of one "important man in the country" his daughter placed at his side "his *Atsatonewai*, that is his package of council sticks, which are all the books and papers of the country."[91] How odd that Brebeuf was fully aware of such records and yet never commented further upon them, almost as if he only felt license to mention them at all as they were being laid to rest in the earth and shut away from his sight forever. One must search painstakingly through the colonial archives to find like pieces of evidence that Natives kept any written account of their laws, religions, customs, and histories.[92] And yet, as Brebeuf launches into a discourse upon the complexities of the Huron language, he fixes upon a paradoxical illustration, asking his readers to consider how the Huron "verb *ahiaton*, meaning 'to write,' is conjugated absolutely in this way: *iehaton*, I write; *chiehiatonic*, you [singular] write; *ihahiatonic*, he writes; *awahiatonic*, we write; *swahiatonic*, you [plural] write; *attihiatonic*, they write."[93] Brebeuf, in conjugating this verb, seems to have unwittnessed a significant implication of his own observation; the implication being that *everybody* writes.

Although the body of firsthand literature built up around every aspect of the colonial endeavor in North America argues persuasively against the idea that Native Americans had any such form of communication, a partial exception comes from the Dutch Moravian missionary Heckewelder who, having lived amongst the Lenape in the 1760s, accustomed himself to the language and traditions of these people. Certainly he repeats the colonial mantra that "the Indians do not possess our art of writing [for] they have no alphabets, nor any mode of representing to the eye the sounds of words spoken," but he, nevertheless, offers one of the rare observations made by a European that is appreciative of an indigenous system of signification. He notes that the Lenape have

> certain hieroglyphics, by which they describe facts in so plain a manner, that those who are conversant with those marks can understand them with the greatest ease, as easily, indeed, as we can understand a piece of writing . . . All Indian nations can do this, although they have not the same marks; yet I have seen the Delawares read with ease the drawings of the Chippeways, Mingoes, Shawanos, and Wyandots.[94]

Heckewelder intimates that Indian writing was not only in ubiquitous use in North America, but that it was in wide circulation between the many nations, employed in trade and diplomacy. And yet we must continue to strain to see this writing, to acknowledge its presence, or get a sense of its overall utility.[95]

As Heckewelder suggests, not only have the grand narratives of many Native cultures been given written form, but Native representation was brought to bear as well on situations of diplomacy, trade, and every day use. In the Northeast carved messages generally known as *awikhigans* were commonly left on trees or prominent places along the trail where passersby would see them. *Awikhigans* might be used to detail the results of a conflict, the success or failure of a hunt, or any other number of eventualities (see figure 1.2). In 1637 Le Jeune wrote of the head counts of Huron prisoners the Iroquois had left on the wooden shaft of a dismantled cross, to inform their enemies of events that had transpired in battle. He recounts how "we

Figure 1.2. Passamaquoddy *awikhigan* found in Garrick Mallory's 1893 *Picture Writing of the American Indians*.

studied it carefully" and notes that "they had also fastened this picture to a branchless tree, so that passers-by could readily see it; the different lines indicated the quality and age of the prisoners, as some Savages who were there explained to us."[96] Le Jeune describes the message in some detail, noting that two pictured heads that were larger than the others represented "two captains they had in their clutches" and that two others were of "young lads being taken to the Seminary." He observes that they "had made stripes in the form of plumes on the heads of the bravest ones" and that "all these heads were scrawled in red, except one, which was painted in black—a sign that this last one had been killed, and that all the others were victims destined, as it were, for the fire."[97] The communication must have, in fact, been quite long and contained a variety of nuances, including the identification of specific individuals. That it needed to be translated to Le Jeune at all, and the fact that it was read so carefully by his Huron companions, signified that what was being observed was not simply a mnemonic device, but a detailed communication of information not previously known to those who read it. Nevertheless, Le Jeune could not refrain from classifying this intelligence once he was done with it, as "grotesque figures (for the Savages are not acquainted with the art of painting)."[98] The writing itself, regardless of its content or utility, is "grotesque" and has the power to appall. For Le Jeune, the fact that this communication was carved out upon a desecrated cross could only have added to his sense of overall revulsion.[99]

Le Jeune, following the winter trek of the Montagnais in the winter of 1633–1634, observed and, to a degree, participated in their daily activities, including the Montagnais' ceremonies and rituals such as the shaking tent ritual and their consultations with the "genii of light."[100] He notes that "the Savages are great singers" and that "they often invited me to sing some song or prayer."[101] He observes that the Montagnais would sing and drum in their suffering, their hunger, and in times of peril. For the Montagnais/Naskapi/Cree the drum was central to daily life and was a means of establishing contact with the manitou that served as intercessors between the human and spirit world. Le Jeune, in his accounts, characterized these manitou as "devils" and made a great show of not being afraid of their power. But, in fact, he either misunderstood or deliberately mischaracterized the nature of such beings, who were not feared so much as revered by the Montagnais. Far from consorting with the devil, the Montagnais were enlisting the aid of their manitou as part of their ritualized order of survival.

According to Canadian ethnographer Adrian Tanner, for the individual most qualified to procure the aid of the manitou, the first thing wanted "was not the traps or the tin stove, but the drum," which was used "to accompany the hunting songs, which come to them through spiritual revelation and which they sing in the evening to the spirits."[102] Such revelations would not only determine where to pursue the hunt, but were integrated into the pattern of the caribou skin coats that the Montagnais wore while hunting. These painted coats were the result of "dreaming and drumming." Dorothy Burnham writes that "the men received instructions in their dreams about the motifs that would give them power when put on their hunting equipment, and the women carried out the work, although it is not known how this partnership, combining the man's dream with the woman's creativity, was worked out."[103]

Caribou coats are still used today by the Montagnais/Naskapi/Cree. Although no longer painted with hieroglyphic characters, they boast geometrical patterns, chevrons, circles, scallops, zigzags, et cetera, that, while bearing symbolic significance, also demonstrate syncretic modes of needlework and design introduced by the Ursuline nuns who came to Quebec shortly on the heels of the Jesuits and played a significant role in the indoctrination of Native women into European norms. Nevertheless, these motifs continue to be determined by the dreams of the hunter and communicated to the artist making the coat.[104] None of the coats in existence today date back to the time of first contacts with the Jesuits, but Le Jeune noted, during a celebration on the day of the "glorious assumption" in 1638, that it was "a beautiful sight to see a company of Savages marching behind the French, in their painted figured robes."[105] This seems to indicate that the robes or coats bore markings, or "figures," similar to the kinds that might be used in birch bark paintings, a symbology that we occasionally glimpse in the Jesuit records, but rarely see straight on.

The paintings, as with the coats themselves, were indicative of the overall respect that the people showed their animal brethren. The labor involved, the songs invoked, and the dreams attended were all ceremonial aspects of a deeply felt reciprocity with the natural world. Offerings and observances were made to the Spirit Leader of the Caribou, Moose, or Beaver (referred to today as "game bosses"), so that they would return year after year.[106] For the Naskapi/Cree hunting is a highly personal journey that must be kept in balance with the sacred relationships and processes of survival. Hans Carlson writes that "the real hunt happened long before the hunter picked up his snowshoes to go to the brush. It happened when he communicated with the animals and asked for their help in feeding his family; their answer would be based on their knowledge of whether he had been grateful for what they had given in the past."[107] Le Jeune was not necessarily unaware of the complex web of relationships involved in the drumming and singing he witnessed, so much as he refused to credit it. He maintained of the Natives in his company that "their superstitions are infinite; their feasts, their medicines, their fishing, their hunting, their wars,—in short, almost their whole life turns upon this pivot; dreams above all, have here great credit."[108] In a sense, he acknowledges how every aspect of Native existence is infused with a spiritual, ritual essence in which experience and vision are incorporated toward survival; it is a system of belief based more on relationships than faith. And yet, in the final analysis, French missionaries like Le Jeune were incapable of crediting what they had witnessed with their own eyes and authorized, if subconsciously, with their own words (see figures 1.3 and 1.4).

One wonders that Le Jeune's own foundational beliefs were not irrevocably altered in the time he spent amongst the Montagnais and Huron of Canada. One can sense how it became difficult to maintain the "true word" of the Christian God in this environment, and even the book, his philosophical and emotional bedrock, began to unhinge itself from the presumed ligatures of certainty. In a passage that one must read as provocatively blurred and evasive Le Jeune recounted how during a winter spent with the Montagnais,

> I sometimes thought I was going blind; my eyes burned like fire, they wept or distilled drops like an alembic; I no longer saw anything distinctly, like the good man who said, *video hominess velut arbores ambulantes*. I repeated the Psalms of my Breviary

Figure 1.3. Naskapi caribou coat. Courtesy of Royal Ontario Museum.

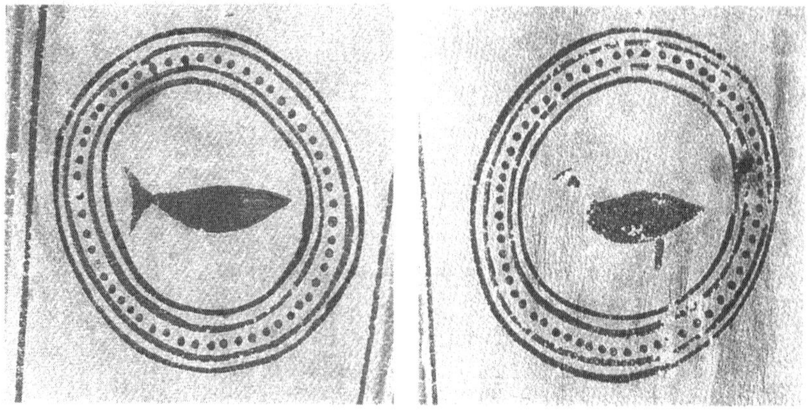

Figure 1.4. Detail from caribou coat.

> the best I could, knowing them half by heart, and waited until the pain might relax a little to recite the lessons; and when I came to read them they seemed written in letters of fire, or of scarlet; I have often closed my book, seeing things so confusedly that it injured my sight.[109]

Certainly there is more than just smoke obstructing the eyes here. In a sense, the passage demonstrates how red ink superimposes itself upon the black ink of his breviary, burning like a fire that confuses meaning, even of those lines he knew "half by heart." A transformation is alluded to, the letters themselves turning from black to red, from ink to flame, and beginning to work in new ways, form new conjunctions that force Le Jeune to turn away from his own book. Even his scriptural insertion (*I see men, like trees, walking around*) is strangely inverted. Read properly, the biblical passage evokes the revelation of a blind man, who, upon encountering Christ, miraculously begins to see more clearly. But Le Jeune is experiencing the opposite effect, his sight apparently dimming in the absence of his spiritual community. His interpretation orients itself instead more toward an origin myth of many Northeastern woodland nations that speaks of the human race first springing from the trees of the forest.[110]

In the years that followed Le Jeune organized a seminary "for the little savages" in Quebec, but it seems to have had little success. Still, at the height of his effort in 1637, Le Jeune could relate the satisfaction of hearing Native children singing the Apostle's creed in their own language. He recalled a moment of multilingual rapture as "the French, the Montangez, and the Hurons all sing together the articles of our belief; and although they used three languages, they harmonized so nicely that it was a great pleasure to hear them."[111] But disease, hunger, and warfare with the Iroquois disrupted every attempt at instructing the few scattered children who were made to attend, and Le Jeune's seminary ultimately had little real influence.

Le Jeune's other effort at instruction involved the persistent European practice of taking Native children from their homes and sending them to France for instruction. Of the three children he sent over in 1636 only one girl survived, and from her he received a letter in her own hand that he quotes in full in his *Relation* for that year. The young woman states, "I am very glad to be in France . . . I hope to have more learning and to cross over to Canada when our Mothers do, to render the debt of hospitality to the women of my nation, if God grants me the grace to do so." Le Jeune also notes a little further along that "she excuses herself if she writes very badly, not yet being able to form the letters." To my knowledge, this is the earliest suggestion of a Native American's engagement with European literacy being directly transcribed in North America, and of course, it is perfectly contained within the rhetorical framework with which Le Jeune presents it to us. The Jesuit responded effusively to the letter from this "poor little child," enquiring of her,

> who has drawn you from your lowly estate to place you in the affection of nobles? What have you rendered to God for your deliverance from slavery, and for your enrollment among the number of his children? Do you remember the resistance you made when your father placed you in my hands? You wished to escape by force, to run after your misery! You would not believe what your countrymen could not yet be convinced of, that we desired to secure for you the greatest of all blessings.[112]

Le Jeune's culturally situated reading of this early specimen of Native letter writing is as egregious as his refusal to read or acknowledge every other form of indigenous literature he encountered during his years in Canada. He perceives the child as having been delivered "from slavery" into the welcoming arms of plenty as though living amongst her own family and extended clan network had been a form of bondage. The lives of women in Native communities often appeared to the Jesuits as nothing less than a kind of enslavement or drudgery. As a result of this bias, Le Jeune cannot perceive the essential plea contained within the girl's correspondence, is utterly blind to the conditions that would engender it, which is nothing more than the pitiful request to be taken back home to her own people. "I hope . . . to cross over to Canada when our mothers do," the girl carefully inserted into the body of her letter. Le Jeune, however, remains fixed upon all the benefits of her having been taken away from the very place to which she longs to return.

The optimism Le Jeune expresses in the prior passage, largely founded upon his own willful suspension of belief, seems to have come unraveled by the close of 1637 when he writes,

> The contagion continued in that country . . . the demons were making open war against us. These tribes believe that we poison and bewitch them, carrying this so far that some of them no longer use the kettles of the French. They say that we have infected the waters, and that the mists which issue thence kill them; that our houses are fatal to them; that we have with us a dead body, which serves us as black magic . . . They go even farther,—they attack our Savior, Jesus Christ; for they publish that there is something, I know not what, in the little tabernacle of our Chapel, which causes them to die miserably.[113]

Le Jeune and the other Jesuits found themselves in the midst of a bitter backlash to their colonial interference, their spiritual impositions and imperial ambitions. He is scornful of the notion that the French have "bewitched" or "poisoned" the Natives with their teachings, but clearly the indigenous communities had studied the relationship between material trade goods and disease and come much closer than the French to understanding the devastating cause and effect that enjoined them.

The swift spread of pandemic disease throughout the areas of settlement and beyond engendered creative responses in the customs and routines of the indigenous peoples of the Northeast, responses that were undoubtedly expressed and countered in indigenous writings. Although Le Jeune does not stoop to scrutinize the signs or impart the details to us in any kind of visible way, he leaves us an interesting passage in which an unreadable text is laid out before our eyes. We are told that in July of 1637, a certain Algonquin came to him with "letters" that spoke of a "Captain" who was coming down to "Kebec" to meet with the "Captain of the French." What are these "letters" of which Le Jeune speaks, who composed them, and how are they deciphered? Le Jeune seems to indicate that the messenger who brought him the "letters" was also the one who communicated their content, for the messenger is quoted as saying that this "Captain" is considered "a grand personage in our country; they say he is a great friend of the Sun, and that he gives letters which prevent one from dying."[114]

Le Jeune confides that he and the governor of Quebec shared a hearty laugh over this story. It does not occur to them that their compulsive habit of baptizing dying Natives with a promise of eternal life sealed in the sign of the cross was little different in character than the described ritual they mocked. Similar anecdotes began to surface although Le Jeune, while compiling all the various reports of the Jesuits under his charge, did not seem to decipher any pattern or pull them together in any cohesive way. When read together, however, it appears that certain Native healers had taken to employing painted coats to combat the sudden catastrophic appearance of new diseases. In a narrative attributed to Father Quentin, who was with the "Algonquin" in 1636, another episode is offered of a young girl "peculiarly loved by her parents" who falls ill and, in accordance with a dream of her uncle's, is laid "upon a sheepskin painted with various figures" that the uncle feels will cure her. The sheepskin is described as painted with "a thousand grotesque figures, canoes, paddles, animals, and such things."[115] In another instance a "Charlatan" insists that a girl will be cured if she is placed upon a blanket "upon which had been drawn pictures of men singing and dancing."[116] It seems these desperate men were invoking their dreams, and using the power of their caribou coats, or some alternative, to combat the sudden inexplicable disease running through their communities, killing their loved ones. If the French book had spread the disease, Native writing was being used to beat it back into remission.

The Jesuits refused to train their vision on the writing of Natives save in the most oblique and transitory references, referring to such inscription as crude "scrawlings" or "grotesque figures." Still the existence of such writing is registered in their accounts and can be accorded a concretized presence, if not actually deciphered from our historical distance. Father Brebeuf relates, during one long winter, how the Jesuits themselves took to "reviving the ancient usage of writing on birch bark, for want of paper."[117] Being somewhat more adaptable than many of his peers, Brebeuf employed this birch bark writing to further his instructions in alphabetic literacy for the Native children in his company.[118] Here Brebeuf can be seen astutely synthesizing his own technology with the technology of the Natives in his presence. It seems self-evident that the very purpose of such writings had always been to transmit narratives of cultural origin, history, and spiritual belief.

One of the more striking examples of the continuance of such a practice may be located amongst the Micmac of Eastern Canada who, for hundreds of years following contact with the Jesuit missionaries, employed a form of hieroglyphic script for use in their recital of prayers. The Micmac called this *Komqwejwi'Kasikl*, or "suckerfish writing," evocative of the impressions left in the river's bed by the bottom-feeding fish. The Jesuit priest Le Clercq noted that these hieroglyphs, far from being highly individualized mnemonic markers, could be deciphered with ease by "Indians who had come from a long distance," suggesting that they had more in common with a form of signification already in place than one developed through interaction with the missionaries. According to the modern-day compilers of these artifacts, this system of hieroglyphs would develop into "one of the most formidable scripts in history with an inventory of approximately 2,700 graphemes."[119]

Le Jeune wished to believe of the Native peoples of Canada that "grace, politeness, the knowledge of the arts, natural sciences, and much less supernatural truths, have as yet no place in this hemisphere, or at least not in these countries."[120] But although the Huron, Montagnais, and other indigenous nations of Canada lived differently than he and perceived the world differently, his own writings couldn't help but betray how little truth resided in his own declaration. Like his Spanish predecessors, Le Jeune refused to be taken in by the possibility of an alternative civilization, and his account actively attempts to efface all evidence of the cultural documents of his Native neighbors, even when relying upon them to move his narrative forward. An indigenous method of writing is referenced, but the imperial gaze rarely lingers upon it or seeks to transcribe its characters. The Jesuits would use the practice of Native birch bark writing to their own ends, but they could not acknowledge the culture represented in these inscriptions. The result has been the entrenched belief that such writings did not exist and that Native *civilization* was itself a prehistorical construct hardly fitting of the title. Contained within Le Jeune's own narrative, however, are the strains that pull against such a discursive construction, the excess moments of represented experience that allow for Native culture to appear between the lines of colonized history as a culture that does in fact know grace, politeness, humor, art, science, truth, and writing. The Jesuits sought to conceal this knowledge from themselves, retreated into their own concretized cultural beliefs, refusing to recognize the transformations of their own characters within the colonial milieu. Like the Spaniards before them, they met each new evidence of a Native civilization similar to their own with a sort of distracted awe, a thing of which they had never heard nor dreamed. Thus it is that by 1673, when Father Marquette traveled down the Mississippi River with La Salle, he had no cognitive precedent for what he encountered along the way. He writes,

> While skirting some rocks, which by their height and length inspired awe, we saw upon one of them two painted monsters which at first made us afraid, and upon which the boldest of savages dare not long rest their eyes. They are as large as a calf; they have horns on their heads like those of a deer, a horrible look, red eyes, a beard like a tiger's, a face somewhat like a man's, a body covered with scales, and so long a tail that it winds all around the body, passing above the head and going back between

> the legs, ending in a fishes tail. Green, red, and black are the three colors composing the picture. Moreover, these 2 monsters are so well painted that we cannot believe that any savage is their author; for good painters in France would find it difficult to paint so well.[121]

In New France as in New Spain, the only answer in response to things never imagined or dreamed of in the New World was to begin to deny Native agency. No "savage" could possibly have been the "author" of such specimens. According to Marquette, even the "boldest" of Natives dared not look upon this sight, thus becoming accomplices in their own unwitnessing. Nevertheless, it becomes apparent that writing was not an essentially foreign concept to the Native peoples of the Northeast. It was simply a technology with different cultural applications. While European adventurers may have labored to deny the existence of indigenous art, culture, and representation, Marquette's own response to it suggests another interpretation that might otherwise be understood to mean "Manittowock They are Gods."

Captive Audiences: New England's Early Native Students or *First Fruits*

The English, too, were invested in representing the cultural encounter at the scene of writing. Thomas Hariot, who joined the Roanoke colony in Virginia during the years 1585–1586, noted that when the native peoples there were confronted with the Bible, they would "be glad to touch it, to embrace it, to kisse it, to holde it to their breastes and heads, and stroke all over their body with it."[122] And according to the Puritan exile Roger Williams, there was really only one appropriate response to the introduction of this product, the European material trade good par excellence. He writes that when Natives were confronted with any "apprehension of excellency in Men, Women, Birds, Beasts, Fish, &c." they would give it the label of "Manittoo, that is, it is a God" and as has been previously noted, this was especially true of books and letters.[123]

Williams, whose intimacy with Narragansett culture made him an occasionally serviceable witness to their lives and customs, apparently did not locate an existing written symbology within Native society. In his *Key into the Language of America* he recounts an episode in which he overhears the Narragansett sachem Miantonomo claiming of the English that they "hath books and writing, and one which God himselfe made, concerning mens soules, and therefore may well know more than wee that have none, but take all upon trust from our forefathers."[124] While we can and should question whether these exact words ever, in fact, left the lips of Miantonomo, the passage itself leaves small doubt that for Williams, at least, alphabetic literacy was an impressive proof of Christian superiority. There was little or no separation between the notions of "writing" itself and "God's Booke." Religion was the form writing took, and books were talismans of spiritual power that Europeans wielded against Natives in their attempt to impress one set of cultural norms upon another. This didn't prevent the Narragansett sachem Canonicus, however, from finding his own use for writing. For, as Williams himself notes, Canonicus would often ask of him "Wussuckwheke, yimmi" or "make me a letter." And this, Williams concedes, he would often do "upon many occasions; for their good and peace," thus in some measure standing in as scribe for the Narragansett sachem.[125]

Williams distinguished two different terms in the Narragansett language, *wussuckwhommin* and *wussuckwheke*—"painting" and "writing," respectively—both derived from the same root, but the former belonging to Native tradition and the later, it is suggested, a newly coined word resulting from colonial engagement.[126] In his chapter on Native clothing Williams notes that their moose and deer skin attire is commonly *wussuckhosu*, or painted "with varietie of formes and colours."[127] He will not train his eye too closely upon such "formes," but one wonders if they bore any resemblance to the painted surfaces of the Montagnais-Naskapi hunting jackets described earlier. In a later section of his *Key* when Williams speaks directly to "*their painting*," he remarks only of "the foolish Custome of all barbarous Nations to paint and figure their Faces and Bodies (as it hath been to our shame and griefe. Wee remember it of some of our Fore-Fathers)."[128] Williams links the custom of face painting to outmoded Western traditions, in keeping with his thesis that the indigenous peoples of America are descended from the lost tribes of Israel. He fails, however, to offer any description of the manner in which the Narragansett "figure" their faces, leaving the impression that there is no quantifiable art to such practices. The only clues that such a tradition may be more intricate and involved than Williams suggests is evidenced in the lexicon for his chapter on painting where, for a second time, he offers the term *wussuckhosu*, meaning "a painted coat," and adds "of this and *wussuckwheke*, (the English Letters, which comes nearest to their painting) I spake before."[129]

In what way, one wonders, are the figures of *wussuckhosu* "nearest" to English letters? The implication, however buried in Williams' circuitous syntax, is that the characters of the *wussuckhosu*, in their similarity to European writing, are not simply ornamental flourishes or face paint liberally applied, à la Mel Gibson in *Braveheart*, but communicative symbols that Williams is hesitant to read. Williams intimates in his work that he was careful not to observe Native rituals firsthand for fear of being a party to blasphemy. "I durst never bee an eye witness, Spectatour, or looker on," he wrote, "least I should have been partaker of Sathans Inventions and Worships."[130] How much more dangerous would it be to engage in a *textualized* encounter with Native belief systems, when texts were the ultimate conveyers of spiritual knowledge, *manittowock*, God? Williams offers us brief glimpses of Native signification in his *Key*, but he also speaks explicitly to his unwitnessing, as he dare not be a witness, spectator, or looker on to Native customs that threaten his own worldview.

Other English settlers offer glimpses of *wussuckwhommin*. William Wood speaks of the "*antic* embroidering" that was painted upon deerskins after they were properly dressed.[131] John Josselyn, too, observes how their "buskins of Deers-skin or moose" were "drest and drawn with lines into several works, the lines being colored with yellow, blew or red."[132] He observed "tobacco pipes of stone with their Imagerie upon them," and wrote of how Prince Philip of the Pokanoket was said to have arrived in Boston with "a Coat on and the Buskins set thick with these Beads [wampum] in pleasant wild works and a broad Belt of the same."[133] Edward Winslow would notice the "many curious mats" that were used to cover deceased sachems in Massachusett burial rituals.[134] What, after all, is "curious" about a mat unless it be the markings upon it, perhaps similar to the markings noted on mats and skins placed over the Huron and Montagnais dead as noted previously? How is it that Williams, Mayhew, Eliot, or any of the other countless eyewitnesses who spent considerable time amongst Native peoples in the seventeenth century failed to see what, for the Moravian missionary Heckewelder, was perfectly evident; that amongst the various nations of the North American continent were, as quoted earlier, "certain hieroglyphics, by which they describe facts in so plain a manner, that those who are conversant with those marks can understand them with the greatest ease, as easily, indeed, as we can understand a piece of writing." Again and again the colonizing eye glosses over such evidences as the *awikhigans*, rock paintings, birch bark scrolls, and wampum records. Indeed, the Puritan minister and hagiographer Cotton Mather noted, "there is a rock or two in the country that has unaccountable characters engraved upon it," but he was quick to dismiss the possibility of their containing any coherent signification.[135]

Such brief acknowledgments often seem merely the exception that proves the rule, and these glimpses of Native writing, cognitively relegated to some primitive classification of cave drawing or ancient graffiti, do not obtain. Ethnographer Henry Rowe Schoolcraft, writing in 1836, expressed surprise even at the fact that Natives kept stories and had "an oral imaginative lore" that passed from generation to generation. He comments, "in the long period in which these tribes have been subjects of observation, we are not aware that powers of this kind [lore-keeping] have been attributed to

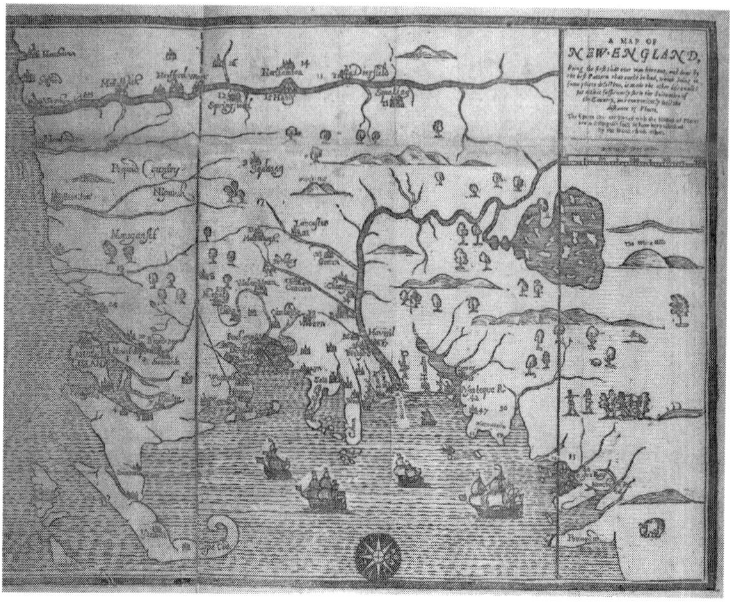

Figure 1.5. Map of New England from Hubbard's 1677 *Narrative of the Indian Wars in New England*. Courtesy of American Antiquarian Society.

them."[136] How might this have gone unnoticed for so long? How did even presumably objective "scientific" observers, some three hundred years after initial contact with indigenous peoples, fail to recognize a rich history of Native narrative tradition? What seems apparent in all these scattered and indirect glances is the likelihood that colonial commentators, whatever their intentions, refused to fully see or acknowledge the validity of an existing system of Native signifiers. As a result of this determination, colonizers felt licensed to use any means necessary in bringing a Christian education to the indigenous peoples of this continent.

W. Deloss Love, a nineteenth-century historian who wrote on the life of the Mohegan and Presbyterian minister Samson Occom, observed that Indian education remained "a common article of the immigrant's creed."[137] Love was amongst the first to point out that all the charters for the various English colonies, beginning with the Virginia Company charter in 1607, contained a clause relating to Indian education. As Love noted, this provision was echoed again and again, including, of course, in the charter of the Massachusetts Bay Company with its suggestive seal of the leaf-bedecked Native asking the Pilgrims to "come over and help us." So often is this summons associated with the particularly Puritan aspects of colonization that we forget the language was precisely that used by the less spiritually ambitious Jamestown settlement as well. While the Virginia settlements lacked the evangelical dedication to Indian education that certain individuals in New England were eventually able to muster, the settlement claimed at least one convert in Pocahontas, daughter of the powerful Powhatan. Pocahontas' education into alphabetic literacy, if it hadn't already begun, was eminent when she died in Gravesend, England, in 1617 while on her way back to America with her English husband John Rolfe. The couple was returning with seed money to begin a school designed to "convert and bring to the knowledge and true worship of Jesus Christ 1000's of poore, wretched and mysbeleiving people."[138] That ambition, for various reasons, was never realized and one supposes the "seed money" went instead to Rolfe's burgeoning tobacco interests.

More instructive, and indicative of the overall process of Christian "education" in the colonies, however, was the original kidnapping of Pocahontas by Samuel Argall in 1612 and her two years spent as a prisoner that predated her "courtship" with Rolfe. The fact that her conversion and subsequent romance results from prolonged captivity has been effectively erased from our cultural repetitions of this foundational American narrative. Pocahontas was almost certainly regarded as a valuable negotiating tool, not only in exchange for English hostages, but in advertising the success of the plantation abroad. As Karen Ordahl Kupperman notes, Pocahontas' capture soon transformed "into the project of making her the first convert in Virginia."[139] There is reason enough to believe that the marriage between Rolfe and Pocahontas was seen as a diplomatic victory on both sides of the Atlantic. But it was a costly gesture on the part of the young Pocahontas, who endured not only prolonged captivity, but had to suffer the ultimate price for her outreach. Though the experiment with Pocahontas ended with her death, Governor Gates (of the Virginia colony) subsequently decreed that other Native children should be kidnapped and brought up in English homes as well with the purpose of educating them.[140] The more congenial language of the propaganda tracts, however, like the language of the charters before them, served to provide institutional cover for such questionable decrees and proved effective in the practice of soliciting money from English patrons for colonial endeavors.

The persuasiveness of such language has a tendency to reverberate through the ages, particularly for those who have compelling reasons to wish to believe it. The nineteenth-century historian Love adequately detailed the phases of Indian education in colonial New England and was sympathetic to the experiences of eighteenth- and nineteenth-century Native Americans in general, yet he fully participated in the common prejudices of his era, failing to recognize the cultural validity of existing Native American traditions and assuming that those who sought to educate the Indians were, by their very vocation, enlightened individuals with humane goals. Therefore, it is completely without irony that he reports of Governor Endicott's decree in 1637 to board young Native students in English homes and how "a general desire was awakened amongst them [the young Natives] to know the God of the English and imitate their government and institutions."[141] Love acknowledges that these first eager students also just happened to be captives of the 1636–1637 event known as the Pequot War. But the fact that they were survivors of a very deliberate genocide resulting in the near extinction of the Pequot as a people is not given its due. How such circumstances might have influenced the so-called "general desire" of young Natives to be Anglicized is anybody's guess, but the process of boarding and educating children who were the human detritus of a war of, perhaps, unprecedented violence on the North American continent could not have occurred without friction, misunderstanding, and heartbreak.

As was the case with the Jamestown settlers, the New England colonists found the reality of training Natives in English customs and manners more complicated than they had initially envisioned. Who could have anticipated from across an ocean that Native peoples, raised "naked" and far from the civilizing light of Christianity, were perfectly happy with their cultural practices, had loving families, durable networks of kinship and trade, and found comfort and security in their traditions both spiritual and cultural? In the early days of the Plymouth settlement the colonists were more in need of Native assistance than the other way around. In fact it took nearly twenty-six years before the colonists could even begin to implement their original charter claims to *help* the Natives, and this was only after disease and the Pequot War had irrevocably altered the overall balance of power in New England, leading John Robinson, the Puritan elder still residing in Leyden, Holland to exhort his wayward flock, "Oh! How happy a thing had it been, if you had converted some before you had killed any."[142]

As one peruses the titles of seventeenth-century Puritan tracts devoted to educating the Natives and bringing them into the fold of Christian knowledge—titles such as *New England's First Fruits, The Day-Breaking if Not the Sun-Rising of the Gospell with the Indians in New-England,* or *The Light Appearing More and More Towards the Perfect Day*—one receives the impression intended by their authors that this was a process of infinite patience and persuasion. Such titles serve to conceal the violence and cultural destructiveness that lay behind the actual initiatives as acted out. In the final analysis, the art of spiritual persuasion had little to do with Natives converting and adopting English customs.

A good deal of that violence can be gleaned from a careful reading of the tracts themselves, even as they seek to advertise and celebrate their presumed successes. *New England's First Fruits* is a 1643 pamphlet written to promote the early evangelical progress of the New England colony while simultaneously soliciting money for the newly established Harvard College situated in what was formerly New Town, but was rechristened Cambridge, Massachusetts for the occasion. The tract begins by providing a catalogue of Native converts who, like many early Jesuit successes, consisted largely of the dead and dying. The children who had come into English homes as a result of Endicott's 1637 decree following the Pequot War became, by default, the most hopeful plants, as they were virtually powerless to change their situations. As the authors of *First Fruits* relate,

> Divers of the Indian Children, Boyes and Girles we have received into our houses, who are long since civilized, and in subjection to us, painful and handy in their businesse, and can speak our language familiarly; divers of whom can read English, and begin to understand in their measure, the grounds they heare, and of the word read and expounded in our Families, and are convinced of their sinfull and miserable Estates, and affected with the sense of Gods displeasure, and the thoughts of Eternity, and will sometimes tremble and melt into teares at our opening and pressing the Word upon their Consciences.[143]

The language, on the one hand, would like to imply a seamless transition, the children being "long since civilized" and under "subjection." The voluntary conversion of the children, who are "convinced of their sinfull and miserable Estates," is a given. When dealing with Puritan discourse, however, it is often difficult to unthread the language of spiritual debasement, which was a staple of their conversion process, from the language of trauma, perhaps because the processes bore some resemblance to one another. Was it merely a convention to suggest that one should "tremble and melt into teares" at the thought of eternity or was this accompanied by an actual physical manifestation of visceral grief? And if the tears and trembling should be taken literally, was such a response an effect of Christian doctrine upon the souls of the young captives or, perhaps, the likely reaction that one might experience following unimaginable loss and hardship?

The children in question had been ripped from their homes, disassociated from their people and cultures, and in some cases had either witnessed, or at the very least endured, the violent deaths of their mothers, fathers, and other relatives. Subsequently they were forced to labor in English homes, a condition of servitude that probably differed little from institutionalized slavery. It would require very little imagination to consider how threats of eternal damnation in hellfire might be equated with the burning deaths of loved ones at the 1637 Pequot fort massacre in present-day Mystic, Connecticut. Even the colonists were incapable, on some level, of entirely purging from their thoughts the overall horror of this event, as seen in this memorable characterization by William Bradford who described it as "a fearfull sight to see them frying in the fryer, and the streams of blood quenching the same and horrible was the stinck & sente their of." Nevertheless, Bradford was able to pull it all into a more palatable perspective, noting how "the victory seemed a sweete sacrifice, and they gave the prays therof to God, who had wrought so wonderfuly for them, thus to inclose their enimise in their hands, and give them so speedy a victory over so proud & insulting an enimie."[144]

First Fruits tells of "An *Indian* Maid at *Salem*, [who] would often come from the Word, crying out with abundance of teares, concluding that she must burne when she die, and would say, she knew her selfe naught for present, and like to be miserable forever, unlesse free Grace should prevent it."[145] For this young maid, exposure to "the Word" summoned her repeatedly voiced fear of death by flame. An expressed desire for Christian grace provides anecdotal cover for what seem to be the traumatic repetitions experienced by certain Native captives and their response to the psychological violence of having God's word *pressed* "upon their consciousness." Conversely, the Puritan historian William Hubbard tells of a Pequot taken prisoner after the war who threatened he "would burn the English alive in their Houses" if he could. Hubbard notes that "when he was told his Sentence was to dye, he said, he liked it well, that he should dye before his Heart was soft, or had spoken anything unworthy of himself."[146] Lacking any compelling reason to conform to Puritan expectations or spiritual rhetoric, this Pequot youth speaks from the otherwise hidden transcript of Native resistance that the other Pequot youth are unable to articulate in their captive condition. In either case, however, whether Hubbard's unrepentant victim or the hopeful young converts of *First Fruits*, Native speech only appears in print when it can be seen as serving a Puritan agenda.

In a sense it becomes a moot point whether the trembling and tears experienced by the captive Pequot children are a result of a foreign cultural discourse being pressed upon them or of the psychic scarring of the recent past. Either event constitutes the kind of narrative rupture that is significant of trauma. For the Native youths who appear in tracts such as *First Fruits* there is no outlet to communicate their feelings, no community of listeners who will legitimate their experience or honor their narratives. The process of silencing affects not only their claim to experience but the very ability to speak in the language and idiom of their lost childhoods. The palimpsestic process of having the word pressed upon the consciousness signifies the writing over of cultural memory, the insinuation of a constructed set of norms over the accumulative sequence of experiences that preceded such an event. For the captive children to "witness" the Christian God they must unwitness the experiences, the beliefs, the cultural assumptions that had led them to this moment, a forced amnesia that was unlikely to have taken hold without serious breakdowns both mental and physical. The effect of all this manifests itself in what Maria Yellow Horse Brave Heart and Lymera DeBruyn refer to as "historical unresolved grief." This is a grief that "cannot be openly acknowledged or publically mourned" as a result of the silences of colonialism and the upsetting nature of its causes and effects, an innate human tendency to want to avoid such painful expressions.[147] As Deborah Madsen points out, however, forgetting is also not an option. She observes, "in Freudian terms even the attempt simply to forget involves repression, melancholia, and the regressive cycle of acting out the symptoms of trauma. The repressed will always return."[148] The return of the repressed is intimated in the tortured language and responses of the young Pequot "converts."

But when Puritan observers recorded these moments, they put their own traumatic displacement on display by insisting upon a version of reality that bluntly denied violent truths and conformed instead to the overall shape of their own hegemonic desires. This insistence meant not only silencing the Native youths who might tell it differently, but silencing their own historical consciousness of these events. Young Native captives were not mourning their tragic losses then, but rather they were visibly shaken and distressed by the blinding truths of Christian doctrine. Their tears and cries were not acts of resistance or grief, but cries to heaven. Their descriptions of flames were not of the past but of a possible future. The descriptions that serve the rhetorical purposes of this discourse are probably not intended to be deceptive. They merely seek to tie a nominally foreign set of cultural responses to the normative responses of Puritan belief. This is accomplished, however, by maintaining an established narrative framework that bluntly disallows any other reason for the described responses than the presumed joy of converting to Christianity.

The fact that the process of "educating" Native youths was not as seamless as *First Fruits* implies was bound to suggest itself in any number of ways, regardless of the framework within which colonial commentators attempted to place it and the even more pressing silence that generally surrounds it. While a dozen or more tracts were written focusing on the education of the Natives in seventeenth-century New England, there is nary a description in any of these accounts of just how that education was administered, what methods were used, and exactly how the youths responded. Typifying the invisibility of these students, the erasure of their presence as individuals, is a remark made by John Winthrop in his *History of New England* wherein he states that, following the smallpox epidemic of 1633, he kept a young Neponset orphan in his home, one of three children who survived. As he glibly reports, he named this luckless orphan "Know-God, (the Indians' usual answer being, when they were put in mind of God, Me no know God)."[149] This boy's very name becomes a callous signifier of the blatant reversals in practice by the colonists, wherein an expression of Native resistance is twisted into one of affirmation. The very conditions of trauma, to know and not know, are enjoined in his given name, and one assumes that the child passes away from disease or a broken heart as Winthrop makes no further mention of him.

Even the most successful students, however, who would serve as interpreters or continue on to help John Eliot in his translations of scripture and other writings into the Algonquian language in the following decade, generally go nameless or surface only briefly in the archives, like earth-divers themselves, coming up for air at sparse intervals. Eliot wrote in 1648 that "there is an Indian living with Mr. Richard Calicott of Dorchester, who was taken in the Pequott Warres, though belonging to Long Island; this Indian is ingenious, can read; and I taught him to write, which he quickly learnt, though I know not what use he now maketh of it."[150] This unnamed youth, later identified as a Montauk named Cockenoe, apparently provided the first key into the Native languages that Eliot needed to jumpstart his mission to the nearby Massachusett tribe. But his contributions barely register in Eliot's writings, and his name appears not once. Cockenoe ultimately abandoned English learning and made a career for himself back on Long Island as a translator between the Indians and the English in a number of land deals. He remained a liminal figure for the rest of his years, moving in and out of Native space and finishing his days as a sailor on the whaling boats that shipped out of New England and New York.[151] In Eliot's short passage, however, one senses the resistance Cockenoe offered to Eliot's teaching. Eliot states, "I know not what use he maketh of it," betraying that Cockenoe, despite his skill at appropriating English literacy, ultimately refused to assist Eliot in his work and deployed his talents for other purposes.

Cockenoe's example is unusual in the sense that he seemed able to make his own choices or proved valuable enough in other capacities to free himself of servitude to Eliot's schemes. He proves an early example of a Native who used his skill with alphabetic writing for his own personal advantage. Others were not so lucky. Many captives of the Pequot War were sold into slavery in Bermuda.[152] Those who were put into English households, far from being adopted as members of the family, were used as servants and forcefully kept from returning to their own people, their own communities. Winthrop reports in 1637, following the war, that "there were sent to Boston forty-eight women and children. There were eighty taken, as before is expressed. These were disposed of to particular persons in the country. Some of them ran away and were brought back again by the Indians our neighbors, and those [we] branded on the shoulder."[153]

Such accounts work against the gentle missionary language brought to bear on the very same situation in *First Fruits*, wherein it is unequivocally asserted that, as far as can be discerned, the Native youths are "much in love with us, and cannot indure to returne any more to the Indians."[154] Winthrop again offers a contrary glimpse in his personal history in a short passage that relates how the young Natives who were "in our families were much frightened with Hobbamock (as they call the devil) appearing to them in diverse shapes, and persuading them to forsake the English, and not to come at the assemblies, nor to learn to read etc."[155] Far from hearing devils, these Indian children being kept in captivity and forcefully assimilated were expressing a desire to maintain some connection to their traditional belief systems while attempting to process the violent uprooting from their homes and families. What emerges in all of these accounts is the unavoidable conclusion that New England's "first fruits," the first crop of educated Natives in the colonies, far from being willing subscribers to a new belief system, were prisoners of an unjust war, kept in bondage and servitude against their wills, and forced to comply with English spiritual beliefs regardless of the psychic toll. Nobody at this point in time should allow themselves the luxury of believing that Native conversions to Christianity in the colonial period occurred freely, willingly, or without violence. While public accounts like *First Fruits* labor to make the process seem voluntary, the violence and coercion seeps through the cracks of the more private records of the times.

Amaleck: The Unwitnessing of Massacre in Puritan Accounts of the Pequot War

The cycles of violence and trauma I describe in the previous section were set into motion by the event known as the Pequot War. The Pequot War was launched for specious reasons that were strongly contested even in their time. It was a preemptive strike that, as with most preemptive strikes, had severely ratcheted up the perceived threat it was so aggressively seeking to tamp down. In his study of the war, Alfred A. Cave reminds us that "Puritan writers advanced interpretations of Pequot character and intentions based on prejudice and supposition rather than hard evidence."[156] But at the heart of the confrontation lay the matter of who would control the wampum trade in the Northeast. In a journal passage of 1633, one can almost see the gears turning in Winthrop's head as he notes of Pequot land that "there they had store of the best wampum-peak, both white and blue. The Indians there are very treacherous people."[157] It would not be a mischaracterization to replace the period between these two short sentences with an = sign. William Bradford, governor of Plymouth colony, saw it differently and wrote to Winthrop at the onset of hostilities, accusing him of having "occasioned a war, etc. by provoking the Pequods, and no more."[158] Winthrop took exception to this and was quick to conflate the presumed Pequot threat to a threat posed by all Indians. He replied to the leaders of Plymouth that if the Pequot were not subdued then that would incite "all the Indians of the country to join to root out all the English."[159]

The conquest of the Pequot would not only secure control of the flow of wampum for the English, which was used as currency in the fur trade with interior indigenous nations, but it would also allow for control of the Connecticut River Valley, which would facilitate travel and trade into the fur-producing regions. Naturally it would free up more land for colonization as well. Captain John Underhill's 1638 account of the war is, without irony, given the subtitle "A discovery of these places, that as yet have very few or no inhabitants which would yeeld speciall accommodation to such as will plant there." The title shifts the focus, in the blink of an eye, from the trouble with the Pequots to the "discovery" of curiously uninhabited lands. As such, his tract is as much a real estate brochure as it is a narrative of military conquest.[160]

The early New England colonists were not immediately aware of the importance of wampum to the local indigenous groups, and would never truly grasp its ceremonial value. Roger Williams, in his *Key*, describes wampum in a chapter entitled "Of their Coyne," where he observes that "they hang these strings of money about their necks and wrists."[161] Wampum was considered merely as Native currency, and as Williams observed, "the Indians bring downe all sorts of Furs, which they take in the Countrey, both to the Indians and to the English for this Indian Money."[162] The real value of wampum was not, of course, as currency but as the ceremonial means of record-keeping, treaty-making, and condolence amongst the Iroquoian- and Algonquian-speaking peoples of the Northeast. Micmac historian Evan Pritchard describes wampum, or "talking belts," as "visual aids in sacred story telling ceremonies in which the history of the people was recounted in full." He notes that many "still use the term wampum to mean currency without realizing it is disrespectful, because its original purpose was a sacred one."[163] According to early twentieth-century ethnographer Frank Speck, who recorded the Lenape Big House Ceremony in 1931, wampum was referred to in the ceremonial life of the Lenape as "our heart." He writes that "to the Delawares wampum stood forth in the light of a covenant. It represented, and still does, a magical power capable of annulling the affects of latent poisonous influences that might pass between persons who exchange gifts or who enter into the transfer of property."[164] It didn't take long, however, for the English to see how they might capitalize upon such an exchange of seemingly worthless shells for expensive furs. Their participation in the wampum trade instantly commoditized it, boosting production amongst indigenous locals and prompting William Bradford to caution that "it may prove a drugg in time."[165] It was a mere three months after the cash-strapped New England colonists declared wampum as legal currency that war against the Pequot was also declared.[166] It was ostensibly a war to control the resources of the Northeast, but given the actual ceremonial and cultural function of wampum, the Pequot War must also be regarded as a war over writing and control over the production of history.

The war began with a dispute over the circumstances that led to the separate deaths of one Captain Stone and a Mr. Oldham. In neither case was there any evidence to support the conclusions of the Massachusetts Bay Colony that the Pequot were responsible for these deaths. In fact, in Oldham's case, the Pequot were known to have not been involved, but were accused of sheltering those who were and so, in the words of the Puritan historian William Hubbard, "became also Guilty themselves of his Blood."[167] Had the colonists held themselves to such a rigorous standard, their crimes would have been innumerable. Perhaps not coincidentally, both Stone and Oldham were early colonial traffickers in wampum. Their attempts to exploit this trade, while meeting with failure, seem to have inspired the English to get involved themselves. The initial dispute between the Pequot and English was smoothed over with an agreement that was, ironically, fortified by strings of wampum. A series of minor skirmishes ensued, however, leading eventually to the capture of two English "maids" in an assault by the Pequot at the fledgling colony in Wethersfield, Connecticut. The maids were ultimately ransomed unharmed, but their initial capture provided the rhetorical outrage needed to justify later acts.

By 1637 the English were able to consolidate their alliances with the other Native groups in the area through the assistance of Roger Williams, who had established friendly relations with the Narragansett during his years in exile. Once these alliances were established, the colonists prepared to strike a decisive blow, culminating in English and Narragansett troops advancing upon a "palisadoed" Pequot village at modern-day Mystic, Connecticut. The fort was surrounded and set on fire during the dawn assault, allowing the English to contain their enemy while flames consumed the roughly six to seven hundred occupants, consisting mostly of old men, women, and children. Anyone attempting to flee the confines of the fort was shot.[168]

A famous illustration of the Mystic fort massacre (accompanying Captain John Underhill's account of the battle) says something about the way in which this conflict was ultimately processed by the settlers. It offers an aerial, or God's eye, view of the Pequot fortress, a circular structure erected of tree trunks stripped of their branches and pounded into the earth with neat rows of huts situated within, each sprouting a precise little lick of flame. Surrounding the fortress in perfect concentric ripples are first an English battalion, their weapons firing, and secondly a ring of Narragansett warriors, each in a like posture with bows drawn. The exterior of the map is decorated with tiny hills and trees that close around the site of carnage with the uniformity of a wallpaper pastoral. While there are a few neatly staged groups of English and Indians engaged in hand to hand combat at each pole of the battle scene, these in no way upset the perfect symmetry of the illustration (see figure 1.6).

Very few depictions of slaughter achieve such aesthetic balance and proportion. One might refer to the de Bry workshop illustration of the 1622 attack of the Powhatan Confederacy against the Virginia colony for a contemporary equivalent in which the degradations and confusion of battle are rendered quite graphically. The frontispiece for the 1656 London edition of Bartolomé de las Casas' *The Tears of the Indians* offers even more horrific examples of the casual dismemberment, flaying, and roasting alive of Indian bodies by the Spaniards. In each of these cases there were strong political incentives to want to bring attention to the horrors being perpetrated. But the lasting image of the Pequot War is striking for its mandala-like beauty, a vision of order and symmetry purposefully abstracting what must have been a frightening scene of chaos and horror.

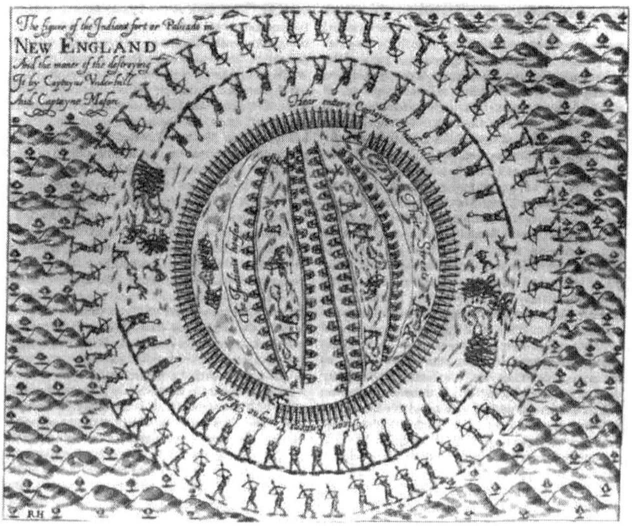

Figure 1.6. Mystic fort massacre from John Underhill's 1638 *Newes of America*. Courtesy of the Mashantucket Pequot Museum and Research Center.

Various contemporaneous accounts of the war perform a quite similar function of trying to distill imagined order from chaos—to construct a narrative of false or inverted continuity from an incident of rupture. Any such attempt, however, is necessarily fraught with an excess of anxiety and tortured justifications. As already noted, Bradford, in his description of the massacre, performs a kind of transubstantiation wherein the reek of bodies "frying in the fryer," becomes a purifying incense, or "sweete sacrifice" in "prays thereof to God." Philip Vincent, another recorder of the event as well as a participant, writes of the massacre that "Pity had hindered further hostile proceedings, had not the remembrance of the bloodshed, the captive maids, and cruel insolency of those Pequets, hardened the hearts of the English, and stopped their ears unto their cries. Mercy mars all sometimes; severe justice must now and then take place."[169]

We should keep in mind here that the "captive maids" in question had been returned unharmed, and the bloodshed to this point had been negligible by most standards of European warfare. Nevertheless, we find here a compelling expression of how a massacre necessarily engenders the exact opposite response of the condolence ceremony at the heart of wampum exchange. Warm hearts of flesh and blood become hardened, the ears must be "stopped," justice itself becomes "severe," and mercy is "marred." In effect, the senses must be dulled in order to facilitate the processes of unwitnessing.

Vincent deliberately minimized the carnage inflicted by the colonists in his relation of the battle, grossly underreporting English casualties as well, and stating "the whole work ended ere the sun was an hour high."[170] Interestingly, only after the narrative of the massacre was concluded does he turn his attention to a seemingly more objective, ethnographically minded description of the Pequot fort. We should note, however, that in doing so, he performs a kind of rhetorical alchemy similar to Bradford's as he writes:

> Let me now describe this military fortress, which natural reason and experience hath taught them to erect, without mathematical skill, or use of iron tool. They choose a piece of ground, dry and of best advantage . . . Here they pitch, close together as they can, young trees and half trees, as thick as a man's calf of his leg. Ten or twelve foot high they are above the ground, and within rammed three foot deep with undermining, the earth being cast up for better shelter against the enemy's dischargements. Betwixt these palisadoes are divers loopholes, through which they let fly their winged messengers . . . The space therein is full of wigwams, wherein their wives and children live with them. These huts or little houses are framed like our garden arbors, something more round, very strong and handsome, covered with close-wrought

> mats, made by their women, of flags, rushes, and hempen threads, so defensive that neither rain . . . nor yet the wind, though never so strong, can enter.[171]

The brief battle scenes that Vincent related speak nothing of woman and children and elide the presence of neat little houses and garden arbors, but what cannot be described amid the scene of battle is offered in repose, as though all were whole again and one might admire the domestic warmth and utility of such a scene. The strange effect this description has, coupled with the earlier description of the massacre, is to perform a task similar to that of the aforementioned illustration. It labors to restore pleasing, dispassionate order to a scene of abject terror. In a sense, this construction mirrors the function of paradise in the Genesis narrative. It encircles a most troubling truth with pleasing descriptive visions of order while placing flaming swords around the perimeter. What lies within is not paradise but undesirable knowledge.

The Mystic massacre, in the Puritan records, becomes something like cognitive ground zero, an event that must be contained and culturally forgotten, per heavenly injunction, even as veiled repetitions of its violent undoing will surface again and again in the literature of the colonists. The fact of the slaughter, its provocations and violence, proved so troubling that it quickly became understood that the Pequot themselves must be made to disappear. Captain Mason, one of the leaders of the engagement, and the one who credited himself with the inspiration for setting fire to the fort, wrote:

> Thus was God seen in the Mount, Crushing his proud enemies and the Enemies of his People: They who were ere while a Terror to all that were round about them, who resolved to Destroy all the English and Root their very name out of this Country . . . bring the Mischief they plotted, and the Violence they offered and exercised, upon their own heads in a moment: burning them up in the fire of his Wrath, and dunging the Ground with their Flesh: It was the Lord's Doings.[172]

Mason viewed this moment of triumph not only as an expression of God's will, a predictable gesture on his part and one in perfect agreement with Governor Bradford in *Of Plymouth Plantation*, but as an all-out battle for the privilege of historical existence. The losers would have their very names rooted from the country and their bones ground into the earth. As he states further on, "The Pequets were then bound by Covenant, That none should inhabit their Native country, nor should any of them be called Pequots anymore."[173] Mason decreed that the privilege of conquest was to write the Pequots out of existence, to blast them into the margins, so to speak.

Of the many narratives relating to the Mystic fort fight, only Underhill's even remotely suggests that the violence actually cut both ways and that the scenes of horror described by its witnesses could not be so readily contained as hoped. As noted, Underhill was no less a land speculator than his compatriots. A military adventurer and opportunist by vocation, he saw the war as a fortunate eventuality by which more land might be opened for settlement. Nor did Underhill have any explicit doubt that God's will was being manifested in this attempt to blot out the Pequots, in both name and corporal presence, from the face of the earth. Nevertheless, in the wake of the battle, he noted that "Great and doleful was the bloudy sight to the view of young souldiers that never had beene in Warre, to see so many soules lie gasping on the ground so thicke in some places, that you could hardly passe along."[174] Underhill felt obliged to relate that the Narragansett who had joined in the battle came to him afterward, and like the young English soldiers, cried "mach it, mach it; that is, it is naught, it is naught, because it is too furious, and slais too many men."[175] While Underhill is likely disdainful of such dainty sensibilities, perhaps the Narragansett were being asked here to express not only the sentiment of local Native communities, but the unspoken sentiments of many a colonist.

In suggesting a justification for the slaughter in which he participated, Underhill states, "It may be demanded, Why should you be so furious (as some have said) should not Christians have more mercy and compassion?"[176] His response was that the acts of certain enemies are so vile, savage, and reprehensible that they do not warrant God's mercy and that, in these times "the scripture declareth women and children must perish with their parents."[177] How it is that the Pequot achieved such terrible fame remains unclear, particularly as Underhill boasted only a few lines later that Indian war was such that "they might fight seven yeares and not kill seven men."[178] The congenial New English commentator William Wood had observed only a few years earlier (prior to any hint of war) that the Pequot were "a stately, warlike people, of whom I never heard any misdemeanor, but that they were just and equal in their dealings, not treacherous either to their countrymen or English, requiters of courtesies, affable towards the English."[179] It is hard to imagine, then, what the Pequot might have done to suddenly attain an infamy requiring the kind of biblical injunction that Underhill, Mason, Bradford, and Vincent all levied upon them. One wonders, however, at what point do the labels "vile, savage, and reprehensible" revert back to their accusers, and are they always in danger of doing so as long as personal agency is suppressed and the actions of men are attributed instead to an unassailable God?

The authors of *First Fruits* compared the Pequots with the nation called Amaleck, a biblical tribe defeated by Moses and his followers as they wandered through the desert, thus offering a typological framework by which to understand and justify the massacre.[180] *First Fruits* claims how

> In that Warre which we made against them Gods hand from heaven was so manifested, that a very few of our men, in a short time pursued through the Wildernesse, slew and took prisoners about 1400 of them, even all they could find, to the great terrour and amazement of all the indians to this day: so that the name of the Pequits (as of Amaleck) is blotted out from under heaven there being not one that is, or, (at least) dare call himself a Pequit.[181]

These efforts to narrate and shape the remembrance of the Pequot War were, no doubt, read eagerly by a Puritan community desirous of a cognitive framework within which they could begin to process this momentous event. The construction of such scenes seems to follow closely the pattern of what Richard Slotkin has called a "regeneration through violence," in which the savage nature projected upon the indigenous peoples of the land is acted out by the so-called civilized forces whose sense of ownership of the land is then reaffirmed and revitalized by their acts. But it left observers back home in England feeling somewhat uneasy as to the colonial endeavor, prompting Roger Williams to wonder in his *Key*, "what Indians have been converted" in New England?[182]

To fulfill their charters and ensure continued funding, the colonists found themselves, in the wake of the Pequot War, under pressure to demonstrate at least some proof of good faith toward their contractual mission. *First Fruits* had used for its case study of progress the example of a Pequot named Wequash, who, as stated by the authors, was actually the "occasion of writing all the rest." Wequash had, at some point, experienced a falling out with Sassacus, the grand sachem of the Pequot during the war, and came to briefly affiliate himself with the Narragansett instead. Williams describes him as a "sachem" in his letters to Winthrop, and indeed, Wequash may have been the leader of a small band of Pequots who, either due to politics, opportunism, or blood ties had grown closer to their Narragansett neighbors.[183] He was said to have been a guide to the English during the devastating attack on the Pequot stronghold in Mystic and is, perhaps, the individual that Captain John Underhill quotes as characterizing the English style of warfare as "mach it, mach it, that is, it is naught, it is naught, because it is too furious, and slais too many men."

Wequash (his name means "swan" according to Williams' *Key*), being a Pequot himself, might have had particular cause for reviling the heavy bloodshed of the attack and probably would not have anticipated the scale of the slaughter he allegedly helped to unleash upon the people in the village at Mystic.[184] He would apparently make a grab for power in the confusion and disarray directly following the war, but after a falling out with the Narragansett sachem Miantonomo, he seems to have become a disenfranchised player in the leadership struggles that followed.[185] Reportedly left to wander "up and down" the settlements invoking the name of the English God in a state of self-loathing and fear, Wequash became the inspiration for two of the earliest manuscripts to come out of New England and a contested figure in the battle over who would frame the overall experience in the colonies.

In *First Fruits* Wequash, despite having been formerly dismissive of English men and gods (referring to their deity as a "Musketto [mosquito] God"), was nevertheless "perswaded" otherwise after witnessing the slaughter at Mystic. He became convinced that the Puritan God was, in fact, "a most dreadfull God" and from that point on "this conviction did pursue and follow him night and day, so that he could have no rest or quiet because hee was ignorant of the *Englishmans God*: he went up and down bemoaning his condition, and filling every place where he came with sighes and groanes."[186] As with the Pequot children living in English homes, what we might today recognize as post-traumatic stress disorder was interpreted by the settlers of Wequash's time as a sort of exemplary spiritual awakening. But the particulars of Wequash's conversion seem suspect, even as related in the propagandistic tract from which they are drawn. Although he apparently wandered the countryside declaiming heathenism and extolling the awesome might of the English God, Wequash acquired little solace from this function and seemed unable to cast off a debased regard for himself. He is described as one who has been hunted and harrowed until his strength has failed, equated with "a Hart panting after the water Brookes."[187] Quite possibly it is nothing more than this haunted and submissive aspect that endeared him so well to the colonists. The authors tell us,

> his manner was to smite his hand on his breast, and to complain sadly of his heart saying it was *much machet* (that is, very evill) and when any spake with him, he would say, *Wequash, no God, Wequash no know Christ*. It pleased the Lord, that in the use of the meanes, he grew greatly in the knowledge of Christ, and became thoroughly reformed according to his light, hating and loathing himselfe for his dearest sinnes which were especially these two *Lust* and *Revenge*.[188]

If any of this can be taken at face value, then Wequash is a figure who is sick at heart, standing in traumatic relation to the imposition of Christian values, both knowing and not knowing God. The result of Wequash's lamentable condition is that he fell ill and suspected he had been poisoned by his enemies. On his death bed, we are told, he commended his soul to the care of Christ and bequeathed his child to the care of the English for "education and instruction."[189] Although the authors of *First Fruits* leave no question that Wequash meets his reward in heaven, having "suffered Martyrdome for Christ,"[190] still it is his acquired docility that impresses. If Wequash was the example that inspired this tract on the spiritual successes of the colonies, it serves as more unintended proof that New England's "First Fruits," far from being the harvest of a civilized education, were, in fact, the wasted ruins of total warfare.

Roger Williams, in the introduction to his *Key*, which went to press in England the following year, directly rebutted the major claims asserted by the authors of *First Fruits*. Williams, as with the Jesuits of New France and the Franciscans in New Spain, felt the only way to make progress was not to teach the "savages" to speak English, but to go amongst them and learn their languages. His *Key* was written largely in response to the claims of Native conversions made in *First Fruits*, and Williams uses the tract to specifically address "that Great point of their Conversion so much to bee longed for, and by all New-English so much pretended."[191] Implicit in Williams' tract was a sense that the settlers of Plymouth and Massachusetts Bay Colony had, in fact, failed in every way to follow through on the stated intention of their charter to civilize the Natives.

Recounting his own experiences concerning this very same Wequash, Williams noted, "I dare not be so confident as others" concerning his conversion.[192] Williams, it just so happened, was present at Wequash's death bed and spoke to the Pequot concerning the condition of his soul in his final hours. According to Williams, Wequash "replyed in broken English: *Me so big naughty Heart, me heart all one stone!*" This picturesque remark, although it carries the hallmark of the metaphorical cadences often attributed to Natives of the period (referred to by some critics as "Tonto speak"), was undoubtedly in response to a scriptural passage Puritan evangelists were fond of quoting, which reads, "I will give you a new heart and put a new spirit within you; I will take the heart of stone out of your flesh and give you a heart of flesh" (Ezekiel 36:26). Wequash seems to have adamantly rejected such an offer, preferring his pre-Christianized heart to the new one.

In response to this exclamation, Williams briefly delves the psychic nature of Wequash's condition, reflecting on such "*Savory expressions . . . from compunct and broken Hearts*, and a fence of *inward hardnesse* and *unbrokenesse*."[193] Everything about Wequash, from his "broken English" to his "broken heart" and "inward unbrokenesse" (alluding to his unrepentant state) shows him to be a shattered spirit. Williams' use of the word "compunct" seems to be derived from "compunction," which aside from indicating uneasiness and guilt, has its root in the Latin *compuntio*, which means a sting, puncture, or wound. Clearly Wequash's wounds were not merely physical but psychological and spiritual. He had been emotionally stung. Paradoxically, however, his wounds, or the absence opened up by historical unresolved grief, became, in effect, the foundation upon which the colonies began to build their literature—the "occasion for writing all the rest" as the authors of *First Fruits* suggested.

Wequash is a simulation of dominance, a site of contested colonial meanings, a construct meant "to replace rather than to represent Indian reality."[194] But if his actions and words, as chronicled, had any trace of actuality, or might be viewed from the longhouse of the archive, it seems possible that what Wequash truly wished for, as he traveled about "bemoaning his condition," was a kind of condolence. It was noted of him, in fact, that in his last days he went "up and downe to those hee had offered violence or wrong unto, confessing it, and making restitution."[195] While the authors of *First Fruits* regard this as a further sign of his embrace of Christian values, he is, in fact, attempting to reinstate a process not unlike the diplomatic rituals of wampum exchange in which all parties offer their narratives in an attempt to clear the path of bloodshed and bad feelings. It is the spirit of "revenge" that Wequash was said to most want to purge from his heart, and for just such a reason, in an effort to purge the cycles of revenge and blood feuds, was the condolence ceremony first initiated.[196] But Wequash was caught between two seemingly irreconcilable spiritual narratives. If, as the ethnographer Frank Speck asserts, the purpose of wampum exchange was to "annul the affects of latent poisonous influences," the Christian rhetoric of the Puritans was in sympathy with Saint Augustine's notion that all of mankind was "poisoned" to the soul by the choices of Adam and Eve in Eden. Wequash was looking for someone to wipe away his tears, remove the dirt from his ears, the obstructions from his mouth, the stone from his heart. In the words of Hiawatha, "this I would do if I found anyone burdened with grief even as I am." But matters were such in the colonies that balance could not be so easily restored and Wequash seems to have found himself politically and spiritually isolated with no one to reciprocate his gesture and help heal his wounds, both psychological and physical.

Wequash stood as a central and contested figure in the first major texts to come out of the colonies in New England. His importance as a rhetorical tool was drowned out, however, by John Eliot's later successes with conversion, in which event Wequash came to be seen as someone who turned on his own people rather than as a feather in the cap of New England's missionary endeavors. Catherine Maria Sedgwick, who retells the story of the Pequot massacre in her 1827 novel *Hope Leslie*, notes that the colonists were "guided to us by the traitor Wequash."[197] Samuel Drake, in his 1841 *Biography and History of the Indians of North America*, described him simply as "Wequash, the traitor. He became a noted praying Indian, after the Pequot War, and was supposed to have died by poison."[198] Wequash's journey from

"First Fruit" to "Christian martyr" to "traitor" was absolute. Whatever the colonists made of him in their textualized containments, however, a common tale can be teased from the overall reportage of a Wequash who seems to have been unable to escape the traumatic ruptures of war, colonization, and the pressures of occupying a liminal space between cultures.

As for the Pequot, they would be remembered for centuries to come as the fiercest of the New England tribes, the flames of their massacre rendered again and again in colonial literature, but always in so vague a manner as to suggest agency had been taken out of the hands of the colonists and placed in the lightning-bolt-hurling arms of a just God. Timothy Dwight offered a chapter entitled "The Destruction of the Pequods" in his 1794 paean to domestic nationalism, "Greenfield Hill." Here he asserts that if the Pequot had only embraced religion, "torture's blaze / Less frequent round thy tender heart had twin'd." In his rendering, the "Mystic flames" that consume the Pequot are flames of anguish that rise up from their own scheming savage hearts. Dwight's contorted sequencing of events asserts that "the victim's blood alone can quench the flames within" as though these internal flames were not only the result of self-destructive tendencies, but were in need of the Pequots' own sacrificial blood to be extinguished.[199] Such a framework, insisting on the irredeemably violent nature of the Pequot, gave license to later historians such as Ola Winslow to justify this egregious violence, asserting that the Pequot were butchered in such a way because "this was a battle after the Indian fashion."[200] Notwithstanding John Underhill's opinion that Indian Wars were such that they could scarcely kill seven men in as many years, or the Native point of view that cried "mach it, mach it . . . it is naught, because it is too furious and slais too many men."[201]

Walter Ong has noted that "print encourages a sense of closure, a sense that what has been found in a text is finalized, has reached a state of completion."[202] Once it reaches this stage it will not be changed, it adheres to a specific order, a contained signification. This often contributes to the illusion that alphabetic writing concretizes truths. But often what it does is simply blot out, or unwitness, that to which it is opposed. When the Puritans typologically justified their own actions in the Pequot War by drawing upon the biblical example of Amaleck, they were demonstrating their knowledge of this, as well as their cultural dexterity with such a tool. The Puritans had learned from their ancient text that alphabetic writing was an act of erasure as well as inscription; but that was still only half the lesson. As related in Exodus, once Amaleck was defeated by the Israelites, "the Lord said unto Moses, Write this for a memorial in a book, and rehearse it in the ears of Joshua: for I will utterly put out the remembrance of Amaleck under heaven" (Exodus 17:14). The passage does not state why the Israelites went to war with these people. It does not say who the Amaleckites were, where they came from, or what might have been their crime, their motivation, their reason for having passed this way. In fact, they are undoubtedly the people indigenous to the region. Their only crime seems to be the fact that they were there, in that place, and they are only mentioned long enough in this particular passage to note that they were defeated and put out of remembrance. They were a warning, an ill omen, a lesson in the consequences of manipulating history, and far from disappearing, they would resurface again and again, like a recurring nightmare. The passage concludes with the oracular awareness that such a nation never vanishes and "the Lord will have war with Amaleck from generation to generation" (Exodus 17:16).

John Eliot would cheerfully assert, time and again, that the Natives "are very desirous to have their children taught, which is one argument that they truly love the knowledge of God."[203] But such an argument only meant that, for better or worse, certain Natives were being forced by circumstances beyond their control to engage with European practices, to acquire efficiency in their tools, and to internalize their norms. The Natives represented in early New England tracts were vehicles of cultural wish fulfillment for the Puritans, bearing little or no resemblance to the actual beings of flesh and blood who dwelled upon these lands. They were mere simulations of dominance. The great majority of Native communities remained outside of this engagement, but they were nevertheless conscious that the power balance had shifted in New England and that they would have to make positive moves to help themselves in order to ensure that their communities remained intact, their traditions preserved. It is only by establishing a longhouse of the archive that we can begin to discern Native motives and acts of resistance in a manner that breaks faith with the established tale of power constructed in the colonial house of the archive. If the first Natives to learn reading and writing in New England were captive children rather than first fruits, Native leaders were quickly deciding upon the efficacy of acquiring this tool of writing for themselves.

2

Praying Indians, Printing Devils

Centers of Indigeneity within Colonial Containments (1643–1665)

Behold, ye Americans, the greatest honour that ever ye were partakers of! This Bible was printed here at our Cambridge; and it is the only Bible that ever was printed in all America, from the very foundation of the world.

—Cotton Mather speaking of the Eliot Bible written in the Massachusett language, *Magnalia Christi Americana*

It were to be wished that both in Grammar Schooles, and in our Colledge also there should be appointed by yourselves a fit salary for schoole maisters and Tutors in the College for every Indian that is instructed by them to incourage them in the worke, wherein they have to deale with such nasty salvages.

—Charles Chauncy, President of Harvard, 1664 Letter to New England Company (in *Correspondence of the New England Company*, ed. Burt Franklin)

Almost any day the students, when passing through the Yard, could peer through the windows of the Indian College, and watch the Indian 'devil' James Printer sweating at the hand lever.

—Samuel Eliot Morison, *Harvard in the Seventeenth Century*

Setting Up Shop: Harvard's Indian College and the Mission of John Eliot among the Natives of New England

Harvard's Indian College is a little known, little discussed cultural experiment of the mid-1600s. Apparently the first brick building to be constructed at the fledgling campus, it was described by the Massachusetts Bay Colony's

Superintendent of Indians, Daniel Gookin, in 1674 as "a structure strong and substantial, though not very capacious . . . large enough to receive and accommodate about twenty scholars with convenient lodgings and studies."[1] The intent was that these hoped for Native scholars would learn enough of Christian doctrine to become teachers themselves, capable of disseminating the word of God amongst their own peoples. Although the plan failed miserably in its stated goals, it set the stage for future endeavors to follow a similar trajectory, as the means and the ends were always, in fact, mutually exclusive. "Who hath despised the day of small things?" (Zach. 4:10), the Puritan fathers of New England were fond of asking when referring to their fledgling efforts at educating and converting Natives, for they knew their efforts to be small, and sure to strike their moneyed patrons overseas as halfhearted at best.[2] Of their poor record they begged, "wonder not that wee mention no more instances at present: but consider, First, their [the Natives'] infinite distance from Christianity, having never been prepared unto by any Civility at all. Secondly, the difficulty of their Language to us, and ours to them; their being no Rules to learn either by."[3] This plea for patience, embedded in the 1643 tract on Indian education entitled *New England's First Fruits*, came some twenty-two years following the Puritans' first landing in Plymouth with their notion of coming over and helping the Indians. The argument was that, if Natives weren't being converted at an acceptable rate, it was due to their own barbaric lifestyles, an overall lack of civility that remained an impediment to Christian learning, and was further compounded by the difficulties of their language. Although the colonists would noticeably renew their sense of mission in the next two decades as a handful of missionaries attempted to learn the Native tongue, the resulting Indian College would never house more than four or five students, and only one Native American student, Caleb Cheeshateaumauk, would actually graduate from Harvard—a pattern of failed objectives that was perpetuated well into the nineteenth century.[4]

A recent excavation of the site of the Indian College unearthed no artifacts that might suggest a Native American occupancy, no emblems of syncretism, no beads of wampum, no arrowheads, no pipes, pots, baskets, blankets or fragments of texts printed in the Algonquian language. What the archeologists on the site *did* excavate, however, were twelve pieces of seventeenth-century type.[5] This type would have belonged to the first printing press in the English colonies which was, either by fate or design, housed in the Indian College building from roughly 1655 when the college was erected, until 1692 when Samuel Green, the steward of the Cambridge Press, died. What at first glance appears to be an arbitrary and, perhaps, ironic intersection of historical interests, on further investigation reveals an almost inevitable association. The early histories of both institutionalized education and printing in the colonies were irrevocably bound to the lives of Native Americans. The oldest and most revered colleges in the present-day United States were instituted with the implicit intent to educate "those poore Indians, who have ever sate in hellish darknesse, adoring the Divell himself for their GOD."[6] In more than one case, the seed money for such institutions was generated by Native fundraisers traveling to England who, by the sheer novelty of their presence, were able to effectively solicit donations for their stated cause. This was the intended outcome of Pocahontas' visit to England in 1616 and, as we will see, it would be the result of Samson Occom's tour of the colonial motherland some one hundred and forty years later to raise the seed money for Dartmouth College. In other cases, as with the founding of Harvard, funds were raised by the mere report of successful Native conversions, even if such reports were thoroughly challenged and debunked by other witnesses, as was the case with the claims made concerning Wequash. Nevertheless, these colonial institutions of higher learning failed in their mission to administer to the needs, both spiritual and educational, of the Native individuals who either sought or were extended their patronage. Native presence was generally tolerated just long enough to garner the proper sympathetic responses needed to fund such endeavors, and then routinely and unceremoniously discarded. One historian summed up the venture neatly in 1720, noting "the Indian College . . . 'tis now converted into a Printing-House, by the direction of the said Corporation; it being found impracticable to persuade the Indian Youth to a Love of Learning."[7]

Embedded in the previous statement is not only a sense of how quickly an isolated experiment in Indian education gave way to entropy, but also a suggestion of how closely the press became linked to, if not quite supplanting, Native American presence in colonial America. The Cambridge Press, though often regarded as an arm of the college, was never much more than a subsidiary of John Eliot's campaign to bring the gospel to the original inhabitants of the area.[8] It was Eliot who staffed the press, with both English and Native workers, and it was Eliot who insured its relative stability over the years, keeping it funded through his constant efforts to print texts in the Algonquian language. A perusal of the titles printed by the Cambridge Press over its initial fifty-year run would offer to any neophyte a surprising catalogue of unaccountably long, indecipherable entries, and help to illustrate the unlikely extent to which printing in the colonies was inscribed in red ink. Samuel Eliot Morison writes that roughly one hundred books were printed at the Indian College location "of which fifteen were in the Indian and eighty-five in the English language."[9] Those fifteen books, however, called for a disproportionately larger amount of paper and printed matter, making the publications in the Algonquian language the mainstay of the press.[10] As a result of the long Indian words and the disproportionate abundance of consonants, special type had to be ordered for these printings so that the equipment itself was geared toward the publishing of Native tracts, further suggesting how the business of the press was determined by Native concerns.[11] Even though such publications remained in the culturally coercive domain of the colonial endeavor, or the house of the archive, the very fact that the press itself was housed in the "Indian College" suggests a certain cohabitation of interests, and demonstrates something of the complex negotiations between the textualized ambitions of the colonists and the real lives of those who were being colonized.

The inner workings of the Indian College offer a surprisingly apt manifestation of the notion Larzer Ziff articulates in his book *Writing in the New Nation* wherein he describes the paradoxical manner "in which the represented self contended with the immanent self both in social conduct and written narratives" in the formation of the United States.[12] Ziff notices the imperial implications of such a phenomenon, as the eventual proliferation of presses and the wide dissemination of printed material on American shores led to a construction of national identity that often steam-rolled over the "immanent" social exigencies of both individuals and cultures. What was "immanent"—in this case the day-to-day lives of Native Americans in the colonies—was systematically upended by the institutional propaganda of the colonial state. One of the most powerful representations to emerge from this process is, of course, the ever present trope of the vanishing Native. Gerald Vizenor apprehends the "immanent" Native identity of the past in "shadows of remembrance" that cast their shapes beyond the absence of the real, or the void that has been left us by colonial unwitnessing.[13] He is appropriately wary of print history and cautions that "to hover over the traces of the presence in literature is not an ecstatic vision."[14] But perhaps print history itself is transformed, acquires a new signification, when interpreted through a "postindian" lens or the longhouse of the archive.

Looking back to the interesting dynamic that located the first press of the colonies directly in a space constructed for Native Americans offers an opportunity to reconsider the role Native Americans played in the early colonial period and how Natives negotiated for their own cultural interests and representation of identity both within and without the totalizing network of the colonists' print discourse. Natives, of course, were not involved in the decisions of what went to print in Cambridge, but, as I hope to elaborate in this chapter, they were involved in nearly every aspect of the actual printing, and only one man, a Nipmuc named James Printer, can be said to have attended the operations of the Cambridge Press from start to finish. Arriving at this awareness, marking the incongruity of it, does nothing to alter the colonial past, but it does suggest a path by which our engagement with the past can begin to break containment and posit a new narrative launching pad, disrupting the traumatic gaps that have left scab-like lesions over the collective memory of this country.

Much of what we now know about the initial attempts by New England colonists to educate and Christianize the Natives can be found in a collection of promotional literature that is probably best summed up as the *Eliot Tracts*. Although Eliot was not responsible for the authorship of each of the ten or eleven texts that comprise this collection, he remains the dominant force behind them and contributed to most of them. Eliot had come over to New England in 1631 and found a post as teacher and sometime preacher at Roxbury. Although not a prominent figure in his early days in the colony, he seems to have emerged as a useful political proponent of John Winthrop's government. As the New England colony found itself nearly split apart during the political struggle known now as "the antinomian crisis" of the mid-1630s, Eliot was a steadfast voice for authoritarian control, surfacing in the records as a harsh critic of Anne Hutchinson during her trial and an outspoken proponent of the controversial Pequot War.[15] Once the colony had stabilized itself again under Winthrop's government, Eliot seems to have worked behind the scenes to help organize the founding and maintenance of Harvard College. It was as a central component to this campaign that *First Fruits* was published in England in 1643 detailing the reported conversion of Wequash and invoking pity for "those poore Heathen that are bleeding to death to eternall death" all for lack of good Christian learning. While the first portion of *First Fruits* was dedicated to the presumed successes at Indian conversion (Wequash being offered up as the model example), the second half detailed the progress of the college, then in its fourth year, offering a summary of the rules, expectations, and disciplines to be mastered. The publicity generated by the tract managed to raise roughly £335, thirty-five of which purportedly went toward the cause of supporting Indian education and the other three hundred toward the college itself.[16] The propaganda tracts that followed *First Fruits* detailed the forays of Eliot, the Mayhews of Martha's Vineyard, and a few other scattered missionaries into the so-called wilderness to bring the word of God to his lost people. As noted by Michael B. Clark, editor of the recently published first edition of these collected documents, *The Eliot Tracts* serve as a "comparatively modest but important counterpart to the Jesuit *Relations* in New France and to the missionary work described as part of the conquistador narratives of New Spain."[17]

As *traditionally* narrated, John Eliot (glowingly referred to by his contemporaries as the "apostle to the Indians"), single-handedly broke the lethargy surrounding the colonial venture and its intended charter to civilize the Natives by venturing out to the nations bordering the United Colonies in the 1640s and winning them over with his sermons and tireless question and answer sessions. In these sessions, he purportedly challenged Native belief systems and convinced the sachems of the superiority of Christian logic. So effective were Eliot's exhortations that it was often reported "what floods of tears fell from the eyes of several amongst those degenerate salvages" upon hearing his sermons.[18] Eliot's enduring claim to fame, however, lay in the 1663 publishing of *Mamusse Wunneetupanatamwe Up-Biblum God Naneeswe Nukkone Testament Kah Wonk Wusku Testament*, or the Christian Bible translated into a local dialect of the Algonquian language. This work, the first Bible to be published in North America, allowed Eliot, along with a few conscripted Native students of "exceptional" ability, to disseminate the gospel in Native space and convince his converts to settle into "praying towns" where they would cultivate the land, live in houses, domesticate animals, and attend services on Sundays. To his contemporaries such as Cotton Mather, Eliot was "a most blessed and a most holy man."[19] His accomplishments were roundly admired, and it was only through the resistance of "several of those nations which refused the gospel" that the work of civilizing the Natives was ultimately unraveled.[20] The revolt of 1675–1676, led by King Philip, the son of Massasoit, was largely believed to have dissolved the praying towns and to have scattered Eliot's converts so that, in the end, nothing remained of his evangelical successes. Following the war, the scattered remnants of New England Natives were imagined to have slowly faded from the scene, driven out by a world that no longer had any place for them, melting away, as many a New England historian would intone, "like snow in the springtime."[21]

As I said, that is the *traditional* narrative. Settler tradition. Simulations of dominance. What should become apparent, however is that the indigenous nations that signed on to Eliot's plan, both before and after King Philip's War, had their own motives quite separate from those articulated by the colonists. The idea that any of Eliot's sermons actually moved the local Natives to spontaneous conversions or uncontrollable tears is somewhat laughable, particularly when one takes into account that Eliot could only barely speak the language at the time of his first reported meeting with the Indians. Even if he had been able to speak it fluently, however, the esoteric content of his delivery would have been all but incomprehensible to his audience. And even granting that the Cohannet Natives to whom he first preached grasped the overall sense of what Eliot was saying, it was never very likely that Native communities would utterly reconfigure long-held belief systems in acknowledgment of Christian superiority, no matter how effective a single sermon. Nor is it very likely that Native converts suddenly huddled into "praying towns" and turned to sweat-of-thy-brow style agriculture in a gesture of abject capitulation to English power. Much of New England's Native population outright refused the idea of the "praying town," and there is ample evidence that those who did congregate into praying towns held onto many of their traditional practices.

The term "praying town" itself is the coinage of colonial interests and needs to be either done away with entirely or reinterpreted through a different framework. The term solidifies a notion that the members of such a community had unambiguously offered themselves up to the devotional practices of the Christian faith, and what's more, implies that "prayer" itself was their dominant activity. The term is a powerful containment, subsuming everything that falls within its discursive properties, and whitewashing, or othering, the Native presence that remains at its locus. But as I hope to demonstrate, "praying towns" were still very much locations of Native presence and traditional activity. If we are to retain the misnomer of "praying" we must regard it outside of its Christian context and think instead of the more universal practice of prayer as, perhaps, the Natives who congregated in these towns were invested in praying for peace and stability more than Jehovah. By holding such a definition in mind, we might begin to remove "praying" from the brackets that surround it and offer it back up freed from without the rhetorics of colonial containment.

The actual motives behind Natives of New England moving into praying towns has been the subject of a long ongoing debate, but the main points of contention remain, in many ways, rhetorical, even if the driving ideologies of the various commentators veer off in different directions. Francis Jennings in his *The Invasion of America* portrays Eliot as something of a charlatan and profiteer who lined his own pockets rather than channeling funds meant for Indian education toward their proper purpose.[22] The Massachusett leader Waban, who became the first Native leader to acquiesce to the strictures of the praying town system, is also regarded by Jennings as an opportunist or false sachem, who joined with the English to acquire personal power.[23] Jennings concludes that Eliot manifested no genuine interest in Native conversion until 1647 when an annuity became available through one Lady Armine in England. While the annuity coincides somewhat with the visible beginnings of Eliot's mission, Jennings' assumption ignores the fact that Eliot must have been studying the language for some time prior to this date in order to prepare himself to deliver a sermon in the Algonquian language in October of 1646. Certainly Eliot required and sought patronage to do his work, but there is no substantial evidence that his motives were purely mercenary. Richard Cogley takes a more charitable view in his comprehensive *John Eliot's Mission to the Indians*, asserting that Eliot actually saw his cause as a way of protecting the Indians from aggressive land-grabbing settlers, and observes that the first attempts at establishing praying towns were closely linked to the wishes of Natives to hold onto the land that was left to them.[24] Ethnohistorian James Axtell, too, notes that Natives converted to Christianity because it provided a "comparatively better" answer to the spiritual exigencies they were facing at the time. Although Axtell concludes that the brand of Christianity adopted by the New England Natives "often lay very lightly on the surface of their lives," still the only choice remaining after pandemic disease, war, and political disenfranchisement was to "revitalize on the spot or die as a culture." The result of such pressures was the adoption of syncretic forms of worship that, while perhaps a disruption of precontact traditions, nevertheless promised the preservation of ethnic identity and continued holdings of ancestral lands. According to Axtell, Natives took what they needed of Christian doctrine to survive, and no more.[25]

What lies at stake in most of these arguments are the motives of the missionaries and the degree of cultural disruption endured by Native peoples at this time. Individual motives are notoriously difficult to read, although my own assumption is that Eliot, for better or worse, grew into his job to a certain extent. Although hopelessly biased toward his own cultural foundations, he desired in his own way to do good for the Native peoples within his sphere of influence. Osage theologian George Tinker asks in his book *Missionary Conquest: The Gospel and Native American Cultural Genocide*, "how could these dedicated spiritual figures [the missionaries in question] not see the role they inevitably played in the exploitation or the political manipulation of the tribal peoples of America?"[26] This remains the vital question of imperialism and cultural hegemony, as pertinent today as it was three hundred and fifty years ago. And yet, why not ask the same of Waban who might have resisted Eliot's advances as other Native groups, like the Narragansett, the Mohegan, and others did at the time? Tinker, like Jennings, suggests that by elevating Waban's authority, Eliot was undermining the Massachusett sachem Cutshumoquin who had previously shunned Eliot's missionary appeals. But Waban himself was under extraordinary pressure. In the final analysis, it is difficult to discern just how much of Native hierarchy was disrupted by the praying town system, since when Natick was ultimately established as the first of these towns in 1653, Cutshumoquin himself emerged as the leader and Waban was designated with the lesser title of "councilor of fifty." In effect, both kept their traditional seats within their own tribal hierarchy. Is it possible that Waban and Cutshumoquin were working in concert, playing good Indian, bad Indian? Or that they held different opinions but came together in the face of pressing political choices the best way they knew how?

The answers to such questions reside in the "shadows of remembrance."[27] Is it possible to delineate their forms and draw new suppositions, removed from the old stale narratives we have been handed? And is it possible that the missionaries, understanding the cultural pressures being brought to bear on Native communities, in some cases were offering the only solution available short of violence, no matter how complicit it made them in an overall scheme of white European dominance? Eliot, himself, would plead in the preface to his *Indian Dialogues*, "suffer not the English to strip them of all their lands."[28] The pragmatic choices of a particular historic moment can have the effect of leaving ideological preferences in the dust, and the arguments tend to become circular. But the arguments must not necessarily conform. What is important is that we find a means of airing them out so that, even given the difficultly of discerning them through the colonial containments by which they come to us, we might hear many parties speaking instead of simply one. This is the theory of the condolence ritual, and I shall try in this chapter to hear different sides of this old story, in order to remove the stale dust of ages.

There can be little if any doubt that Natives congregated into praying towns as a cultural expediency. How they retained their own traditions within this system, the ligaments of language, culture, and cognition that formed their group identity, remains largely unavailable to us. The fact that the missionaries, like Eliot, Mayhew, and Gookin, were complicit in an act of cultural containment and erasure should not in any way be brushed aside, but also does not preclude a case-by-case evaluation of their personal efforts and accomplishments. The so-called praying towns and the Indian College, however, were as much Native space as they were spaces of colonial containment. It strikes me as self-evident that Natives like Waban, James Printer, and Caleb Cheeshateaumauk, author of the first extant example of a Native's alphabetic writing in North America, were involved in acts of continuance as well as accommodation when they engaged with European cultural conditions. When encountering the traces of their presence left within the archival troves, we ourselves are brought into a space of containment, where texts reside within texts, fragments remain fragmented, and Native agency is thoroughly encircled by the discursive boundaries maintained by the colonist. But by allowing a Native-friendly framework to project itself over these archival materials, thereby reconfiguring the contextual boundaries, containment can be broken and previously overlooked agendas can begin to surface. Written texts and fragments like Caleb Cheeshateaumauk's 1663 letter to Robert Boyle, or the speeches transcribed in Eliot's "Tears of Repentance," have something to tell us about Native lives in seventeenth-century America. Many Native individuals did learn to read and write in New England at this time, both in English and in their own language, while simultaneously maintaining ligaments of their own traditions. Some, as I have previously stated, were captive children forcefully assimilated and given no choice in the matter of conforming to English ways. Others acquainted themselves with Western literacy as a conscious survival strategy. In either case, these individuals were engaging with a system of power negotiation that they hoped would benefit themselves and their communities in the years to come.

Although *The Eliot Tracts* comprise the most comprehensive record of missionary outreach in seventeenth-century New England, they lack the vital narrative immediacy and surprising personal detail of the *Jesuit Relations*. These tightly focused missives rarely allow themselves to stray from the master narratives of their Puritan authors to either take in the scenery, both human and natural, or appreciate the picturesque nature of the encounters described. Eliot, Thomas Shepherd, Thomas Mayhew, and the other authors involved were more focused on framing promotional talking points than maintaining any fidelity to the complexity of human interactions. The general framework of the earliest tracts is to describe an encounter in which a sermon was offered to a group of Natives, and then to detail the questions and answers that followed. Occasionally the rudiments of Native customs and beliefs are given a halting description, or the actions of a few *exceptional* converts might be highlighted, but the unerring agenda of these writings was to garner patronage by recording "progress," and little attention was given to anything that detracted from that vision. Nevertheless this tight ideological focus is compromised, fortunately it turns out, by complications of translation and transcription. As Eliot attempts in the later tracts to shepherd his heathen flock into the official embrace of the church, he relies more and more upon the transcribed confessions of his converts. These transcriptions, often taken on the spot by a Native translator, offer an intriguing glimpse into the mindset of the praying Indians who negotiated this tricky cultural terrain. Although their responses often strain toward the formulaic, they reflect a hybrid dialogue of conflicting concerns and agendas, and might be considered Native oratories translated by Native editors. While they were originally published to suggest the readiness of the participants to be accepted into the church, an entirely separate agenda presents itself in these texts—an agenda that was to remain one of the crucial touchstones of Native sovereignty. The praying Indians, as I mean to demonstrate, hoped to keep their traditional lands and regarded their compliance with Christian doctrine as a formality toward achieving such an end. Eliot, in the meantime, proceeded to print documents in the Algonquian language, as though the material fact of the texts themselves somehow offered an accounting of the authenticity of Native conversions.

What did it look like as all this printed material made its way into Native space in colonial America? How was it conveyed, and how improbable must it be that the very same *word* that the colonists hoped to bestow upon the Indians in their efforts at hegemonic control originated through the operation of the Cambridge Press from within Harvard's Indian College, an ostensibly Native space as well? If the enterprise remains an emblem of colonial domination, there is nevertheless cause to suspect that Natives had something to gain in this exchange as well and were not simply passive receptors of a new discursive medium. Alphabetic writing and its dissemination through printed texts was one of the most powerful tools the colonists brought with them to Native America. If it was unable to offer the immediate satisfactions made available through other trade goods, it nevertheless defined the parameters upon which the ultimate battles for cultural identity would be, and still are, waged. When the Natives of North America encountered printed texts, all available evidence indicates they understood they were encountering *manittowock*, or power.

A Town Called "Rejoycing": Reenvisioning the "Praying Town" as Native Space

By October of 1645 the Massachusetts Bay Colony, experiencing both population growth and, perhaps, a greater sense of its collective strength, felt the necessity once more of taking up its original mission to convert the Natives of the land. A decree issued by the General Court ordered that the court,

> being mindfull of their dutyes, to endeavor as much as in them lyeth, that all meanes may be used to bring the natives to the knowledge of God & his wayes, to civilize them as speedily as may be, & that some such course be taken as may cause them to observe those rules, order, [that] notice be given to ye reverend elders, in their severall shiers . . . to enacte what shall be thought meete hereabouts.[29]

Responding to the call were Thomas Shepherd and John Eliot who, in the course of a year, began to open up a discourse with the Natives bordering closely on their town of Cambridge where the new college had been formed. In the fall of 1646 these two men organized an expedition to meet with their indigenous neighbors and convey what they could of their colonial mandate.

The community of Massachusett and Nipmuc Natives living in the village of Cohannet (in the area of present-day Newton, Massachusetts) in October of 1646 probably heard the welcoming cry rise up prior to actually seeing the white men entering the village that morning. Whether or not they were expecting the visitors, a meal was likely to have been prepared of parched or boiled corn from the recent harvest to feed the guests.[30] The leaders of the community would have gathered to hear what the *chauquaquock* (knife men) or English, in their beards, long black frock coats, and white collars, had to say.[31] And the women and children would have gathered as well to see what gifts the white men would bring.

Without a doubt, the Massachusett were a people in crisis in the 1640s. They had seen their numbers decimated by a series of unknown diseases in the past twenty years with heavy epidemics in 1616 and again in 1633. The dead had piled up so quickly that there hadn't been time to offer proper burials, to go through the established rituals, and mourn in the traditional manner.[32] Such devastation had been unknown. The dead took with them their stories, their knowledge, their power. There hadn't been time to pass it all along in the ceremonial manner. Having been intermittently at odds with the Narragansett and Mohegan, the Massachusett now found themselves increasingly unable to defend their own interests.[33] In response, they had sought to establish relations with the newly arrived Europeans, resulting in an uneasy peace and a steady loss of ground. It was probably understood that, for better or worse, these were times of historic change, and on that October morning their eyes may have fastened momentarily upon the black, leather-bound books prominently displayed in the hands of the approaching travelers. The villagers were hardly unfamiliar with the preferred discourse of their settler neighbors, and although the persistence with which this discourse was pursued may have struck the Cohannet villagers as inexplicable and needlessly abrupt, they resigned themselves to extending a polite audience as was their custom. Amongst those who waited to hear what the English would say were Waban, the principal leader of the village, and his son, Weegramomenit, also known as Thomas Waban, who was roughly sixteen years old at the time and stood there "amongst the rest of his Indian brethren" although "in English clothes."[34]

Tradition generally has it that Eliot preached to the Natives from a stone pulpit, in keeping with the antiquated notion of Native peoples living like wild animals in the gloom of the forest (see figure 2.1). This session, however, of utmost spiritual significance, was most likely held in a longhouse erected specifically for the occasion. As the Puritan account of this meeting makes clear, upon being greeted by five or six of the chief men of the village, the visitors were led "into the principal Wigwam of Waaubon," who is identified at this moment as the "chief minister of justice" and one who "gives more grounded hopes of serious respect to the things of God." Far from being a small, cramped enclosure, the wigwam accommodated "many more Indians, men, women, children, gathered together from all quarters round about, according to appointment, to meet with us, and learn of us."[35] If Eliot was persuaded that he was bringing Christian light to the Massachusett, Waban was inviting the Puritan preacher into his own indigenous sphere of power and influence.

Figure 2.1. F. O. C. Darley sketch of John Eliot preaching to Waban and the Massachusett Natives at Cohannet.

According to the 1646 tract "The Day Breaking, if not The Sun Rising of the Gospell with the Indians in New England," a sermon was then delivered, its focus on the ten laws or commandments that the English purported to hold above all others, for they had been passed down to men directly from God, inscribed upon cold hard tablets of stone. Most important of these ten laws or prohibitions was the notion that, above all, the English God was to be regarded as the most powerful, or, in King James parlance, "thou shalt have no other Gods before me" (Exodus 20:3). The Massachusett thought they knew something of this God, and believed that he *was*, in fact, powerful, but that he was a *moosquantum*, or angry God. The English often heard this to mean he was a *muskeetoo* God, regarded by the Natives as small and annoying. Such misunderstandings were no doubt par for the course on both sides in the almost comically fractured discourse engendered by the Puritan missionary efforts.

Following the sermon the English were curious to know "whether all of them in the Wigwam did understand their discourse or only a few." The villagers responded as one that they had understood well enough. Then the English encouraged them to ask questions. Apprehending what was desired, someone finally asked how it came about that one might speak with the

Christ Manitou in the book. The English responded by saying, "if they [the Natives] were able to read our Bible, the book of God, therein they should see most cleerely what Jesuschrist was." But because they could not do this thing the Natives might try to "sigh and groane, and say thus; Lord make me know Jesuschrist, for I know him not." We can only assume the villagers nodded their heads in polite accord and struggled not to appear baffled by such talk. Another enquired as to how it was that images of God were made if this was clearly forbidden by the second commandment. The English responded by noting that, when an Indian drew a picture of another Indian on a tree "with such little eyes and such faire hands," this was "not an Indian but the Picture or image of an Indian." Not only was this a singular rare acknowledgment that the English were aware of the Native practice of making *awikhigans*, but it anticipated Rene Magritte's postmodernist conceit, "ceci n'est pas une pipe," by a couple of centuries. The English were careful to elaborate, however, that only "wicked men," otherwise known as Catholics, would create such images of God.[36]

The session went on for some three hours, after which the English finally expressed that they were weary. Waban had all along one vital question he intended to ask, but as was customary he waited until he was quite sure the English had concluded their discourse before asking it. As the authors of the "The Day Breaking" recount it,

> the chiefe of them seeing us conclude with prayer, desired to know when wee would come again, so wee appointed the time, and having given the children some apples, and the men some tobacco and what else we then had at hand, they desired some more ground to build a Town together, which wee did much like of, promising to speake for them to the generall Court, that they might possesse all the compasse of that hill, upon which their wigwams then stood.[37]

The difficulty in this passage is in discerning whose agenda is being articulated here at the conclusion of this session. The opening page of "The Day Breaking" seeks to assure the reader that "he that pen'd these following Relations, is a Minister of Christ in New England, so eminently godly and faithful, that what he here reports, as an eye or an eare witnesse, is not to be questioned."[38] That such a qualifier exists at all attests to the rampant anxieties concerning the reliability of written discourse that lay submerged in the European consciousness at this time. The anxiety was deeply enough rooted in the culture that bearing false witness was ninth of the ten prohibitions of the English religious code (Exodus 20:16). Nevertheless, we must question the integrity of much of the dialogue as offered. Although something approximating the particulars given by the text may have taken place, the opportunities for misunderstanding were enormous and the need to manufacture a successful and coherent encounter was equally pressing. The dialogue, in its presentation, is wooden and unnaturally precise. The Native audience is made to ask the very questions that the English were most eager to answer. But Waban's final question is framed in such a way as to stand outside the bulk of the recorded dialogue. Having been asked following the distribution of English gifts, which generally signaled the close of the session, it holds a separate status, which might imply that it was either not quite central to the concerns of the colonizers, or, conversely, that it was of the greatest importance. Either way, it seems to have entered the discourse as an afterthought, inserted as the English were preparing to leave.

Nothing had been written prior to this about setting aside guaranteed tracts of land for Natives willing to convert. This is not to say that it hadn't been discussed, however, and the writing on the wall appeared perfectly legible to Waban. The English had established a policy of *vacuum domicillum* in New England, meaning that any lands not being used, according to the English interpretation of "use," automatically fell into the possession of the Crown. The English, while aware of the tricky legalities of simply claiming foreign land as their own, did not necessarily let this prevent them from doing it anyway, and regarded it as a "remarkable" blessing that God had "swept away great multitudes of the Natives by the small Pox a little before we went thither, that he might make room for us."[39] Native claims to land were recognized by the English only if there were "improvements" made thereon, which explicitly meant clearing the land for agriculture and building permanent dwellings. In such a case allotments were presumably granted. From Waban's point of view, then, the implications seem clear. He is not concerned with the religious content of the visit so much as he is interested in receiving some assurance from the English that they will not encroach further on his lands. While, Thomas Shepherd, the presumed author of "Day Breaking," is fixed upon the idea that the Natives desire a "town" of their own, this is more than likely a poor translation. What Waban desires is to keep the lands that have always belonged to him and his people. He wishes for the land upon "all the compasse of that hill, upon which the wigwams then stood." And he seems to understand that he must attain such an assurance in writing.[40]

While Eliot is often credited for the inspiration of rounding the Natives of New England up into praying villages, he in fact appears to have been following the lead of Waban and others who agreed to engage with Christian discourse for the price of receiving some guarantee of retaining Massachusett lands. If anything, the settlers were more interested in moving the Natives to a new location further west, as is expressed in later tracts.[41] In a sense,

Waban gains the best of this initial bargain, for he must ask no tangible sacrifice from his villagers. He offers no promise that he or his people will become Christians (in fact he explicitly expresses his doubt that such a thing will come to pass), but only that they will welcome more visits from the Christians. In return he bargains to keep the lands that he already inhabits. And temporarily, at least, the General Court seems to comply. Waban did give up one thing, however. He did "voluntarily offer his eldest son to be educated and trained up in the knowledge of God, hoping as hee told us, that he might come to know him, although he despaired much concerning himself; and accordingly his son was accepted and is now at school in *Dedham*."

The "Day Breaking" tract appears to recount the first tentative moves toward Native education in the colonies, discounting the fact that Thomas Mayhew had already made significant inroads with the Natives of Martha's Vineyard by this point. It also appears evident, however, that some aspects of the 1646 visit were predetermined. After all, if we can take any of this at face value, then Waban's son was already dressed in English clothes at the time of the meeting and attending school in Cambridge. Quite possibly he had assisted Eliot in the translation of the sermon delivered, although this role is often attributed to Cockenoe, the Montauk captive of the Pequot War who was "indentured" with Richard Callicot at the time, and whom Eliot cited as his first language tutor.[42] Either way, we must acknowledge that Waban's compliance, to some degree, had already been anticipated and perhaps formalized when Eliot and his cohorts arrived on that day in October.

Eliot and his compatriots returned to "the wigwam of Waaubon" no less than two weeks later to attempt another sermon and to resume the obtusely metaphysical series of questions and answers they had begun in the first meeting. In the give and take that followed not only was the matter of how to best serve and worship God discussed, but apparently the Natives were curious to know why the sea was made of salt, and why the "water was higher than the earth."[43] There is no indication of whether or not they were satisfied with the answers provided. Perhaps within their own cosmology were stories to explain such things and they wished to see how the English answers would either correspond or differ. The Massachusett held to a tradition that the world had been flooded once, and that one *Powaw*, having foreseen this event, fled to the White Mountains where he and his people weathered the storm and then repopulated the earth. Others believed that the beaver was their father, having restored the earth by scoring mud from the bottom of the sea and placing it on the back of a turtle.[44] Still others told of a time when

> much water flooded the valleys and arose above the hills; achooak; much penetrated and much destroyed. Finally, it arose

> far above the highest mountains. Nanabush (the great hare) was born creeping, ready to move and dwelt at Tula, an island. All the beings were struggling in the water for Tulapin, turtle back. Nanabush discovered the great turtle and got safely on his back, as did several other beings, aided by the noble Nanabush, and were saved. After the waters had gone down, the giant turtle's feet were upon land at Talli. So there dwelt the many men, descendants of Nanabush, also the turtle beings.[45]

Regardless of the beliefs of the Natives gathered in the village, however, the English answer to each question posed amounted to the simple, and equally unscientific, assertion that it was "God that made them so."[46]

Quite possibly the dialogues recounted in these missionary tracts are mere fictions and should not be given over to interpretive investigations of Native motives, as many have argued. Rather than take these dialogues as literal translations of an encounter, however, they can be seen as an outline for a larger political and cultural discourse taking place. Such an outline is unquestionably determined by colonial forces and agendas, and yet is likely to intimate something of the indigenous response to those agendas. If we can think through such intimations from a perspective that takes into account the situation of the Massachusett, their political objectives and cultural exigencies, it becomes possible to disentangle their recorded responses from colonial frameworks and regard them from a position in Native space. In fact, it is incumbent upon us to perform such acts of translation or forever let the colonial representation, with all its clearly staked biases, stand.

The Puritan tracts that arose from these meetings, with their progressively more hopeful titles, that is: "The Day Breaking if not The Sun Rising of the Gospell with the Indians in New England," "The Clear Sunshine of the Gospel Breaking Forth Upon the Indians," "The Glorious Progress of the Gospel amongst the Indians," "The Light Appearing more and more towards the perfect Day," and so forth, tell a tale of a curiously stuttered forward progress, a glorious day that was constantly on the verge of breaking but never seems to reach high noon. They rationalized their perpetual lack of success with caveats such as, "for what Nation or people ever so deeply degenerated since *Adams* fall as these Indians; and yet the spirit of God is working upon them."[47] But the Natives of the Northeast, too, were oriented toward the rising sun, and built their wigwams with their entrances facing east. The missionaries found a seemingly receptive audience in Waban and believed his name came from "the Indian word for Wind," which they saw as fitting, for Mr. Eliot had preached from Ezekiel 37: 9, 10, wherein it is stated "that by prophesying to the wind, the wind came and the dry bones lived."[48] But this was yet another mistranslation. *Waban* is, in fact, the Algonquian word for "East" or "Dawn."

Red Shell, a Martha's Vineyard Wampanoag historian from the turn of the nineteenth century, explains that "Wampanoags, or *waban-noak*, [meant] 'easterners,' or 'people of the east.' Waban, from which *wampan* is derived, means 'east,' and *noak* is 'they live' making the name 'they live east (of us).' By that name the Pokanoks were known to the Pilgrims and other early settlers as the 'great Wampanoag nation.'"[49] The word *Waban* is also linguistically linked to *wabos*, the great white hare, who is a trickster figure in Algonquian myth and closely related to the culture hero Nanabush or Weetucks.[50] As Roger Williams noted of the Narragansett in his *Key*, "they have many strange Relations of one *Wetucks*, a man that wrought great Miracles amongst them, and walking upon waters, &c. with some kind of broken Resemblance to the Sonne of God."[51] Weetucks or *wautuckques*, in Williams' "broken" Algonquian, means conie or rabbit, and he notes, "they have a reverend esteeme of this Creature, and conceive there is some deity in it."[52] The late nineteenth-century ethnographer James Mooney also notes that

> *waban* . . . the Great White Rabbit is really the incarnation of the eastern dawn that brings light and life and drives away the dark shadows which have held the world in chains. The animal itself seems to be regarded by the Indians as the fitting type of defenseless weakness protected and made safe by constantly alert vigilance, and with a disposition, moreover, for turning up at unexpected moments.[53]

With this in mind, it might be asserted that both the English and the Indians were culturally invested in notions of the day-breaking if not the sun-rising with the Indians in New England. Waban's name, perhaps adopted for this new stage in the lives of the Massachusett, seems to signal a rekindling, the hope of a new dawn for his people after suffering the combined floods of disease, destabilization, colonization, and warfare that had marked the previous thirty years, or the bulk of Waban's adult life. His name is also associated with *wampan*, or wampum, denoting history, survival, life (see figure 2.2).

If Waban's name signified hope, it was nevertheless readily apparent to him that a colonial ring of containment was closing around the Massachusett. A great deal of land had already been sacrificed through trade agreements and, whether officially or not, a great deal of power had been ceded as well. His people would have entertained more than a simple intuition of how events with the Pequot a decade earlier might easily replicate themselves in their own territories. The Pequot War had not only resulted in colonial control of the wampum trade, but it led to an extensive reallocation of

Figure 2.2. Tomah Josephs' (Passamaquoddy) birch bark "scrapings" found in Charles Leland's 1884 *Algonquian Legends*.

lands, with a new colony chartered to none other than John Winthrop Jr. in May of 1646. The invigorated interest in missionary outreach on the part of the English in the autumn of 1646 was in most ways an ill omen, but one that Waban seems to have encountered with skill and forethought. When the missionaries met with the Massachusett at Waban's wigwam a third time on November 26 of that same year there again followed a series of questions and answers at this gathering. But above all, Shepherd informs us, their "great desire this time was to have a place for a Towne."[54] Waban was understandably anxious to receive some official confirmation from the General Court that their traditional holdings had actually been granted them.

According to "The Day Breaking if not The Sun Rising," it was announced to the Massachusett that their request for a town had been granted, and as Shepherd notes, "the Indians are much taken" with the prospect of remaining on their land.[55] But there was a distinct disconnect between what the Natives were told and what the court had actually decided and it seems evident that a removal was being contemplated from the start. As a direct result of the discussions that had taken place during the first October meeting, the Massachusetts General Court had, in fact, put aside money to purchase "parcels of land" for the Natives so that they might "live in an orderly way amongst us." In the irony defying language of the court, this was regarded as the colony's "first guift for ye good of Indians."[56] The missionaries, however, kept from the villagers the knowledge that they would not remain long on the grounds they presently inhabited. Shepherd writes that "while the court were considering where to lay out their towne, the Indians (not knowing of anything) were about that time consulting," making plans based upon their understanding that they would stay where they were.[57] Eliot supplied the Massachusett with tools and provisions in "hope" that they might begin "improving" the land. And despite all of these unsettling machinations, he chose to mark the occasion by deciding on a name for the newly established township (disregarding the fact that it already had a name).[58] They settled upon "Noonantenum," meaning "rejoicing," "because they [the Natives] hearing the word, and seeking to know God, the English did rejoyce at it."[59] The English concluded their visit with the recitation of a short prayer in the local language that read "Amanaomen Jehovah tehassen metagh / Take away, lord, my stone heart."[60]

Shadow Printer: The Invisible Native Hand on the Lever of the Press

Before the English left on this third encounter in November of 1646, four young children were placed in the hands of the missionaries by a prominent Native at Cohannet named Wampas, with the intention that they, too, would receive an English education.[61] These children, according to the authors, were promised "acceptance and an education of them either in learning or in some other trade of life." The authors of "Day Breaking," it seemed, were not quite sure how to dispose of the children put in their charge, noting that "they are not yet placed out because it is most meet to doe nothing that way too suddenly."[62] But the choice for a home for two of the Native youths seems to have landed on Henry Dunster, the first president of Harvard College. Dunster had become recognized as a proponent of Indian education, particularly efforts at teaching the Natives in their own language, and much of the fundraising surrounding these efforts was being channeled directly through the college as it was in keeping with its original charter.[63] One of the children Wampas handed over to the English must have been his son, John Wampas, whose checkered career would include a brief term at Harvard, a stint in colonial prison, and a life as fugitive mariner. Although it is difficult to prove with absolute certainty, another of the young children handed over that day was probably James Printer (obviously "Printer" is a later designation given to James when he came into his trade. He is quite probably the first Native of New England to acquire an English surname derived from his given employment). Yet another may have been Job Nesuton who would later help Eliot with the translation of the Old and New Testaments.

There is also some reason to believe, however, that James at least had already been placed in an English home prior to the Nonantum visits. Samuel Eliot Morison notes that in October of 1646 Dunster wrote a letter to the Massachusetts Council asking for compensation for expenses paid toward his boarding of two Indian children, Jonathan and James. The letter offers an audit of what was spent, informing us that the two boys were provided with £16 worth of food, £64 worth of clothing, and that both became ill early on in their residency for some five or six weeks. Dunster also notes that he spent £60 on James' schooling. If the dates offered by Morison are correct, then James was brought to Dunster prior to Eliot's trip to Cohannet. But it also seems plausible that the "Jonathan" mentioned is John Wampas, and therefore another one of the children most likely to have been offered up at the Nonantum lectures. Probably, as was the case with Thomas Waban, it is the chronology offered in "Day Breaking" that is off. Whatever the circumstances, Dunster seems not to have been happy with these "hopeful young plants" and the expenses that accompanied them. He wrote to the governing council that "the Indians with me be so small as that they [are] incapable of the benefit of learning as was my desire to impart to them, and therefore they being an hindrance to mee and I no furtherance to them, I desire they may be somewhere else disposed of with all convenient speed." The magistrates of New England agreed to compensate Dunster some £22 for his efforts, but were silent on the matter of how to dispose of the two Indian boys.[64]

It may have been understandable that Dunster, despite his stated advocacy for Indian education, didn't want two Indian children cluttering the works. He had only a few years earlier married one Elizabeth Glover and inherited not only her five children from a previous husband, but a bouncing baby printing press that she had brought to America with her in 1638. To establish a press in New England had been the goal of her first husband, the Reverend Jose Glover. Glover died on the passage over, however, and the press was maintained for the next few years by Stephen Day at the house of Elizabeth Glover. Stephen Day, a locksmith by trade, land speculator at heart, and printer by conscription, oversaw the printing of the first published materials in New England including *The Freeman's Oath*, a 1639 almanac, *The Bay Psalm Book*, and the first Harvard Commencement theses. Although trained by Glover and brought over as an indenture, Day proved a less than adequate printer and did not find approval with the tightly wound Puritan community in New England. When Elizabeth Glover married Dunster in 1641, the press became Dunster's own private venture, whether he desired it or not. To complicate matters further, Elizabeth Glover (now Dunster) died in 1643 after bearing Dunster a son. Dunster remarried the next year, and soon another baby was on the way.[65] To summarize, somewhere in the years of 1645–1646, Dunster, along with overseeing the fledgling college, had to make room in his newly erected house for his first son and five step-children through Elizabeth Glover, a new baby from the second marriage, a printing press, and two Indian youths that he didn't know how to "dispose of." Morison notes that the press presumably "occupied the ground floor of a lean-to or addition on the north side" of the house. Quite possibly the two Indian boys were made to sleep in the same room alongside the press, as there would have been a lack of space and the lean-to was probably built as a servants quarters to begin with.[66]

If Dunster wished to unload the children on someone else, he may have been discouraged by the fact that money being allocated to the college from Parliament, according to a 1649 proclamation, was inextricably tied up in the encouragement of "the preaching and propagating of the Gospel of Jesus Christ amongst the Natives, and also for maintaining of schools and nurseries of learning, for the better educating of the children of the Natives."[67] Thus his boarding of the two children remained a public relations gesture that had been, from the start, the most effective manner of winning money from England for support of the college. Perhaps another incentive, as Cogley asserts, was that the money raised by the Weld-Peters commission, which was responsible for the publication of *New England's First Fruits*, had gone toward building Dunster's new house rather than any demonstrable help for the Natives. Therefore Dunster owed his present quarters to the very cause of Indian education.[68] This was undoubtedly what had motivated Eliot to bring the children to Dunster in the first place.

As for the press, Stephen Day proved unmanageable and unreliable in his office as printer, and his son Matthew was quickly hired in his place to run the operation. Matthew Day died only three years later, however, leaving the bay colony with a press but no one to run it. And yet it *did* keep running, even without the famed Samuel Green, who was to step in soon after and take over the day-to-day business of keeping it going. Samuel Green has become something of a beloved figure in colonial lore, fondly described by Morison as "one of those popular, versatile, faithful and energetic characters necessary to the good conduct of any college town."[69] Rarely, however is he commended for his skill as a printer. Green wrote to John Winthrop Jr. in 1675 that "printing was the employment I was called unto when there was none in the country to carry it along . . . and although I was not used unto it yett being urged thereunto by one and another of place did what by my own endeavors and help that I gott from some others that was procured, I undertook the work."[70] His phrasing alone punctuates some of the difficulties he might have faced as printer.

As George Parker Winship notes in his 1946 history, *The Cambridge Press*, Matthew Day died on May 10, 1649. Green took over the press in October. But some ghost printer seems to have kept things going in the interim as the summer of 1649 saw the publishing of the Harvard Commencement Programs in the absence of a proprietor. Winship imagines that some journeymen who had been with the press all along managed to get these publications out, but doesn't trouble himself to offer up any likely candidates. Green himself admits to the help from "some others that was procured," but also offers no names, nor is there any record of anyone being compensated for such work. There is good reason to believe that this invisible, unpaid printer who kept things running in the absence of a "real" printer was none other than James Printer himself. Gookin would write some years later that James, unlike his brothers, "was bred among the English, and employed as a press man in printing the Indian bible."[71] If Printer had been living with Dunster, as most historians assume, and had been placed there to learn a trade, as Eliot insists, then it seems more than likely that he was trained by Matthew Day and had actually acquired some remedial printing skills in the three years that he had slept in the same house as the press, and presumably in the same room. That he remains an invisible presence is not surprising, as any Native contributions to the workings of the colony were bound to be overlooked or unwitnessed. In fact, the very invisibility of this interim printer, or the historical shadow cast in his place, suggests that James was the immanent presence behind it. James, who would have been roughly eleven or twelve at the time of Day's death, and had probably learned to read and write a little English in the fledgling grammar school Eliot established in Cambridge, was old enough, and probably experienced enough at this point, to have gotten the job done.[72] Certainly it was considered no great feat for Ben Franklin to have done as much when he was a printing devil in his youth, working for his brother some sixty years later.[73]

Margaret Connell Szasz, in agreement with recent scholarly consensus, writes that "one of the most remarkable aspects of Green's long and successful career was his association with James. By teaching this young Nipmuc the skills of the craft, he insured Indian involvement in one of the most crucial aspects of the Massachusetts publishing venture."[74] I would posit, however, that it was James Printer who trained Green, a man who, by his own admission, knew nothing of printing when Dunster singled him out for the job in 1649. In fact, prior to taking over the press, Green had been a general handyman around the campus, prominent in the militia, and at various times doorkeeper to the House of Deputies, clerk of writs, stationer, and college barber.[75] Lacking a definitive trade of his own, he seems to have eagerly answered whatever call was demanded of him. That Green's status as printer would initiate a publishing legacy stretching for generations and accounting for many of the most important documents of the colonial period owes more than a bit to blind chance and the assistance of one barely perceptible "printing devil" whose contributions became absorbed in the identity of his white master.[76]

By 1650 a new charter for Harvard signed by Dunster and then-governor Dudley was incorporated for "the advancement . . . and to the maintenance of . . . all other necessary provisions that may conduce to the education of the English & Indian youths of this Country in knowledge: and godliness."[77] As Harvard struggled to establish itself as an institution, it increasingly acknowledged the utility of attaching itself to goals of Native education. In 1651 Dunster proposed that the building for the Indian College be funded. The Indian College was the first brick building at Harvard, described by Gookin as "strong and substantial but not very capacious," costing between £300 and £400, and "able to accommodate about twenty scholars with convenient lodgings and studies."[78] Aside from the obvious educational goals, however, Dunster may have had the alternative motive of needing a place to house his long-term boarders, and the rising generation of Native students who had been studying all along at the local grammar school (see figure 2.3).

The Indian College was built sometime between 1654 and 1656, the general period of its construction interestingly coinciding with a number of concurrent events. First of all, Dunster resigned as president of Harvard in 1654, and was replaced by Charles Chauncy in November of that year.[79] Dunster was more or less forced out of his position following legal troubles that concerned the royalties of the printing press, and claims by the Glover family—the original owners of the press—that they were entitled to a share of its overall profits. Forced out of his home in the winter of the following year, Dunster moved his family to Scituate, leaving the press behind.[80] One wonders if the incoming Harvard president, Charles Chauncy, inherited Jonathan and James as well. There is no record of either of them throughout this period. Probably they divided their time between their homes in the Indian village of Hassanamesit and Cambridge. Nevertheless, Chauncy seems to have regarded the inherited printing press in his quarters as a nuisance, even describing it as "dangerous and hurtful," words more commonly used to describe Indian "savages" than printing presses. Therefore the press was moved to the new Indian College building probably in the spring of 1655.[81] This was most likely a solution of greatest convenience since not only was there a noticeable amount of vacant space in the two-story, thirty-by-twenty-foot-long house, but this would allow the Native printer, James, to continue living in direct proximity to the press and keep it maintained.[82] The year before,1654, also happened to be the year that the first text in

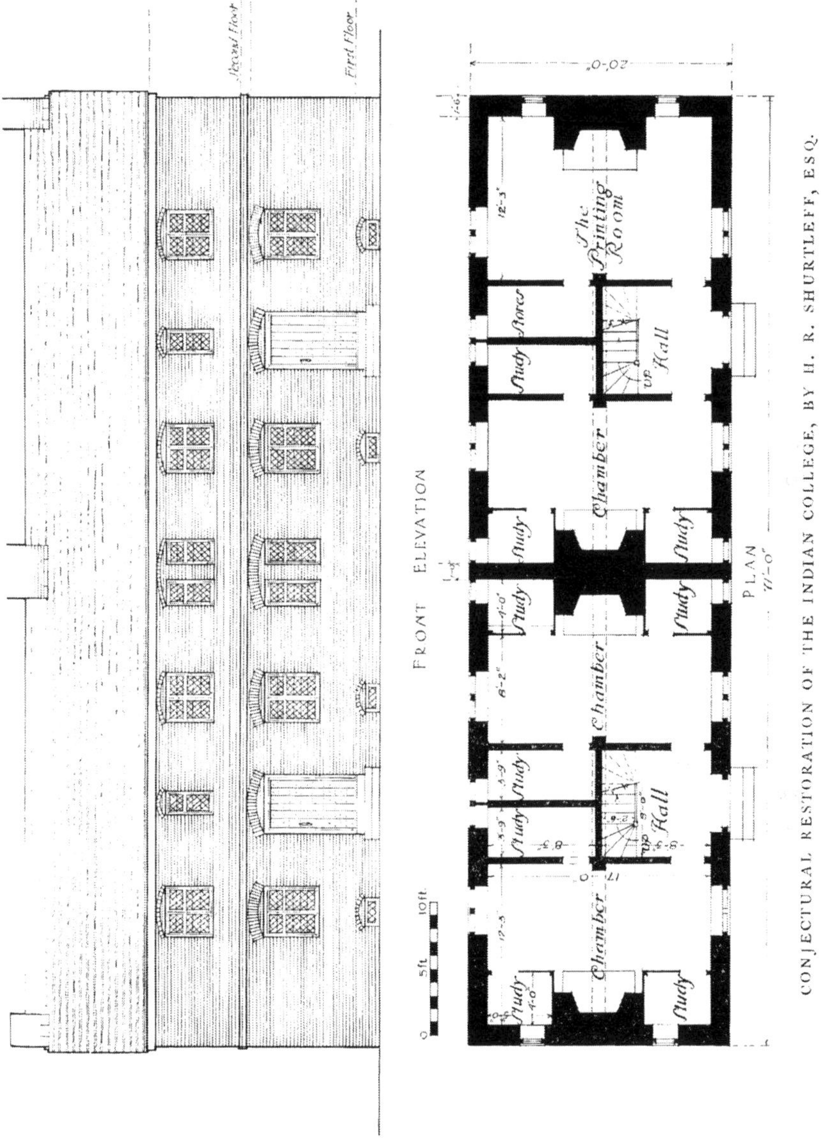

Figure 2.3. Indian College building as imagined by H. R. Shurtleff found in Samuel Eliot Morison's *Harvard College in the Seventeenth Century*.

the Native language, *The Indian Primer*, was printed by Eliot, presumably with the help of Job and James. Chauncy was never a champion of the project of printing texts in the Native language and probably considered it a major inconvenience to have such an operation ongoing in his own quarters. This was one more reason to have it, and its associates, relocated. Once the press was situated in an Indian space, with an Indian printer and Indian translator on board, it could continue its production of texts in the Indian language unabated.

James Printer does not emerge in the archives again with any reasonable certainty until 1659, when it is noted by the commissioners of the New England Company that "two of the Indian youthes formerly brought up to reed and writ are put apprentice; the one to a carpenter, the other to Mr. Green the Printer."[83] This doesn't necessarily mean, however, that James was actually made an apprentice in 1659, but merely that the commissioners chose to "officially" remark upon his "apprenticeship" at this point as they were in the process of soliciting for a new press with which to make the first Indian Bibles. It may be that James had finished studying at Corlett's grammar school by this point and could turn his full attention to his designated trade. But to call him an "apprentice" implies a codified relationship that was not truly open to Native American youths. As nineteenth-century historian and antiquarian book dealer Samuel Drake notes in his *Biography and History of the Indians of North America*, James was *still* considered an "apprentice" when he later became swept up in the conflict known as King Philip's War in 1675. Drake wryly comments that "if after an apprenticeship of sixteen years one could not leave his master without the charge of absconding, at least, both the master and the apprentice should be pitied."[84] In all likelihood, James' "apprenticeship" had, at that point, been a full *twenty-six* years in the making. James, with his skill in printing and his ability to read and write in both English and Massachusett, was probably on hand for the printing of the 1654 *Indian Primer*, and therefore was likely to have had a hand in every text produced in the Indian language from the Cambridge Press over a 53-year period.

All the while that James was learning the printing trade and teaching it to Samuel Green, Job Nesuton was learning more specifically to read and write, and was busy teaching the Massachusett language to Eliot. Job had probably received some two or three seasons of schooling at one of the secondary schools in the colony by the time Eliot announced in 1650 that "I have one already who can write, so that I can read his writing well, and he (with some pains and teaching) can read mine."[85] Eliot had made it clear in his letters to the newly established, London-based Society for Propagation of the Gospel in New England that "I do very much desire to translate some parts of the Scriptures into their language, and to print some primer in their language wherein to initiate and teach them to read, which some of the men do much also desire." But Eliot was quick to note that, despite the fact that he had been dabbling in the Massachusett language for some four or five years, he had "yet but little skill in their language . . . I must have some Indians, and it may be other help around me to try and examine Translations, which I look at as a sacred and holy work, and to be regarded with much fear, care, and reverence."[86]

Neal Salisbury intimates that it was the Indian interpreters who were responsible for the actual translations of the biblical texts, with Eliot merely spearheading the project.[87] And Szasz strongly asserts that "for too many years this Indian contribution to the publications has been ignored."[88] These scholars have appropriately sought to locate and recognize the high degree of Native input into this colonial endeavor. In response to their remarks, however, Richard Cogley has sought to realign the discussion once more, acknowledging that such contributions took place, but arguing that Eliot, himself, must have done the actual translating as the texts in question "required a command of English and a theological erudition that no Native at the time possessed."[89] Cogley does a good job bringing to light the interpretive complexities of this massive undertaking, noting how words like "horse," "brass," "psalm" and others had no equivalent in the Algonquian. The word "lattice" for instance, was substituted with the word "eelpot," as the Native eel pot seemed closest in design. There is no verb *to be* in the Algonquian language, which created many challenging problems. A passage in Matthew referring to "ten wise and foolish virgins" was transformed into a male-gendered reference, as it was perceived that chastity was a masculine rather than feminine virtue in the culture of the New England Natives.[90] Absent from Cogley's overall assessment, however, is the acknowledgment that it would have taken a similarly sophisticated internalization of the Massachusett language to effect the translation, particularly if Native audiences were to have any hope of overcoming cultural differences and grasping its content. Just as the Native translators were not expertly fluent in English and the esoteric conceptual framework of Judeo-Christian traditions, Eliot was hardly fluent in Algonquian and the spiritual and traditional equivalents that were brought to bear in juxtaposing such disparate cultural realities. One can only surmise then that the translations were a truly collaborative effort.

Regardless of the fact that Eliot openly admitted his need for constant assistance in completing this work, never does he cite by name the individuals who assisted him on specific projects. They too are historical shadows, their names filled in by years of historical inquiry and research. We know from an accounting bill sent to the New England Company in 1662 that Job was paid for his help as "interpreter," to Eliot.[91] And in his 1677 *An Historical Account of the Christian Indians in New England*, Daniel

Gookin remarks upon Job's death (fighting alongside the English in the first major battle of King Philip's War in 1775) that "he was a very good linguist in the English tongue, and he was Mr. Eliot's assistant and interpreter in his translations of the Bible, and other books of the Indian language."[92] Gookin's comment, alongside other references to the help received, point to the fact that the work of translating all of these materials into the Native language was not the work of a single white man, nor, is it likely, a single Native interpreter. John Sassamon, whose alleged murder would spark the events leading up to King Philip's War, probably had a hand in some of the translation as we will see in the following chapter. The aforementioned Cockenoe must have been involved in some early translation work as well. And James Printer was apparently indispensable in bringing these materials to press. Job, however, seemed to have been the mainstay in providing Indian translations over the years, despite a few isolated incidents of his, to use Eliot's term, "backsliding."

Eliot, as is clear in his comments concerning transcription in "Tears of Repentance" and elsewhere, simply did not possess enough fluency in the Algonquian language to receive sole credit for the accomplishment of translating the Bible. Even as late as 1683 when the second edition of the Bible was proposed, Eliot wrote to the commissioners "we have but one man, viz. the *Indian Printer*, that is able to compose the sheets, and correct the press with understanding."[93] The translations had to have been a joint venture in every way, requiring as much Native input as English. While it shouldn't be surprising that Eliot's name alone appears on the frontispiece of these works (along with Samuel Green's as printer), the Indian translations were the handiwork of Native individuals whose labor and input went largely unnoted (see figure 2.4).

Tears and Testimonies: "Tears of Repentance" and "A Further Account of the Progress of the Gospel"

The Natives who dwelt in proximity to English rule often found themselves in a thankless and precarious situation. As Wampas expressed it, "because we pray to God, other Indians abroad in the countrey hate us and oppose us, the English on the other side suspect us, and feare us to be still such as doe not pray at all."[94] The political and psychological pressures attendant upon such a situation, when added to the other psychological pressures these communities had already withstood, must have created an atmosphere of nearly unbearable tension and grief. Even Waban, who seems to have led the movement of Natives congregating into praying towns, testified in

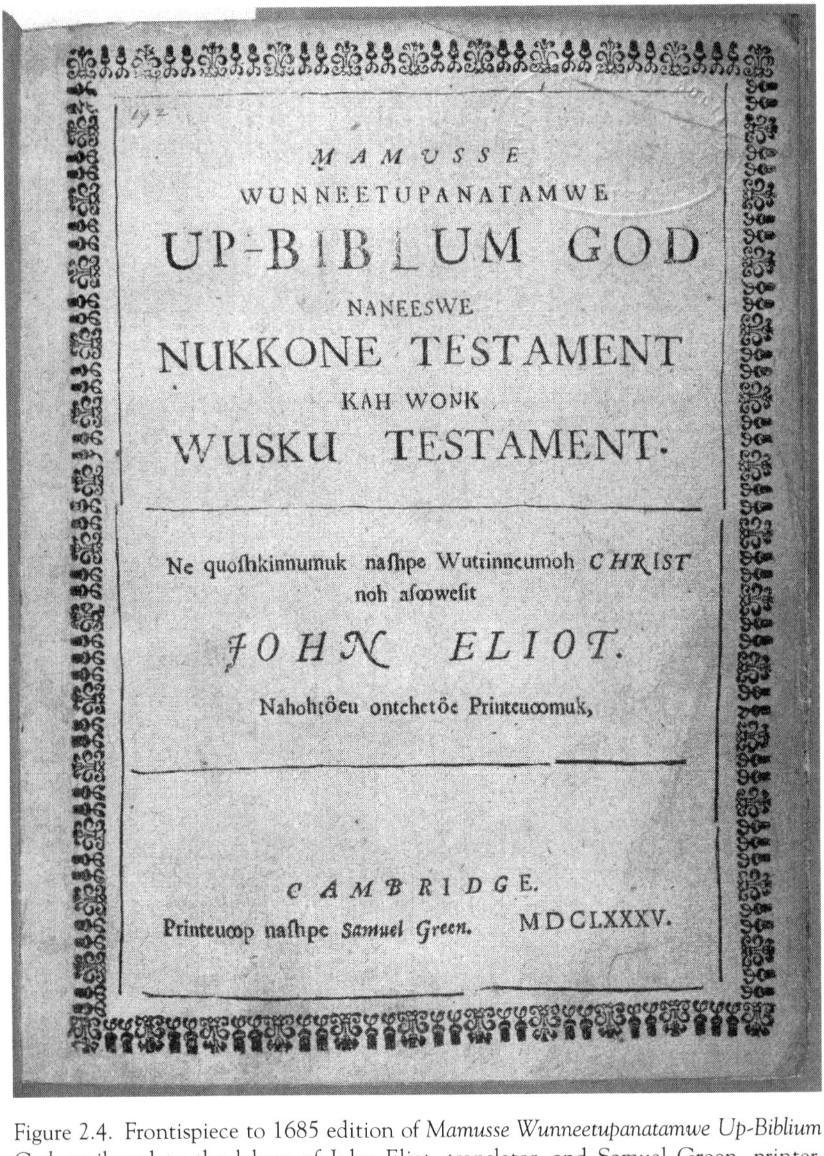

MAMUSSE
WUNNEETUPANATAMWE
UP-BIBLUM GOD
NANEESWE
NUKKONE TESTAMENT
KAH WONK
WUSKU TESTAMENT.

Ne quoshkinnumuk nashpe Wuttinneumoh CHRIST
noh asoowesit
JOHN ELIOT.
Nahohtôeu ontchetôe Printeucomuk,

CAMBRIDGE.
Printeucop nashpe Samuel Green. MDCLXXXV.

Figure 2.4. Frontispiece to 1685 edition of *Mamusse Wunneetupanatamwe Up-Biblium God* attributed to the labors of John Eliot, translator, and Samuel Green, printer. Courtesy of American Antiquarian Society.

1652, "when the English taught me of God (I coming to their Houses) I would go out of their doors, and many years I knew nothing; when the English taught me I was angry with them."[95] This statement, offered up in the 1653 tract "Tears of Repentance," allows a compelling glimpse into the conflicted process of Native conversions. While Eliot continued to conjure up seamlessly optimistic assessments of the emerging dawning of Christianity amongst the Natives, Waban and others, when allowed to speak from within a different context, presented a much more complicated response. More than likely, contained within Waban's brief pronouncement is a world of turmoil. One intuits a rift in the public visage and the private one he wears when "out of their doors." Within the confines of Puritan print discourse Waban remains a dedicated convert and precious "first fruit," but in private he wrestles with the cultural tensions he has taken it upon himself to bear. This separation between the immanent and the idealized Native is made apparent somewhat when one looks at Eliot's paradoxical testimonial of Native confessions, entitled "Tears of Repentance."

In 1651 it was decided that the Nonantum Natives who had signed on to Eliot's missionary outfit should be relocated, and two thousand acres of land were opened up for that purpose in nearby Natick. Little has been said concerning how such a move, even a move of only some fifteen miles, might have resounded with the Natives themselves or affected their political infrastructure. Waban's band understood they had been promised the land at Nonantum and had begun to, in a sense, reorganize their lives there in accordance to the dictates of the Puritan missionaries. But now, without being consulted or given a choice, they were forced to reorganize again within newly proscribed geographical boundaries. One gets a sense of what scant consideration this topic has generated when reading George Emery Littlefield's account in his *The Early Massachusetts Press*, wherein he concludes simply that "the Indians were favorably disposed toward this proposition and soon became anxious to remove."[96] It brings to mind General Winfield Scott's callous observation concerning the forced removal of the Cherokee in 1838, of which he concluded "they took their way, if not rejoicing, at least in comfort."[97] Cogley writes that the "Nonantum Natives were pleased with the location" and notes that John and Robin Speene, two prominent praying Indians of the time, held an "inheritance" there. He states that "Wamporas" or Wampas "also approved of the location."[98] Many, however, were still very much attached to the ancestral lands they thought had been promised them at Cohannet, or Nonantum, as the colonists preferred to call it (although it could no longer be considered a place of "rejoicing," but rather a cause for mourning). Waban seems to have opted to remain silent on this subject in "Tears of Repentance," although it remains clear from his earlier statements made in "Clear Sunshine" and "Glorious Progress," that he had lobbied to remain in Nonantum. While "Tears of Repentance" is a tract published directly in the service of Eliot's missionary endeavors, it reveals some of the growing tensions arising from coerced conversions and removals.

The notion of Native "tears" in relation to Christian conversion had already become a popular convention by the 1650s, suggesting to European audiences the pitiful state of a godless people and the utter despondency with which they embraced the Christian faith. As suggested in the previous chapter, such tears might also have had a great deal to do with the trauma of wartime loss and dislocation. But the convention also speaks to how Natives searched for a response to Christian doctrine from within their own cultural response mechanisms. In certain settings, many Native peoples would express themselves through ritual tears, meant to demonstrate the reciprocation of grief and mourning. Ceremonial tears in response to Christian teaching must have somehow seemed an appropriate response to the grief-wracked message of death and sin that informed the words of the English missionaries. But it was a response perpetually misunderstood and sentimentalized by the settlers.

On October 13, 1652 a number of converts (a term that must be applied loosely here) were brought together in front of a small committee of church elders in Natick to offer confessions and demonstrate the depth and comprehension of their gospel learning. Waban was one of five who testified. Curiously, the text offers not one, but two confessions for each of the Natives who spoke that day (save for Waban who, for reasons unexplained, is only represented by his single testimony). The first versions presented were recorded in conversations prior to the meeting, and the second versions drawn from the testimonies extemporaneously presented on the day of the meeting. It is a bit of a mystery why dual confessions were deemed necessary, although perhaps the first written testimonies were composed because, as Eliot suggests, his converts "were daunted much to speak before so great and grave an assembly."[99] If so, this would have been a rare inhibition for Native elders accustomed to delivering orations and speaking in councils. Eliot, more likely, felt some anxiety concerning the ability of his converts to stick with the script, and hoped that the written confessions might be read in lieu of live performances. Or perhaps he mistrusted his own skill as translator, as it was his job to see the confessions recorded as they were being spoken. At any rate, the council of Puritan elders who had come to witness the proceedings voted to do away with the prescripted versions, perhaps sensing that they had been overly determined by Eliot's coaching. The end result was that, even though two versions of each Native confession ended up in print, only the live testimonies were actually offered that day.

One might justifiably wonder if Eliot and the Native confessors shared the same rhetorical objectives, as the testimonies offer little evidence of what might be considered sincere conversions. At the very least, however, the Natives had been drilled in particular aspects of the confessional ritual, and therefore focused upon their own sinfulness, expressing the types of sins that were presumed to be a staple of the Native diet such as uncontrollable lust, greed, and devil worship. Such perceived failings, of course, had everything to do with how Europeans misinterpreted Native customs, and nothing to do with any actual individual transgressions, therefore offering the confessors little space for personal reflection as to what their "sins" signified or how they might be repaired.

A broadside printed at the Cambridge Press in 1660 entitled "Christians Oonoowae Sampoowaonk" or "A Christian Covenanting Confession," although printed after the proceedings in "Tears," offered the script for a proper confession, as Eliot saw it, in both the Indian and English languages. It called for an explicit declaration of one's love of God, intoning "I believe with my heart and confess with my mouth," and offered some foundational passages of scripture that would be helpful in such a situation. The broadside concluded with a sample testimony that read:

> For these causes, wee that dwell in this towne called _________ are gladly willing to bind our selves to God, to remember the Sabbath day and keep it holy, so long as we live. And also to bind ourselves to each other, to meet together every Sabbath day (when it may be done) to doe all our Sabbath day Services, prayers & c. according to the word of God, the holy Spirit of God helping us. By this Gospel covenant, we doe give ourselves and our Children to Jesus Christ, to walk with him in Church order so long as we live.[100]

The objectives of such a statement were clear. As Salisbury notes, "Indian converts were expected to renounce their individual and collective pasts and to adopt a new identity created for them by the representatives of an entirely foreign culture."[101]

If the script as articulated in the broadside was not followed, the proceedings at Natick, nevertheless, offered up a satisfying performance of abject self-loathing by a people presumed to be savages, preventing the audience from concentrating on other more troubling or ambivalent aspects of the confessions. For instance, Waban began his testimony admitting to having wished to be a sachem and a "witch" before the English came, and claimed that he desired riches for himself and harbored evils in his heart. All this language, however mangled in cultural translation, would have met with approval. Yet Waban concluded his speech by noting that "I do not truly pray to God in my heart: no matter for good words, all is the true heart;

and this day I do not so much desire good words, as throughly to open my heart: I confess I can do nothing, but deserve damnation; Only Christ can help me and do for me. But I have nothing to say for myself that is good."[102]

Such a confession could hardly have met with the specifications for church admittance, which asked for one to acknowledge belief with the mouth *and* the heart, nor does it seem so designed. Waban concedes to offering "good words," as he says, but they are naught for his heart is not yet in it. Salisbury, in attempting to explain this confession, makes the argument that part of the task for the Native confessor was to recognize "how just it is for God to deny them the knowledge of Jesus Christ." In other words, he feels this is in keeping with the script. But in a postscript to Waban's speech, Eliot himself notes that the confession was "not so satisfactory as was desired."[103] Waban, however, proves an adept orator. He demonstrates a sophisticated understanding of the expectations of the ritual, performing contriteness in the face of English religious customs while saying nothing that isn't ostensibly true. If he desires Christ on some level, and recognizes human failings and desires, nevertheless he lays bare the sentiments of his heart, wherein he does "not truly pray to God," enfolding this statement within an acceptable framework of repentance. Although Cogley refers to Waban's confession as "incoherent,"[104] Waban's performance is, in fact, one of measured engagement, diplomatically threading the needle between English expectations and his own goals for his people.

Waban may have made concessions to Eliot and the English in a grab for power outside the recognized bounds of Native succession, as some have argued, but it becomes apparent that Waban was influential enough in his own right to be a necessary figure for the English. As such the English found themselves having to overlook his lackluster spiritual awakening. As Eliot remarks, "his gift is not so much expressing himself this way, but in . . . Ruling, Judging of Cases, wherein he is patient, constant and prudent insomuch that he is respected among them." Apparently those very gifts were on display in Natick that day, and being used in relation to the ceremony in question. As one Puritan auditor noticed, Waban "spake these latter expressions with tears," thereby expressing his sincerity even while denying personal acceptance of Christ.[105]

Eliot's postscript notes following some of the speeches give us a fortuitous glimpse into aspects of the oral delivery that go missing from the previously mentioned *prescripted* testimonies. Waban's tears, probably in keeping with certain ritualized aspects of oral performance, were but one example of this. We learn in another postscript note that the next speaker, Monequassun, seems to have been cut off by Eliot in the middle of his speech, Eliot perceiving he had taken too long in his delivery. Monequassun, like Waban, confesses that, of Christ "my heart of my self cannot believe," and it is not long after this unsettling revelation that Eliot decides to terminate his performance. Although the auditors were unable to understand what the Natives were actually saying until Eliot read the words back from his own notes, they apparently were aware that Monequassun's delivery had been cut short and Eliot was forced to explain himself. He writes that the great assembly "understanding nothing he [Monequassun] said, only waiting for my interpretation, many of them went forth, others whispered, and a great confusion was in the house and abroad."[106] One wonders if Monequassun's physical gestures helped stir the audience into such great confusion, if he expressed anger or disappointment at being interrupted, or if the "great confusion" was simply a result of Eliot's putting an abrupt end to his oration. Either way, it seems to have been conveyed to the audience that something was amiss. Perhaps Eliot was not so much concerned with the length of the speech as he was with the content. Not only did Monequassun deny any acceptance of Christ in his heart (a denial that is conspicuously absent from the prescripted version), but he folded into his testimony a protest against being moved from Nonantum. He confesses that the only reason he agreed to hear God's word at all was because "I loved the place of my dwelling [Cohannet], and therefore I thought I wil rather pray to God" than run away. In the prescripted version he asserts, "being called to confess, to prepare to make a Church at Natick, I loved Cohannet . . . I was not willing to follow Christ to Natick." He repeats this sentiment in his oral testimony saying, "hearing that we must make a town in Natick, and gather a Church at Natick, my heart disliked that place . . . I was much troubled because I had not believed Christ, for I would not follow him to make a Church."[107]

Monequassun is not simply a disgruntled traditionalist unwilling to bend with the times. He was, in fact, "schoolmaster" at Natick and had learned to read and write despite the sacrifices such an acquisition demanded of him. He tells of his struggle, asking "how should I, my wife, and child be cloathed, if I spend my time in learning to reade?"[108] But his heart was apparently in conflict, and he acknowledges that he ultimately accepted the conditions of the praying town only after his wife and child died of disease while still at Nonantum (Rejoicing). Monequassun was clearly an anguished and eloquent figure, who had employed his natural talents to sincerely investigate what was within the English teachings. On that day in Natick he was prepared to deliver an oration that not only addressed the concerns of the Puritan elders in attendance, but laid out his own concerns and misgivings as well. The forum may have appeared to him as something more than a "confession." It may have appeared a rare opportunity to speak directly to Puritan authorities. According to local, indigenous custom it would have been unthinkable to arrest such a speech in midsentence. Eliot, however, shut off Monequassun's words before they could do further damage to his own agenda.[109]

The conclusion of the elders and auditors who had sat through the 1652 orations that day was one of cautious encouragement. While it was concurred there was reason for optimism, the sanctioning of the Natick church was put off for a later time. The so-called praying town would have to wait another eight years before a church was finally established in 1660. The text of "Tears of Repentance" remains something of a curiosity, however, as it inhabits the rhetorical boundaries between Native and colonial agendas. While certain Native speakers like Waban and Monequassun were more skilled at holding their rhetorical ground and inserting their own concerns into the discourse, the other speeches also register tensions. One of the testimonies, that of Ephraim, goes so far as to conclude, "I do not truly in my heart repent, and I think that God wil not forgive my sins . . . I pray outwardly with my mouth but not my heart."[110] This subversive statement, once again, stood in open defiance to the sentiment offered in Eliot's 1660 broadside script that rehearsed, "I believe with my heart and confess with my mouth." Surely these lines from Romans 10:10 had been drilled into the confessors. William of Sudbury, also known as Nataous, father of James Printer, concludes his testimony with the stinging words, "I am angry with myself, because I do not believe the word of God, and gospel of Jesus Christ."[111] Such statements hardly fulfilled the promise of the tract's title page, which advertises a "manifestation of their Faith and Hope in Jesus Christ and the Work of Grace upon their Hearts."[112] Nevertheless, the Native tensions in "Tears of Repentance," couched as they are in the linguistics of Christian piety and framed on either end by validating letters from Eliot, Thomas, Mayhew, and Richard Mather, failed to fully register to their English audiences who were simply impressed that such a strange spectacle could even take place in the American "wilderness."

Eight years later the bad feelings concerning the removal from Cohannet were still fresh in the minds of the Natick Indians and can be apprehended in the tract "A Further Account of the Progress of the Gospel." As Eliot once again sought admission for Natick into the church in 1659, a speech delivered by Nishokou offered additional insight into the tensions that not only persisted, but might be couched within the framework of a Christian confession. Like Monequassun in his earlier confession, Nishokou regrets having been forced to leave Cohannet. He states, "I desired to pray to God and would not go away, but it was because I loved our place and dwelling." When elected as a leader at Natick, he initially withdrew in resistance to the forced removal. But as he states, "then the Souldiers came upon us on the Sabbath-day, while we were at meeting, and took away our Guns, and caused us to bring them to Roxbury." This is the only hint, in any of the surviving accounts, that the removal from Cohannet was forced at gunpoint. Nishokou questions how it could be that the soldiers performed such a task on the Sabbath of all days, but clearly he is placing the invasive act of the soldiers in the form of a rebuke that might be heard by his English audience.[113] Not only were they forcefully removed, but the soldiers appeared while the praying Indians were living up to their namesake. Nishokou concludes, "I desired to be in Christ's hand, as in a Fort, in a Fort we are safe from exercise, they cannot easily catch us; out of a Fort we are open to them." Such a statement appears to succinctly express the sentiments of most if not all the Natick villagers. They had chosen this course because it offered them the most protection against outside forces. Nishokou does not specifically identify the "they" from whom he needs protection, but his earlier statements seem to suggest that it is the English themselves. Therefore Christianity, and the praying town system, is seen as a protective armor, the adopting of European rhetoric to protect oneself from European colonization. It is a telling example of spiritual and psychological extortion. He notes that "when my heart is troubled about our Land and about riches, I quiet my heart with these meditations."[114] Certainly Eliot's translations downplay the grievances concerning removal from Cohannet. That the grievances were genuine, however, is indicated by his own admission in a 1655 tract entitled "A Late and Further Manifestation of the Progress of the Gospel Amongst the Indians in New England." Here Eliot speaks of a falling out amongst his converts, and notes that

> the Cohannet Indians desired a place which they had reserved for themselves, and I finding that I could not at that time pitch there without opposition from some English, I refused that place, and pitched at Natick, where I found no opposition at present. This choice of mine did move in the Cohannet Indians a jealousie that I had more affection unto those other Indians, then unto them. By which occasion . . . their minds were quite alienated from the place of Natick.[115]

Ironically, had the confessions at Natick, in either occasion, met with approval it would have raised the status of the Natives there, in Puritan parlance, to that of "visible saints" and this would stand at direct odds with the larger unvoiced project of making Indians "invisible." Nevertheless the revelation of such widespread discontentment amongst the praying Indians reflects the conditions under which "Tears of Repentance" and "A Further Account" were recorded. The conventions for admission into the Puritan Church called for a precise accounting process, as it was crucial for the auditors to sift through the confessions for intimations of divine grace. Therefore the spontaneous nature of the spoken testimonies was allowed to stand. Naturally some issues arise concerning the reliability of Eliot's translations and transcriptions, but Eliot, himself, seems to have been attuned to many of our contemporary concerns of translation, and in his notes to "Tears" we can begin to apprehend the anxiousness with which he doted on these proceedings. He comments that

> in writing and reading their Confessions, I have not knowingly, or willingly made them better, than the Lord helped themselves to make them, but am verily perswaded on good grounds, that I have rendered them weaker (for the most part) than they delivered them; partly by missing some words of weight in some Sentences, partly by short and curt touches of what they more fully spake, and partly by reason of the different Idioms of their Language and ours.[116]

One might imagine that Eliot was inclined to downplay the moments of obvious resistance and to give greater emphasis to the statements that conformed most conspicuously with church doctrine. Such an understanding reveals, in part, just how crucial it was for skilled orators like Waban to negotiate a steady path, so that his words might be recorded, and his meaning remain intact without giving pause and allowing Eliot a reason to lift his pen from the page or cut short his speech. Nearly elided in the tract, however, is the fact that Eliot was not directly translating the words of the confessors himself. In one place only does he note that "oft I was forced to inquire of my interpreter (who sat by me) because I did not perfectly understand some sentences."[117] Eliot was not confident enough in his ability with the Algonquian language to translate the orations by himself, and so he must have had a Native speaker on hand to assist him in this important endeavor. I am inclined to imagine that the interpreter was Thomas Waban, although it may have been any of Eliot's cadre of Indian helpers. He had intended to use Job Nesuton as interpreter that day except Nesuton had fallen out of Eliot's good graces for having intoxicated the son of Totherswamp a day or two prior to the proceedings.[118] As a result of Nesuton's "backsliding," another interpreter had to be recruited to take his place. Whoever that interpreter may have been, the very fact of his presence on the stage suggests that the translations were likely more faithful to the actual words delivered than if a white interpreter, alone, were involved. Therefore "Tears of Repentance," as spoken by Natives and translated by a Native, has as much claim to being an authentic Native text as many another "as told to" document, and perhaps more of a claim. Despite its frankly coercive outer framework, "Tears of Repentance" offers significant and historically unacknowledged expressions of Native sentiment and resistance during the period of colonization in seventeenth-century New England.

Thresholds of Change: Caleb Cheeshateaumauk's "Honoratissimi Benefactores"

For the Natives of New England, the years leading up to King Philip's War were marked by traumatic changes and continuous mourning. When Waban delivered an oration in the Christian mode, he would observe that "we have many at this time sick in body, for which cause we do fast and pray this day, and cry to God . . . we have a great many diseases and sicknesses in our souls." Locating avenues of Christian discourse that bore some relation to the exigencies of his people, he latched onto the tradition of Christ as a "Physitian," who "healed men's bodies but he can heale souls also." Waban called on Christ to "heale all our diseases of soul and body."[119] Whether or not Waban had fully accepted Christianity as a spiritual belief system, he indicates a willingness to appeal to the God of the Europeans in a time of hardship. Rhetorically he seeks a path by which he might invoke Christian concerns and combine this with a healing message rooted in the concerns and beliefs of his own people. Christ, like a shaman or powwow in Native tradition, is called upon to play the role of spiritual leader and healer to draw out the sickness that has invaded the souls of so many. He is a powerful figure who crosses barriers between spheres of reality and prepares one's passage into the next world.

But to appeal to Christ at all in New England was also to welcome in the technological invasion of writing. By the 1660s there were a number of Natives in New England who were conversant in the concepts of Western literacy, capable of reading and writing in their own language, and a few who were even capable of translating between the two languages. As early as 1647, following Eliot's first successful mission, the colony had passed an ordinance requiring that "schools for the education of youth be settled and continued among them."[120] That meant that some Native students had spent upward of thirteen years with at least some exposure to European teaching. In Martha's Vineyard, Thomas Mayhew had been preaching Christianity to the Natives since 1643, and had quietly racked up some successes of his own amongst the Wampanoag there, particularly through his association with Hiacoomes.

Hiacoomes was a Native of no particular influence on Martha's Vineyard, described by some as "slow" in speech, a "mean" person, "scarce worthy of notice," but who responded to Mayhew's instruction and deliberately took on the sachems of his island, apparently prevailing through a number of extraordinary circumstances to gain power and authority within that community during a time of sickness and mourning.[121] His eldest son Joel would be amongst the first Native students to attend Harvard. Still, it is difficult to gauge the kind of progress in reading and writing that was made in these years, aside from the recognition that it was all, of course, "glorious." Eliot was still seeking money from Parliament for schooling in 1650 when he wrote

> Let me, I beseech you, trouble you a little further with some considerations about this great Indian work which lyeth upon me, as my continual care, prayer, desire and endeavor to carry on, namely for their schooling and education of youth in learning, which is the principal means for promoting of it for future times . . . We must have special care to have Schools for the instruction of the youth in reading, that they may be able to read the Scriptures at least.[122]

Certainly by 1651 schooling had taken hold to a certain degree as Eliot writes,

> it hath pleased God to stirre up the hearts of many of them this winter to learne to read and write, wherein they do very much profit with a very little helpe, especially some of them, for they are very ingenuous. And whereas I had thoughts that we must have an Englishman to be their Schoole-Master, I now hope that the Lord will raise up some of themselves.[123]

As a result of these many encouragements the Indian College was built in 1655 or 1656, with some expectation that Indian scholars would be rising up through the ranks to attend classes at Harvard. If the building wasn't soon put to its intended use, perhaps it was, as Daniel Gookin cited, because even though "the design was prudent, noble, and good . . . it proved ineffectual to the ends proposed. For several of the youth died after they had been sundry years at learning, and made good proficiency therein. Others were disheartened and left learning, after they were almost ready for the college. And some returned to live amongst their countrymen."[124]

For Native youths a sudden removal to Cambridge meant exposure to a cosmopolitan breeding ground of germs and viruses for which they had no genetic immunity. And, of course, many who survived the initial biological onslaught could readily discover other reasons to forsake a Puritan education and melt back into their respective communities. The prospect of permanently boarding in Cambridge, away from the comfort of kinship networks and familiar traditions, in order to devote oneself to an exacting textualized relationship with the Christian world, must have appeared on the horizon like the most oppressive of black clouds. Surely it was adequate to have learned enough of the alphabetic system so that one could read, write a little, and confirm the details of a recorded land transaction. A residency at Harvard, on the other hand, would have entailed mastering Latin, Greek, Hebrew, and extensive coursework in the classical Western traditions of rhetoric, physics, metaphysics, ethics, and logic.[125] Such a life is not for everyone, in any culture, and none of this was likely to be put to any practical use back in Native communities where entirely different notions of these schools of thought were practiced. As a result, what had at first seemed a hopeful harvest to the Puritan educators was soon winnowed down to two or three potential prospects. In 1658 Harvard president Charles Chauncy would testify

> that two of the Indians that are trained up at the grammar-Schoole in Cambridge of New England, whose names are Caleb and Joel, were called forth upon tryall at the publick Commencement before the Magistrates and Elders, and in the face of the Country, and thereupon very little warning gave good contentment (for their time) to them that were present, being examined by the Praesident of the Colledge in turning a part of a chapter in Isaiah into Latine, and shewing the construction of it so that they gave great hope for the future of their perfecting.[126]

Can there be any doubt that the Isaiah passage in question spoke of exchanging hearts of stone for a "new heart" of flesh and blood?

Joel Hiacoomes and Caleb Cheeshateaumauk were Wampanoags of Martha's Vineyard who would enter Harvard's Indian College in 1661. They had been schooled on the Vineyard by Peter Folger, maternal grandfather to Benjamin Franklin, and then sent to Elijah Corlett's grammar school in Cambridge in 1657 or 1658. One wonders if they were classmates with Job Nesuton, James Printer, John Wampas, Monequassun, or any other of the praying Indians who might have attended during this decade. It seems probable that many of these individuals would have been acquainted by the time Caleb, Joel, and John Wampas enrolled at Harvard. They would have been approximately the same age, have moved in similar circles, and might have felt some sort of camaraderie regardless of their different tribal affiliations.[127] Certainly James Printer would have been working the press in the Indian College at this time, and was probably boarding there as well when Joel and Caleb became residents. Nipmucs and Wampanoags had close tribal relations and shared many of the same traditions. There is little reason not to think that a companionship would have been forged amongst them. Although it isn't precisely evident when Wampas entered the school, he and James Printer both had relations in Cohannet. Job Nesuton must also have made regular appearances, as he was assisting Eliot with the translation of the first "Indian Bible," which was being put to press at this time.

These youths must have understood the precarious nature of their times and would have had a rare appreciation of the particular burdens of occupying a liminal space in the heart of the colonizer's stronghold. One wonders if they shared stories in the evenings, told jokes, drummed and sang, gambled (New England Natives, according to William Wood, played a game called hubbub in which wagers were made over throwing bones), or did any of the other things that college students generally do.[128] Or were their lives so overshadowed by their conflicted upbringings and the pressures placed upon them as representatives of their people, pulled from their homes and struggling to master a foreign discourse, that they were inadvertently estranged from one another? Had they shared similar experiences, either growing up in such close proximity to the English, or in keeping with the traditional aspects of their cultures? Did they keep medicine bundles, or share tobacco that they themselves had grown and harvested? Did they hunt for food, or lament their absence from home during ceremonies such as the green corn dance at harvest time? In Wampanoag tradition youths of a certain age were sent out on something like a vision quest, in which they would seek communion with animal or guardian spirits—manitou. Such a quest might involve fasting and the imbibing of hallucinatory mixtures that facilitated dreaming and visions.[129] There is no way of knowing whether the occupants of the Indian College had passed through such ceremonies, or if they partook of another kind of vision quest in which they sought the power of the English God. In Wampanoag tradition, the hero figure Weetucks had performed miracles and was said to have walked upon the water.[130] According to Wampanoag lore it was Weetucks who had carved the "mysterious" symbols to be found on nearby Dighton Rock, advising his people to maintain their ways in the oncoming rush of colonization.[131] Was it possible to pray to Christ and Weetucks at the same time, or to see one within the other? One wonders if the students took notes, kept journals, wrote letters. Had they learned the writing of their own people, and did they ever take to composing in that symbology over the long nights in their dormitory?

The Indian College was more than a just a liminal space, however, where individuals labored to internalize and synthesize the codes of competing cultures. It was a space of production. As house to the Cambridge Press it was a place of textualized production, full of the noises and smells of a printing house, and for nearly the entire time that Caleb and Joel were there, its sole product was the Indian Bible. According to Littlefield, the printing of the New Testament had begun in 1660 and the printing of the Old Testament was not finished until sometime in 1663. A 1660 letter from the New England Company requested that, for the "happy progresse" of the project, "all other business [be] laid aside that might hinder it."[132] But the Indian College was also a place where identity was being manufactured and refined, the Native students as its soul product, giving hope, as Chauncy wrote, for "the future of their perfecting." Gookin spoke in glowing terms of Joel Hiacooms, forwarding an opinion of him as

> a good scholar and a pious man, as I judge. I knew him well for he lived and was taught in the same town where I dwell. I observed him for several years, after he was grown to years of discretion, to be not only a diligent student, but an attentive hearer of God's word; diligently writing the sermons, and frequenting lectures; grave and sober in his conversation.[133]

But as we know, the face that a Native showed to the colonizer was not the same face shown in private or amongst his or her own people. Nevertheless, whether a product or the image of a product was being manufactured, the Indian College stood as the point of production.

Perhaps the residents of the Indian College also viewed their tenure as a time of production and transformation within the framework of their own cultures. The Natives of the Northeast maintained a sense of the thresholds between worlds, such thresholds often existing in close metaphorical association with geographically disparate changes in the landscape, such as where land meets sea, earth meets rock, or forest meets open space. The crossing of these thresholds, whether in dream or some other visionary state, could be regarded in correspondence with physical, spiritual, and social transformations. Those who had formed the most powerful relationships with their manitous, known to the English as shamans or powwows, could bring these transformations about as an act of will and enter into the upper spirit world or the underwater realms most associated with dangerous or uncontainable powers. In keeping with such notions, all space, whether social or natural, was negotiated in terms of its cosmological significance and relation with other realms. Lodges and longhouses were built in accordance with their place in the cosmos and were designed to represent symbolic thresholds between worlds. The sweat lodge in particular was placed in special relation to the spiritual center of a people.[134] The Indian College building might have felt to its occupants like a threshold too, if not between worlds, then between epistemological walks of life. It was a new kind of longhouse. Although, perhaps not in the ways that their English "benefactors" regarded it, in some respects the Indian students were at Harvard seeking transformation, and a redefined relationship with the powers that made up their universe. This understanding was probably lodged deep inside of them with no real need to be articulated to their English patrons. But they may have held such an understanding in common amongst themselves. They were engaged in a process of restoration. Whatever they brought back home with them would be threaded into a cultural framework with the design to clothe and protect a people who had experienced great hardship. While their communities may not have been in full agreement with the path they chose, they could see evidence that transformations were actually occurring. Within their lodging the European's writing had been transformed into the Algonquian language, largely as a result of their own agency. Sheets upon sheets of it emerged fresh from the press every hour. James Printer would finish each day with the ink still permanently smeared upon his hands. It seems likely to me that the Natives at Harvard Indian College would have bonded together in this moment, recognizing that they stood in the center of something momentous, and would have depended upon one another for emotional support. Whatever allegiances they may have forged, however, would shatter into waves of grief, as only Printer and John Wampas, of all these young men, would survive the tumultuous times directly ahead.

Only one document is extant from this period to suggest Joel and Caleb's proficiency as scholars at Harvard. On November 3, 1663 John Winthrop Jr. wrote a letter to Robert Boyle in England containing a handwritten text said to have been composed by Caleb Cheeshateaumauk under the heading "Honoratissimi Benefactores." The short letter within a letter was a demonstration of the progress being made at Harvard's Indian College, and was part of an appeal for continued funding of the newly erected institution. "Honoratissimi Benefactores" is the first of only two known texts to have survived Harvard's early experiment in educating the local Natives, the second coming some twelve years later, penned by a Native named Eleazar who was the next to last of the praying Indians to attend Harvard.[135] Cheeshateaumauk's composition is, at once, a testament to the rigors of the program at Cambridge and an emblem of its ultimate failure. But it also poses typical problems in terms of locating Cheeshateaumauk's agency within the letter itself. Not only is the text in Latin, the language of the Western scholarly elite, but it is peppered with references to Greek mythology, the "ancient philosophers," and Christian ideology. The stated goal of the letter is to illuminate "the way of truth and of life" in the Lord Jesus Christ, and to honor the English patrons who have supported (or, perhaps, it is hoped, will continue to support) this most worthy endeavor.[136]

The first paragraph of the letter proceeds as follows:

> Most honored benefactors,
>
> Historians tell us of Orpheus, the musician and outstanding poet, that he received a lyre from Apollo, and that he was so excellent with it that he moved the forests and rocks by his song. He made huge trees follow behind him, and indeed rendered tamer the most ferocious beasts. After he took up the lyre he descended into the nether world, lulled Pluto and Prosperina with his song, and led Eurydice, his wife, out of the underworld into the upper. The ancient philosophers say that this serves as a symbol to show how powerful are the force of virtue of education and refined literature in the transformation of barbarians. They are like trees, rocks, and brute beasts, and a substantive change must be effected in them. They have to be secured like tigers and must be induced to follow.[137]

That Cheeshateaumauk's letter would have appeared as an impressive proof of progress for its intended audience back in England seems certain. The letter is problematic, however, for any number of reasons. One might ask if it is an authentic text that can be accurately attributed to Cheeshateaumauk. Was the letter a product of his own mind, his own pen, or something dictated to him by his white overseers? And even if we assume the letter to be authentic, its content, at least upon a surface reading, seems to defeat any assumption that a Native identity or sense of indigenous tradition has survived the educational pilgrimage from orality to literacy. As a cultural artifact it reads as a particularly impenetrable example of a subsumed discourse, leading some critics to assert that any attempt "to ascribe undercurrents of traditional Indian cultures to these works does not make sense."[138]

Let us first take Cheeshateaumauk's letter at face value. The letter works within a motif of Western classicism, suggesting that the Greek bard Orpheus, through the animating powers of his music, "made huge trees follow behind him, and indeed rendered tamer the most ferocious beasts." In case there was any doubt, Cheeshateaumauk makes it clear that herein lies a useful metaphor relating to his own experience. He writes, "the ancient philosophers say that this serves as a symbol to show how powerful are the force and virtue of education and refined literature in the transformation of the nature of barbarians." Furthermore, Orpheus' powers to spread cultivation and refinement are, in a later paragraph, directly likened to the efforts of the colonists, alongside their honored English benefactors, to educate "us pagans" who formerly were "naked in soul and body, alien from all humanity, led around in the desert by all sorts of errors."

Quite possibly Cheeshateaumauk, like many an other student in my experience, was conscious of assuming a particular role when he wrote this letter of thanks and praise, and was fully aware of the academic forms and expectations that accompanied the assignment. He was probably even well aware of the pragmatic expectations, and the use to which his letter would be put. On the verge of graduating Harvard, Cheeshateaumauk did not lack sophistication. If one can assume, for a moment, that Cheeshateaumauk is performing a role, putting on a suit of clothes, so to speak, that he has learned to wear over a period of years, and knowing full well that he will shed them once he is finished and return to his more comfortable skin, then we might also see where his own cultural leanings might be reflected in the text—the Native skin beneath the colonial cloth, so to speak.

Orpheus stands in as the bearer of literary civilization in Cheeshateaumauk's letter, but it is interesting that a character from an oral tradition was chosen to fulfill this role. While this is perhaps unintentional, it might be by way of a certain sympathetic recognition or familiarity that Cheeshateaumauk chooses not only a nonliterate figure to represent the gift of literacy, but one who is particularly noted for being the keeper of oral traditions. William S. Simmons, who has extensively studied and recorded the folklore and myths of Northeastern Natives, writes that "Indian converts traced aspects of Christian belief and practice to aboriginal sources, thus representing change as continuity with their own past."[139] As a bard, Orpheus would have trafficked in stories and songs chanted in a communal setting. His gift is recognized as "excellent" which we may recall was the common exclamation of the Native when they recognized something as "Manittowock, or God." And by "moving the rocks and trees" and taming the wild beasts with his song, Orpheus might be regarded as performing the very role of shaman or powwow, who also calls upon the power in rocks, trees, and other spirit guardians. As William Wood commented in his *New England's Prospect*, the "powwow" Passaconaway was reported to be able to make "the water burn, the rocks move, trees dance, metamorposize himself into a flaming man."[140] Such performances were not simply meant to elicit amazed responses from their audiences. Many Natives of the Northeast saw themselves in a specific kinship relation with natural objects, enlisting their power in ceremonies and rituals. Far from being inanimate objects, trees were regarded by many Native peoples as their ancestors.

The trip to the underworld would have been recognized as the shaman's ability to cross thresholds and enter into other realms. Such feats were not only ingrained in Native belief systems, but were a staple of stories and legends. Jarold Ramsey has written that "the Orphic story, of a hero's unsuccessful quest to bring back a loved one from the Land of the Dead, is apparently universal among American Indian tribes."[141] In a comprehensive

1957 study of Native traditions that resemble the Orpheus narrative, Ake Hultkrantz concludes that such legends are "connected with shamanistic ideology" and have their roots in the role of the shaman, or medicine man, as healer or one who guards against "soul loss."[142] Such a narrative, particularly in a time of such inexplicable sickness and death, might have served the function of consoling the grief of a people, while observing the ritualistic necessities of accompanying spirits to the afterworld, even if they ultimately could not be brought back home. Knowing the path and how to avoid obstacles between worlds remained an important feature of this narrative. As one ethnographer notes, "singing after a death was an advantage to a traveling soul for it illuminated the trail, and according to the Haida, permitted the soul to enter its new abode with its head up."[143] It probably is worth noting that the Christ narrative performs a similar function, in that Jesus, the "phisitian" travels between life and death, and illuminates a path to redemption that had been barred since the time of original sin. Caleb may have been conscious of these similar functions and drawn upon them, deliberately or not.

Finally, it is of note that Orpheus is ultimately dismembered, and, according to some traditions, his head is carried off to its island home, still singing. If the figure of Orpheus has been interpreted as the harbinger of Western civilization, the story is more strongly suggestive of the endurance of cultural narratives whose stories and songs survive despite violent ruptures and displacement. A later Wampanoag tradition has it that the head of King Philip was secreted away after his death and buried between Taunton and Mount Hope. Simmons reports that "every three generations the ghost of Philip walks abroad, and reveals to a medicine man this spot."[144]

I do not mean to suggest that Cheeshateaumauk was consciously toying with all of these allusions (although I do not discount such a possibility), but only that the details of Orpheus' life may have been what drew Caleb to the tale in the first place. He is quite possibly engaging in a process of weaving the elements of two traditions together in an attempt to locate common ground. Such a process may have informed the manner in which his kin on Martha's Vinyard approached Christianity from the very start. Either way, there is something of a cognitive lapse in the parable as written, for if the Orpheus of ancient times clearly induces a passive transformation through linguistic charms, it remains to be explained why Cheeshateaumauk's "barbarians" need to be "secured like tigers and must be induced to follow." In this slippage we may detect something of the internal struggle of Cheeshateaumauk's own experience. Perhaps he was not so much charmed by European culture as dragged kicking and screaming.

Cheeshateaumauk's narrative, considered to be the first extant writing by a Native American from the North American continent, cannot be read strictly as one of continuance. Clearly it is infected with "manifest manners," the rhetorical conventions that, whether intentionally or not, play into the master narrative of a white European hegemon that views its destiny on the American continent as manifest. Certainly Caleb is not explicitly writing about his community, tribal sovereignty, or the strengthening of Native traditions. There was no venue for Caleb to publish such things in seventeenth-century New England, even if he wanted to. Nor could they be openly expressed amongst his Puritan *benefactores*. Nevertheless his short missive, plucked from the embers, so to speak, of a largely forgotten episode in history, stands at the forefront of a Native presence that is endeavoring to open up such a discourse in the only medium that seems to matter to its aggressive neighbors. Caleb's intentions are always to return to his community, to live with his people, and, perhaps, spread the word of the Christian Bible. But it shouldn't be doubted that such an engagement with Christianity will be folded into traditional practices as well, and Caleb's letter offers some awareness of the syncretic forms that will take root in future communities and future discourses.

Caleb was the only Native American to graduate from Harvard's Indian College. According to Gookin, not long after he took his bachelor of the arts in 1665, he "died of a consumption in Charlestown . . . where he wanted not for the best means the country could afford, both of food and physic." Joel Hiacooms returned home to Martha's Vineyard before his commencement to visit his father and kindred, but his ship apparently wrecked near Nantucket on the return trip. Gookin writes that, in all probability, "the people in it came on shore alive, but afterwards were murthered by some wicked Indians of that place," and he laments "thus perished our hopeful young prophet, Joel."[145] The incidents surrounding Joel's death remain vague. Historically, the assumption seems to persist that Joel was killed as a result of his association with the English and his efforts at assimilation. As Jill Lepore maintains in *The Name of War*, writing was a dangerous pastime for New England Indians and placed them in "a particularly perilous" position.[146] But the ship in question carried both English and Wampanoag passengers, and it is unclear whether Joel's status as a "praying Indian" had any role in his death, or if he was merely the victim of unfortunate circumstances. The trial of the case at Nantucket consisted of a joint court of English and Wampanoag officials, with the Wampanoag leader Philip called in from the mainland to oversee the proceedings. The offending Indians were sentenced and hanged.[147] The deaths of Joel and Caleb did not signal the absolute end of the Harvard Indian College, but it was a symbolic end and the building was probably never again used for its originally stated purpose.

Within ten years of Joel's death, all-out warfare would consume the peoples of the American Northeast and disrupt further attempts at Indian education. King Philip's War, the pan-Indian assault from 1675–1676 organized and led by the Wampanoag sachem, Philip or Metacom, would be understood by the Puritans as the last word on Native and English relations within New England's colonial boundaries. The Natives were supposed to have disappeared in its wake, like snow in springtime, just as the Pequots were rhetorically erased following the war bearing (and paradoxically perpetuating) their name. Of course they didn't go away. Isolated communities of Native Americans struggled to maintain themselves on the ground still available to them. The Pequot and Mohegan managed to remain neutral throughout King Philip's War and their communities were still intact in the aftermath, if in a more tightly enclosed ring of colonial presence. Waban and Thomas Waban, who had both been rounded up, despite their declared allegiance to the English, and forced to endure a long harsh winter of interment on Deer Island throughout much of the war, returned with their people in the spring of 1676 to live on a patch of land offered by a Mr. Thomas Oliver along the Charles River outside of Cambridge. Waban, in his seventies by now, was sick with dysentery and close to death. But he recovered his health before the summer was out and lived for another eight years, well into his eighties.[148]

Gookin writes that the Deer Island refugees remained on Thomas Oliver's land through the summer of 1676, and then "scattered to places adjacent, to work for the English in harvest time. But toward October they removed; some to the falls of Charles river, and some settled about Hoanantum Hill; not far from Mr. Oliver's, near the very place where they first began to pray to God, and Mr. Elliot first taught them, which was about thirty years since."[149] Hoanantum was none other than Nonantum, or a place of rejoicing, formerly known as Cohannet. Here Anthony Speene, having come full circle, built a large wigwam or longhouse, reclaiming what had been the spiritual center of his community back in his childhood days before the coming of the English. Waban and his son Thomas, however, eventually made their way back to Natick, where, as we will see in chapter 4, the younger Waban presided and kept town records in his own language for a number of years.

To engage in writing and print discourse in the seventeenth century was to move the narrative of indigenous continuance from Native space to colonial space, an enterprise that endangered the integrity of Native agency, Native forms of giving and receiving knowledge, by containing such expressions within colonial contexts. In many ways, the praying Indians themselves have become a text within a text. Their lives and words have been sandwiched into the propagandistic discourse of the settler population, so that their own speech seems to turn against them. Nevertheless, Waban and others, by engaging with European literacy, had bought themselves a generation of peace and relative stability—no small accomplishment in violent and uncertain times. As we will see in the next chapter, when war did break out, Natives started writing back. Just little notes at first, left on bridge posts and trees. They wanted the English to understand that they hadn't started this war after all, that they had negotiated for peace and done everything in their power to sustain agreeable relations, and it was the English with their houses and cattle and Bibles that had stirred things up and made life untenable. Such protestations survive as fragments, or containments, texts within texts, preserved between the covers of musty colonial history books and collections, in the service of a colonial agenda. And yet their composition occurred within circumstances that allowed for the first historically visible manifestations of a hidden transcript, or the breaking of containment on the part of Native peoples.

As for the Indian College, Samuel Sewall would lament in 1698 that "the old Brick College, Commonly called the *Indian* College is pull'd to the ground." Like the great libraries and temples of the Aztecs, this Native space was reconstituted, its bricks collected and employed in the erection of yet another edifice of European intellectual hegemony, Stoughton College.[150] Discarded in the rubble of its dismantling were the remnants of type from the old Cambridge Press that had been used to disseminate the Christian word in the Algonquian language.

3

King Philip's Signature

Ascribing Philip's Name to Land, War, and History in Native New England (1660–1709)

Surely then we have many of us cause to tremble. How sad it is to consider, that an Indian should write a letter to an Englishman and thus express himself, "When any hurt is done, you say that we have done it though we never did wronge to English-men and hope we never shall."

—Increase Mather, *An Earnest Exhortation to the Inhabitants of New England*

To all Christian People to whom these presents shall come, Phillip, allies [alias] Metacom Cheiffe Sachem of Pocanakett in the Collonie of New Plymouth in New England sendeth Greeting.

—Philip (Metacom), opening refrain in numerous land transactions between Philip and the colonists

Written in Stone: Colonial Contests for Meaning

On November 20, 1701, the Puritan minister Cotton Mather wrote in his diary how "I dare not go any longer, without my old Methods, of Praying with Fasting in secret Places . . . [to] address the Lord for His Blessing on my Church-History . . . which He has helped me to write, of His glorious Works in these American churches."[1] Mather had embarked upon the writing of the *Magnalia Christi Americana*, his massive deterministic history of the Church of New England, and was engaging in something not unlike a vision quest, a secret fast, calling upon his God in a most private ritual to grant him the power and strength for the task ahead. Some twenty-five years earlier the sachem of the Wampanoag Nation, Metacom or Philip, may have undertaken a similar quest to determine the history of his people as well as a course of action that might lead them through the treacherous space of his contested, increasingly colonized homeland. He too must have fasted and sweat, sought spiritual counsel and called upon his spirit helper, or manitou, for power and strength to plot the difficult path before him. In the time of crisis, when the struggle for peaceful coexistence on the land seemed to reach its breaking point, Philip is said to have rehearsed this history, at least in part, to then Rhode Island deputy governor John Easton and the English ambassadors in his presence. His words were recorded as follows:

> The English who came first to this country were but an handful of people, forlorn, poor and distressed. My father was then sachem, he relieved their distresses in the most kind and hospitable manner. He gave them land to plant and build upon . . . they flourished and increased. By various means they got possession of a great part of his territory. But he still remained their friend till he died. My elder brother became a sachem . . . He was seized and confined and thereby thrown into illness and died. Soon after I became sachem they disarmed all my people . . . their land was taken. But a small part of the dominion of my ancestors remains.[2]

Both Mather and Philip were engaged in projects of constructing and safeguarding history, but while Mather's signature adheres to his inscribed vision, Philip's vision has been largely held captive over time by the manifest manners of the colonizers whose records co-opt his words and image, making of him the sometimes vile, sometimes tragic catalyst of a divisive war.

The caretaking of tradition is, of course, a prominent concern of all cultures and remains as central to the expression of Wampanoag identity as a nation today as it did in the seventeenth century. A legend in Wampanoag country touching upon the anxieties of losing one's cultural autonomy remains inscribed upon the surface of Dighton Rock, a large, forty-ton boulder once located at the mouth of the Assonet River across the bay from Mount Hope which was the seat of Philip's sachemship.[3] According to the Wampanoag elder Manitonquat (Medicine Story), Dighton Rock carries the details of a prophecy made by the Wampanoag culture hero Weetucks. A version of this story, recorded by Edward J. Lenik in 1998, goes as follows:

> Weetucks led the people down to the river bank and showed them a large rock . . . On the smooth southern face of this rock he had . . . carved a large figure, which he told them represented Kiehtan, the Creator. Next to that was a smaller figure which Weetucks said represented their Kiehtan's helper first-teacher Maushop. Across the center of the rock he had carved many fantastic shapes, animals and birds and fish and plants that were known to no one. This, he said, represented the vast unknown

> variety of beings in the Creation. At the eastern edge there were two human beings standing together. The first was looking back towards the Creator and Maushop and the marvelous figures of Creation. But the other was looking away, looking off the rock towards something beyond, toward the east. And over the head of this last person was carved a lightning bolt pointing down right above him, pointing down to the top of his head.
>
> Weetucks . . . told them of the new way that would come to them from the east, from beyond where the sun rises. He told them that they would follow different ways and that the people of the Morning Light [the Wampanoag] would be tempted to follow these new ways, for they would seem attractive and good. People would actually begin to learn the new ways and forsake the old ways. But eventually it would be seen that these ways were destructive, that because of them the forest and the creatures of the forest, including the human people, would begin to be destroyed. That was what was meant by the lightning bolt above the head of the outer figure on the rock.

Manitonquat concludes by noting that "those who continue to follow in a sacred path, the way of the Creator, and also those who saw their mistake in time and turned around to find Creation's way again, these would survive to help heal the earth and restore the balance of life" (see figure 3.1).[4]

Figure 3.1. Photograph of Dighton Rock with Henry Rowe Schoolcraft on top. Photo taken by Seth Eastman.

The story bears some small relation to the story of Nana'b'oozoo restoring the earth after the flood, in the sense that it teaches how one must hold onto the filaments of tradition in order to discern proper action in the present. The fact that the rock carvings were located in a tidal zone suggests that they could only be seen, or read, at low tide, and so part of the ritual involved in honoring this tradition was noting the fluctuation of the earth's waters, and how in times of flood or crisis, meaning can easily become obscured. The Wampanoag, following the example of Weetucks, would come down to the water's edge at the proper season and wait for the tides to once again reveal the rock's mysteries. This might have been accompanied by clambakes, dances, and other festivities that are still carried out today.[5]

Worth noting, however, is that the story of Dighton Rock, as Manitonquat tells it, also carries the mark of a priori construction, safeguarding a pure Wampanoag identity against the hegemony of settler culture. In doing so, it hews closely to what Chadwick Allen has characterized as a "blood/land/memory complex" which attempts to construct representations of indigenous authenticity by essentially linking land and memory to issues of identity.[6] By remembering what the markings on Dighton Rock are meant to signify, Manitonquat lays a hereditary claim to both Wampanoag identity and the geographical and spiritual origins of that identity. If such a translation may, itself, be overly deterministic, it nevertheless makes a bid to keep Dighton Rock within a sphere of Wampanoag narrative concerns.

John Danforth, in the wake of King Philip's War in 1680, made a meticulous copy of the markings on Dighton Rock. Curious as to what the markings meant, he apparently made enquiries amongst some of the local Wampanoag as to its origin. He writes, "it is reported from the tradition of the old Indians, that there came a wooden house (and men of another country in it) swimming up the river Assonet, that fought the Indians and slew their Sauchem." Danforth assumes that the story is "ancient," ignoring the fact that it corresponds precisely to the events of English colonization leading up to King Philip's War. Either history was repeating itself (not an unlikely outcome of colonial intrusion) or Danforth was being offered a version of "history" that was much more recent than he supposed. Danforth ultimately sent the markings along to his colleague Cotton Mather, who, in turn, sent this text to a correspondent in England, noting its "strange characters" and "odd shapes" engendering "odd thoughts." In his wry commentary, Mather hoped that the colonists would express their gratitude to their English fellows and patrons back home "not less durably, but more Intelligibly . . . than what the Indian People have Engraved upon Rocks."[7] Mather rejected any attempt at interpretation out of hand, simply concluding of the "deeply engraved" marks that "no man alive knows how or when" they were made. For Mather, the markings were unintelligible, foreclosing any attempt at coherent signification. Both Danforth and Mather, in their own manner, effectively sought to contain and discredit this marker of Wampanoag memory and spirituality. But if Mather assumed the markings to be beyond translation, he nevertheless, could not shake the "odd thoughts" engendered by such "strange characters." The existence of these markings—in effect, Native writing—was clearly troubling to him, signifying chaos, a glimpse of Erebus, an uncertainty of meanings that cut to the core of his bedrock beliefs. He was therefore motivated to unwitness the Native hand behind any such inscription. By removing Native agency from the picture ("no man alive knows how or when they were made") and declaring the marks "unintelligible," Mather made a bid to cast Native stories, writings, and people outside the pale of history.[8]

The history of colonialism is nothing more than the history of how strength defines and rhetorically maintains itself, how the exercise of power is made to seem necessary, appropriate, and even humane, and how the violent excesses of power are discursively dislocated, and in most every case reconfigured to perpetuate the sense that the colonized bring such violence upon themselves. While power is exercised through pressure and force, the normalization of power is exercised rhetorically through "manifest manners." Therefore, as Robert Gray asserts in *A Good Speed to Virginia* in 1609, it is perfectly lawful to make war "upon barbarous and savage people, and such as live under no lawfull or warrantable government" so long as the goal is to "reclaime and reduce those savages from their barbarous kinde of life."[9] In this quite common tautology (still being dusted off on occasion and used in our own times) what makes a people barbarous is the fact that they have no law or warrantable government. The reason they are perceived to lack these things is not because they offer no discernable manifestation of the principles of law and government—the Powhatan confederation was easily recognizable to Gray's countrymen as hierarchical and under an unquestionably greater civic management than the unruly Jamestown colony—but rather that the people in question have been predetermined to be savage and barbarous.[10]

Edward Said notes in his influential *Orientalism*, that "to simply say that Orientalism was a rationalization of colonial rule is to ignore the extent to which colonial rule was justified in advance by Orientalism, rather than after the fact."[11] In the case of the colonization of the Americas, this equation was reinforced by the unavailable evidence of a written legal code for Native culture. In fact, such an absence would become one more justification for violence, as it was supposed that domination and forced assimilation would help to introduce the writing that might codify the laws, which would then be able to assert a warrantable government. In Vietnam War era parlance, the village needed to be destroyed in order to save it, or as Gray surmises, "those people are vanquished to their unspeakable profite and gaine."[12] Gray is correct in part. The combined elements that make such an equation possible are, in fact, "unspeakable," as they become surrounded by the silences of historical trauma and unwitnessing.

The presumed lack of law, culture, art, and religion on the part of the "other" is the constant mantra of the colonizing regime, and it persists throughout the centuries, for it is upon this supposition alone that violent domination for humanitarian ends remains viable. Europeans were either incapable or unwilling to recognize a system of customs circulated and perpetuated through oral tradition. This might be regarded as a kind of *Oralentalism*. Law, in order to be legitimate, had to be preserved through phonetic indicators as were the laws of the Judeo-Christian tradition, which were fundamentally structured around the laws God had passed down to Moses, words inscribed in stone by God's own hand.[13] Located somewhere within this narrative tradition is the decision of so-called Western culture that oral law was no longer adequate—even God's dictums needed to be codified in writing. As Walter Ong suggests, a primarily literate culture "moves speech from the oral-aural to a new sensory world, that of vision."[14] The biblical figure of Moses stands at an interesting discursive crossroads in which God still speaks directly to humans, but his words immediately transubstantiate into text.[15] Quite possibly this need came about as a result of exposure in captivity to the "pagan" Egyptians who used hieroglyphic writing to record their histories and religion. It is only as the Jewish people flee Egyptian captivity that the need for scriptural law seems to manifest itself. Be that as it may, a common belief of the seventeenth and eighteenth centuries was that "alphabetic" writing was bestowed to humans when God spoke to Moses on Mount Sinai. Daniel Defoe wrote in 1726 that a Divine power impresses "those Words on the two tablets of stone and at the same time no doubt instructed Moses in the reading of them, and in the knowledge of their sounds; so we have unquestioned authority to assign the knowledge of Letters, and the Art of writing them to a Divine original."[16] This understanding of the origins of alphabetic literacy spoke not only to the "unquestioned authority" of spreading the written "word" of God to those who had yet to hear it, but it reinforced a European sense of cultural superiority, granting Christians the exclusive right of constructing meaning and imposing it upon others. The result is that alphabetic writing has been employed to this end since the first moments of contact.

Jill Lepore notes in *The Name of War* that the conflict that would be known as King Philip's War was itself a battle over interpretations or "a contest for meaning—and the colonists won."[17] The contest in question, however, had been in motion from the very start of colonization, a struggle of epistemological values and hermeneutics that was to determine how the land and its occupancy would be envisioned and regulated. The contest only erupted into all-out war when it became clear that meaning could not be imposed through peacetime coercion or the thinly veiled threat of institutional force that lay directly behind the missionary efforts of those like Eliot, Shepherd, Mayhew, Gookin, and others. Although Philip has historically been portrayed as the aggressor in this war, it might readily be argued that the real war started in the summer of 1671 when Plymouth Colony, forming a "Councill of Warr," endeavored to bring all the Native communities in the region under their authority and began marshalling men into service to achieve this end. Although Philip held out as long as he could, appealing to both the Rhode Island and Massachusetts Bay colonies for support, he was ultimately forced to acquiesce to the terms pressed upon him by Plymouth Colony officials.[18] The war, in effect, had already begun. As noted in the introduction to this work, however, the victors of such wars not only get to write history, they are, in the very same act, sentenced to forget it. While meaning can be forcefully codified and contained in texts bearing the signatures of all the various players, it requires cultural amnesia to ensure continued containment. The dominant culture becomes motivated to unwitness the filaments of tragic wisdom that retain their autonomous ability to overlay the archive with suggestions of undetermined meaning. As such, the extremes of colonial violence needed to be unwitnessed alongside Native legitimacy, Native inscription, and even Native presence. These processes of cognitive dissonance were already in operation well before King Philip's War officially broke out. While Eliot and his fellow missionaries were busy constructing a progressive, overly optimistic narrative of Native conversion in colonial New England, Natives themselves were finding the coercive pressures of colonization more and more untenable.

Renarrativizing Native Space: From the Age of Massasoit to the Age of Philip

The years 1660–1665 must have felt like banner years for John Eliot. His long hours of working with Native students to learn their language, of training up Native youths and positioning them in the proper places, of preparing his moneyed patrons back in England so that they were in full support of his projects, had finally culminated in a complete translation of the Old and New Testaments into the Algonquian language, the full text finally appearing in 1663. These were the years of hope in the young "prophets" Joel and Caleb as they launched on their college careers, their untimely deaths as of yet unforeseen. The New England Company for Promoting the Gospel in New England was granted a renewed official charter in the first months of 1661 (a contingency made necessary by the return of the monarchy to English government in 1660), ensuring continued institutional backing from the mother country. For a company seal, a variation on the old Massachusetts Bay Company logo was adopted, only this time the friendly Native figure, as if in response to Cheeshateaumauk's letter, had placed his bow and arrow on the ground, donned a cape, and held an open book in his hands (could it be any other than the Indian Bible?), with the familiar cry issuing from his lips, "Come over and help us" (see figure 3.2).[19] In addition to all this, the town of Natick had finally been granted permission to establish its church in 1660, following the second round of confessions by praying Indians recorded in "A Further Account of the Progress of the Gospel" (1659). A handful of these Natives were able to read and write in their own language, could preach to their own congregations, and had been provided primers alongside the translated chapters of Genesis and Matthew. Now they had their own complete editions of the Christian Bible to read from as well.

For Native communities in southern New England, however, these years remained a time of extreme tension and transition. The year 1660

Figure 3.2. Seal of the New England Company, 1661.

witnessed the death of Massasoit, or Osamequin as he was known amongst the Wampanoag ("Massasoit" may have simply been a term or title denoting a leadership role), an important figure in Native and English relations. The Puritan historian William Hubbard claims that Massasoit, "a little before his death," formally introduced his sons Alexander and Philip to the New England magistrates at his home in Mount Hope, "desiring that there might be Love and Amity after his Death between his Sons and them." But Hubbard also notes that, despite Massasoit's famed kindness to the original pilgrims who landed in Plymouth and the forty years of peace between them, the sachem still "maintained no small Displacency of Spirit against them as they were Christians." Hubbard continues that,

> in his last Treaty with his neighbors at Plimouth, when they were with him about purchasing some land in Swanzy, He [Massasoit] had them engage never to attempt to draw away any of his People from their old Pagan Superstition, and devilish Idolatry to the Christian Religion, and did much insist upon it till he saw the English were resolved never to make any Treaty with him more on that Account; which when he discerned, he did not further urge it.

Hubbard concludes by noting that this exchange was "a bad omen," and so it was, though arguably more for the Wampanoag than the Puritans.[20]

Hubbard, of course, was thoroughly steeped in the prejudices of his time and people. Though he regarded himself as a mere "compiler" of the war's events, who could do no more than gather the existing materials and "methodize" them in some sort of coherent order, he thought little enough of the local Natives as to regard their subsequent revolt undeserving the title of "war." These were rather "Massacres, barbarous inhumane Outrages" that had no warrant in the world of rational thought or motivation. Hubbard openly wondered if a report of Indian acts could even merit the "Title of an History."[21] Hubbard was at once writing that history and yet unwitnessing any Native title to such processes.

Massasoit almost certainly perceived, in his final years, how his passing would bring about a period of anxiety and turmoil, and, consequently, he made moves to try to smooth over that difficult passage using the diplomatic skills that had served him well over a forty-year period. But he seems also to have anticipated how concerns of land ownership and spirituality were coming into conflict with one another in an intractable manner. In a very real sense, land—Native space—was the only remaining buffer between the Wampanoag and the spiritual and cultural incursions of the colonists. The more Massasoit found himself in need of ceding land, the greater were his concerns about European belief systems being foisted upon his people. What Hubbard obtusely regards as "displacency of spirit," or a stubborn hostility to Christian belief, is in fact Massasoit's last attempt as sachem to preserve Wampanoag culture and see that peace and prosperity might be handed down to the next generation. Hubbard, however, repurposes this moment in an attempt to sever the historical obligations brought about by Massasoit's original hospitality to the colonists, for indeed, he writes, "they [the colonists] had repayed his former kindnes to them, by protecting him afterwards from the insolencies of the Narragansett."[22]

Preserving Wampanoag culture was of vital concern to Massasoit, but he must have become perfectly cognizant of the fact that Europeans posed a greater overall threat to Wampanoag culture than the Narragansett ever had. Massasoit was not resistant to European innovations, ideas, or trade goods. He did not endeavor to hermetically seal Wampanoag culture in an impenetrable time capsule resistant to change and syncretic growth. His willingness to accommodate strangers in such close proximity on the land remains a historical marker of the overall confidence he had in his own cultural moorings. By insisting, however, that the Europeans never "attempt to draw away any of his People from their old Pagan Superstition," Massasoit seems to have been arguing for intellectual and spiritual sovereignty—the basic right to maintain traditions and practices that had grown up organically with the Wampanoag people in that particular place.

The figure of Massasoit has become thoroughly co-opted by settler culture in narratives endlessly rehearsed in children's histories, cartoons, and Thanksgiving pageants. As such, the tensions that broke out after his death have occurred to us strangely as the result of Philip's fatally "flawed" character, sketched by settler tradition as a savage intractability more in keeping with what was presumed to be the general haughtiness of his race. The historian Leach sums this mode of thought up well when, in relating events leading up the war, he refers to Osamequin as "the long-time friend of the English," and to Philip as "ambitious, proud-spirited, quick to resent an affront to his dignity. Within his breast there burned a sullen spark of dissatisfaction fed by the ever-growing power of the white men."[23] Such language would become *de rigueur* following King Philip's War, inviting the interpretation that the conflict was not the result of unbearable political, economic, and cultural pressures, but rather the caprice of Philip's "haughty" temperament. Massasoit is cast in the familiar role of "good Indian" or Indian helper (a role filled by other famous simulations of Native identity such as Pocahontas, Squanto, and Sacagawea), while Philip is cast in the familiar role of resistant savage, armed and dangerous, closed to all Christian teaching (see figure 3.3). A close look at Hubbard's narrative, however, intimates that tensions leading up to the war were already reaching a breaking point in Massasoit's own

Figure 3.3. Paul Revere's engraving of King Philip as seen in the 1772 edition of Benjamin Church's *The Entertaining History of King Philip's War*. Courtesy of American Antiquarian Society.

time, and that the elder sachem was every bit as invested in the "sullen" task of preserving Wampanoag culture and sovereignty as was his son.

Upon Massasoit's death, his eldest son, Wamsutta, also known as "Allexander Pokanokett," became sachem of the Pokanoket Wampanoag. The role of sachem was largely hereditary for Natives of the Northeast although, as with all regimes determined by lineage, prominent leaders seem to have arisen from time to time from without those bloodlines. A sachem's domain stretched no further than what Kathleen Bragdon refers to as "the face to face community in which social relationships were forged," or the bounds defined by kinship networks that lived, farmed, hunted, intermarried, and shared one another's fortunes together.[24] Certain leaders, however, seem to have risen to a kind of status that reached beyond these bounds, either through a regional recognition of their deliberative ability or as a result of their prowess in warfare. Although the power of sachems within this system of government was considerable, it is probably best articulated by Roger Williams, who notes, "although they have an absolute Monarchie over the people; yet they will not conclude of ought that concerns all, either Lawes, or Subsides, or warres, unto which the people are averse, and by gentle perswasion cannot be brought."[25]

The names Alexander and Philip, acquired for diplomatic purposes when Wamsutta assumed his leadership role, were not issued for their martial connotations as is commonly assumed, but seem to have been designated by virtue of the fact that these were the most memorable Macedonians in Western tradition, and it was the Macedonian cry to the apostle Paul that is echoed in the colonial mantra of the Massachusetts Bay Company, "Come over and help us."[26] Nevertheless, Eliot was undoubtedly speaking of Wamsutta when he wrote in 1649 that "Young Ousamequin is an enemy to praying to God, and the old man too wise to look after it."[27] Wamsutta's reign was short lived. He died suddenly of unknown causes in July of 1662 after being forcibly disarmed and detained by the English for specious reasons. It has been argued that he was poisoned by the colonists or in some other way harmed, but even if this were not so, his humiliating detainment and interrogation, designed to intimidate him in his newly acquired role as sachem, was enough to cast a pall on the relationship that had been so carefully cultivated and maintained by Massasoit.[28] Wamsutta's leadership position in the tribe was filled by Metacom, or Pometacom, known to the English as "King" Philip.

Philip, ascending to the position of sachem, not only found himself having to deal with the fallout from his brother's untimely death and the cultural pressures attendant upon the colonial situation, but he inherited a number of land disputes with the colonists as well, some of which had been dragged out over a period of many years. The authority sachems held to sell land out from under their people will probably never be properly understood. That different Native groups designated and observed boundaries is well established, but it is questionable that sachems had the full backing of their tribes when and if they sold lands. Complicating the question is the fact that Natives and colonists had different notions of land use and ownership. It was within the sachem's bounds to grant use of the land to particular groups or individuals in return for tribute payments, but the idea that land could simply change hands based on the decisions of private individuals may have been intrinsically foreign to the Native sense of occupancy. Extended offers of mutual occupation were routinely understood, however, as "sales" by the English. Bragdon notes that "while Native notions of land ownership were superficially similar to those of the English, the power of decision-making with respect to land alienation rested with the community as a whole."[29] This seems in keeping, at least, with Roger Williams' judgment that a sachem would make no decision that could not be brought about without the consent of the community or "by gentle perswasion."

Nevertheless, Philip's father and brother had both been involved in numerous land transactions—a practice in which Philip, too, would necessarily partake. But because Native negotiators, for the most part, could not actually read the documents to which they gave their marks, there was always ample room for disagreement and foul play (see figure 3.4). Also invisible in the documents is the amount of pressure being placed upon sachems to let go of their lands. This invisible pressure is intimated in a 1668 entry in the Plymouth Colony Record books where it is stated, "Harry [Wosako] desires that neither Tuspaquin nor his sone be prest to sell their lands [obscured word] by any English or others whatsoever: The lands mentioned which Tuspaquin possesseth [obscured words] Wosako with as long as he lives."[30] Although aspects of such records may remain open to interpretation, it appears as though Wosako is making a plea that Tuspaquin, often referred to as the Black Sachem, not be "pressed" or coerced into selling lands that had traditionally been used by Wosako and his family. The legal implications of such "sales" were, perhaps, not well understood by sachems constantly being "prest" by colonial authorities to cede "unimproved" hunting grounds that didn't appear to be under any colonially validated definitions of usage. The resulting ambiguities inherent in these transactions are suggested by a 1668 deed in which Philip claims, "I am willing to sell the Land within this draught; but the Indians that are upon it may live upon it still."[31]

It might safely be concluded that many of the land transactions between colonists and Natives at this time, whether written or verbal, were not honored or properly interpreted, leading to an atmosphere of distrust and discouragement between the parties involved. The Wampanoag became caught in disputes they had little control over, and such disputes became

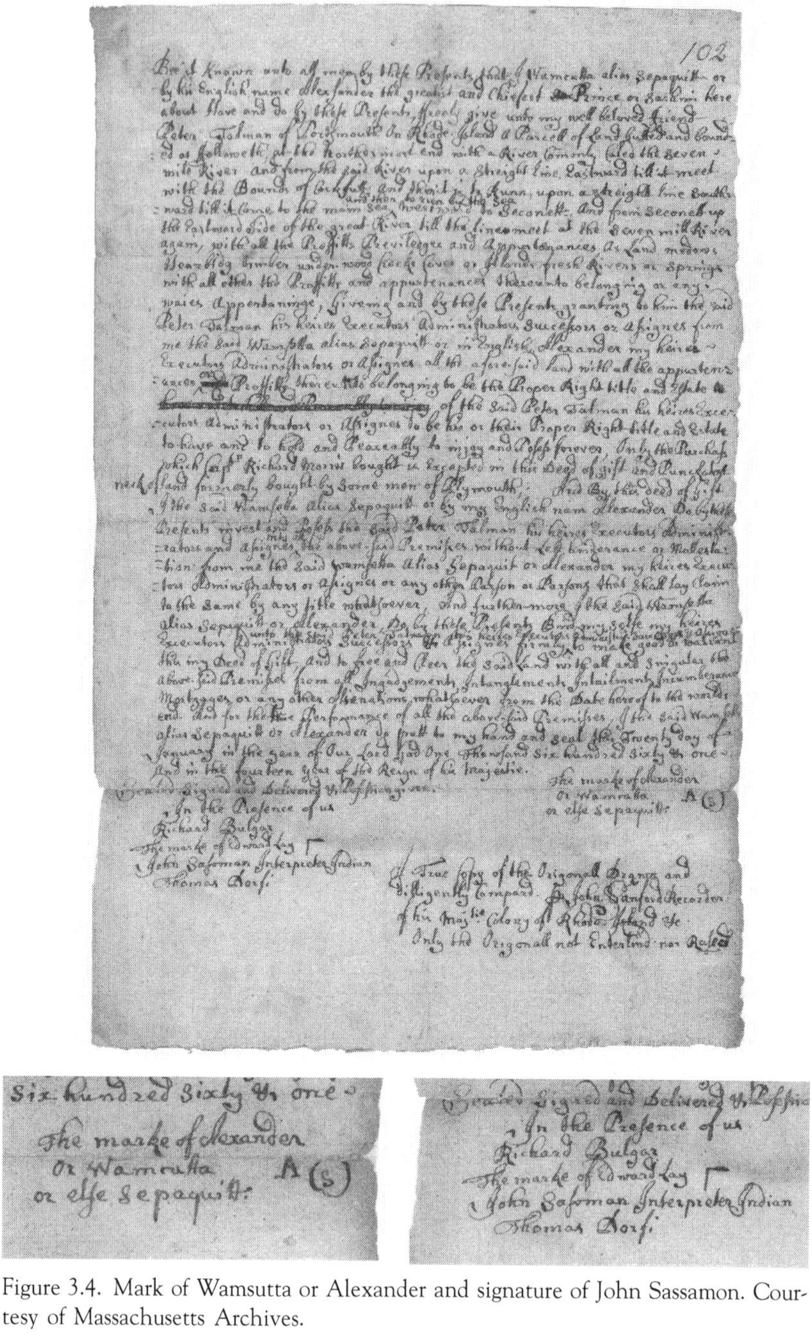

Figure 3.4. Mark of Wamsutta or Alexander and signature of John Sassamon. Courtesy of Massachusetts Archives.

the grounds for great disruption and resentment.[32] As one frustrated Wampanoag commentator wrote some years later in his own language, "yeunuh wussukquohwonog wutche nummukkoukounganun Englishmananog yeh ahquombi" or "this writing is about our being robbed by the English at this time."[33] Regardless of all these difficulties, however, in at least a dozen land transactions in this period to which Philip gave his name and mark, one can apprehend remnants of the ceremonial regularity and order with which these meetings were attended. In each case Philip seems to have brought a determined goodwill to the proceedings, his customary preamble in the surviving documents reading, "To all Christian People to whom these presents shall come, Phillip, allies [alias] Metacom Cheiffe Sachem of Pocanakett in the Collonie of New Plymouth in New England sendeth Greeting."[34] Of course, this was a variant of a stock opening phrase used by colonists in many land transactions of the time, and therefore risks being interpreted as just another moment of colonial ventriloquism. It is difficult to determine if such a statement is a record of compliance and goodwill or coercion.

Whichever interpretation we apply, the record confirms that Philip, like many other sachems of the region, was in a position, whether reluctantly or no, to let land go to his English neighbors (see figure 3.4). Certain historians still cling to these records as proof of the overall fairness of the transactions, as though the fact that the deeds are written and preserved somehow legitimates all colonial claims or erases the levels of coercion that necessitated the sale of land in the first place.[35] In the speeches attributed to Natives from the time, however, as well as in certain recorded passages by colonists, we find corroborated at least the impression of misdealing. Interesting to note is one undated entry preserved in the Plymouth town records that was apparently written by a Native hand, and seems to have been delivered in Philip's name. It reads,

> Philip would intreat that favor of [you] and any of the maiestrats if aney English or engians sp[e]ak about aney land he preay you to give them no ansewer at all this last sumer he maid that promis with you that he would not sell no land in 7 years time before in that time he has not forgot that you promis him. He will come asune as possible to speak with you and so greet your verey loving frind philip dwelling at mount hope neck.[36]

This 1674 letter, which may have been written by a "privy councilor" of Philip's, suggests that the legitimacy of some of these transactions remained in question and that Philip was attempting, as had his father, to retain control over the process.[37] Meeting with John Easton, the deputy governor of Rhode Island, only a week before the war started, Philip was reported to have charged that "when their [the Native's] kings sold land the English would say it was more than they agreed to and a writing must be proof against them all."[38] Easton, who had come to propose negotiations to prevent the war, was in full agreement with Philip's grievances, simply confiding, "We knew it to be true."[39]

Narragansett and Mohegan communities found themselves in similar situations, defending their traditional grounds against a rapidly expanding colonial presence that remained disrespectful of the notion that untilled lands, inhabited only seasonally, could be considered *in use* or under any legally recognized ownership. In 1652, acknowledging that "there hath been a question . . . about the Indjans title of lands," the Massachusetts General Court decreed that "what lands any of the Indeans within this jurisdiccon have by possession or improovement, by subdouing of the same, they have just right thereunto, according to Genesis, 1 and 28, chapt 9:1, and psalms 115:16." As for those lands that were not properly "subdoued" or under the pronounced "qualification of right to the Indeans," these would be "accoumpted the just right of such English as already have, or hereafter shall have, graunt of lands from the Court and the authorite thereof from that of Genesis 1: 28, and the invitacion of the Indians."[40]

This declaration was, in effect, a renarrativizing of Native space. It helped justify territorial usurpation by superimposing the spiritual narrative of Genesis over that of "Turtle Island." Such a narrative not only insisted upon God's injunction in Eden that Adam and Eve "subdue" the land, but it invoked the later pronouncement of Isaac to his son Jacob, that he "mayest inherit the land wherein thou art a stranger" (Genesis 28:4). Natives that were brought into "civilitie" and were willing to live "according to the custome of the English" were presumably to be rewarded an allotment. Groups of Natives who were to conform to Christian practice might be rewarded with townships.[41] But the decree also laid the groundwork to simply dismiss the multitude of existing disputes by proclaiming a new set of principles upon which ownership would be based. Such were the geographical and spiritual incursions commented upon by Massasoit. Where the English felt they had the power and jurisdiction to enforce such laws, Native claim and custom was disregarded. Native space became colonized space. Sites of Native power, such as Dighton Rock, as they came under colonial control, became Edenic—sites of forbidden knowledge, engendering "odd thoughts," that needed to be geographically and cognitively displaced.

His Name and Mark (P): Philip or Metacom as Both Signifier and Signified

Some of the disagreements and tensions arising from the aforementioned laws and arrangements may have been exacerbated even more by the subsequent adoption of nominal Christianity by some indigenous groups and their division into fourteen separate praying towns. Daniel Gookin notes that there were upward of 1,100 souls in praying towns by 1674 and a couple hundred more in the Vineyard, Nantucket, and Plymouth. Of those who were designated "praying Indians" by the colonists, it was believed that several hundred could read. These estimates were probably optimistic. Many of the so-called praying towns had achieved their legitimation in the eyes of the Puritans simply by virtue of one or two prominent men confessing some allegiance to the English.[42] Thomas Mayhew would report in 1674 that there were very few on the Vineyard who could actually read and write, "not above three or four, and those do it brokenly."[43] Nevertheless, the creation of these towns marks the determined rise of European hegemony in the region, brought about not by spiritual persuasion as their rhetoric implied, but rather by legal and institutional force.

George Tinker writes that the praying Indians, by seeking protection from the English, became "cut off" from the more traditional Natives, both economically and in terms of kinship relations.[44] But, perhaps, this isn't as inevitable as it has historically appeared. Gookin, who, aside from Eliot, was the Englishman most intimate with the workings of the praying towns, acknowledges that many of their inhabitants had yet to convert to Christianity. Of the newly formed Indian parishes, he writes, "many . . . being not yet come so far, as to be able or willing to profess their faith in Christ . . . are not admitted to partake in the ordinances of God, proper and peculiar to the church of Christ; which is a garden enclosed, as the scripture saith."[45] Even village leaders such as Waban and Nishokou had failed to offer any concrete allegiance to the colonizer's creed. For those who had adopted Christian practices, their engagement with the European religion was unlikely to constitute a complete overwriting of the traditions and beliefs that had informed their prior lives, no matter how much Europeans insisted on regarding it as such.

In his 1674 *Historical Collections*, Gookin offers his detailed description of the praying towns in general and Natick in particular. Gookin was a close associate with Eliot in the project of converting Natives and organizing them into Christian containments. He seems to have risen to his position in the New England hierarchy as a result of his military prowess, although it is not entirely clear where he attained such credentials. Coming to New England in 1644, after having spent some time in the Virginia Colony, Gookin was immediately placed in command of the military forces in Cambridge and later rose to the position of major-general as well as becoming the town's representative to the General Court. His affairs in Cambridge apparently placed him in close association with the newly instituted college and the aims of Dunster and Eliot to convert the Natives. In 1656 Gookin was appointed to the position of overseeing Indian affairs within the jurisdiction of the Massachusetts colony. In a document following the war a number of Native signatories refer to Gookin as he "who hath been a ruler to us aboute twenty yeares."[46] Aside from Eliot, he knew more about the lives of the Christian Indians in New England than any other English reporter.[47]

Gookin notes that the town of Natick was either surrounded by, or held within its borders, a "handsome round fort, palisaded with trees" in the manner of many Native villages in the Northeast. He observes that, although there was one large building constructed after the English manner that served as both meeting house and school, the other buildings at Natick were all "after their old mode," the English houses "being more chargeable to build and not so warm." Gookin also notes that the English house "cannot be removed so easily as their wigwams, wherein there is not a nail used, to avoid annoyance by fleas, and themselves being generally artists in building and finishing their own wigwams: for these and like reasons, they do incline to keep their old fashioned houses." An important implication here is not only that the Natick Natives maintained traditional lodgings, but that they were still in the habit of seasonally removing to other locations, despite English claims to the contrary.[48] If Natick was equipped with a framed structure for a church, most of the other praying towns were not likely to have had capital for such an investment and we can well imagine from Gookin's descriptions that church services were held in traditional longhouses, or structures that were "spacious, about sixty feet in length, and twenty in width."[49] English frame houses would have imposed a true permanence on their places of dwelling, but traditional wigwams could be taken down and moved with little effort. In the spring many of the Massachusett, Nipmuc, and Wampanoag, whether from the praying towns or not, would travel up the Concord River to Wamesit on the Merrimack to fish, "this place being an ancient and capital seat of Indians." Eliot would follow there each May to preach to the many "strange Indians" who arrived.[50]

On church days and meeting days the villagers were called to worship by the beating of a drum (for lack of a bell in the colonies) in the yard of the meeting house.[51] This house, the one anomaly in the Native village, had two floors, the bottom floor being an open hall and the top floor serving as a tanning area described by Gookin as "a kind of wardrobe, where the Indians hang up their skins, and other things of value." Eliot kept a chamber partitioned off in a corner of the upstairs room where he would sleep when he was in town.[52] Samuel Eliot Morison claims that not only did the Natives of Natick retain their traditional style of dress, but that Eliot adopted "the Indian undress himself in his wilderness visitations."[53] The idea of Eliot in leather stockings seems to defy the conception of him as the culturally anchored "apostle" so elaborately constructed by Cotton Mather in the *Magnalia Christi Americana*, and perhaps points to the level of assimilation occurring in Eliot's own life. Over the years he had arguably become as attached to the Native American communities to whom he preached as the English community of his origins. Although Eliot is typically rendered in his Puritan frock coat, Bible in hand upon some pulpit rock, the stern proselytizer of Puritan values to the Indian, there is reason to believe that he, too, had made accommodations to Native communal structures and that the lines of cultural separation ever so gently blurred in his later years.

Natick remained at the center of Indian schooling, with Monequassun as the school teacher, and after 1666, Anthony and John Speene as well as Thomas Waban, John Wampas, Job Nesuton, John Sassamon, and others who had learned to read and write also in residence.[54] It is hard to know exactly what occurred in these schools. The recent discovery of small European manufactured thimbles at the site of the praying village in Magunkaquog suggests that, aside from literacy and Bible learning, young girls were being taught to sew within the main meeting house there. The same archeological dig, however, unearthed a significant number of quartz crystals alongside the thimbles—crystals that were commonly used by Eastern woodland Natives in spiritual contexts, suggesting that traditional practices were also being kept intact.[55] It might be surmised that the community at Natick, as well as in other praying communities, did their best to achieve a balance between the demands of colonial indoctrination and the exigencies of day-to-day life and seasonal practices. This is not to suggest that dramatic changes had not been forced upon Native communities in this time, but there are reasons to believe that "praying Indians" were in constant contact with their cultural traditions in ways that later commentators often blotted out of official memory.

While one of the steadfast rules of the praying towns was that the Indians refrain from "pawauwing," it would have been a simple thing to cross over to the next Indian village and join in rituals and celebrations there. Praying towns were not organized in any kind of specific strategic groupings, but were interspersed randomly between the traditional villages of their bands and the English frontier settlements that were sprouting up right alongside them. In a sense, they formed a perimeter around the colony that Gookin later argued might have provided a first line of defense against hostile Native forces.[56] Nevertheless, from the records that Gookin and Eliot kept, there is reason to believe that there was much movement between these sites and a continued flow of traditional practices was ensured. In his 1671 promotional tract, *Indian Dialogues*, Eliot even makes mention of a "subtle endeavor to have mingled the praying and non-praying Indians."[57] While Eliot sees this as a Native scheme to disenfranchise the praying towns from within, it was probably a case of Eliot having stumbled upon the hidden transcript of resistance that had always been in place in these villages. In other words, the concept of the "praying town" has operated as another colonial containment that serves a purpose in the archive quite separate from the actual character of these Native spaces. The phrase suggests a kind of totality of belief within its presumed walls (a garden enclosed), but the lived experience was not so well defined by such forced dichotomies of praying/pagan.

There was a deep communitist aesthetic at work in the manner in which Natives reorganized themselves in this period, and the acquisition of writing played an important role in affecting the outcome. It was invariably, however, a colonial insistence upon separating Natives between those who had assimilated and those who remained presumably savage that produced the illusion of two separate classes of Indian in the seventeenth century. Most often, the construction proved false and, in turn, bitterly disappointed the colonists who were so tightly wedded to this cognitive binary. Native converts were constantly accused of "backsliding" and "apostasy" and by the time King Philip's War broke out, the so-called praying Indians were arguably more reviled than those who had all along rejected Christian overtures. They were reviled precisely because their Christian conversions couldn't stop them from being Indians.[58]

Despite all this, the production of a class of praying Indians remained a politically expedient construct, and forced true tensions and divisions upon groups that otherwise were not in contention with one another, but in fact were grappling with the same pressures and conditions in similar manner. In short, the line between "traditional" and "praying Indian" was probably never quite so well drawn in Native space as it appeared in colonized space. Clearly these spaces were in the process of overlapping and coexisting, and the battle to control and define identity was ongoing. Apparently some Native communities could exist within each sphere of influence simultaneously, and were able to survive in such an environment, at least up until the point when war broke out and individuals were forced to definitively choose sides as a matter of survival. But even then, as we will see, the cultural affiliations and individual subject positions remained fluid and interchangeable.

Even for the colonists, the lines between traditional and praying, friendly and hostile Indian, though codified, were not absolutely defined just prior to the war. Eliot, for one, continued to believe that his work amongst the Natives was tied into a narrative of forward progress and would ultimately yield a rich harvest. Although few of his efforts could be thought of as unqualified successes, and many colonial leaders remained doubtful of the overall utility of his project, Eliot was hopeful that Native communities could be perfectly contained within Puritan culture. This hope is expressed most poignantly, perhaps, in his tract *Indian Dialogues*, the first conscious work of fiction produced and published in the colonies (or at least the first work that acknowledges fictitious content). One can sense a clear contrast in this work from what had been expressed in the earlier "Tears of Repentance." If in tracts like "Tears" Native speakers were presumably offering up their own words, *Indian Dialogues* seems to allow a renarrativizing of these cross-cultural encounters that conformed more closely to the outcomes for which Eliot had originally hoped. Eliot admits up front in this work that the dialogues are "partly historical, of some things that were done and said, and partly instructive, to show what might or should have been said, upon the like occasion." In a sense the *Dialogues* are a correction for tracts like "Tears of Repentance" that, with their immanent Native orators and Native translators, never seemed to go off completely as planned.

One of the central characters in *Indian Dialogues* is, in fact, Waban, who appears to be a composite of Waban the elder, his son Thomas Waban, and no Waban that ever was. We first encounter him as he is sauntering through the forest and chances upon a Native acquaintance by the name of Peneovot. After a brief opening volley of polite greetings is exchanged between the two, Waban brings the conversation to a point, declaring,

> I am a praying Indian. I have left our old Indian customs, laws, fashions, lusts, pauwauings and whatever else is contrary to the right knowledge of the true God, and of Jesus Christ our redeemer. It repenteth me of all my fore-past life, the lusts, vanities, pleasures, and carnal delights that were formerly very sweet and very delightful to me, are now bitter as gall unto me. I hate and loathe them. All the works of darkness in which I was wont to take pleasure, I do now forsake and abandon. I am come into the light. I now see things as they are indeed, and not as they seemed to be in the dark. I now know the word of God, which showeth me the way of eternal life . . . I now know Jesus Christ, who hath died for us, to procure a pardon for us, and to open a door and way of eternal life and salvation for us. Into this way I have entered. Herein I walk, and I have promised to God, that I will live and walk in this way all the days of my life.[59]

It is quite probable that if Eliot could have placed the words directly into the mouth of Waban in the earlier "Tears of Repentance," then this is precisely what would have been said. Absent now are the tortured confessions of self-loathing that seemed to emanate from some twisted negotiation between Native traditions and Puritan expectations, and the ambiguous declarations concerning an ability to "know Christ" in one's heart. Waban's assertions here are seamlessly acculturated and he can declare with great confidence that "I now know Jesus Christ." Perhaps even more fantastical than Waban's speech here, however, is the response it garners from Peneovot, who immediately exclaims, "Oh, I am surprised, I am amazed. You have ravished my soul. You brought a light into my soul. I wonder at myself. Where have I been? What have I done? I am like one raised from out of a dark pit."[60] The only thing apparently missing from this most affable of exchanges is Waban proffering to his companion a friendly jar of Grey Poupon to seal the deal.

These Natives, far from representing anything of flesh and blood, bear a striking resemblance to the one-dimensional figure in the New England Company seal who has laid down his bow and arrow and now holds a book in hand, asking the Puritans to come over and continue with their much needed assistance (refer to figure 3.2). Eliot's Natives are products of Puritan fantasy, pretend human creatures that offer up no psychic resistance to the challenge of a newly opened cultural paradigm. In a sense, *Indian Dialogues* lays bare the cognitive rift still very much in place some fifty-one years after initial contacts between Puritans and Indians. While the Waban of "Tears of Repentance" is all too aware of the difficult philosophical terrain between the two cultural discourses and negotiates it with studied care, Eliot continues to see (or unsee) Native culture as a hot bed of human error so fundamentally base that it has no viable defense, no ready response, to the superimposition of Christian values.

It is worth noting that, not only is the Waban of *Indian Dialogues* a fully converted, card-carrying member of the Puritan church, ready to spread the gospel amongst the Indian nations, but this Waban, like Thomas Waban, can read and write and therefore speak authoritatively of scripture, quoting passages at will. It speaks to Eliot's overall optimism, and, perhaps, his own incremental familiarity with Native lives and custom, that he has one of Waban's hopeful converts respond to his teachings with the exclamation, "I doubt it will be difficult for me to learn to read. I am full of capacity."[61] One would be hard pressed to find a similarly positive claim being made by a Puritan concerning Native potentiality during this period. But even taking into account such a positive portrayal and the, perhaps, good intentions inscribed therein, *Indian Dialogues* remains a work of violent erasure in lockstep with the simulations of dominance. The Waban of *Indian Dialogues* is revitalized, irrepressible, reborn through Christian learning. By comparison, the Nipmuc sachem Nishokou, upon whom Waban trains his later discourse, is portrayed as listless and culturally enervated. He laments that Waban "can read and understand these things. I am old and cold and dry, and half dead already. I have not strength enough left to be whetted to a new edge." Nishokou equates himself with the "dry bones" of scripture, too far gone to receive the requickening of Christian love. He is made all too aware of the inadequacy of his cultural framework and accepts Waban's preachings without argument, offering his children up for English education.

Certainly we must appreciate that this is a deliberate work of propaganda, and yet, where it aspires to be persuasive, it is in fact psychologically flat, lacking sophistication of both argument and human understanding. If it is meant to be instructional, as Eliot claims, and to suggest what "should have been said" in certain situations, its affect is just the opposite. *Indian Dialogues* seems to assume it can afford such simplicity because Native culture has nothing sophisticated of its own with which to meet the Christian rhetoric being forwarded. Nowhere in this work does a Native speaker find cause to defend his traditional beliefs or customs. Eliot sees no need to frame a debate or set up a kind of straw man to represent the Native worldview. As virtual Waban exclaims, the old ways "are now bitter as gall unto me. I hate and loathe them."

In the final interaction of *Indian Dialogues* even Philip Keitasscot, whom we are to understand is the Wampanoag leader King Philip or Metacom, sachem at "*Pagan*oehket" (italics mine) is quickly turned round by a conversation with the young missionary convert, Anthony. Their dialogue prompts Philip to observe, "I perceive also that in your worshipping of God morning and night, you read in that book. I pray tell me what book that is? What is written in it? And how do you know it is the word of God?"[62] This, of course, was the question that missionaries from day one were dying to be asked by Indians, as evidenced by the fact that they had reframed it countless times in their recorded conversations. The assumption obviously remained that Native peoples had no corresponding practice by which to comprehend the value of books and letters and Philip is made to parrot this sentiment. It is reasonable to assume, however, that by 1671 when *Indian Dialogues* was published Philip not only fully grasped the meaning and significance of alphabetic literacy, but had a reasonably sophisticated understanding of what Christian scripture was about. He had been exposed to books, had negotiated treaties and land sales, and would have been kept abreast of the Native-language works being produced at the Indian College in Cambridge. Arguably, as will be seen later in this chapter, he even played a small role in seeing these works through to their publication.

Nevertheless, the Philip of *Indian Dialogues* is constructed in accordance with the typological necessities that Eliot and his cohorts had envisioned as part of their colonial mandate and their covenant, as a people, with God. In that scheme of things, Philip was like the Macedonian pagans of old who, when confronted with Christian truths, were desirous to know more and ultimately became willing converts. Once Philip is reassured, in *Indian Dialogues*, that converting to Christianity will not cause him to forfeit the wampum tributes due him as sachem, he withdraws all opposition to converting, exclaiming, "I feel your words sink into my heart and stick there. You speak arrows. I feel that you wound me, but I do not think you hurt me. Nor do you mean me any hurt, but good."[63] Eliot has, rhetorically at least, killed the Indian but saved the man. Such a sentiment, placed in the mouth, injected into the very body even, of Philip again shows the utter disregard for the types of tensions that were coming to a boil at this particular moment. The true Philip, if we can call him that, was in an embattled state, pressured into conceding one indigenous right after another, forced by the colonists to surrender his arms even though no violation of their decades-long peace could be demonstrated, forced to surrender lands that had once been part of his unquestioned domain. Far from seeing the light, this Philip would declare war on the colonists just a few years after *Indian Dialogues* was published. But in this precarious moment, prior to the ruptures of war, Philip was still regarded as a hopeful convert and potential first fruit.

In the wake of the war, historians like Hubbard and Increase Mather would begin to recast Philip in a new image, as the "sullen," "haughty," and "rebellious" son, "brooding" on his mountain seat like a certain figure out of Milton's *Paradise Lost*. Cotton Mather, in his bid to construct a revised cultural narrative for both Puritan and Native, would take care to reenvision the "Indian dialogue" between Philip and Eliot, but this time within a new framework informed by Philip's ultimate resistance. In his *Magnalia Christi Americana* Mather recounts,

> it was particularly remarked in Philip the ring-leader of the most calamitous war that ever they made upon us; our Eliot made a tender of the everlasting salvation to that king; but the monster entertained it with contempt and anger, and after the Indian mode of joining signs with words, he took a button upon the coat of the reverend man, adding, That he cared for his gospel, just as much as he cared for that button.[64]

The shift from hopeful convert to irreconcilable fiend was complete. What seems clear, however, is that both textualized Philips were mere ciphers employed to feed whatever was the current agenda or prevailing sentiment of the colonists.

If Eliot was busy imagining Philip's cheerful and seamless conversion to Christianity in 1671, the United Colonies were still intent on demonstrating their hegemony over the region and called Philip to a council in Taunton on April 10th of that year. Once again, there had been rumors of an Indian uprising and the colonists used such rumors to justify their ever increasing breaches of Wampanoag sovereignty. Whatever their attempts to evangelize the Natives, the colonists were unable to separate themselves from the notion that they were surrounded by non-Christian peoples who seemed to them, in general, savage and unholy, and this condition fostered a great sense of anxiety amongst them, so that threats, whether real or imagined, were always perceived and generally acted upon. Philip and his men, arriving in Taunton for the meeting, were forced to surrender their arms, and the document of this meeting purports to express Philip's acquiescence to the charges against him in his own words. It reads:

> Whereas my Father, my Brother, and my self, have formally submitted ourselves and our People unto the Kings Majesty of England, and to the Colony of New Plimouth, by solemn Covenant under our Hand; but I having of late through my Indiscretion, and the Naughtiness of my Heart, violated and broken this my Covenant with my Friends, by taking up Arms, with evil intent against them, and that groundlessly; I being now deeply sensible of my unfaithfulness and Folly, do desire at this Time solemnly to renew my Covenant with my ancient Friends, and my Father's Friends above mentioned, and do desire that this may testifie to the World against me if ever I shall again fail in my Faithfullness towards them (that I have now, and at all Times found so kind to me) or any other of the English Colonies; and as a real Pledg of my true intentions for the Future to be Faithful and Friendly, I do freely engage to resign up unto the Government of New plimouth, all my English Arms, to be kept by them for their Security, so long as they shall see Reason. For true Performance of the promises, I have hereunto set my Hand, together with the Rest of my Council.[65]

The mark of "P" for Philip (and, simultaneously, Pometacom), chief sachem of Pokanoket, was given here along with the marks of the other Native and colonial witnesses on hand. Unlike the other sachems, Philip signaled his understanding of English literacy by fashioning his mark to the letter of the alphabet that begins his name, a decision on his part that has fascinating implications. We should no more consider the aforementioned words to belong to Philip, however, than we should credit the aforementioned testimonies attributed to Philip by Mather and Eliot. In each case, the record offers up what can only be thought of as a fictive semblance of Philip, absent any trace of human complexity.

For the next two hundred years Philip, or Metacom, would probably become the most textualized Native figure in American letters, being employed with each new representation as a vehicle for the shifting ideologies of America's process of self-identification, each time serving as a mirror for settler desires and anxieties, each time offering American audiences a way out of their own apprehensions of guilt, wrongdoing, or excessive violence.

But the sentiments to which Philip gave his mark in the 1671 treaty, under duress, offers only the official transcript of power. That these were by no means Philip's real sentiments is evident not only in his subsequent actions, but in statements recorded by the neutral John Easton, mentioned earlier, just prior to the breaking out of the war which would also come to bear Philip's name. What remains indisputable, however, is that for Philip, or Metacom, picking up the pen in colonial New England meant invariably signing away lands, arms, and rights, despite the warmest greetings with which these transactions were generally initiated (see figure 3.5).

Death by Writing: Exhuming the Narrative of John Sassamon

As demonstrated in chapter 1, almost all historical and literary commentary for three hundred years following the Pequot War attempted to redirect blame for the 1637 fort massacre on the Pequot themselves, who, in a poem by the Puritan minister Samuel Danforth, were consumed by "Mystic Flames" as a result of their innate haughtiness and pride.[66] One would have

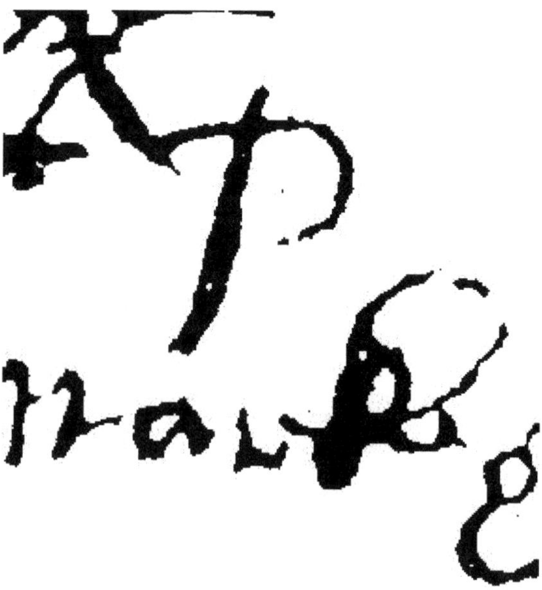

Figure 3.5. Mark of King Philip or Metacom on 1666 land transaction. Courtesy of Plymouth Registry of Deeds.

to move outside the colonies of Plymouth and Massachusetts Bay to find an explicit discordant voice, like that of Roger Williams, for instance, who noted after the war that if the colonists would restrict themselves to fighting only defensive wars, "it would be very easie for ye English to live & die in peace with all ye Nations of this Country."[67] Nevertheless, against all logic, the Pequot, rather than the English, came to be known as the most warlike and aggressive of all peoples in the region. Such incongruous efforts at containment were called upon again in the response to King Philip's War, and the colonists found themselves reaching into the same old, if slightly refined, bag of tricks. As William Hubbard reminded his readers on the frontispiece to his 1677 *Narrative of the Troubles with the Indians in New England*, which began with a brief summation of the Pequot War, "the Lord said unto Moses, write this for a Memoriall in a Book, and rehearse it in the ears of Joshua; for I will utterly put out the Remembrance of Amelek from under heaven."

King Philip's War would be a much broader engagement than the Pequot War, stretching out over a longer period of time, and inflicting a great many more casualties on either side, leaving a more permanent scar on the overall cultural landscape of New England. As such, the near perfect ring of containment we saw placed around the events of the Pequot War would be more difficult for the colonists to maintain and would require much more elaborate explanations than simply invoking God's will. Many of the primary documents to emerge from the conflict, such as Mary Rowlandson's famous *The Sovereignty and Goodness of God*, betray interesting ruptures as individual witnesses often found it difficult to sustain the tightly wound parameters of the war's prevailing discourse, even despite their emotional and philosophical allegiance to it.[68] Nevertheless, the Puritan community that emerged from this conflict was one that had permanently hardened its stance against Native presence in New England. The war, with all of its devastation to the colonists, came to be seen as a trial inflicted by God upon a backsliding people. The colonists ultimately drew up a remarkable master narrative in which they had been severely rebuked, but after a period of violent penance, were brought back into the good graces of the Lord.[69] Natives were regarded as a scourge in this conflict, the tool that God used to afflict his chosen people. In the words of Daniel Gookin, God had made "a rod of the barbarous heathen to chastise and punish the English for their sins."[70]

The events of King Philip's War have been duly chronicled in any number of books and essays and my intention here is not to rehearse these circumstances in full but to concentrate on the written testimonies of its Native participants and to consider the contexts and consequences of these testimonies. Many of the causes leading up to the war have been alluded to already in this chapter. Philip had seen his brother die under suspicious circumstances, he had repeatedly been called to court to surrender his weapons and the weapons of his people despite having caused no demonstrable offense, he had been cheated in land deals and watched Wampanoag landholdings quickly get whittled away. There were complaints of English cattle repeatedly destroying Native corn and of the English selling liquor to the Natives despite prohibitions against it, causing unrest in both Native and settler townships. When Rhode Island's deputy governor, John Easton, in his attempt to negotiate peace with Philip a week before fighting broke out, suggested that, perhaps these matters could be settled through arbitration, Philip responded that "all English agreed against them and so by arbitration they [the Wampanoag] had had much wrong, many square miles of land so taken from them for English would have English Arbitrators . . . and now they had not so much land or money, that they were as good be killed as leave all their livelihood."[71] Philip apparently concluded this meeting with the wish that "the English should do to them as thay did when thay wear to strong for the english."[72] Or in other words, it would be nice if the English treated the Indians now, the way Philip's father, Massasoit, had treated the Pilgrim settlers when they first arrived on these shores, too weak and unskilled to support themselves. Easton, in his account, refutes none of this, noting only that "we sate veri frindly together" and that "we departed without any discurtiousnes."[73]

If the causes for war had been building for well over a decade, the death of John Sassamon, a prominent Christian Indian who had likely assisted in the translation of the Eliot Bible, has often been pinpointed as the ultimate catalyst for King Philip's War or, at least, the final straw in the long mounting tensions. In January of 1675, Sassamon's body was found in Assawomset Pond near Middleborough where he had apparently fallen through the ice while fishing. After further inquiry, his body was ordered exhumed and it was noted that there were contusions on Sassamon's head suggestive of foul play. Witnesses were found, accusations made, and three of Philip's top advisers were accused of having orchestrated Sassamon's murder. They were subsequently hanged for the offense. Philip maintained their innocence throughout, but as he had told Easton, "all English agreed against them and so by arbitration they [the Natives] had had much wrong."

Colonists, and subsequent historians, interpreted Sassamon's suspicious death as a result of Wampanoag resentment at his having turned to Christianity. It was said that Sassamon had, just prior to his death, warned the Plymouth governor, Josiah Winslow, of Philip's plans for attacking the colony. It is also reported by Easton that, according to a rumor in circulation, Sassamon had deceitfully inserted clauses in Philip's will that would have deeded land to himself upon Philip's death. Perhaps Sassamon had begun to internalize some of the more pernicious particulars of the land deal from the many times he had played the role of mediator and witness to transactions between Indians and English. Nevertheless, Easton allows the possibility that Philip, upon discovering the deceit, may have sought Sassamon's death. This is often offered as the reason that Sassamon apparently fled to the English for protection.

The Puritan historian William Hubbard saw these events in starker terms, however, and describes Sassamon as

> a very cunning and plausible Indian, well skilled in the English Language, and bred up in Profession of Christian Religion, imployed as Schoolmaster at Natick, the Indian Town, who upon some Misdemeanour fled from his Place to Philip, by whom he was entertained in the Room and Office of Secretary, and his chief Councellor, whom he trusted with all his Affairs and Secret Counsels.[74]

According to Hubbard, then, Sassamon, being "cunning and plausible" had fled *to* Philip, not to the English, but, as Hubbard further elaborates, it is Sassamon's Christian conscience, aided by the solicitations of Mr. Eliot, that finally "sting" him and bring him back into the Christian fold prior to his death. These strained explanations succeed, in either case, of making Sassamon a liminal figure, accused in both Native and colonized space of various infractions and misdemeanors, fleeing from one side to the other and back again. And yet, one might ascertain from the confusion of reports that Sassamon was never simply on one or the other side of this cultural divide, a constant fugitive to identity politics. It is quite possible that he moved comfortably from one realm to the next, not in flight, but existing in both simultaneously, perhaps not apprehending that this somehow endangered his existence or placed him in a compromised psychological space. Consider that, whether murdered or accidentally drowned, Sassamon was not a fugitive seeking shelter amongst the English at the time of his death as most reports suggest. He remained firmly in Native space, had found the time to go ice-fishing, and the pond where he fished was no hideout or refuge in colonized space, but simply his home, on land that had been gifted to him by Philip's close ally Tuspaquin, the so-called black sachem, in 1673.[75]

While relatively little is known about Sassamon, his picking up the pen and venturing into the world of the archive allows us to piece together a few serviceable assumptions. Although probably too young to fight, he had apparently acted in some capacity alongside the English during the Pequot War, serving under Richard Callicot. More than likely he was used as a runner to deliver messages between colonial troops and parties. Roger Williams, in his correspondences, makes mention of having used Sassamon in this capacity. From an early age, therefore, he had been in proximity to Christian spheres of influence and proved himself a useful and capable intermediary. At some point he received schooling in Cambridge in the 1660s, either at the grammar schools, at Harvard, or both. Upon ending his education a few years later, he was sent to teach at Natick.[76] Sassamon has been viewed as both victim and self-interested manipulator of a cultural divide that only a handful of skilled individuals were capable of negotiating in late seventeenth-century New England. Certainly his exposure to the English and the education he received amongst them gave him the tools to mediate between peoples and perhaps take advantage of the lines of misunderstanding and confusion that resulted from cultural differences on either side. What is rarely offered up for consideration, however, is the possibility that Sassamon's acquired standing in his community was not so much a result of his affiliation with the English, or the result of shrewd cultural manipulations, as it was a mark of his service to the Wampanoag and his usefulness as a bilingual code-breaker.

The assumption has been that Philip would have naturally resented Sassamon for his accommodations to Christian practices. Nathaniel Saltonstall, a Boston merchant who wrote about these events in a 1675 letter, noted that Sassamon had been sent to preach the gospel to Philip, "but King Philip (Heathen-like) instead of receiving the Gospel, would immediately have killed this Sosomon, but by the Perswasion of some about him not to do it."[77] Increase Mather, writing about the war, observed, "no doubt but one reason why the Indians murthered John Sausaman, was out of hatred against him for his Religion, for he was Christianized and baptiz'd, and was a Preacher amongst the Indians, being of very excellent parts, he translated some of the bible into the Indian language."[78] The assumption is clearly that Sassamon's professed Christianity would have been enough to provoke his death warrant in the eyes of the "haughty" Philip.

These culturally biased hypothesis, written during or just after the war when antipathy for the Indian was at its high watermark in New England, have been furthered by more contemporary historians who rightly view Sassamon's death as one of the major catalysts for the war, but have largely failed to disentangle Sassamon in any meaningful way from the simulations of dominance through which he materializes before us as a Native figure of great and pivotal interest to colonial authors. In *Flintlock and Tomahawk*, Leach maintained that "the suspicion of his [Sassamon's] murder was greatly strengthened by the known facts of Sassamon's life."[79] Leach describes Sassamon as a figure drawn to opposite extremes, "having been raised under the Christian influence of Massachusetts Puritanism," before fleeing "to the wilderness" to become "a valuable aid to Philip," and then returning once more "like the Prodigal Son" to be readmitted to the Christian Indian community at Natick.[80] In other words, his code switching, crossing from one cultural extreme to the other, seems to have occasioned resentment and ultimately a death warrant. James D. Drake, in a more recent history of the war, describes Sassamon as probably "one of the slipperiest characters in seventeenth-century New England history." Why this characterization applies, Drake does not clarify, although the assumption is that Sassamon, like a shapeshifter, slipped from one cultural set of identity markers to another with the greatest of ease. Drake reiterates the known details of Sassamon's life and suggests that because of the obvious conflict of interests manifested by his cultural fence leaping, "Philip must have always suspected his [Sassamon's] loyalty."[81]

Drake argues that the praying Indians and the traditional Indians, represented by Philip, were in constant competition with one another for followers prior to the war. By placing themselves under the protectorate of the colonies, the praying Indians were apparently detracting from the number of subjects that Philip could claim as his own, thereby diminishing his status and draining his yearly tribute.[82] While there were admitted tensions between praying Indians and non-Christian Indians, it is difficult to gauge just how strong they ran or if such tensions were felt by one and all. Although Philip is often regarded as being a "King" of the Wampanoag, in fact his sachemship, like that of his father's, was confined to his particular band of Pokanokets. His actual influence probably spread further than this, and given the overall situation, he may have perceived the determination of neighboring bands to seek protection under the English as a loss of Native power and influence in the region. But his hostility to Christianity itself was unlikely to have been a motivating factor, particularly when Eliot and others had made it clear that praying Indians would continue to pay wampum tributes to Philip. Furthermore, as has been argued, the line between Christian and non-Christian Indian was never so well drawn as the commentators at the time labored to suggest. Maybe the real foundation of the tensions between groups was the question of who the Christian Indians would side with if war were to break out. But as has been intimated, even this question proves misleading. The more relevant question turned out to be, who would actually claim the Christian Indians in the event of war?

For good or ill, John Sassamon serves as a useful case study of the shifting grounds of identity politics for Natives in colonial New England. In her book, *The Name of War*, Jill Lepore describes Sassamon in particular as an agent caught in liminal space, one whose situation necessitated the dangerous task of existing in both colonial and indigenous cultures at once, while never belonging to either. Lepore refers to literate Natives at the time of King Philip's War as "neither English nor Indian," as though the conditions of acquiring literacy completely scoured one of his or her cultural identity.[83] In her skillful historical account, Lepore correctly acknowledges the difficulties involved in mastering the cultural discourse of alphabetic literacy and the forced concessions that were surely made by Native communities. And yet she falls victim to an unfortunate historical stereotype when she claims that "literacy killed John Sassamon."[84] While Lepore's is, perhaps, the most nuanced version of Sassamon's role in the period leading up to King Philip's War, there is still room to question the degree of liminality, or in other words, to wonder how truly different Sassamon's situation was from every other indigenous individual trying to exist within the transforming space of Native New England. It wasn't just "literacy" that was deadly in this period. Simply being indigenous was more than enough to place one's life at risk. In many cases, access to the tool of alphabetic literacy was what preserved both individuals and entire Native communities.

What is evident is that Sassamon had played a vital role in Philip's sachemship from the very start. He appears to have been living amongst the Wampanoag at Montaup (Mount Hope) during Wamsutta's reign, probably fulfilling the role of interpreter. He would come to play the same role for Philip as well, leaving his signature as witness on the peace treaty that Philip was made to sign with the Plymouth colonists in 1662.[85] According to Saltonstall, Sassamon had been "brought up (among others) an Indian at the Colleg at Cambridg" some six or seven years prior to King Philip's War.[86] If so, his residence at Harvard would have coincided with the period that Caleb Cheeshateaumauk, Joel Hiacoomes, James Printer, Job Nesuton, and John Wampas were there in the mid-1660s, as this seems to have been the time of greatest activity for Indian education at the college level. The chronology implies, however, that Sassamon served as a counselor for Philip prior to his time at Harvard, and that he continued in such a role after leaving Harvard, as evidenced by his signature as "scribe" alongside Philip's in many of the subsequent land deals. In other words, it would seem that, rather than "fleeing" his people in disgrace to attend the Christian academy at Harvard, as most historians have suggested, Sassamon moved freely back and forth amongst the Wampanoag and the English during this period. It is quite possible that he was actually sent by Philip to master English writing at the college, just as Waban had sent his son Thomas to do and, presumably, as Printer, Nesuton, Cheeshateaumauk, Hiacoomes, and Wampas had also been sent. As with other Native leaders of the time, Philip would have wanted a representative who knew something of English customs, language, and writing. By appointing Sassamon to this task, Philip not only gained a diplomatic edge, but he indirectly participated in the translations of the Christian Bibles on which Sassamon reportedly assisted.

Sassamon's signature appears alongside Philip's "P" in nearly all of the land transactions and councils that Philip engaged in at this time prior to the war. Hubbard refers to Sassamon as Philip's "Secretary and chief Councellor."[87] Others have referred to Sassamon simply as Philip's "scribe."[88] Whatever the extent of his role, it was probably understood that indoctrination into Christian values was part of the price of an English education in letters. Far from playing a part that was at odds with his Wampanoag community, it might be presumed that Sassamon was being asked to serve a vital role for Philip and the Wampanoag in learning to compose and translate documents and mediating Wampanoag and English transactions. John Eliot wrote to the United Colonies Commissioners in 1664 requesting "encouragement" for Sassamon who was, as Eliot claimed, teaching "Phillip and his men to read." To this end, Philip had even, apparently, sent to Eliot for books.[89] The assumption has always been that Sassamon performed these services for the colonies and yet, Eliot's letter implies that Philip was a willing participant in this endeavor and, as such, it is just as likely that Sassamon was working for the benefit of the Wampanoag. In return, he was rewarded with twenty-seven acres in Assawomset by the "black sachem," so named because of his loyalty to Philip during the war.

Sassamon apparently began a ministry at Nemasket, a nearby township, and as a result of this James Drake feels "the man upon whom Philip had placed his hopes was now an avowed enemy."[90] But this assumption again rests upon the forced language of the colonizers at the time of the war, who regarded praying Indians and their traditional counterpoints as absolute polar opposites. Nemasket was not a designated "praying town" when Sassamon went to "teach" there, and despite his earlier association with Eliot, he would have been quite at home in this more traditional Native space. It wasn't until his death was reconfigured as a murder, his body literally exhumed and renarrativized, that Sassamon suddenly became a key in the master narrative of the Puritan war effort. He was labeled as an informer, having tipped off Governor Winslow that Philip was planning an attack. Interestingly, Gookin, who was intimately knowledgeable of these affairs, makes no note of Sassamon's alleged perfidy and claims instead that it was Waban who tipped off the colonists.[91] Perhaps it was permissible for colonial commentators to insert the name of any likely "praying Indian" into this role of informant. In fact, all Natives within the Plymouth Colony had been brought under oaths to inform colonial officials of any rumors of a "plott or designe contrived against the English."[92] That such a plot would ultimately be "uncovered" by a government so actively pursuing one seems a foregone conclusion. Commentators like Hubbard, Saltonstall, and Increase and Cotton Mather have colored our view of Sassamon, ordaining him "the first Christian martyr" amongst the Indians. Such claims were rooted in strategic rhetorical biases meant to inflame passions. Sassamon, however, was as much a cipher for colonial causes as was Wequash, Massasoit, and Philip.

As Hilary Wyss astutely observes in her book *Writing Indians*, "it was only as a dead Indian that Sassamon acquired status among the English; those Christian Indians who were still alive were accorded none of the respect that Sassamon received."[93]

Sassamon's death is invariably referred to as a "mystery," but a mistrial would be a more effective term to bring to bear. We will never know the exact circumstances surrounding his death, just as we will never know with complete assurance most things that happened in colonial times. We can conclude, however, that the assumption of Philip's complicity in the death and the subsequent execution of his warriors, who maintained their innocence unto the end, was not an act of justice so much as it was an act of war. John Easton, who provides the least biased transcript of the grievances of the Indians at this time, ultimately weighs in that, based on the testimony of "sum indians I judged intelegabell and impartiall" it seemed reasonable to believe that Sassamon had, in fact, drowned. While Easton acknowledges that sometimes "naty [nasty] Indians wold kill others," he had never known them to "obscuer as if the dead indian was not murdered."[94] He further notes that, since Philip was king, if he had "dun it it was ther Law so to execute home [whom] their kings judged deserved it that he had no case to hide it."[95] All told, these arguments not only bring into question the presumption that Sassamon was murdered, but they question the right of the English to prosecute such a murder. The fact that three of Philip's men were tried and hung for this crime should only be seen as one more direct provocation to Philip whom the colonists had been hoping to disarm, convert, and thereby disenfranchise, for at least a decade.

"Know by this paper": Native Writing in King Philip's War

The result of all this is that, whether by design, decree, or default, a group of Wampanoag made an assault on the town of Swansea near Philip's seat at Mount Hope on June 20, 1675. An even fiercer attack was made four days later and the war was suddenly on, proving to be a longer and infinitely more costly conflict than either side could have anticipated at the start. It would stretch out over a year and three months and take a toll in lives lost and resources plundered that remains unprecedented on North American soil in relation to the overall population of the region. At the height of the conflict, Philip's confederation of Native warriors (if it can be thought of as such) consisting of Wampanoag, Nipmuc, Narragansett, Pocasset, and others, were able to push back the western edge of English settlement all the way to the Charles River, ransacking at least a third of the established English townships. Philip, however, was ultimately unsuccessful in his attempts to enlist the French, the Dutch, Mohawk, or other outlying Indian nations into the war. Without this help Philip could not sustain his successes, and by spring of 1676 his armies were depleted, his people were exhausted from their condition as refugees constantly foraging and on the run, and the life had largely drained out of the cause. By August 12th of that year Philip had been pursued to his death and the war, though it would drag out in places for a few more months, was effectively over.

James Drake and Neal Salisbury, both of whom have contributed in important ways to the body of knowledge surrounding this conflict, have referred to King Philip's War as a kind of Civil War. What both authors would like to establish is that this war was not the inevitable existential crisis between savage and civilized forces that history, in a not too distant past, had so beautifully, consistently, and meticulously rendered for its reading audiences. As has been reasserted here, the Natives of New England and the colonists, despite their concerns, conflicts, disagreements, and grievances, had existed side by side as neighbors for many years, mostly in a state of peace, involved in economic and cultural transactions that were more complex, ritualized, and tightly integrated than has been generally credited. Nevertheless, the conditions of New England in the 1670s were not those of a civil war. It was a war created by an environment of constant pressure, coercion, and forced capitulations. The English did everything within their power to work their will amongst the indigenous peoples in their midst, and though they would continue to assert their will "peaceably" if able, they were not opposed to forcing the issue or shedding even innocent blood to achieve their ends. No doubt, they hadn't predicted just how costly in blood and treasure such a conflict would be. But regardless of this ill-fated miscalculation, the desired outcome was achieved. An entire people, whose claims to the land were problematic in terms of English desires for growth and hegemony, were brought into containment through concerted efforts that ultimately reached their fruition through the violence of war. The indigenous groups, on the other hand, did all they could to uphold their title to the land and their right for coexistence in this space, submitting to countless threats, losses, and indignities. Many of those indignities bore the mark of Philip's insignia, the "P" that presided over each capitulation. When the breaking point finally came, many Natives of New England would begin to express themselves by other means, not only through acts of retaliation and violence, but by using writing to voice their dissent rather than their spiritual compliance.

One might think that during this time of heated accusations and choosing sides, the previously (as I maintain) fluid line between praying and traditional Native would quicken, but in fact it was just the opposite. For the colonist, at least, distinctions between traditional and praying Indian largely collapsed beneath the more comprehensive historical view that all

Figure 3.6. Map of New England and native settlements, 1675. Map design by Terry Stigers.

Natives were "savage," "beastly," "hell-fiends," and not to be trusted.[96] This, even though many praying Indians would, in fact, choose to fight side by side with the English against Philip once war broke out. Not only Job Nesuton, Eliot's most effective translator, but a number of other praying Indians gave up their lives defending colonial interests in King Philip's War. Gookin and Eliot stood more or less alone amongst the English in defending the praying Indians, honoring their contributions, and condemning "the animosity and rage of the common people" that was indiscriminately directed toward them.[97] Gookin's 1677 *Historical Account of the Christian Indians* is, in fact, an impassioned condemnation of the treatment that praying Indians received at the hands of the colonists, delineating nothing less than the contours of an all-out race war being played out within the arena of the larger conflict. " 'T is no strange thing for men's reason to be darkened, if not almost lost, when the mists of passion and temptation do prevail," Gookin charges, describing a situation in which violent injustices were heaped one on top of another in a climate of unbridled intolerance.[98]

Gookin was, no doubt, startled by the ease with which his own people suddenly rejected the Christian Indians in their midst, spurning his years of faithful work by willfully and indiscriminately lumping the praying Indians in with Philip's so-called renegades. Such sentiments openly violated every assurance he and Eliot had made to the Native communities in thirteen praying towns. Although the praying Indians were, as a whole, guilty of nothing, and had sworn allegiance to the colonists, a decree was passed two months after the war broke out, forcing "all Indians that are desirous to approve themselves faithful to the English, be confined" to within a mile radius of the center of their towns. Any Natives found outside these confines could expect to be shot on sight, and "their blood, or other damage by them sustained, will be upon their own heads."[99] Gookin argued that the Indians therefore had no way to hunt or bring in their crops. Damages were inflicted on their properties by covetous English neighbors. Many were captured and made prisoners and then slaves. Gookin and Eliot, themselves, despite their years of respected service to the colony, suddenly found their lives threatened. Gookin writes of how

> The clamors and animosity amongst the common people increased daily, not only against those Indians, but also all such English as were judged to be charitable to them. And particularly many harsh reflections and speeches were uttered against Major Daniel Gookin, and Mr. John Eliot, the former of whom had been appointed by the authority of the General Court of Massachusetts . . . for Gospelizing those Indians . . . for neither had any of our Christian Indians been justly charged, either with

> unfaithfulness, or treachery towards the English . . . but on the contrary, some of them had discovered the treachery . . . of Philip . . . and since the war have served the English faithfully, but yet must be content to receive such retribution from too many, (at whose hands they have deserved other things,) but now both the Christian Indians, and all that favored them are enemies to the English . . . so great was the rage and unreasonable prejudice of many at this time.[100]

Gookin was experiencing nothing less than the total betrayal of his missionary endeavor and found himself suddenly and unexpectedly well outside the discursive boundaries made permissible by warfare. One local magistrate threatened Gookin "that he ought rather be confined amongst his Indians" and that "his taking the Indians Part so much hath made him a Byword both amongst Men and Boys." Gookin was heard to say at the time that hostility was so great against him that he was afraid to go out in the streets.[101] Such events would lead Gookin to characterize his 1677 defense of the praying Indians, written directly after the war, as a text "clothed in a wilderness dress."[102] He refers here not only to the hasty nature by which he pulled these materials together for publication, but to the distressed state of consciousness informing his historical account. Unfortunately neither Gookin nor Eliot, despite their sensitivity to what the praying Indians were made to endure, were capable of divining how their own passions biased them against those allied with Philip, who were regarded as insolent barbarians rather than members of sovereign nations with legitimate grievances. Philip's plight varied little from that of the praying Indians, but his people were labeled the aggressors in this war, even though, as John Easton points out, the English had already determined "in arms to conform Philip," prior to Philip's initial assault on Swansea in June of 1675.[103]

The peacetime containment of the praying towns gave way to the wartime internment of praying Indians on Deer Island in Boston Harbor, where many of the Natives who had allied themselves with the English spent a tragic eight months from October of 1675 to May of 1676, without provisions of food or shelter. With no more than a few hours warning, the people of Natick, "about two hundred souls of all sorts," quietly submitted as they were forced from their homes and led to boats which awaited them on the Charles River, just above the town of Cambridge. In a rarely rehearsed scene that bears an uncanny relation to the later removal of the Cherokee on boats from Ross's Landing in June of 1838, the Natives waited until midnight, with Eliot preaching to them in the interim, counseling patience and prayer, before the tide turned and the boats could carry the dazed refugees to their new island prison.[104] Many other Natives, erroneously labeled as "enemy combatants," were immediately sold into slavery in the West Indies.[105] Eliot fiercely protested this practice, exhorting the council at Boston that Christ's design was "not to extirpate nations, but to gospelize them."[106] Both he and Gookin came under continued fire, not only for advocating for their converts, but for having provided them with weapons and ammunition in the days leading up to the war so the villagers might defend themselves from unprovoked attacks.[107]

If Eliot and Gookin were complicit in the overall violence of cultural containment inflicted upon Natives of this century, they became steadfast in rejecting the physical violence that sought a final solution to Native presence in New England. Eliot, who as a young man had argued strongly in favor of the Pequot War forty years earlier, now found himself pleading to the New England Company on behalf of the Deer Island internees, writing, "ther be 350 soules or thereabout, put upon a bleake bare Iland . . . Where yet suffer hunger and could. There is neither foode nor competent fuel to be had, and yet are bare in clouthing."[108] The prisoners were told by the General Court to grow corn to feed themselves, an impossible suggestion given that by the time of their internment it was already too late in the season to plant and even under the best conditions, Deer Island was not an ideal location to grow anything. The Natives were forced to subsist upon clams which, as Gookin relates, "did occasion fluxes and other diseases."[109] They had no proper clothes for the winter months and passed this season in want and misery, many dying along the way.

For those who did not submit to the internment, life in the war-torn colony became just as treacherous. Any Native seen wandering the countryside was in danger of being considered hostile by the colonists and could be legally shot on sight.[110] The only remaining options were to surrender to the conditions of starvation and disease on Deer Island and risk being sold into slavery, or to join up with Philip's armies and attempt to drive the English off their lands and back into the sea. Such were the choices facing James Printer, who was living in Hassanamesit in 1675, fulfilling the role of "teacher" when war broke out. It remains unclear why or when Printer left the Cambridge Press, although with the deaths of Joel and Caleb, the Indian College had more or less ceased to exist and was possibly being occupied by English students instead, as had been President Chauncy's stated intention from the start.[111] Certainly, by 1674, any thoughts of educating and boarding Natives there had been abandoned. Gookin writes that "by reason of the death and failing of Indian scholars . . . it hath hitherto been principally improved for to accommodate English scholars."[112] This transformation of space would undoubtedly have made the college an unwelcoming climate for James. Whatever the reasons for his departure, James' name appears in a declaration written in the summer of 1675 assuring the Massachusetts

General Court that the undersigned were "not to assist Philip." James' sudden stature as both scribe and councilor is suggested by the prominence of his signature, alongside the Nipmuc sachem Pianboo's, on this document. This is the first time that James appears in the public record as "Wawas" or Wowaus, and he is, perhaps, surprisingly designated one of "the rulers of Hassanamesit."[113]

With the war fully started, and in the wake of provocations like the ones detailed previously, some praying Indians recognized the precarious nature of their situation and opted to flee to the French. One group of praying Indians at Wamesit, rather than "be under the harsh dealings of cruel men,"[114] left a letter for the English which clearly states their concerns and regrets. Signed by John Numphow and John Lyne who designated themselves "their rulers," the letter reads as follows:

> I, Numphow, and John a Line, we send the messenger to you again (Wecoposit) with this answer, we cannot come home again, we go towards the French, we go where Wannalansit is; the reason is, we went away from our home, we had help from the Council, but that did not do us good, but we had wrong by the English. 2ndly. The reason is we went away from the English, for when there was any harm done in Chelmsford, they laid it to us and said we did it, but we know ourselves we never did harm to the English, but we go away peaceably and quietly. 3rdly. As for the Island, we say there is no safety for us, because many English be not good, and may be they come to us and kill us, as in the other case. We are not sorry for what we leave behind, but we are sorry the English have driven us from our praying to God and from our teacher. We did begin to understand a little of praying to God. We thank humbly the Council. We remember our love to Mr. Henchman and James Richardson.[115]

When the writers initially assert "we went away from our home, we had help from the council, but that did not do us good," they seem to be referencing their initial removal from their ancestral grounds to the praying town of Wamesit. As with those who had been forced to abandon Cohannet for Natick, this original grievance had not been forgotten as they offered their chronology of reasons for abandoning colonial New England. But they also saw that they would be treated cruelly by the English if they remained in place, either by being sent to Deer Island or by being exposed to the caprices of the hostile colonists who had been their neighbors. While they were willing to note a few rare exceptions, it seemed to them that the English were "not good," and that they would have better luck throwing their lot in with the French.

Philip, in the meantime, had allied himself with the squaw-sachem of the Pocasset, Weetamoo, who had been his brother Alexander's wife (Philip was also married to Weetamoo's sister Wootonekanuske). Weetamoo further strengthened the alliances of the New England Indian Nations through her wartime marriage with Quinnapin, a sachem of the Narragansett, and nephew of Miantonomo as well as great-nephew of Canonicus. Although the Narragansett attempted to remain neutral during the war, by the winter of 1675 they were violently pulled into the conflict when the colonists preemptively launched what has been called the Swamp Fight, or more recently the Great Swamp Fort massacre. This battle was reminiscent in many ways of the Pequot massacre at Mystic some forty years earlier. As stated, the Narragansett had not yet entered the war and had never, in fact, been at war with the English. Quite the opposite, they had sided with the English during the Pequot War. Nevertheless there was a general reluctance amongst the Narragansett to swear allegiance to the English cause. First of all, the English had presided over the murder of their sachem Miantonomo in 1644. Deep resentments still lingered over this affair and Canochet, the current Narragansett sachem and son to Miantonomo, although seeking neutrality, was disinclined to be forced into an agreement with the colonists. Writing for the *Narragansett Dawn*, a newspaper written and published by the Narragansett themselves in the early half of the twentieth century, Fred B. Brown comments upon a treaty that the English forced the Narragansett to sign at the outbreak of the war. The treaty asked that the Narragansett use "all acts of hostility against [Philip and his subjects] and kill them wherever found." According to Brown, who was the Narragansett tribal historian at the time, "this treaty was made at the point of gun and sword, and made with inferior Sachems" as the more influential members of the tribe made themselves hard to find when the English began pedaling it.[116]

In fact, Canochet had gone so far as to allow the old men, women, and children of the Wampanoag to shelter with the Narragansett during the hostilities, which allowed Philip the freedom of movement that was crucial to some of his early successes in attacking English towns and eluding the English army. Brown notes that "some writers have referred to the Sachem's action as Canochet's perfidy."[117] But he also notes that "the Indian was much given to hospitality, and the treatment of a guest was a very sacred consideration." When Canochet was pressured once again by the English to bring in any Wampanoag he might have in his midst, he was said to have replied "not a Wampanoag, nor the paring of a Wampanoag'[s] nail shall be delivered up."[118] The result was the attack on the fort by the English on December 12th, on a brutally cold night, during which the bone dry fort was set to flames, killing the hundreds of men, women, and children of both Wampanoag and Narragansett descent who sheltered there. The fire not only destroyed the human lives of those within, but a great deal of the stores put aside for the winter were consumed, leaving the survivors to struggle, forage, and starve out the remainder of that winter. Brown notes that "the suffering of the [English] troops has been too often portrayed to be repeated . . . but it is only an occasional unprejudiced writer that has sought to describe the heaps of butchered and burned women and children many left to die in the wintry blast without shelter or care."[119] As a result of this ill-advised attack, the Narragansett were suddenly but irrevocably drawn into the deadly conflict, and played a large role in the subsequent sackings of Lancaster, Medfield, Sudbury, and a number of other English towns over the course of the next few months.

On the trail with the Nipmucs, James Printer, now Wowaus, would most likely have crossed paths and joined with the Narragansett. Lepore suggests that he was being held captive by his own people, but his position was more complex than that of prisoner of war and his loyalties may not have been so simply defined by his years of service to the English. James Quannapaquait, a praying Indian who served as a spy for the English during the war, would report that "these praying Indians were carried away by the enemy somewhat willingly, others of them unwillingly . . . for before they went away they were in a great strait, for if they came to the English they knew they should be sent to Deere Iland, as others were . . . And others feared they should bee sent away to Barbados and other places."[120] The threat of slavery or internment aside, the fact that many of the "praying" Natives were ready to join up "somewhat willingly" with the non-praying Natives is probably indicative of cultural loyalties that had always been in place. Quannapaquait mentioned that Printer's brother, Joseph Tukuppawillin, "would fain have come back to the English," but he does not say as much for James Printer whom he also spies amongst the Nipmuc.[121] Another account notes of Printer that he was one of the "Revolters" and "a fellow that had done much mischief."[122] Whatever Printer's situation, it was evident that his years of living with the English afforded him no protective status, and he was quick to find a new status amongst Philip's armies.

Whether by choice or lack of choice, James landed in the position of scribe to Philip during the war, fulfilling the role that had belonged to his old Indian College acquaintance, John Sassamon, before him. Although many writing Natives had been swept up in the conflict, it has been supposed that Printer was responsible for a note left on the post of a bridge for the English to read after the sacking of Medfield in 1676. The note read, "Know by this paper, that the Indians that thou hast provoked to wrath and anger, will war this twenty one years if you will; there are many Indians yet, we come 300 at this time. You must consider the Indians lost nothing but their life; you must lose your fair houses and cattle."[123] Gookin provides us a few other examples of Native messages posted during the war, and Lepore notes how these messages communicated a Native awareness of the English attachment to property and material things, and therefore emphasize the destruction of these prized items.[124] By using the communal "we," these written messages also seemed to be expressing not the sentiment of one leader, but many combined individuals—the tribe as single entity. I would add that these notes can also be viewed as an extension of the practice of leaving *awikhigans*, or records of wartime accomplishments carved upon bark or trees along pathways that others were sure to pass. *Awikhigans* were typically used in hunting expeditions to detail the location of game and a description of what exactly was killed, but they clearly proved useful in time of war as well. Printer and others, by posting such messages in prominent places after a battle were, in fact, engaging in a traditional form of communication, detailing the number of troops involved and the damage inflicted.

Printer would come to play an important role in the famous captivity and redemption of Mary Rowlandson, whose 1682 narrative became, in many ways, the landmark text of King Philip's War. As scribe to Philip, Printer would take part in the written negotiations for Rowlandson's release, composing a letter that claimed, "I am sorrow that I have done much to wrong you and yet I say the falte is lay upon you, for when we began quarrel at first with Plimouth men I did not think that you should have as much truble as now is: therefore I am willing to hear your desires about the Captives."[125] This letter, with its mixed signals of blame and regret suggested the uncertain position that the Native insurgents were in at this phase of the war. Hilary Wyss suggests that the "I" in the letter refers to James, himself, and that he is privately and covertly signaling to the colonists regret for his actions in hopes of being treated leniently.[126] But it seems more likely that the letter is meant to speak for all the sachems who had gathered at Wachusset to discuss the fate of the English hostages. Its intrusion of the pronoun "I" (where in the previous note there is only "we") seems to speak specifically for Philip, whose initial "quarrel" with the Plymouth magistrates originally led to the outbreak of hostilities. It suggests that Philip had not reckoned upon a drawn-out and bloody conflict and that he was looking for a way out of the war. But such a path would not be opened for him.

As for James Printer, with the war winding down and everywhere disarray, he "came in" to the English of his own volition sometime in the late spring or early summer of 1676, at which point he was made to swear his allegiance to the English yet again.[127] Cotton Mather would report that "James an Indian, who could not only reade, and write, but had learned the Art of Printing, notwithstanding his Apostasie, did venture upon the mercy and truth of the English Declaration which he had seen and read, promising in the future to venture his life against the common Enemy."[128] Hubbard also relates this moment, noting that

> amongst the sundry that came in was one named James the printer, the superadded Title distinguishing him from others of that Name; who being a notorious Apostate, that had learned so much of the English, as not only to read and write, but had attained likewise some Skill in Printing, and might have attained more (had he not like a false Villain ran away from his Master before his Time was out).[129]

Like every other repatriated praying Indian, James was made to swear an oath of fidelity to the English after "coming in," and was asked by the General Court to bring in "som of the enimies heads" to prove his devotion.[130] Lepore speculates on the possibility of James actually having had to perform this horrific absolution of bringing in heads as trophies, and what that might say about his allegiance to a Nipmuc identity and the tragic consequences of his having played both sides of the fence in the cultural struggles of the last fifty years. There is enough reason to believe that James was, in fact, sent back out into the field in early July, but when he returned two months later, it was with living "heads," so to speak. A letter to the "Court of Assistants" dated September 5, 1676 speaks of two brothers, William and Joseph (Quannuckhow?) being brought in "at the bequest of James the Printer" with offers of "grace" for returning.[131] James had probably brought others in as well, attempting to reassure those who were still out in the field that they might return home without risk of fatal retribution. Whether or not such assurances were kept by the colonists, James, himself, was apparently reinstated into colonial life, and almost certainly did, as Lepore suggests, set the type for Rowlandson's 1682 narrative *The Sovereignty and Goodness of God*, imprinting his own name and deeds into the colonial record.

Other Natives also vigorously lobbied for peace, relying on the talents of their writing brethren to communicate their distress. A petition probably written by Job Kattatnanit, who had served as a spy amongst the Indians for the English, nevertheless makes a request for the release of prisoners, listing three reasons "for this our humble supplication," amongst them that "the persons we beg pardon for, as we are informed, are innocent; and have not done any wrong or injury unto the English, all this war time, only were against their wills, taken and kept amongst the enemy."[132] The letter concludes by asking that, if not the release of all the prisoners "yet if you shall please to grant the women and children, it will be a favour unto us."[133] Another letter, written by one Simon Pottoquam on July 6, also pleads for the release of certain prisoners and requests of the English that

> you will consider about the making of Peace: We have spoken to the people of Nashobah (viz Tom Dublet and Peter) that we

> would agree with you and make a covenant of Peace with you. We have been destroyed by your soldiers, but still we remember it now to sit still: do you consider it again: we do earnestly entreat you, that it may be so by Jesus Christ. O let it be so: Amen Amen.[134]

Pottoquam makes his plea not only to the English officials, but to "My Lord, Mr. Waban," and asks that all Englishmen and Indians "hear Mr. Waban and Mr. Eliott" apparently in recognition that both Waban and Eliot were actively working behind the scenes to negotiate for a lenient response to the praying Indians who had been swept up in the conflict.

While the aforementioned letter is written on behalf of a number of Native figures, the letter concludes with a postscript attributed solely to the words of the Nipmuc sachem Shoshanim or Sam Sachem, who claimed:

> After we were destroyed then Philip and Quanipun went away into their own Countrey againe: and I knew they were much afraid, because of our offer to joyn with the English, and therefore they went back into their own Countrey and I know they will make no warre: therefore because when some English men came to us Philip and Quanipun sent to kill them: but I said if any kill them, I'll kill them.[135]

Although what is meant by the final statement of this communication is unclear, it does, overall, suggest that Philip sensed the war was nearing its end, and that perhaps Shoshanim was attempting to express his fidelity to the English while also begging for some leniency for Philip in the same breath. "I know they will make no warre," he tells the General Court, implying that the will to continue the conflict had gone out of all parties involved. Perhaps he intends that, should Philip contradict him and continue to make war, then Shoshanim would take matters into his own hands and have Philip killed himself. While, perhaps, this may read as a kind of betrayal, it is also a plea for a return to Native sovereignty, with Natives once again prosecuting their own internal affairs.

Dream Wampum: A Final Exchange

The fate of Philip has been recounted in many places and I will not retrace it in full detail, except to say that he was shot and killed by one of Captain Benjamin Church's Native scouts on August 12, 1676. His body was desecrated, quartered so that it could never rest whole again, and by

Church's fiat it was decided "for asmuch as he had caused many an English mans body to lye unburied and rot above ground, that not one of his bones should be buried."[136] If the bones of the Pequot were to be dunged into the earth and written out of the book of memory following that previous war, it was decreed that the outrage of Philip's rebellion should be kept in plain sight, his severed head remaining impaled upon the gates of Plymouth for the next two decades, a grisly physical reminder of full colonial dominance in the region.

Philip had made his way back home in the dwindling days of the conflict, to Mount Hope or Montaup, and it was here in the swamps near his "ancestral seat" that he was finally hunted down and killed. Many reporters have found a kind of bitter irony in the fact that Philip came home only to meet his end. As Leach writes, there seemed almost "some great compelling sense of tragic drama" that led him back to this place as it was "here he first raised the tomahawk against the hated English," and here he would die.[137] This explanation has a kind of fatalistic resonance and symmetry when narrated from the colonial archive, like something that had been plotted out or ordained, but Philip was unlikely to have been motivated by a heightened sense of either tragedy or drama. Montaup had sacred significance to Philip. It was likely pronounced Uppaquontup in Algonquian, meaning "at the high place, or, the head."[138] It stands some two hundred and fifty feet above sea level and from its summit one could survey all the local English settlements. Although we can really only speculate, there were a number of possible reasons for Philip to return here at this point in the war. It was the terrain with which he was most familiar, containing a number of large swamps and forests where he and his men could hide and forage for food and supplies. More than likely, Philip was done with war as Sam Sachem had suggested. He might have attempted to sue for peace if anyone would listen, but the climate amongst the colonists was such that there would be no peace for Philip. After failing to make alliances with the Dutch or Mohawk to the west or the French and Abenaki to the north, Philip returned to Montaup where he had maintained friendly relations in the past, not only with neighboring bands of Wampanoag, Massachusett, and Nipmuc, but with the Rhode Island settlement which, although joined with the United Colonies in the war, had been historically more sympathetic to Native concerns than any of the other colonies. He may have hoped to acquire some kind of amnesty or refuge here, or, in fact, he may have been planning to launch another offensive as some suspected, particularly on the town of Taunton, so soon as he could rest his armies and recover strength. But there may also have been simply, finally, a strong impulse to be on home turf, the high ground of his ancestors where the stories and songs of his people resided. It may be he came home because history was on his mind.

In the days before his death, Philip was holed up in the swamps on Assawomset Neck not far from the entrance to the Taunton River in the Assonet Bay. It was here that Church unexpectedly encountered Philip sitting on a stump early one morning, but failed to recognize him at first due to the fact that Philip's hair had been newly shorn. Although Church doesn't say as much, this was probably done by Philip in mourning for his uncle, Akkompoin, who had been shot and killed by Church's men the day before. Philip managed to escape before Church could get off a shot, but Church's account establishes Philip's presence in the stretch of land between Assawomset (also the location where Sassamon drowned) and Assonet Bay, the location of Dighton Rock, just days before his death (Assonet, in fact, means "place of the rock," suggesting the significance of Dighton Rock to local tradition). In the ensuing hours Church would not only capture Philip's wife and nine-year-old son, but he would also come across Quinnapin, leader of the Narragansett forces, who was apparently "drawing off from that country," and taking his people home. The coalition of Native forces was splitting and Philip had become politically and personally isolated as Church's portrait of the morning encounter seems eager to suggest.[139]

The area around Dighton was, in a sense, the bread basket of the Pokanoket domain. Not only was it a fertile region, but it was a traditional site of conferences and ceremonies. Aside from being the location of Dighton Rock, it is also near what is known as the Dighton "Council Oak," a great, hundreds-year-old oak tree, approximately six feet in diameter, used by the Wampanoag as a council site (it remains a symbol and loci of Wampanoag presence today). Given the overall significance of this region and of Dighton Rock in particular as a spiritual site for the Wampanoag, there is an altogether different kind of symmetry to Philip's being there at the end of the war that bears his name. As stated at the start of this chapter, in the legend recounted by Medicine Story (Manitonquat), the Wampanoag culture hero Weetucks had reportedly forewarned the Wampanoag that "the people of the Morning Light would be tempted to follow these new ways" of the strangers from the east, "for they would seem attractive and good. People would actually begin to learn the new ways and forsake the old ways," and this would bring about the near destruction of the Wampanoag. Philip, now faced with this very real potentiality, was seeking not only refuge, but power and guidance to move forward.

It is too simplistic to suggest that Philip had attempted to stem the tides of change that he faced in his own time. He, too, had engaged in many of the practices brought over by the colonizers, had bought and sold land, kept domestic animals (pigs), had sent envoys like John Sassamon to be schooled in English ways, and had attempted in some fashion to carry out the mission of peaceful coexistence initiated by his father. It was never *change* that threatened so much as the condition of difference imposed from without, the unwillingness of the colonists to regard their indigenous neighbors as fully human or deserving of a place on the same soil. But Philip, whatever else might be presumed of him from the shadow traces of archival memory, had tried to preserve the Wampanoag as a sovereign entity upon their own ancestral grounds, and the Dighton Rock site remains symbolic of this in some way. There obtains to it a cultural/ritual significance that probably drew him there at this particular time. As such, coming home was an act of survivance.

We might pause here to take into account the interpretation of Dighton Rock's inscription offered by the Ojibwe medicine man Chingwauk. In 1839, the nascent ethnographer Henry Rowe Schoolcraft made the relatively unusual move of submitting a drawing of the "mysterious" rock to this "Algonquian Priest" and Ojibwe political leader, who immediately claimed to recognize the symbols and, regardless of Cotton Mather's claim to the unintelligibility of such characters, did not hesitate to translate their content.[140] Characterizing it as "muz-zin-na-bik," which Schoolcraft translates simply as "rock-writing," Chingwauk offered a complex reading that is paraphrased by Schoolcraft in his account and detailed with numbers and letters designating the various features being described. Chingwauk interprets that the figures on the rock speak of two nations at war with one another. The first figure,

> represents an ancient prophet and war captain. He records his exploits and prophetic arts. The lines of plumes from his head denote his power and character. No. 2 represents his sister. She has been his assistant and confidant in some of his prophetical arts. She is also the Boon of Success in the contemplated enterprise, and she is held out, as a gift, to the first man who shall strike, or touch a dead body in battle.[141]

Schoolcraft's paraphrasing obviously reflected a number of his own cultural assumptions. Given that Chingwauk was surely not burdened by the perception that rock writing or *muz-zin-na-bik* was, as many Americans assumed by then, the forgotten art of a "lost civilization," there is no reason to believe he would have characterized the war captain as "ancient" in his reading. Nor is it likely that the "sister" was held out as a "boon of success" to the bravest warrior as in some Homeric epic. The language here is obviously Schoolcraft's own interpretation. Nevertheless, Chingwauk opens up a reading of the images on Dighton Rock that offers intriguing possibilities. While lacking in the historical particulars like names and dates so integral to Western modes of history-keeping, his reading nevertheless provides many more intimate details. He observes that

> Part *a* denotes the vapor-bath, or secret sweating lodge, marked by Crossed war-clubs. The three dots, in the center of the apartment *b*, denote three large stones used for heating water to make steam, and are supposed to be endowed with magical virtues. The sacred apartment, *c*, from which oracular responses are made, contains a consecrated pole or ballista . . . the semicircle of six dots, signifies so many moons, marking the time he devoted to perfect himself for the exploit, or actually consumed in its accomplishment. 6 is the symbol of a warrior's heart.[142]

Chingwauk also identifies the spirit animal that came to assist the war captain (the Pighoo, or northern lynx—a powerful figure in Algonquian and Haudenosaunee culture). He believes that the prophet is named for a sea bird called Mong, or the loon, and he offers details of the battles fought and the number of men who died in the confrontation. Eventually a truce was negotiated, denoted by a belt of peace, and this too is all part of the inscription.[143]

Chingwauk's reading was hardly credited in his own time, with one expert commentator asserting (in an eerie rearticulation of Mather's view) that "the Indian is no better qualified to interpret petroglyphs than the [the more civilized investigator] . . . and in many respects, indeed, is far less qualified, even though the rock pictures may have been made by his forbears."[144] The reasoning seems to be thus: even though Indians may have produced the glyphs in question, they are less qualified to interpret them than the "civilized investigator," because, by definition, they are a people without writing, laws, or history.[145] How could a people without writing be expected to interpret their own writing? But if such writings were universally understood from indigenous nation to indigenous nation, as the eighteenth-century missionary Heckewelder proposed, there is little reason to question the basic framework of Chingwauk's interpretation.

For Philip, Dighton Rock was a center of power, its spiritual significance in every way relevant to the situation he was currently facing. Chingwauk's reading describes the "sacred apartment" with its "consecrated pole" that would relate to the center pole of the longhouse, or the center of Wampanoag spirituality. The reading also speaks of the months of preparations, including sweating, purification, prayer, and strategizing that a Wampanoag chief would have engaged in prior to the war. It speaks to the existence of a peace treaty, not unlike the covenant that existed between Philip's father Massasoit and the English. And it speaks of establishing an alliance with a powerful women or "sister," just as Philip had formed an alliance with the female sachem Weetamoo, his sister-in-law and the former wife of Wamsutta. Certain markings on the rock that have often been interpreted as Roman numerals by European reporters, are more likely figures suggesting the number of warriors that died in battle, as would typically be seen on an *awikhigan*. There is little reason not to believe that the figures on the rock tell a local history rooted in indigenous traditions. The markings are similar enough to most other indigenous rock drawings, birch bark writings, or *wussuckwhommin* to place this fact well beyond doubt. Whether or not Dighton Rock constituted Philip's own history, it offers a narrative of Wampanoag identity, a framework by which Philip oriented his place in the world both geographically and epistemologically, and it bears the still-contested signature of the Wampanoag people. By coming home, Philip was recentering himself within that particular narrative and framework.

Philip made his way in the following days from Assawomset to Mount Hope, and it was there in the swamplands on the southwestern side of his "ancestral seat" that he was unceremoniously shot and killed on August 12, 1676. Church was in the habit of enlisting captured Natives into his army and it was, in a perhaps ironic historical twist, one of these men who ultimately fired the shot that killed Philip. In Church's firsthand account, Philip's captured forces are rendered as strangely compliant when it came to swearing allegiance to his cause. His report redounds with a kind of unflappable energy, as though the war's end game were all one merry pursuit and everyone he came into contact with was either won over by his charisma or richly deserving of their fatal end. It is worth keeping in mind, however, that by refusing Church's offer to join the campaign, his Native conscriptees were faced with the choices of imprisonment, slavery, or death. The Pequot minister William Apess, meditating upon these events some one hundred and sixty years later surmises that Philip's Native executioner must have either been "hired or compelled" to perform such an act. Nevertheless, he concludes, "I rejoice that it was even so, that the Pilgrims did not have the pleasure of tormenting him."[146]

Following Philip's horrific death, Captain Benjamin Church continued his prosecution of the war into the swamps of Mattaposet Neck, where he finally encountered the last of Philip's army as well as Philip's spiritual advisor and "chief Captain," Annawon.[147] There seems to be little record of Annawon outside of Church's 1716 account, and contemporary historians tend to hew fairly closely to Church's description of him. Apparently Annawon managed to keep a low profile in the colonies despite the fact that he played such a prominent role in Wampanoag affairs. Prior to his capture by Church his name appeared in the colonial archive only as witness to two land deals made by Philip in 1672.[148] Richard Slotkin, who offers the most comprehensive critical reading of Church's encounter with Annawon, describes him as a "subchief" regarded as "the true embodiment of Indian resistance to the English and the real war leader of the Wampanoag, his true stature being invisible to historians bemused by their own symbolism."[149] Church himself refers to Annawon as "a very subtle man, and of great resolution" who had often said "he would never be taken alive."[150] It was said of him that he never slept two nights in the same place and that he had been "a valiant captain under Asuhmequn [Osamequin or Massasoit] as well."[151] If Chingwauk's interpretation of Dighton Rock pointed toward the emergence of a powerful prophet or medicine man identifying himself with the loon, Annawon played just such a role in the Wampanoag community. His name may have referred to the broken, or gunshot, wing of a bird.[152] Annawon, however, has also been translated to mean "rock."[153] In all likelihood, Annawon was a *pniese*, a man of special status amongst the Wampanoag who acquired his powers through visionary gifts and belonged to a secret society well versed in both war and medicine.[154]

After Church made his surprise assault upon Annawon's secret refuge, he describes a remarkable meeting between himself and Annawon during which Philip's advisor, recognizing his defeat and the ultimate defeat of his people, handed over to Church what were described as "Philip's Royalties, which he was wont to adorn himself with when he sat in State."[155] Richard Slotkin, in his fascinating analysis of this moment, regards it as Annawon's "transfer" of his own people's power "to a proven worthy successor. The King of the Woods has died, and his slayer is crowned in his place."[156] Slotkin's romantic reconstruction of this scene properly interprets the colonial mindset, and the prevailing myth/fantasy of conquest and succession in which there is an ultimately satisfying justice to this transfer of power, a mutual recognition of a new hierarchy and order that echoes many passages in James Fenimore Cooper, not to mention James Frazier's *The Golden Bough*. But Slotkin, overly invested in untangling the myth archetypes of American culture, fails at this moment to fully differentiate between Church's own conscious self-mythologizing and the historical reliability of his offered narrative.

As Church constructs this scene for us, he had so exhausted himself following the capture of Annawon and his army that he had to lie down for a spell before bringing his captives back to Plymouth colony. And so we find Church still tucked away in Annawon's secret forest lair when he awakens some hours later to find his Indian guards, who were supposed to be keeping watch, all fallen asleep at their posts. The hostile Natives, save for Annawon, were asleep as well, and it is in this liminal zone, between sleeping and waking, with no witnesses about (and in particular no English witnesses), that Church has his mystical encounter, he and Annawon "looking one upon the other perhaps an hour" in silence. Annawon finally gets up to leave, but rather than move to stop him or alert his guards as one might suppose he would do, Church simply waits at attention until with

> the moon shining bright, he saw him [Annawon] at a distance coming with something in his hands, and coming up to Capt.

> Church, he fell upon his knees before him, and offer'd him what he had bro't, and speaking in plain English, said Great Captain, you have killed Philip, and conquered his Country, for I believe, that I & my company are the last that War against the English, so suppose the War is ended by your means; and therefore these things belong unto you.

These "royalties" consisted of

> Philip's belt curiously wrought with Wompom, being nine inches broad, wrought with black and white Wompom, in various figures and flowers, and pictures of many birds and beasts. This when hung upon Capt. Churches shoulders [Church refers to himself in the third person here] it reached his ancles. And another belt of Wompom he presented him with, wrought after the former manner, which Philip was wont to put upon his head; it had two flags on the back part which hung down on his back: and another smaller belt with a Star upon the end of it.[157]

This description is, without a doubt, the most focused examination of Native representation to appear in the English colonial record up to this point. The particulars of the Covenant Chain and the complex rituals of diplomatic negotiation that the English colonists would engage in with the Iroquois and Lenape involving the exchange of wampum belts were still well in the future. And while previous accounts had spoken of "grotesque figures" and "antic designs," they had not stooped to clarify, or dignify, such references with detailed description. And yet these were the same "royalties" that John Josselyn had spoken of in an earlier tract when he recalled "Prince Philip's . . . Buskins set thick with these Beads in pleasant wild works and a broad belt of the same."[158] Church offers something different here. Not only does he acknowledge the well "wrought" designs upon the wampum belts of birds, beasts, and flowers, but he distinguishes one from another, and ultimately refers to their function, not only as peace offering, but as historical record (for an artist's rendering of Philip's belt, refer to Paul Revere's engraving earlier in this chapter, figure 3.3). After handing over the belts, Annawon is said to have given "an account of what mighty successes he had formerly in Wars against many Nations of Indians, when he served Asuhmequin, Philip's Father."[159] Although Slotkin describes what ensues as a conversation between two kindred spirits who have earned a mutual regard for one another in time of war, Church, whether consciously or not, is recounting how Annawon read the wampum records to him, taking the entire night to recount the history of his people inscribed therein.

It remains doubtful that this encounter ever occurred as Church describes it. Even as recounted, it appears to us as a dream, a fantasy, Church's own self-indulgent reordering of events some forty years after the fact, imbuing his own participation in the deaths of Philip and Annawon with a sense of righteous closure. Church is simply rendering for his historical legacy and personal conscience what the country as a whole will soon embrace as its own literary/historical master narrative. In this narrative, the Native willingly hands over the land and all of its resources to the white man whom he has acknowledged as his better. It is the gift before departure, like Hiawatha in the poem by Longfellow, paddling away into the good night once the Blackrobes arrive to take rightful control of the land and its people.[160]

If Annawon truly did formally present the wampum records to Church, it may have been for reasons Church was incapable of fathoming. The offer may have, in fact, been a diplomatic one in which Annawon was suing for peace. Frank Speck has noted that

> wampum functions as a spiritual antiseptic . . . in transactions of a personal nature as well as in negotiations between political bodies. Going a step further we see how the Indians regarded the belts and strings of wampum which were transferred between parties entering into negotiations as the necessary pledges of sincerity of spirit and purity of purpose.[161]

The records Annawon held out would have undoubtedly contained mention of all the treaties between the English and the Wampanoag, dating back to Massasoit. The information they offered was one of repeated wrongdoings and violations on the part of the English. Annawon, in this desperate moment, was either holding these facts out to be audited by Church and the other Wampanoag who accompanied him, or he was offering one last reading of Wampanoag history and belief in an oration that demonstrated sincerity of spirit and purity of purpose in a recital that, according to Church, lasted "the remainder of the night."[162] Then again, maybe Church simply confiscated these materials from Annawon, but had been well enough acquainted with Native diplomacy and ritual that he was able to fabricate this final encounter in his later years as he looked back on his war experiences and attempted to render them into an enjoyable romanticized story for family and friends. It is precisely because the scene is a dream, unwitnessed by the other English soldiers and the Natives about him who were all sleeping, that Church can offer this encounter in any detail at all. Whatever the truth about how the wampum changed hands, the war was now officially over and Annawon's gesture of reconciliation went unheeded. Although Church seems to have made some motions to have Annawon's life spared by the General Council, Annawon was promptly tried, executed, and beheaded roughly a week after his capture, his head placed upon a stake alongside Philip's at the gates of Plymouth.

Philip's "royalties" were apparently handed over by Church to Josiah Winslow, then governor of Plymouth Colony, who in turn shipped them to England as a gift to King Charles II. In a letter written by Church on September 10, 1676, he notes he had received from Annawon

> a bundle of deerskin containing the symbols of office of Annawon's predecessor, King Philip. Included were a broad wampum belt containing a pictoral history of the Wampanoag Tribe and a smaller trimmed with red hair (obtained from the Nipmuc Country) with a design depicting the "Totem of the Wolf," the emblem of the Federation, two glazed powder horns, and a red blanket.

Furthermore, in a letter dated June 26, 1677, Winslow writes to King Charles that he

> craves His Majesty's acceptance of these few Indian rarities, being the best of our spoils and the best of the ornaments and treasures of the Sachem Philip, the grand rebel; a belt of wampum nine inches (width) wrought with black and white wampum in figures and flowers, and pictures of many birds and beasts; (This, when hung upon Captain Church's shoulder, it reached the ankles).[163]

Note how closely Winslow's language in 1677 mirrors the language Church used in his 1716 account. It is nearly a verbatim reproduction, suggesting that Church must have had a copy of Winslow's letter to the king by which to recall these events when he later penned them. Therefore, at least part of the description of Philip's "royalties" was Winslow's and not Church's. The letter also parenthetically demonstrates that Church was in the habit of donning the wampum belt ("this, when hung upon Captain Church's shoulder, it reached the ankles"), suggestive of his own sense at least that this legacy of Wampanoag history had been bequeathed him personally. Perhaps knowing that these rarities were being passed on to English royalty simply inspired Church to inflate his own role in the proceedings. Whatever the case, the wampum belts, a most valuable testament to Wampanoag history and culture, seem never to have made it to England or were lost once they got there. Their trail ends, for the time being at least, with Winslow's 1677 letter.[164]

There is a final interpretation of the inscription on Dighton Rock that is worth mentioning. William Simmons relates this story in which a number of white men appeared in the Assonet Bay in a great white bird, "probably a European ship," and after a struggle during which "thunder and lightning issued from the bird," it carried off Wampanoag children in its talons.[165] The legacy of colonists taking Natives as slaves was established from the earliest moments of contact. But the project flourished in the wake of King Philip's War, sweeping up hundreds of traditional and Christian Natives in its grasp, including, as mentioned earlier, Philip's own wife and son. Of those who weren't executed or enslaved, many, particularly children, were sold into bondage in New England, effectively removing them from their kinship networks and the traditional practices of their people. Nipmuc historian Thomas Doughton, in his *Notes on the Nipmuc Reservation at Hassanamesit*, traces the fate of some seventy indigenous children indentured to English families after the war, whose parents had been killed in battle, executed, sold into slavery, or imprisoned. Like the child survivors of the Pequot War, New England's "First Fruits," these children were to be "religiously educated & taught to read the English tongue." Doughton writes, "we know from native informants that life as a servant in white households was often bleak."[166] But perhaps not as bleak as the fate of Native slaves sent to labor out the remainder of their days on sugar plantations in the West Indies.

Native land also went up for grabs following the war. John Wampas, who had been trained to read and write at Harvard, took advantage of the opportunistic atmosphere and sold off great tracts of Nipmuc land to eager white buyers. Gookin intervened to try to repair these wrongs, but it was difficult to get the English courts to backpedal on what had already been deeded. In 1681, while James Printer was laying the type for Mary Rowlandson's captivity narrative for the Cambridge Press, Nipmuc land was officially divided into three sections which were then to be purchased from the Nipmuc who it could be agreed held a legitimate title to those parcels. Retaining this land for themselves was not an option, although a small tract was set aside for their continued use at Hassanamesit.

Printer's name, "James Printer, also Wowaus," can be found undersigned to a number of these transactions relating to the "nipmugs" or Nipmucs in the years directly following King Philip's War.[167] The presence of his signature should not suggest that he was eager to give up these lands for his own gain, any more than Philip or Massasoit had been. The General Court had removed the possibility of Natives orchestrating their own land transactions in order "to prevent further troubles & pretensions that may arise."[168] Nevertheless, Printer or Wowaus seems to have risen to a position of standing amongst his people and was reportedly still serving in the role of teacher at Hassanamesit when he died in 1717.[169] The Nipmuc had been relieved from their "confinement at Natick" in 1698, and James was able to finally return to his traditional home with five other Nipmuc families. His proficiency in English allowed that this remaining bit of Nipmuc land would pass along to his sons Moses and Ami, who in turn were able to read and write and ensure that the Nipmuc would not be entirely divested of their lands. Moses and Ami appear to have been instrumental in arranging a treaty for the setting aside of 7,600 acres equally divided amongst the Nipmuc families residing at Grafton/Hassanamesit in 1728. While the treaty also, once again, ceded a great deal of land to the English, it made provisions for the construction of a schoolhouse and mandated that a school teacher be appointed to instruct both the Indian and English children "without cost or charge to the said Indians." According to the treaty these lands were to remain in the possession of the Nipmuc "forever."[170] As testament to this one can find today the sign on the Grafton Hassanamesit Reservation testifying "These four and one-half acres have never belonged to the white man, having been set aside in 1728 as an Indian Reservation by the forty proprietors who purchased the praying Town of Hassanamesit." If writing was a hazard to the Natives of King Philip's time, it also remained a tool of cultural and historical preservation.

In *The Name of War*, Jill Lepore wonders how it is that, of all the praying Indians who had acquired literacy and were capable of writing independently, not one left an account of the war, a history as seen from the Native perspective. In response to her own question, she speculates that the consequences of literacy for Native Americans in seventeenth-century New England were deadly, and she draws upon the life of John Sassamon as a case study. Certainly there were hazards for those who found themselves in the liminal space between colonial and Native culture. The question still lingers, however. African Americans, enslaved for generations, and systematically distanced from kinship and community networks, were often able to acquire literary efficiency (and even eloquence) within a system that strictly forbade it, and many slaves lived to write, despite their lack of formal training in letters, involved narratives of their lives and the vicious institution within which they had been reared. Perhaps the reason that Native Americans saw little need for this in the seventeenth century is because they still retained their own historical and cultural traditions within their own communities. Wampum, petroglyphs, and other forms of Native writing remained useful mediums for recording Native histories. They did not seek to disseminate such histories amongst the wider "white" community, and even if they had, the colonial community was incapable of hearing them or seeing them. Unlike the nineteenth century that saw the publication of hundreds of slave narratives from black writers who had educated themselves and relished the opportunity to tell their stories to a reading public, there was no political faction amongst the seventeenth-century colonists willing or desirous to hear the Native version of these events. Certainly Native accounts of King Philip's War were told and retold in Native space long after the war was over. But the publishing outlets for a Native account of the war were nonexistent. James Printer had his hand closest to the machinery that might offer up such an account, but he was forced to manufacture Rowlandson's account instead, and presumably many others that generally characterized the Christian Indians who had been caught up in this war as "wicked and cruel."[171]

Though the printer Samuel Green died in 1692, James was still working the Cambridge Press in 1709 when he was asked by the New England Company to produce a new translation of the Psalms. Samuel Sewall, the new superintendent of Indian affairs to the colonies, would write, "James Printer is chiefly taken up in Printing and gains a youthfull cheeriness in your service."[172] In an unprecedented move, Printer's name would finally appear on the frontispiece of this edition of psalms, next to the name of Bartholomew Green, son of Samuel Green, in acknowledgment of the central role he played, over a fifty-year period, in the establishing and maintenance of a press in the colonies (see figure 3.7).

Maſſachuſee PSALTER:
ASUH,
Uk-kuttoohomaongaſh
DAVID
Weche
WUNNAUNCHEMOOKAONK
Ne anſukhogup JOHN,
Ut *Indiane* kah *Engliſhe* Nepatuhquonkaſh.
Ne woh ſogkompagunukhettit Kakokerahteaekuppannegk, aketamunnat, kah wohwohtamunat Wunnetuppantamwe Wuſſukwhongaſh.

John v. 39.
Natinneakontamook Wuſſukwhonkanaſh, newutche ut yeuſh kuttunnantamumwoo kuttahtomwoo micheme pomantammooonk; kah niſh naſhog wauwaonukqueniſh.

BOSTON, N. E.
Upprinthomunneau *B. Green*, kah *J. Printer*, wutche quhtiantamwe CHAPANUKKEG wutche onchekehtouunnat wunnaunchummookaonk ut *New-England*, &c. 1709.

THE
Maſſachuſet PSALTER:
OR,
PSALMS of DAVID
With the
GOSPEL
According to JOHN,
In Columns of *Indian* and *Engliſh*.
BEING
An Introduction for Training up the Aboriginal Natives, in Reading and Underſtanding the HOLY SCRIPTURES.

John v. 39.
Search the Scriptures, for in them ye think ye have eternal Life, and they are they which teſtifie of Me.

BOSTON, N. E.
Printed by *B. Green*, and *J. Printer*, for the Honourable COMPANY for the Propagation of the Goſpel in *New-England*, &c.
1709.

Figure 3.7. Frontispiece to 1709 *Massachusetts Psalter*, printed by B. Green and J. Printer. Courtesy of American Antiquarian Society.

4

Beneath the Wave

The Maintenance of Native Tradition in Hidden Transcripts (1709–1768)

And here town records, old tattered, time-worn, weather-stained chronicles, contain the Indian sachem's mark perchance, an arrow or a beaver, and the few fatal words by which he deeded his hunting grounds away.

—Henry David Thoreau, A *Week on the Concord and Merrimack Rivers*

This is my book, and I own this forever.

—Annotation by Nannahdinnoo written beneath the book of Revelation in one of the original Eliot Bibles

Leave me not to Practice the Works of these People.

—Samson Occom, *Collected Writings*

Diving into the Wreck: Locating the Hidden Transcripts of Resistance in Native Writings of the Eighteenth Century

In her history of the Mohegan Nation, *The Lasting of the Mohegans*, Melissa Jayne Fawcett recounts a story told her by Bill Wakole, an elder of the Sac and Fox Nation. In this story Wakole relates how

> when the Europeans first came to the eastern shores, it was as if a giant tidal wave had hit the Native people and knocked them all flat. As the wave made its way west, the devastation was not as great; for, the wave was not as strong. As the waters subsided, there were no obvious signs of life along the eastern shore, so it was assumed that all the creatures who had lived there, before

> the wave came, were dead and gone. But after a while, tiny bubbles were seen on the surface of these eastern waters, and it was realized that the creatures of the eastern shore had not died at all. They had simply learned to live underwater. These creatures—amongst whom were the Mohegans—are now rising to the surface. They are wise creatures, for they have learned to live well within the wave that now surrounds them. Their experience beneath the wave has made them strong, and they are destined to grow and prosper.[1]

As with the earth-diver myth related in chapter 1, this narrative offers a metaphorical explanation of how culture and tradition maintain themselves in the face of calamity. The arrival of Europeans, the phenomenon often referred to as "contact" that brought with it war and disease in untold measure, is likened to a tidal force that seems to obliterate everything in its path. But in Wakole's story Native culture itself becomes the earth-diver, remaining submerged just long enough to ride out the initial force of the wave, only to restore itself again in the surface world once the flood has subsided. This is not only a story of survival, but one of continuance, for if indigenous traditions appear vanquished in this underwater time, it is only that they have fallen out of sight for a while, they have sheltered somewhere beneath the frothing white wave of European hegemony until able to breach into sunlight once more, stronger, wiser, rekindled. It is a story of continuance for it frames itself within the existing narrative / myth structure of Algonquian culture. It recalls narratives central to indigenous literary traditions and places them in the service of regeneration in contemporary times. The telling of the story is part of a process that reenergizes life in the present. The retelling of the story in different forms and settings, I believe, helps to affirm and perpetuate that regeneration through survivance.

Certainly Natives persevered and survived in the era following contact, but as detailed in previous chapters, Eastern indigenous culture was often constrained to take on new forms, to reorganize itself in unfamiliar ways, and to present a face to the outside world that might appease the aggressive expectations of an ever-expanding European population base. With indigenous culture rendered virtually invisible to the colonist in the wake of King Philip's War, the political assertion was facilitated that "all the creatures who had lived there, before the wave came, were dead and gone." The process was one of elaborate and violent *unwitnessing* with the dominant culture systematically denying the continued existence of that which threatened the fabric of its own emerging national narrative. The construction of the colonial archive with its inherent ability to maintain such illusions, to suppress what it could not bear to incorporate in its self-inscribing, and to contain that which must not insinuate itself into official memory, reinforced the ideology that indigenous civilization was vanishing, had vanished, was, in fact, never a quantifiable entity to begin with.

Wakole's story brings back into focus the illusory nature of this assertion. While Native culture may have been forced in many ways to assume the role of its own demise, still it maintained itself in its submerged state until such a time when "it was realized that the creatures of the eastern shore had not died at all." As with many indigenous narratives, this tale does not draw a marked distinction between the human and animal worlds. "All the creatures" of the Eastern seaboard are taken into account in the telling, as they are equally threatened by the enveloping wave, equally engaged in the subsequent act of renewal. Even European culture, for which the wave is both simile and metaphor, remains a passive presence in the story once having fulfilled its violent and inchoate task. Though it is the fact of European presence that catalyzes the violence, the colonial perspective becomes folded into the larger perspective of the storyteller so that the all-consuming European gaze is effectively averted. There is no determinate voice to notice how "there were no obvious signs of life" in the wake of the flood, or how "it was assumed that all the creatures who had lived there . . . were dead and gone." These are not colonial or imperial eyes that do the seeing. The narrative stands outside the gaze of identifiable human agency, achieving a tone that is at once nonjudgmental, all inclusive, and yet extremely cognizant of the political exigencies it invokes. It affirms, in some sense, Craig Womack's notion that oral tradition (understanding this to be an oral narrative that Fawcett has paraphrased for us in writing) "has always contained within it the level of political critique."[2] Or, to further quote Womack, "from the Indian worldview, the song contains the medicine that sets the cure into motion."[3]

On the surface level, or from the perspective of the keepers of the archive, there is no cohesive narrative explaining how Native culture in New England maintained itself through the colonial invasion until present times. As stated in the colonial records for October 25, 1676, "there now scarce remaynes a name or family of them in their former habitations but are either slayne, captivated [sold into slavery], or fled into remote parts of the wilderness, or lye hid, dispayring their first intentions against us."[4] Native identity, in terms of political and national continuity, simply ceased to be. This perspective has had significant implications for indigenous nations attempting to reestablish themselves within the hegemonic containment of contemporary tribal recognition. But Wakole's explanation begins to elaborate how continuity "lyes hid," lies beyond the purview of the archive or creates of itself a "hidden transcript." As he observes of the Eastern seaboard nations, "they had simply learned to live underwater."

That Eastern Algonquian culture now makes its impressions above water, on dry earth once more, might be confirmed by the presence of Native studies programs in universities across the country, the calls from Native scholars to locate and study the intellectual traditions of their nations (and of American Indians in general), in the continuing revival of indigenous languages, the maintenance of reservation schools that work from within the parameters of tribal tradition, or in the economic revival that has taken place amongst the Mohegan, Pequot, and many other nations, in large part assisted by the opening of casinos on their lands. But these are still tentative steps, often, if not always, essayed on contested ground. As Fawcett writes, "today, Mohegans walk along the eastern shores mindful of the time they spent below the surface of the Great Wave." Fawcett herself, as tribal historian for the Mohegan, is mindful of the fact that while Natives remained an actual presence on the land throughout this "wave-time," the stories preserved in the "voices of grandmothers and grandfathers" that make up the oral tradition of all nations were passed along as "whispering lessons," barely audible in their submerged state.[5]

Like the oral traditions that spent time under the wave, noticeable only when "tiny bubbles were seen on the surface of the eastern waters," the written testimonies, the inscribed transactions of Natives who put pen to paper for deliberate reasons in previous centuries, might be considered part of what Fawcett calls the "chain of duty and remembrance that links contemporary Mohegans to their ancient past."[6] If there is a difficulty in engaging with these texts, or fully recognizing them as part of a Native tradition of survival and resistance, it is a difficulty that comes from our having encountered them from so firmly within the colonial containments through which they have surfaced. In some ways these texts are like the bubbles mentioned earlier—isolated expulsions of oxygen indicative of a greater, richer life still residing unseen beneath the wave. But the more scholars engage with these texts and relocate them within a tradition of Native continuity, the more the texts in question begin to resist the parameters of their former containments. As Robert Warrior notes,

> although we may have no immediately accessible tradition that informs us how to confront present challenges, we do have many examples of Native writers and scholars who have confronted similar situations. When we take that tradition seriously, I will argue, we empower our work . . . we are doing something that Natives have done for hundreds of years.[7]

Warrior observes that "Native written intellectual tradition reaches back at least to Samson Occom's missionary writings in the 1700s" and, as

I hope I have demonstrated, perhaps even earlier. Warrior is not suggesting that anyone should become slavishly dependent upon such traditions from wherever they emerge, but that components of a tradition be recognized, based on "what humans have created and how they created it."[8] For, in fact, this is all tradition is, regardless of its implications to identity and culture: a human construction delineating a path through life founded in practice, belief, and ritual, considered by many to be good. Alphabetic literacy became a part of Native American tradition in seventeenth-century America and, in fact, was a vital tool in the act of withstanding an epoch of violence and loss brought on by the colonial encounter.

In this chapter I will look at a number of eighteenth-century texts that, while appearing as components of the "public transcript," speak, in part, to what anthropologist James C. Scott refers to as the "hidden transcript of resistance" and continuance in Native New England. As Natives make their first autonomous entries into the Western archive, they are consciously molding their message to conform to the discourse of the colonizer. But I will argue that such forms are deployed to serve the agenda of a hidden transcript that allows for Native culture to survive in this time beneath the wave of colonization. I do not argue that the texts appearing in the archive are deliberately masked or attempt to misrepresent a point of view. I do argue, however, that for these texts to appear at all in the public record they must be constructed in a certain manner, hyper-aware of the particular discursive avenues of expression that are available within the dominant culture. Native writers in the eighteenth century had to perform within the theater of dominance while still keeping in mind cultural objectives, which are apprehended by the hidden transcript and necessitate the need for the public appearance in the first place. I will begin by looking at early land transactions written in the Massachusett language and translated by Kathleen Bragdon and Ives Goddard. These writings afford us a glimpse into the internal workings of Native communities at Natick and on Martha's Vineyard, as well as a few other Native strongholds in colonial New England. The chapter concludes with an examination of the writings of Samson Occom, focusing mainly on his prepublication writings, and in particular his 1768 a "Short Narrative of My Life." Occom emerges in America's revolutionary period as a Christian leader of the Mohegan and a figure fully capable of negotiating the textual exchanges between colonizers and Natives. Within the textual productions of these Native spaces, I will be looking especially for the discursive practices that allow these Native writers to appear in the public transcript while working to perpetuate the hidden transcript of indigenous tradition and political action. Two private inscriptions, written in the Massachusett dialect and found within the margins of two separate Eliot Bibles, speak most poignantly to this phenomenon. The first reads, "it is a storm but we

Indians still survive well on this morning." The other reads, "Know ye all people, there is going to be a new storm."[9]

"This Indian Land": Writings in the Massachusett Language and Sustaining Native Space

By many accounts, Native literacy, alongside Native resistance in New England, melted away in the wake of King Philip's War "like snow in the springtime."[10] King Philip's War seems to serve as one of those interesting historical markers beyond which the dominant culture attempts to erase any further suggestion of continued Native presence. It simplified the task of historians over the first two hundred years of this country's existence to allow this formulation to stand, although in her book *Dispossession by Degrees*, Jean O'Brien adeptly demonstrates how Natives didn't simply fall off the face of the earth following the war, but were, in fact, gradually squeezed out of their landholdings and economically and socially marginalized through legal (and extralegal) maneuvers over the period of a century. O'Brien notes that "by the end of the eighteenth century neither the English minister nor the English town clerk took care to record the beginnings and ends of Indian lives."[11] Property transactions in Natick, however, in which Natives were systematically divested of their lands, were well documented in the decades after King Philip's War. According to O'Brien, these records themselves comprise a discursive construct that could only "reproduce the extinction narrative that has dominated the traditional account" of Natives in New England.[12] But her research also uncovers the even more complicated machinations of unwitnessing in which Native presence must be acknowledged before it can be stricken. With one colonial hand the existence of Natives in New England was being erased through the absence of birth records and death certificates, while the other greedily acknowledged the actual presence of Natives through the contractual disenfranchisement of Native capital. Native presence lies at the center of a traumatic knowledge that is at once seen and unseen.

The reality was, of course, that Natives had not disappeared from the New England landscape at all. The mortality rate for Natives during the war had, in fact, been devastating, estimated by historians to be as high as 40 percent of the population. As James Drake astutely points out, one reason the percentage of Native deaths was so high was not a simple result of English military superiority, but rather because Natives had fought on either side of the conflict.[13] Many Natives did flee the containment of colonial control in New England following the war and a significant number were also sold into slavery. As for the rest, they were either forced into indentured servitude or corralled into a few small enclaves or plantations to be kept under colonial surveillance.[14] Harold W. Van Lonkhuyzen notes, in his 1999 essay on the reappraisal of the praying village, that "the continuing processes of internal and external change in the post-war period rapidly dissolved the social organization underpinning Indian identity." In Van Lonkhuyzen's estimation, Natives brought irreversible changes upon themselves by craving European goods and buying into the "praying cult" that European missionaries offered as a strategic escape from the traditional domination of sachems. Natives were "undone in their desire to interact with the English while maintaining their traditional social structure and goals."[15]

Another way of reading indigenous presence in Natick in this period, however, is to recognize the town as a center of Native influence within a colonial containment, that far from dissolving or assimilating itself into irrelevance, achieved a level of brief autonomy following King Philip's War. With the passing of John Eliot in 1690 there was no one person committed to performing the kind of outreach at Natick that insured a continuation of European-style worship. Kathleen Bragdon and Ives Goddard report that church membership fell in this time to only seven men and three women, more or less confirming just how "lightly" Natick converts had worn their Christianity.[16] Nevertheless the town remained under Native leadership until the 1720s, with Thomas Waban maintaining a central role in the government and keeping town records in the Massachusett language. Might these records, as translated by Bragdon and Goddard in their compilation *Native Writings in Massachusett*, also be considered a hidden transcript—for who, indeed, could read this archive outside the community itself, save for a small and already dwindling number of missionaries who had schooled themselves in the language? The records Thomas Waban kept detail a regularity of affairs in the daily life of the village—outside the realm of Anglo oversight—that defies the historical perception of Native community and culture as melting into the water table in a single season.[17]

A few sources have made much of an apocryphal story in which Waban, the elder, boasting of how he handled drunk and quarrelsome Indians, claimed he would "tie 'um all up, and whip um plaintiff, and whip um fendant, and whip um witness."[18] In this account Waban is made the agent of colonial wish fulfillment: first, by removing the violence necessary to enforce dominant codes out of the colonial sphere and meting out punishment to deserving Indians himself; second, by being too ignorant to understand basic principles of justice; and third, by affirming that *all* Indians must be guilty of something and therefore ought to be treated as such regardless of their designation in the legal process. Upon reading the actual translated town records of Natick, however, one finds that the most severe judgments meted out concern a five-shilling penalty levied on the town representatives themselves for failing to appear at an appointed meeting, and six shillings awarded to one Moshontanum for an apparently false accusation made against her.[19] There is no mention of any other punishments, corporal or otherwise, and one suspects the practice of whipping drunken Indians was more in keeping with Puritan notions of retribution and rehabilitation than anything Waban relished enforcing.

Of course the Natick Indians were unable to retain complete legal autonomy and many of their affairs were presided over by the colonial courts. Most of these cases involved accusations of theft and drunken disorderliness. A deposition filed by the citizens of Dedham in 1680 asserted that the Natick Indians "rob us of our corn and other provisions out of our fields; that cattle in the woods have been torn by their dogs . . . and in their drunken fits [they] have affrighted some women."[20] Such accusations, vague and difficult to prove, demonstrate the level of distrust toward the Indian that had been fanned into open hatred during the war and persisted into the next century and beyond. One wonders, for instance, how exactly it was that the Natick Natives went about "affrighting" white women. Were actual acts of hostility involved or was it simply by their presence and proximity? On top of these accusations, it was claimed by the colonial residents of Dedham that the Natick Indians were "proud and surly," refusing "to take notice of an Englishman if they meet him in the street."[21] If these complaints were subjective in nature and difficult to verify, they nevertheless helped to undermine Native jurisdiction by insinuating that the Natives "cannot govern or have any command" over their own people.[22]

The external colonial documents concerning Natick may suggest discord and relative anarchy within this Native space, but the internal proceedings of the town seem to have occurred without rancor. The Natick documents written in the Algonquian language mostly concern the results of town elections and the parceling out of land to Native citizens, alongside various other land transactions. An allotment that appears to have been granted by the town in 1720 affords a glimpse into the tenor of these proceedings. It reads,

> Then the proprietors jointly and willingly released one piece of land (it lies at the south side of this house and this river) to the one named Muttassonshq or Susannoh, the wife of Josiah Ephriam. And that land lies between the boundary of Samuel Commacho and the northwestern corner where the fort used to be, and from that straight towards the northwest to the boundary further on, the boundary of Andrew Ephriam, and between that: that land towards the north up to the river, about 20 acres or perhaps less. And this has been lovingly given to Muttassonshq. She has that property forever. By Thomas Waban, Town Clerk here.[23]

Despite the more or less official and pragmatic tone of this document, it allows us to make some tentative observations into the life of the town in this period of partial autonomy. For instance, it tells us that women were allowed to possess land in their own name in Natick. While English law allowed women to own land only under special circumstances, such as when a husband passed away with no son to assume the title, the aforementioned document suggests that Muttassonshq's husband is still alive and that she will, nevertheless, have sole title to the land in question.[24] We might also notice that no currency appears to exchange hands in the offering. The "proprietors," who we may believe are the town authorities, collectively "release" the land to Muttassonshq, suggesting something of a hybrid articulation of collective and private ownership. In fact, of the fifty-one documents dealing with land transactions that Bragdon and Goddard translated from the Natick town records, only one mentions a monetary exchange, and this seems to occur outside the realm of the town's authority as Waban records how a certain stretch of land was allotted to one John Thomas, "but he sold that for three pounds."[25] We also learn from the aforementioned document that, although the woman who is allotted her own tract of land has a baptized name, "Susannoh," she is clearly known by her Native name of Muttassonshq. "Susannoh" seems to appear as an afterthought, in recognition of the official nature of the document and an acknowledgment of the external authority for which such documents are ostensibly kept.

And finally we notice that the parcel of land is given to Muttassonshq "lovingly," and that she is bequeathed that property "forever." The adverb "lovingly" is not found in any of the other recorded allotments, but it allows us to imagine, at least, a sense of community and warmth in these transactions that bespeaks a relative period of peace and security. The word *micheme* or "forever," which appears in a great many of the Native documents, assumes that the land will remain in the hands of its original owners for perpetuity despite the hard lessons of the last one hundred years spent as neighbors with the acquisitive-minded English.

That such claims to perpetuity were bound to come under threat might be apprehended, however, in a 1715 decree stating "now no one (shall) sell any more wood to the English from this time. If anyone henceforth contrarily does that, he sells trees to the English, he shall pay twenty shillings for one tree. This was done. By Thomas Waban Town Clerk here. This is a law." The decree is undersigned by Samuel Abraham, Josiah Speene, and John Wamsquon. We do not know the exact circumstances that would require such a law to be passed, but we can readily imagine that a process is being set in motion in which unfair dealings with the English led to disputes that often resulted in Natives losing land and rights in English courts. Daniel Gookin's son, also named Daniel, who took over some of the preaching duties once both his father and John Eliot had passed away, came to operate the sawmill at Natick in the 1690s. He seems not to have been valued by the indigenous community in the same manner that his predecessors were, however, and in a 1695 deposition he was accused by the Natick residents of encroaching beyond his allotted lands. Nevertheless, by 1696 Gookin Jr. had acquired some 1,700 acres of Natick real estate.[26] The injunction against selling wood to the English was more than likely an attempt to curtail the plundering of Native resources by acquisitive-minded colonists like Gookin Jr. As always, the best way to avoid such circumstances was to avoid the lure of commerce with the colonists altogether.

A final point about the Natick town records as compiled by Thomas Waban is that nowhere is there a mention of God. The topic simply does not arise despite the fact that the matter of religious belief was central to nearly every document produced by Native peoples prior to these writings. If the Massachusett and other Native groups who found themselves in Natick in the late seventeenth and eighteenth centuries had indeed constructed "a new cosmos," as Van Lonkhuyzen suggests, it was a cosmos less affected by Christian ritual than by the pressures of maintaining culture within a colonial containment. Native ritual, belief, and practice were not bound to remain static throughout this period, any more than European practice and belief remained static. The struggle for survival imposes its own norms on one and all, and the world made *new* by European presence imposed new normative values on European and Indian alike. But the achievement of yet one more generation of cultural unity and relative peace was no small thing, in this or any other time, and in Natick, at least, there seems to have been a forty- to fifty-year period in which the Massachusett, alongside other Native individuals who resided there, carved out a quiet path of survivance.

The documents translated in Goddard and Bragdon attest to the thread of Native proficiency in alphabetic literacy that continued from the seventeenth into the eighteenth century and how it began to achieve a certain autonomy from the immediate concerns of the colonists. Their compilation of records suggests that, to a significant extent, written documents had come to stand alongside verbal agreements for Natives, not just in Natick, but throughout New England.[27] The authors estimate that, by 1698, 30 percent of Natives living in praying towns had acquired some form of literacy, and that this was comparable to the number of English settlers who could read at the time. This may or may not be true. In 1714 Samuel Sewall put this question to the test on a visit to Martha's Vineyard, enquiring, "if any could read English." He records that "at last only two young men were produced. I set him to read in my Psalm-book with red Covers, and then gave it him. Promised a Testament to the 2nd."[28] Of course there may have been compelling reasons for individuals to keep such knowledge to themselves. Nevertheless, literacy for the Natives of this period was most likely of a "restricted" type, consisting of the ability to read, not necessarily accompanied with the ability to write, and was limited to the "Massachusett" language, a dialect of Algonquian, which naturally meant there were few actual texts available for consumption.[29] By the 1720s the argument for publishing texts in the Native dialect that Eliot had hammered into being had few remaining adherents.[30] But the surviving documents in the Massachusett language from this period, while mostly of a pragmatic nature, suggest that Native peoples who had acquired literacy still found occasion to use this skill in Native space. These writings offer a glimpse into the syncretic usage of oral and literate traditions, what Bernd Peyer refers to as "orature," that continued with the "Massachusett" or Algonquian-speaking Natives who, by the end of the seventeenth century, were producing written documents in their own language to record land dealings, not only with the colonists, but amongst themselves.[31]

In one such document we have the landholder voicing the words "I do not sell this land, but I bequeath this Island Mashinneah, entirely, everything (of) land, all trees, and all grass and everything that is there; I bequeath it all to my four children." The speaker goes on to emphasize once more, "my bequest is not sold, this island forever, as long as the earth exists, but only they use it, these four children of mine, and in all their posterity forever and ever as long as they have descendants. This is my true declaration."[32] There is an insistent idea expressed within this document that the title to the land is hereditary and that the land remain in the hands of those who have traditionally held it. The speech act being recorded seems intent upon denying the concept that the land is being sold—a strictly European notion. Instead it stresses a sense of continuance, a prerogative of usage that has always been and always should be. The transaction has both the sense of an oration and a dynamic engagement with the present. "I do this," the speaker is quoted as saying, "I Quateattashshit."[33] With his words he is making it so. Many of the documents that Bragdon and Goddard translated are invested with a similar quality of spoken exchange and the insistence that these agreements, whether understood to be written or not (as some, at least, were written after the fact), would be binding *micheme micheme*, "forever and ever."

Another interesting document written in the Massachusett language was a 1752 petition by the Mashpee to their self-proclaimed overseers in Boston. Though the document is written out, it is clearly transcribed from a speech rather than composed in the act of writing, and in keeping with the tradition of treaty oration, there is frequent repetition, with the communal "we" employed throughout. What results is, perhaps, an event unique to the North American continent of the eighteenth century: a Native oration that has no attendant audience. The document earnestly beseeches its Boston overseers to hear its plea, crying "Oh! Oh!, gentlemen, hear us now, Oh! ye, us poor Indians . . . Oh! Hear our weeping, and hear our beseeching you, Oh!" The cadence, which might sound peculiar to us and certainly strange to the conventions of alphabetic literacy, strikes one as doubtless in keeping with traditional oratorical practices, despite its having been transcribed, and despite the insertion of certain obsequious rituals of English-Indian relations (for example, the speaker refers to himself and his people as us "poor Indians," a popular expression amongst the English when assuming Christian responsibility for Native welfare). What the document establishes is a right of tribal ownership, regardless of the fact that a few members of the Mashpee community had acted as sole agents in selling the land out from under the rest. It reads,

> what they conveyed to you was this piece of land. This was conveyed to us by Indian sachems. Our former Indian sachems were called Sachem Wuttammohkin and Sachem Quettatsett, in Barnstable County, the Mashpee Indian place. This Indian land, this was conveyed to us by these former sachems of ours. We shall not give it away, nor shall it be sold, nor shall it be lent, but we shall always use it as long as we live, we together with all our children, and our children's children, and our descendants, and together with all their descendants.[34]

Although the Mashpee had acquired the tools of literacy and now attempted to gain political leverage through its application, they refer back to traditional oral arrangements as legal precedent, "that unwritten tenure of nomadic tribal authority," as indeed this is their only recourse.[35] They insist upon the legitimacy of a tribal understanding of land occupancy, reaffirming that they shall use the land forever "unless we all peacefully agree to give it away or sell it. But as of now not one of all of us Indians has yet agreed to give away, or sell, or lend this Indian land, or marsh, or wood. Fairly, then, it is this: we state frankly we have never conveyed them away."[36]

The apparently "traditional" understanding conveyed in this document might easily lead us to forget that these, too, are so-called praying Indians, who had presumably turned away from communal land ownership in favor of individual lots that the owners might do with as they pleased. What is repeatedly reaffirmed, however, is that the individuals who sold property to the English had no right to do so under Native custom. Any decision to sell land—*this Indian land*, consisting not only of farmed lots, but of marsh and wood—needed to be made collectively, and as is clearly stated, "*we* never have conveyed them away." It is further asserted that they "shall always use it as long [as] Christian Indians live. We shall use it forever and ever."[37] The Mashpee Indians would continue to fend off white speculators, squatters, and thieves from their lands, using whatever means were available to them, and have managed to maintain their presence in Mashpee to this day despite unrelenting challenges from their white neighbors.

Natives who lived in praying towns in the late seventeenth and early eighteenth centuries, despite having adopted a semiliterate culture, managed to retain certain vestiges of their traditional lives. As historian David Silverman puts it, if they were becoming Christians, "by any reasonable standard, it was a distinctly Indian kind."[38] The towns were structured under a system of communal decision-making, often presided over by leaders who were still part of traditional ruling lineages.[39] Christiantown, one of the praying towns at Martha's Vineyard, maintained a "dancing field" where ceremonies continued to be held.[40] As the aforementioned document demonstrates, land was often understood to be held communally and not by allotment. At least until the nineteenth century, residents continued to speak and even write in their traditional languages, and literacy was used to secure legal ownership of lands and solidify a sense of tribal identity.[41] One document in particular, drawn up by the Gay Head Indians of Martha's Vineyard, contains a provision that the signers "with all our children and all our (common) people, have agreed that no one (shall) sell land. But if anyone larcenously sells land, you shall take (back) your land, because it is forever your possession." In this short but poignant document the word "forever" appears no less than twelve times.[42] It speaks not only to the cultural tensions from without the Gay Head community, but the extreme pressure from within as sachems were sometimes tempted to sell off vast tracts that were not previously thought to be individually "owned." Such sales legitimated the colonial processes by which Natives were divested of their land, but often created internal rifts within the Native communities themselves, as many strongly objected to this overlaying of colonial law upon indigenous custom and used writing as a means to try and reinstate their own practice and privilege.

Evangelism and Eye-Strain: Samson Occom's Native-Centered Vision of Evangelism

The problems facing Mohegan in the mid-eighteenth century were very similar to those facing the Natives at Martha's Vineyard. Whereas the Martha's Vineyard Natives attempted to rely upon former oral agreements to contest the purchases of the English, however, the Mohegan carried the ball a step further into the colonial court.[43] The career of Samson Occom, while in some ways complicated by his lifelong affiliation with the Presbyterian

Church and his perceived status as "the Indian Moses," offers a study in how Native communities in this time began to negotiate the public and private realms of colonized space through literary engagements.[44] Interestingly, the "Moses" appellation is in reference to the exodus Occom helped to initiate, in which many New England Natives relocated to Oneida territory in the late eighteenth century. It is an appellation that attempts to enfold within the dominant paradigm of Christian conversion what was, in fact, an act of Native resistance and communitism. But Occom might also be remembered for initiating an engagement with alphabetic literacy in many Native communities, in a sense performing this other function sometimes attributed to Moses.

Occom's only recognized publications in his lifetime, his entries into the public transcript, were a sermon that he delivered at the execution of a fellow Mohegan, Moses Paul, in 1772 (*A Sermon Preached by Samson Occom, Minister of the Gospel, and Missionary to the Indians at the Execution of Moses Paul an Indian*) and a book of hymns in 1774 entitled *Collection of Hymns and Spiritual Songs*. An early draft of his autobiographical sketch also appeared in newspapers prior to his voyage to England 1766.[45] The appearance of these texts in the public transcript suggests that they were well-formulated performances of Native compliance and assimilation. If they gestured toward the hidden transcript of Mohegan tradition and resistance in any way, it was in a manner subdued enough not to upset the colonial establishment or the printing offices of Timothy Green, descended of the late Samuel Green, who brought editions of both of Occom's books into print. That both his sermon and his book of hymns were quite successful in their time attests once again to their level of conformity to colonial expectations.

The narrative of how Occom came to ascendancy as a prominent Native figure of his time has been obscured somewhat by this perceived conformity alongside the framing of his life as a kind of appendage to the overall narrative of Eleazar Wheelock's founding of Dartmouth College and the fuzzy traditions of Native advocacy that still adhere to the origins of this institution. The narrative typically begins with Wheelock, a Connecticut minister with ties to the New Light revival movement of the period, who, following in the footsteps of John Eliot and foreshadowing Richard Henry Pratt, opened up a charity school for Indians in 1754. Here he would train young Natives to act as missionaries who would venture out into the wilderness and convert their fellow heathens. Occom stands out in this effort as Wheelock's first and, arguably, only success.

Occom's career, which received mostly a warm reception in his day, has been chronicled since the late nineteenth century, starting with well-researched and sympathetic biographies, first by William Deloss Love in 1899, and again by William Harold Blodgett in 1935. If sympathetic, however, both authors were nevertheless invested in perpetuating a narrative that viewed the civilizing of Natives through Christian doctrine as both necessary and inevitable, leading to the familiar "assimilation or extinction" narrative that had been dominant since colonial times when representing Native lives. Love writes, "it is hardly possible that an Indian, with all the defects of his race, could grow to the full stature of a civilized man without struggles against his hereditary weaknesses."[46] Nevertheless their focus on the particulars of Occom's life begins, in both cases, to apprehend the ruptures in that discourse, and Love is at least able to offer the partial recognition that Wheelock, "the father at Lebanon had not dealt kindly by his Indian son."[47] Despite the blatant paternalism ingrained in such statements, both historians come to a similar awareness of how the civilizing program was rigged against Occom and his people. Both Love and Blodgett also performed a surprising and valuable service in printing large portions of Occom's journals and letters, making these unique documents accessible to future generations and allowing Occom to speak "in his own voice."

It would have to wait until contemporary times, however, before Occom's life would receive a substantial critical reassessment. Bernd Peyer was the first to publish Occom's "A Short Narrative" in its full and final version in 1982. In a summarization of Occom's life in *American Indian Quarterly* that same year, Peyer labels Occom "the 'father' of modern Native American literature."[48] Nevertheless, Occom's writings were mainly regarded as belonging to a genre of literature described by Arnold Krupat as "salvationist," or a discourse subsumed by the monologism of colonial hegemony. David Murray and Dana D. Nelson, while noting the inherent acts of resistance in Occom's writings, both firmly question Occom's ability to forge an "autonomous expression or an authentic voice."[49] Perhaps it isn't until Jace Weaver reevaluates Occom's life in *That the People Might Live*, that we begin to receive an unqualified assessment of Occom as a Native advocating for Native causes. His voice is not subsumed, in Weaver's notion, but "communitarian," wholly invested in the project of preserving his community of Mohegan.[50] Approaches that consider Native intellectual sovereignty a legitimate force have allowed for a new lens through which to interpret Occom's work. This has been pursued most fruitfully, I believe, by Abenaki historian Lisa Brooks who, in her book *The Common Pot*, performs extensive archival research on Occom's career, and regards his contributions from "Native space." Informed by perspectives made available from such a vantage, we see how the particulars of Occom's life and how it has been represented to us begin to reverse themselves in significant ways. These approaches have broken vital new ground for interpreting Occom's career, as has the recent compilation of most of Occom's known writings by Joanna Brooks in *The Collected Writings of Samson Occom, Mohegan*. The very size of this volume alone is enough to give one pause, and force many to reconsider what was the Native engagement with literature in the eighteenth century.

One way we begin to reimagine Occom's life and reverse the historical current, so to speak, is by recognizing that it was Occom who came to Wheelock on December 6, 1743, and not the other way around. Still, we are often left with the sense that Occom was a lone operative, working in isolation from his people, drawn like a moth to a brighter flame. Even his name, Occom, or Ockham (if we can trust Love on this point) meant "on the other side" in the Algonquian language.[51] It seems to have been a given that, to cross over to Wheelock's side of the woods, Occom must have necessarily abandoned his own traditions, his own heritage. Occom, himself, offers the story in the familiar framework of a religious conversion narrative, beginning his 1768 "A Short Narrative of My Life" with the declaration, "I was born a heathen and brought up in heathenism," and with the rest of the Mohegans, "lived a wandering life." After having been exposed to the teachings of the itinerant New Light ministers sometime around 1740, Occom, in his own words, "was Awakened & Converted . . . & Continued under Trouble of Mind about 6 months; at which time I began to Learn the English Letters." Putting his trust in the life and salvation of Jesus Christ, he felt "the Distress and Burden of my mind was removed, and I found serenity and Pleasure of Soul, in Serving God." Under these circumstances Occom reached the conclusion that "if I Could once Learn to Read I would Instruct the poor Children in Reading,—and used frequently to talk with our Indians Concerning Religion." Having had some knowledge of Wheelock, and knowing that he instructed English youths, Occom had "a great Inclination to go to him and be with him a week or a Fortnight, and Desired my Mother to Ask Mr. Wheelock, Whether he would take me a little while to Instruct me in Reading."[52]

Taken up to this point, Occom's narrative demonstrates a facility in the desired idiom to use if one were a Native American in eighteenth-century New England hoping to make an impression on local authorities upon whom one relied for financial resources and institutional backing. More so than Waban and his other indigenous predecessors, Occom seemed to have mastered and internalized the language of Christian conversion, striking a tone that was neither overly devotional nor utterly debasing, but conforming to the proscribed movement from a state of abject darkness to one of superior light. Occom's contemporary and acquaintance David McClure put it in terms even more suited to the rhetorical conventions of colonial powers. In his *Memoirs of the Reverend Eleazar Wheelock*, he writes that Occom,

> was of the Mohegan nation, and born a pagan. Living in the vicinity of the English, he, in 1741, at the age of eighteen, became acquainted with the Christian religion, forsook the

> vices of his countrymen, and became devout and zealous. He was deeply affected by the deplorable ignorance and vices of the Indians, and was industrious in qualifying himself to teach and reform them.[53]

In other words, the literature of the time, to which Occom contributed, seems to emphasize a deliberate divide between Occom and his fellow Mohegans who were presumably plagued by "vices," "hereditary weaknesses," and still dwelt in "deplorable ignorance." Perhaps the only indication in these brief notices that Occom himself does not perceive such a dramatic split can be found in his aforementioned admission that he "used frequently to talk with our Indians Concerning Religion." Not "exhort" or "preach," but "talk." If the colonial powers preferred to regard Occom as coming into exclusive dialogue with themselves, Occom still saw himself in dialogue with his own people. But as with Caleb Cheeshateaumauk, James Printer, John Sassamon, Thomas Waban, and many others before him, he had been sent out as an emissary to "Learn the English Letters," a skill that he could take back to his people and attempt to use to their advantage.

Despite his tendency to privilege a Christian worldview and seeming to favor certain Eurocentric conventions in his public writings, Occom viewed himself as a Mohegan first, and his considerable intellect and energy were applied toward furthering Mohegan goals to the best of his abilities. Occom was a member of the Mohegan Tribal Council before he reached the age of twenty. He was active in his community and served under the sachemships of both Ben Uncas II and Ben Uncas III.[54] And prior to his leaving for England to raise monies for an Indian college, he was seen by the colonists as the most visible agitator in the Mason land case, which had been the cause of a great deal of controversy in southern New England throughout the eighteenth century.

The general details of the Mason case help to illustrate the complicated tensions surrounding Native land rights, and, in some ways, can be seen to break down the insistent dichotomy between the Christian and the traditional Native. It was understood, by some at least, that Mohegan land was held in trust by the Mason family of Connecticut, and that by treaty these lands could not be sold. But as the colonists continued to forcefully assert their presence in the region, these former treaties were regarded as ambiguous at best, and it became conveniently unclear who had lawful authority over the territories in question, or what the original intent of the treaties might have been. Because colonists preferred to deal with individual "kings" rather than tribal structures, they had maneuvered to influence the succession of sachems to insure that the Mohegan at least nominally in power, Ben Uncas III, was sympathetic to their own desires. Some years later Occom would post his objection to this practice in a letter to Sir William Johnson, superintendent of Indian affairs for the crown at that time. Occom petitioned bitterly that the English continued to view Uncas as the Mohegan sachem, "but We have a Law and a Custom to make a sachem over us Without the help of any People or Nation in the World, and When he makes himself unworthy of his Station we put him down ourselves."[55] The English, however, refused to acknowledge the elected sachem at Mohegan, John Uncas, and continued to deal solely with Ben Uncas III.[56]

Occom seems to have aligned himself with those of the Mohegan nation who were against the sale of lands from an early date. Lisa Brooks notes that the mark of young Occom can be found on a Mohegan/Niantic petition dated September 1736, in which it is stated that the

> whole body of them did renounce Ben Uncas as Sachem . . . And by virtue of these presents, we do disapprove of and make void whatever Ben Uncas has acted or may act in the capacity of Sachem or King over us in the conveyance of any lands, rights, and privileges whatsoever belonging to us.[57]

Fawcett tells us that when the colonial government refused to recognize the elected sachem at Mohegan, the majority of the tribe chose to recognize no sachem at all. Mohegan itself split into two factions divided between Ben's Town and John's Town, a rift that would continue to fragment an already embattled community.[58] As with the Wampanoag in Martha's Vineyard, the people found themselves at odds with the recognized sachems who were siphoning off their lands, and traditional Native hierarchies were being forcefully splintered.

There is a, perhaps, apocryphal story that when the largely discredited Ben Uncas III died in 1769, his pallbearers, Occom amongst them, dropped his coffin to the ground in front of the Connecticut officials who had come to pay their respects, in protest of their supporting his sachemship. Sources closer to home noted that as Reverend Jewett, the white appointed minister at Mohegan, was delivering the eulogy, Occom rose and left the room, "though for what cause was not stated; and his example was followed by many others." It was reported that so many left the service, following Occom's example, that of those remaining, there were not enough to carry the body to its designated resting place in Norwich."[59] In the colonial telling of this event, there seems no rational explanation as to why the Mohegan would simply walk out on their own king. An act of resistance is made to seem arbitrary and depoliticized. Such actions, given no voice, no archival articulation by the Mohegan themselves, nevertheless simmer up through the archival depths, awaiting contextualization, awaiting the emergence of new narrative strategies to articulate their resistance. They are in some sense para-archival, having been displaced from a coherent cultural framework, and serve only as mute doorstops in the colonial archive until the ruptures of colonialism can be repaired or reconstructed by the longhouse of the archive.

One can argue that, within Native tradition, sachems had always held the right to apportion tribal lands without the consent of the tribe. David Silverman makes a case that for Native New England, the concept that lands were held communally was, in fact, a result of continued exposure "to English private-property ways, missionaries, and especially threats against the Native land base," rather than any traditional conviction.[60] There is a splendid irony in this claim: that it was the rather rabid imposition of private property values on the part of the English that led to Native Americans adopting an articulated ethic of communal land holding. But then, I imagine the English would have responded in precisely the same manner had the King or Queen suddenly begun selling off chunks of the motherland to foreigners for personal gain. Across the board, Native communities in New England stood up and tried to stop their sachems from selling off land. Whether this was in keeping with traditional responses or not, and whether or not sachems were operating under a misunderstood notion of the types of agreements into which they were entering, one thing remains clear: the people of Native New England objected to the practice, and in their writings we can determine that they at least attempted to exercise their sovereignty as a people to put a stop to it.

Lisa Brooks argues that we should not be so quick to understand that sachems were simply selling out their nations for personal gain in these related transactions. Her notion that Natives of the Northeast viewed the land as a "common pot," the contents of which were shared by all with one spoon, stands in contrast to Silverman's theory. She observes that "considerable confusion erupted when English deed making began to enter the space of Algonquian councils and the practices of Algonquian sachems began to enter the space of colonial land transactions." Going back to the original treaty language, or the "League of Amnity" between the Mohegan and the English in 1681, Brooks concludes that the first Uncas granted only "the rights of shared inhabitation" to the English, and not an outright purchase. The treaty Uncas put his mark to states, "I do resign up to the Colony of Connecticut all my Lands and Territories, hereby, for myself, my Heirs and Successors, binding myself and them that I will make no other Dispose of them to any person or people whatsoever, without their Grant and Allowance first had and obtained." Brooks understands this to mean that Uncas granted to the English, as a recognized power in the region, the right to mutual inhabitation and use of resources. While Uncas retained sachem rights to occasionally open a parcel of land for English settlement, he had not, by any means, ceded the distribution of Mohegan lands over to the colonists. Brooks states that "for Uncas, the agreement laid out the terms for sharing the space of the watershed." She observes that writing, "like wampum, solidified the 'binds' between the two groups that would enable their mutual habitation."[61] The misunderstandings that followed would have been in keeping with the patterns of land distribution, obfuscation, and forced concession that occurred in other Native regions of New England, resulting in disputes similar to those that led to King Philip's War in 1676.

Treaties or contracts such as these seem to have had little purpose other than to impose a protectorate relationship between Natives and the colonies that, regardless of the spirit with which a given sachem entered into it, could only deliberately confuse the issue of who had legal title to the land. In a sense, it placed Native property rights into what Kevin Bruyneel refers to as the "third place of sovereignty" or a kind of liminal space of jurisprudence that constructs a purposeful ambiguity around legal protections and definitions for Native space that carries into current times.[62] We shouldn't assume, however, that the English had only one way of interpreting such agreements once they were made. There were continuous disputes about what original claim the Natives had to the land in the first place, and what right European powers had to simply come over and assume control of indigenous lands for themselves. Because such acts had legal implications beyond the realm of colonial land grabs, it became important for the English to establish precedent and retroactively negotiate land transactions that had been determined orally or by vaguely worded treaties.

In 1724 the Reverend John Bulkley of Colchester, Connecticut openly acknowledged the many disagreements concerning rightful ownership of land on the North American continent. In a treatise entitled "An Inquiry Into the Right of the Aboriginal Natives to the Lands of America," he argues that "this is a matter more talked about than understood," and he takes the stance that there is, in fact, "a native right" (although he feels compelled to refer to this as "the vulgar phrase" for the matter at hand).[63] Bulkley argues that the Native right is synonymous with John Locke's articulation of "natural rights," or the rights that adhere to those who exist in "a state of nature." Locke had argued that the law of reason "makes the deer the Indian's who had killed it, it is allowed to be his goods, who has bestowed his labor upon it." But to substantiate a claim that open, unimproved land (read: wilderness) could be properly said to belong to anyone in "a state of nature" was absurd. As to the "pretended claims" of "the Moheags," Bulkley affirms that any agreement made with them was made while they were in such a state of nature, and therefore was unbinding, regardless of how anyone interpreted it now. "Instead of such large territories they have been ignorantly . . . thought by some to have, they had really good right or title but to here and there a few spots of it, viz. only to so much as by the means of the abovementioned they had separated and enclosed from the rest of the country." That the Mohegan were, in fact, in "a state of nature" at the time of these treaties, he argued, could be affirmed by the "manners of the more uncivilized part of their survivors at this day, who I imagine may reasonably be thought the liveliest images of their ancestors, and most to retain their customs."[64]

To reiterate Bulkley's tortured syntax, the Colchester minister was trotting out the familiar *vacuum domicilum* policy argued by the Puritans that declared open, unimproved lands to have no clear ownership as a result of "natural law." But, in a new twist, he was using this idea to render invalid previous land transactions and treaties. He argued that the Mohegan in particular had nothing that could be called "civilization" and, knowing virtually nothing of Mohegan culture beyond the fact that he disapproved of what he saw, he referred to the current Mohegan residents as the best proof of this. Lacking culture, art, history, and particularly writing, Native land title instantly became "perplexed and in the dark [so] that nothing can be known."[65] In a sense, Mohegan identity was itself an unimproved wilderness. Bulkley wondered where the proof was to decide the many conflicting claims that various sachems made concerning the bounds of particular villages and nations, and tellingly, he asserts that any attempt to find such proofs was "like a search for the living among the dead." Mohegan land claims, for Bulkley and a number of like-minded colonists, became "a mere chimera of fiction."[66]

For whatever reasons, the Mason family (relations of the same Major John Mason who ordered the burning of the Pequot fort in the previous century and declared that the English would "root their very name out of this country") came to side with the Mohegan in the particulars of this case.[67] The Masons took their arguments to the king of England and it was during this decision in 1743 that the aforementioned treaty with Uncas was unveiled. But the English court rejected the view of the Mohegan that the treaty called for mutual habitation. The decision went to the colonists, arguing that the lands had been ceded outright, and that because settlers had already made improvements upon the land, it would be detrimental to scale back, robbing these settlers of their legal purchase and risking that the land fall "once again into a Wilderness."[68]

By this point it was probably impressed upon the Mohegan that their claims to sovereignty and their traditional memory of treaties made in the past would remain under contestation by aggressive colonial powers until they themselves could gain some control of the legal process by which the colonists claimed authority. As Lisa Brooks suggests, "the best route to protecting their lands was for the Mohegans to acquire the power of literacy for themselves."[69] And so it was that, in the same year their court case failed in England and the Mohegan split into two factions, Samson Occom "crossed over" to Eleazar Wheelock's residence in order to acquire an English education.

Occom most certainly already knew how to read and write by the time he came to Wheelock to be tutored in 1743. He had learned these skills on his own, or with the help of English neighbors, as he claims in his narrative. But he hoped to advance his learning, and in the first passage of a journal that he started that year (a journal he would continue to keep intermittently for the remainder of his life), he wrote in an already strong hand that he had come to Wheelock "to learn something of the Latin tongue and was there about a week."[70] His journal details his frequent comings and goings between Wheelock's and Mohegan while offering few peripheral details or internal musings. Perhaps he hoped to learn Latin because it was used in so many legal books and documents. Or perhaps he had other motives. Like most writers of the colonial period, Occom didn't seem to feel much of an inclination to unburden his thought process in his personal writings, but opted, for the most part, to keep a simple record of his travels. One early passage from 1745, typical in its lack of explicit introspection, merely states, "I lodged at Deacon Wheelock's at night and the Next day at Windham, and in ye 18th of Dec. between 2 & 3 Clock in the after Noon the Poor Girl was Executed and I went right home to Lebanon that Day."[71] The lack of detail here, as in other places, is frustrating. Much could be read between the lines of such a passage, although without knowing the precise context of the event, it remains difficult to enter into. Why would Occom go out of his way to witness an execution and mark it so pointedly in his journals? Does the stock epithet "poor" suggest that the execution was of an Indian girl (as in a "poor Indian")? And do we read disapproval and dissent in the bleak silences that crackle up through this passage and his solitary journey home? Although some confusion exists as to who exactly it was Occom saw executed that day, there is reason to believe it was one Elizabeth Shaw, executed for murdering her infant child. The fact that this event was somehow significant to Occom is suggested by the fact that on the outside cover of this particular journal he has scrawled the word "Elizabeth" over and over. Some degree of intentionality always adheres to the hidden transcript, but its availability is further complicated by the controlled reticence that sustains itself even within Occom's private journals.[72] Nevertheless, this early passage, in some furtive mechanization of fate, foreshadows Occom's later appearance on the scaffold in 1772 alongside the accused murderer, Moses Paul, some twenty-seven years later.

Occom stayed on with Wheelock just shy of four years, although, by his own account, he was sickly for nearly a year of this time, and at least some of that time was spent under the tutelage of Benjamin Pomeroy, minister at Hebron, who helped prepare Occom for the ministry and continued his training in Latin and Greek.[73] At other times Occom was involved in the seasonal subsistence routines of his community. Love suggests that, according to local tradition, Occom stayed in a "hut," or more accurately a wigwam, that he built somewhere on the periphery of Wheelock's property, while he was attending school.[74] But his comings and goings were frequent. He wrote how somewhere around the 17th of September in 1745 a number of Mohegan traveled by boat to Montauk, Long Island and that they were "kindly entertained." Already beginning to think, or at least write, like a missionary, he noted, "there was Some Stir among 'em."[75] The expedition to Montauk was almost certainly part of a seasonal pattern, and not simply a random excursion. Montauk was known for its fishing and hunting grounds and had been a traditional fall destination for the Mohegan and many other Native groups.[76] For Occom, however, the trip to Montauk was of particular interest as he would soon elect to enter into this community, first as teacher, and later as husband, father, and spiritual leader.

The expectation was that Occom, having proven himself a promising student, would continue on to Yale, but after four years under Wheelock's tutelage he claimed that excessive "eye-strain" had hampered his studies. Love tells us that "indeed he at length so overstrained his eyes by his earnest application to his books that he was unable to take the course which had been designed in preparation for the ministry."[77] Perhaps a "smoky wigwam" was not the ideal place to conduct a crash course in Western civilization and its customs. Or perhaps Occom had his own ideas about how he wanted to use the education that had been extended him. But it was no easy matter to disentangle himself from the colonial/missionary machinery once having been implicated in its processes. Our old friend, the Society for Propagating the Gospel in New England, had taken on the charge of defraying Wheelock's expenses for Occom's education, and wondered if Occom couldn't be kept occupied by "engaging in manual labor" until the time that his eyes recovered, and in the meantime they would kindly "allow what is necessary toward effecting a cure."[78] There seems to have been definite resistance to the idea of Occom, after having personally benefited so much from the charity of the society, simply branching off on his own.

Perhaps we have to strain our own eyes as well to see how Occom, himself, negotiated such conflicts. If there was, as Love suggests, a "misunderstanding," concerning Occom's career opportunities, that misunderstanding most certainly lay in the lap of the "Society," which presumed to dictate Occom's future for him. It is often assumed from Occom's later writings, when he spoke of the gross salary inequities between himself and other white missionaries in his "Short Narrative," that he went to Montauk with the understanding that he would be compensated for his efforts. But, as I will elaborate upon later, the strong possibility exists that Occom was simply making a rhetorical point when he brought up the imbalance of pay retroactively. Money had not been the motivating factor for Occom to go to Montauk, nor would it ever serve as the axis upon which his decision-making turned. His decision to go to Montauk appears to have been made independently, following a 1749 fishing trip during which the people there invited him to be their teacher. In all likelihood he asked for and expected no external recompense for his efforts. He was not necessarily seeking the imprimatur of Wheelock or the missionary societies that had initially supported him. The fact that he stayed on with the Montauk for upward of eleven years bears this out. In his narrative he writes not only that the Montauk were "very desirous to have me keep a school amongst them," but that he "left it with them to give me what they Pleased; and they took turns to Provide Food for me."[79] By his own account, then, the terms of his stay were agreed upon between himself and the Montauk. Occom warmly entered into the patterns of community, kinship, and subsistence that were in accordance with his own upbringing as "a heathen" and with ongoing traditions at Montauk. He lived in a wigwam for the next eleven years (as he had all his previous years), farmed his own land, moved as the community moved, kept a school for the children (and probably the adults as well), tended to the sick, and provided church services and counsel. In most material aspects he was still very much living the life of the so-called "wandering heathen" that he had presumably left behind when he first became interested in Christianity.

He married Mary Fowler sometime around 1752, entering into one of the more influential families of the Montauk. In his 1761 report to the colonial government entitled "An Account of the Montauk Indians on Long Island," he offered a description of a traditional marriage, observing how "young people and others are allowed to choose companions for themselves. When a young couple conclude to have each other, they acquaint their parents of it, or near relations: and they assist them in it, they generally make a feast &c. Sometimes the couple themselves make a small feast, and so call few neighbors to eat and drink with them." Marriage is the very first issue Occom addresses in this account ("I shall begin with their MARRAIGES" he writes) and one wonders if he isn't describing the particulars of his own marriage ceremony in this passage.[80]

Occom fully immersed himself in the rhythms and routines of Montauk life, becoming something of a community leader in that time, performing the roles of minister, schoolmaster, scribe, healer, and judge. That his role transcended the parameters of a typical Christian preacher might be apprehended in a 1754 catalogue of "Herbs and Roots" Occom recorded in his notes that lists various herbal remedies to ailments as varied as pleurisy, headaches, and heavy menstruation. He notes here that a Montauk named

Ocus "has now learnt me 52 roots—and I have paid him in all 27 York money."[81] Occom, in keeping with traditional Algonquian custom, sought to expand his knowledge and fulfill the role of spiritual leader as well as medicine man. Only after a number of years, as Occom's family grew and his responsibilities as an important figure to the Montauk community expanded, did he perceive that he was performing a valuable service for the Society for the Propagation of the Gospel as well, prompting him to bring up the issue of recompense.

As for the society itself, it was unwilling to loosen its grasp on Occom and in 1750 Wheelock wrote him that "if you are well to pursue your studies I can't but think it advisable to return to them." He concluded the letter by cautioning that Occom "watch against pride & self-esteem."[82] Apparently Occom's "eye-strain" had yet to remedy itself because he did not return to his studies, or at least not in the official capacity that was hoped for by his professed mentors. Alongside his many other activities, Occom notes in his autobiography how in his spare time he made extra money binding books for the colonial residents of Long Island.[83] It can only be assumed that this occupation allowed him to pursue a course of study on his own regardless of eyestrain, as book learning, to at least some extent, remained an important feature of Occom's life. He continued to improve upon his skills as writer, preacher, and scholar, and when Occom built his house at Mohegan years later, a visiting David McClure would note that adjoining the guest room was Occom's "library of a handsome collection, brought by him, principally from Great Britain."[84] Occom often gave books out as gifts when he visited amongst the youth in his parish, and had in his collection an Eliot Bible that had been in his possession since his early schooling days.[85] That he continued to remain intellectually engaged with reading and writing throughout his life is evidenced by a 1792 edition of *The Writings of Thomas Paine*, in which, within the list of subscribers, appears the name "Samson Occom, Brothertown, NY."[86]

Despite Occom's continued resistance to the wishes of Wheelock and the society, he remained all too effective as a Christian emissary for them to simply brush him off and cut their losses. Previous missionary efforts amongst the Montauk and Shinnecock had made little or no headway. So in the summer of his eighth year as the default minister to the Indians at Montauk, Occom was given an ordination hearing so that he might continue his work in a more official capacity. That this event was of some significance to Occom as both a personal and a moral victory is perhaps signaled by the fact that it occasioned his most comprehensive journal passage to date, on June 28, 1757. In fact, there was a six-year gap in Occom's journals leading up to this point, suggestive of the fact that Occom saw little need to record his daily life in Montauk as a free agent. But as he entered back into the realm of colonial space and control he reemerges into the textualized realm as well.

For various reasons it took yet another two years for Occom's official ordination as a Presbyterian minister to occur, on August 29, 1759. Love notes that on this occasion a text was given to Occom from which he was to compose a trial sermon.[87] The text was Psalms 72:9, which reads, "they that dwell in the wilderness shall bow before him; and his enemies shall lick the dust." While such a text probably felt like a natural fit to the Suffolk Presbytery that ordained him, the passage was likely to have driven home for Occom an acute sense of double consciousness. We do not know how he negotiated the subtleties of this assignment, fulfilling the obligations of Christian rhetoric while raising the aspect of his people as, perhaps, something more than savage dust-lickers bowing to colonial dogma. Although he gamely delivered the sermon and received the blessing of the church, his concluding remark in his journal that day bore the deadpan traces of ironic reflection typical of Occom, as he penned "thus the solemnity ended, *Laus te Deum*."[88]

Shortly after his ordination, the society asked of Occom to begin a ministry to the Indians of Oneida in what was still considered to be the wilderness of present-day Upstate New York. Occom set out on this mission in the summer of 1761, accompanied by his brother-in-law David Fowler, who had been one of the first graduates of Wheelock's recently established Moor's Charity School. Of interest is a passage dated June 14 as he and Fowler headed south toward New York City in order to catch a ferry back north up the Hudson River. Coming within five miles proximity of the great city, Occom and Fowler were held back on account of a smallpox scare. But they were close enough to observe, as Occom writes, the sight of "drunkards Realing and Stagaring in the Streets, others tumbling off their Horses . . . And [if] ever a People under the Heavens spoke Hell Language these people did, for their mouths were full of Cursings, Prophaning God, Holy Holy Name—I greatly mistake if these are not the sons and Daughters of Belial." And all this on a Sabbath day. Either the spectacle of white urban life made a huge impression on Occom, or he had been forewarned that the city would present a scene slightly contrary to what Christian practice demanded of its practitioners and he felt obliged to confirm such an apprehension. I find it unlikely that Occom had yet to witness, firsthand, the strains of hypocrisy that fairly spilled over the lid of colonial dogma wherever one cared to look. But perhaps he had yet to see it to such a degree, and he prayed to his God, "Leave me not to Practice the Works of these People."[89]

I wonder if Occom's ordination sermon, in which he was forced into an exhortation rooted in the civilization/savagery binary of his colonial professors, wasn't still on his mind when he penned in his journal that day in New York, "I have thought there were no heathen but the Wild Indians, but think there is some English Heathen, where they Enjoy the Gospel of Jesus Christ. Yea I believe they are worse than ye Savage Heathen of the Wildernesse."[90] If such an observation played directly into the oppositional binaries of colonialism, it also labored to reverse the equation. Occom wrote these lines as though his reaction were spontaneous, a private revelation. But Occom's habitual reticence, viewed alongside such occasional outbursts, takes on a new context when one understands that his journals were perused by at least one other pair of eyes peering over his shoulder. In a letter from Wheelock to the Reverend George Whitefield dated November 25, 1761, Wheelock writes, "My black son Mr. Occom has lately returned from his Mission to the Onoyadas, and the last week I had the Pleasure to see him with one of that nation (who designs to winter with him and Learn the English Language & teach Mr. Occom Mohawke) and I was agreeably entertained by Mr. Occom's Journal."[91] We might understand from this that, at least up through this trip to Oneida, Wheelock was in the habit of reading Occom's journals (and also in the habit of obscuring Occom's ethnicity if it suited his mood, casting him in the same category as the "black" slaves he kept on his estate). If so, then Occom's profound silences, his lack of personal introspection, take on a more meaningful weight, while his rare effusions might be seen in a more strategic light. It was standard practice, of course, for itinerant ministers to keep a journal of their labors in the field, but Occom's status as Native interlocutor made this practice fraught with potential pitfalls and opportunities to betray what his mentors regarded as instances of Native pride and haughtiness.

What this unveils for us is yet another layer of transcription that shifts between the hidden and the public, delineating the levels of colonial surveillance under which Occom performed, while hinting at the edges of an articulated resistance. Occom not only found a means of subverting the colonial binary of savagery and civilization within an acceptable framework, but (as evidenced in Wheelock's letter), he could be seen nurturing separate alliances from both within and without the missionary context. One wonders what sort of relationship Occom forged with the Oneida representative with whom he planned to "winter." Was this part of his own diplomatic endeavor that would lead to his eventually carving out a place for himself in the territory of the Iroquois? And for whom else but Wheelock does he write in his journal, "I am glad there is one defect in the Indian Language and I believe in all their Language i.e. they can't curse or swear or take god's Name in Vain in their own Tongue."[92] This observation, expressed for the first time in his journal that day outside the city of New York, would become a repeated theme of Occom's that he often included in his sermons to mixed Native and white audiences. But, for the moment at least, Wheelock was the sole audience for Occom's journals. And apparently he was "agreeably entertained" by the performance offered, even if the epithet of "black son" strangely colors his appreciation of their intrinsic value.

The first mission to Oneida lasted only nine weeks in the summer and early fall of 1761. Upon his departure, Occom was presented with a belt of wampum put in his trust by a congress of leaders from the Iroquois Confederacy. The wampum belt signified that the parties involved wished to reaffirm their relationship with the English so that they would be bound "fast together in perpetual Love and Friendship."[93] It also seems to have, in some measure, spoken to the effectiveness of Occom's short ministry there. In the speech given by the Haudenosaunee leaders at the time of his departure, it was noted of Occom's preaching that "these things were never heard of before in such clear light."[94] That Occom was still fluent in the cultural traditions of exchange between Native peoples is evidenced by a claim made by Nathaniel Whitaker some years later while both he and Occom were on their way to England to raise money for an Indian College. Whitaker asked that the "religious belt" be procured as "it would be of great use to us as Mr. Occom remembers the Speech."[95] The Mohegan people had long stationed themselves at the source of the wampum trade, and the protocols of its exchange, including the use of wampum as a mnemonic device to recall oral testimony, were probably still well understood by Occom's generation.

As a missionary to the Indians, Occom was able to model an idea of English Christianity that did not stand in absolute abhorrence of Native practice. Although he understood well enough the oppositional binaries under which colonial rule asserted itself, and knew how to articulate his spirituality under sincere and acceptable terms, Occom's own rhetoric was designed to erase such binaries or ease their tensions. He had a facility for drawing the hierarchal imperatives of Christian dogma into a space of Native engagement, writing in his account of the Montauk that "they had a notion of one great and good God, that was over all the rest of the gods, which they called CAUHLUNTOOWUT, which signifies one that is possessed with supreme power."[96] After death, he maintained, their souls departed westward, "where the righteous, or those that behaved themselves well in this world, will exercise themselves in pleasurable singing and dancing forever."[97] Any English reporter, including even Roger Williams, who wrote in quite similar language of Narragansett belief systems, would have been repulsed by the whiff of paganism embedded within the image of eternal "singing and dancing," and have chosen an adjective other than "pleasurable" to describe such an afterlife. Occom concluded of Montauk customs however that "I don't see for my part, why it is not as true, as the English."[98] Occom's gentle and engaging discourse, as we shall see, offered a syncretic approach to Native and English rhetorical traditions, avoiding harshly oppositional language. Such an approach was apparently as effective amongst Native peoples as it was with the English, as his preaching was well received in either camp. He would make brief return trips to the Oneida in 1762 and 1763, but this final mission was cut short by the outbreak of the event known as Pontiac's War. When he returned home to Mohegan he was able to secure a post teaching to the Niantic in Connecticut and so Occom took this opportunity to move himself and his family back to the country of his birth after having lived away for well over a decade.

There can be little doubt that when Occom returned to Mohegan, he quickly established a leadership role for himself within the community, despite the fact that he hadn't actually kept a permanent residence there for some twelve years. His very presence seems to have helped galvanize an already tacit resistance to ongoing colonial encroachments made at Mohegan. Occom, merely by setting up shop as he had elsewhere as both teacher and minister, siphoned off what little cooperation had been afforded the existing white missionary efforts at Mohegan, as led by David Jewett, and the schoolmaster Robert Clelland. Clelland appears, by all accounts, to have been ineffectual as schoolmaster, and Jewett held property in Mohegan that he stood to forfeit if the Mason land case, newly reopened, went to the Natives. Both were inclined to see Occom as a threat, even prior to his arrival, as evidenced by an apprehensive letter Clelland wrote to Wheelock in February of 1763, asserting that "Mr. Occom is to be over with his family this Spring and drive Mr. Jewett & I from Mohegan."[99]

The letters surrounding this new conflict seem to suggest that even the English population at New London preferred Occom over Jewett. As Wheelock would write to George Whitefield, on October 10, 1764,

> the breach between Mr. Jewett and Mr. Occom grows wider—Mr. Jewett's People and a great Number from other neighboring Parishes flock to hear Mr. Occom on Lord's Day at Mohegan &c the Effect of which you may easily guess. And Mr. Jewett is like to lose all his Land in the parish, if the Indians there should gain their point in their Suit against the Government in an old affair called Mason's Case lately revived . . . This together with their Controversy with their School Master has made a great Ferment among them, and Mr. Occom is blamed by some that he will advise the Indians [and] that he will suffer the English to flock to hear him.[100]

Occom, upon returning home, had reengaged with the Mason land case, as Wheeler's letter supposes, and the various conflicts swirling around Mohegan found an inevitable point of intersection in these proceedings. The community was fractured. Ben Uncas III, sachem by colonial fiat only, had become little more than a pawn in the interests of the European power structure of the region. The missionary hierarchy at Mohegan and New London, put in place by the Society for the Propagation of the Gospel, was economically invested in the disenfranchisement of Mohegans from their land. And Occom stood in the middle of it all, not as one representing the religious practices of a foreign culture, but as an advocate for the continued cohesiveness of Mohegan community. If the people preferred him over Jewett as spiritual advisor, and over Uncas as counselor in political affairs, it had the effect of destabilizing the entire colonial power structure at Mohegan. As Wheelock saw it, this occasioned a clamor that "spread through the government, and almost everyone cried out against Mr. Occom as a very bad, mischievous, and designing man."[101]

Perhaps it is not too cynical, then, to suggest that Wheelock stumbled upon a fortuitous means of getting Occom out of the picture when it was determined to send the Indian preacher to England in 1766 to raise money for a proposed Indian College. The idea seems to have been floated out as early as 1764, when one Charles Smith, an associate of Wheelock's and onetime headmaster of Wheelock's school, suggested, "would it not be best to send Mr. Occom with another Person home a begging?" Smith astutely noted that "an Indian minister in England might get a Bushel of Money."[102] Wheelock quickly embraced this notion, even while disseminating derogatory comments about Occom to anyone who might listen in an effort to discredit Occom's growing popularity in Mohegan and the surrounding area. In a letter to John Brainerd he asserts that "the blow" given to his school by "sending Mr. Occom back from New York was beyond any it has received from the first." But in the very next breath he advises Brainerd to keep quiet about the plans of "Mr. Occom going with you" to England.[103] Wheelock at once admits to the symbolic and practical indispensability of Occom, even while acknowledging him as the single largest threat to his own endeavors. The silence counseled by Wheelock in this private correspondence begins to reveal the hidden transcript of power that stood in direct opposition to the more public pronouncements of Wheelock's missionary endeavors with the Indians.

Before Occom could be sent to England, an attempt had to be made to smooth out the controversy that had been built up around him. Occom himself must have sensed the utility of this, and felt that his traveling to England would be worth the hardships risked, because he ultimately voices what was deemed an acceptable degree of regret over his actions in Mohegan in order to clear a path for himself. The Board of Connecticut Correspondents (a board of Connecticut representatives overseeing Wheelock's missionary efforts, and of which Wheelock was a member, in league with the Society for the Propagation of the Gospel), had accused Occom of misconduct toward "the overseers in the Affair of leasing the Indian Lands, and some proud and haughty Threatenings to turn Episcopalian . . . And disrespectful Treatment of the Reverend Mr. Jewet, and illegal proceedings again[st] the School Master at Mohegan, and engaging in the Mason Controversy."[104] Of all these charges he was acquitted save for the one of most significance to the board, which was the charge of meddling in the Mason land case. Of course, it wasn't in any way illegal for Occom to be involved in this case. It was simply inconvenient from the point of view of the board. With this understanding, Occom offered a carefully worded apology, which is transcribed as follows:

> Although, as a Member of the Mohegan Tribe and, for many years, one of their Council, I thought I had not only a natural and civil Right, but that it was my Duty, to acquaint myself with their *temporal affairs*; Yet I am, upon serious and close Reflexion, convinced, that as there was no absolute Necessity for it, it was very imprudent in me, and offensive to the *Public*, that I should so far engage as of late I have done, in the Mason Controversy: which has injured my Ministerial Character, hurt my Usefulness, and brought Dishonour upon Mr Wheelock's School and the Correspondents. For this imprudent, rash, and offensive Conduct of mine, I am heartily sorry, and beg Forgiveness of God—of this honorable Board of Correspondents, of whom I ought to have asked farther Advice—and of the Public; determining, that I will not for the future act in that Affair, unless called thereto and obliged by lawful Authority.

The apology is quite thorough, and has been characterized as "humble" and an example of "the firm hand which Wheelock maintained over his disciples."[105] And yet it is worth pointing out that it also has a number of dry, almost sardonic, touches that are typical of Occom. He makes a point of establishing the fact that his involvement in the Mason case was not only his legal right, but, as he perceived it, a "duty." And although he allows that "serious and close Reflexion" has convinced him that there was no "absolute Necessity" for such conduct, nevertheless he has succeeded in establishing his own context for his actions and positioning himself as a representative of Native space rather than simply a pawn of the committee. He concludes to not act further on the case "unless called thereto and obliged by lawful Authority," but as he already made clear in letters to William Johnson and the king of England, he firmly believed that the Mohegan had that lawful authority, and it was the colonial correspondents who had no rightful claim to Mohegan lands. Therefore, it is by no means a stretch to conclude that

Occom had promised absolutely nothing. His only consideration seems to be whether or not his persistence in the Mason land case, at that particular time, will "hurt my Usefulness." The apology is a means to an end for Occom, the public transcript that allows him to pursue the next step of his career, while remaining at the same time suggestive of the hidden transcript of Native resistance to colonial power.

While this transcript is clothed in appropriate English language, its inherent tensions cannot be utterly erased. It is reported by Ben Uncas III that Occom, himself, "told a squa he had outwitted the ministers"[106] in this event. While this may have been mere hearsay, a rumor Uncas put in motion to further damage Occom's reputation, the fact stands that Occom did continue to pursue his involvement in the Mason land case in England and elsewhere and as Lisa Brooks relates, this "revelation gives weight to the subtext of Occom's confession, which asserts the primacy of his nativity and his obligation as a councilor to his community."[107] Nevertheless, the path had been cleared for him to go to England and it was decided that he would be accompanied by Nathaniel Whitaker (rather than John Brainerd, the original choice) who was minister of the church at Norwich, Connecticut.

Occom, despite the undeniable tensions inherent in his self-presentations, was ever conscious of the persona he was forwarding in his writings and the social operations it performed.[108] The first draft of his "Short Narrative" was written as he set out for England in the fall of 1765, amid claims from his detractors that his "heathen" credentials were forged. A campaign was underway suggesting that Occom, rather than converting to Christianity in his late teens, had been raised and educated in the Christian religion from birth. Like many non-whites who sought to appropriate and master the white lexicon, Occom proved too expert at his endeavor and therefore found his origins contested.[109]

Occom was placed in the position of emphasizing his "Indianess" to a largely foreign Christian audience that knew nothing about Native culture or customs. As he wrote in the shorter 1765 draft of his autobiography, "Since there is great miss Representation by Some Concerning my Life and Education; I take this opportunity to give the World in few Words, the true Account of my Education." Whether with a sense of irony or not, he bluntly overstates his "heathenism" here and speaks in abject terms of his pre-Christian life spent wandering "up and down in the wilderness." He claims, "I was born a Heathen in Mmoyouheeunnuck alias Mohegan in N. London—North America. My Parents were altogether Heathens, and I was educated by them in their Heathenish Notions." He notes that "my Parents in particular Were very Strong in the Customs of their fore Fathers."[110] Because his goal was to raise money for the proposed Indian school, he felt compelled to present himself in the manner that he knew to be most efficacious toward achieving this goal. Introducing himself as a converted heathen served the purpose of positing the redeemable nature of Natives in general, forwarding his own life story as a successful example. As we shall see, however, when he extended this autobiographical sketch upon his return from England in 1768, although he would leave many of these troublesome phrases intact, the tone of his account became much more openly critical of the white European practices that had pressured him into making such concessions.

Still, as Occom waited to set sail from Boston, doubts persisted. In a letter to Wheelock, written shortly before his ship set sail, he comments that the Boston commissioners of the Society for the Propagation of the Gospel "think it is nothing but a Shame to Send me over the great Water . . . They further affirm, I was bro't up Regularly and a Christian all my Days, Some say, I cant Talk Indian, others Say I cant read—In short I believe the old Devil is in Boston to oppose our Design."[111] The letter demonstrates the difficult position Occom was in, as an Indian who had embraced Christianity. While some clearly doubted that an Indian could attain Occom's level of education and regarded him as a sham, others proposed that, as a result of his education, he was not *Indian* enough. He had to labor to convince those concerned with the mission that he was the genuine article, sprung from the heart of heathenism, despite his refined outer appearance, and it probably began to dawn on him that, as he entered onto a larger stage, a more nuanced performance would be required of him. I find it unlikely, for instance, that Occom was in the habit of calling the ocean "The Great Water," but such turns of phrase seem to have crept into his rhetorical mode and became part of the syncretic discourse, or orature, he was adopting as a Native skilled in alphabetic literacy.

The fact that Occom felt personally invested in this trip to England is suggested by the fact that, rather than characterizing it as solely Wheelock's scheme in his aforementioned letter, he refers to "*our* Design." He further writes, "I have a Struggle in my Mind At times, knowing not where I am going, I don't know but I am Looking for a Spot of ground where my Bones must be Buried, and never to see my Poor Family again, but I verily believe I am called of God by Strange Providence and that is Enough."[112] Perhaps he was familiar with the story of an earlier Native representative sent to England, named Pocahontas, who never made it home and whose bones were interred far from the land of her own people at Gravesend. Or, just as likely, he was familiar with the fate of Mahomet Weyonomon, a Mohegan sachem who traveled to England thirty years earlier in 1735 and died of smallpox while waiting to see George II concerning the Mason land case. Mahomet was buried in an unmarked grave in a south London churchyard.[113]

As Occom and Whitaker waited to ship out, we learn that the ship was being held up because of the complications of the Stamp Act controversy and an embargo taking place. There was unrest in the port city. Occom, an

Indian dressed as an Englishman, waited to ship out to London. But when he returned, it would be to white men dressed as Indians, throwing tea in the harbor and calling for a new political power structure in the colonies.

"An Undoubted Call": Divining a Native Agency for Occom's Tour of England

Occom set sail on December 23, 1765 and reached Bricksham, England safely on February 3 of the new year. As he made his way to London he seems to have been impressed, but also steadily appalled, by the severe disparity between rich and poor that he witnessed, the overwhelming opulence of the noble classes and the absolute squalor of London's beggar class. He observed "what great difference there is Between the Rich and the Poor— and What Difference there is Between God's poor and the Devil's Rich." In the streets he noticed "some Cursing, Swaring & Damning one another, others was hollowing, Whestling, talking giggling, & Laughing, & Coaches and footmen passing and repassing, Crossing and Cross-Crossing, and the poor Begars Praying, Crying, and Beging upon their knees."[114] After being brought to watch the pageantry of Queen Charlotte's birthday, he commented to himself in his journal, "O Lord God Amighty let not my Eyes be Dazled with the glitering Toys of this World."[115]

Occom's trip to England was a financial success and something of a public relations coup for Wheelock, despite the fact that Nathaniel Whitaker, the other half of this missionary tandem, was poorly received and quickly overshadowed by Occom's presence. If Indians were a common enough sight in the colonies, they were still a novelty to the Englishman. And Occom was ever aware of the fact that he was putting on something of a dog and pony show, even if he refused to fully pander to such expectations. The fact is, he was well liked in England. People came to see one thing, perhaps, but were gratified by the unexpected something *other* that Occom delivered. He was not the wild man of colonial lore, dressed in buckskins, face paints, and feather dresses. He didn't dance and howl and make wild incantations. He bore little resemblance, in fact, to previous Native dignitaries who had been journeying to England over the last two hundred years. And still, audiences came to see an Indian, and there were certain stereotypical traits attributed to the Indian character that were bound to shine through to his audiences, whether for good or ill. One can sense the inherent tension between the expectations of English audiences and the actual impression Occom made in a 1767 letter by Reverend Peter Jillard to Wheelock that reads,

> It was right to send over Mr. Occom, as a Specimen of the benefit of ye School—As far as I hear he pleases in every Town & city—So much simplicity appears in the man: So honest, guiless a Temper, with Seriousness in his public Service; So well he speaks in publick, & so well he acts in private among his friends & mankind, that he engages their hearts.[116]

The English people were willing to pay good money to see an "authentic" Indian, and although Occom may have subverted their expectations, he nevertheless delivered, offering to their eyes the image of the converted yet noble savage, simple, without guile, incapable of uttering a lie in his orations (see figure 4.1), in the words of Love, his sermons still retained "the indescribable scent of the forest in them."[117] The overall demand that grew for Occom amongst the evangelistic set might be intuited in a dialogue

Figure 4.1. 1768 portrait of Samson Occom by Moses Chamberlain.

recounted in Occom's diary on July 13, 1766. He writes, while he was at tea, "I seriously asked Mr. Cocks who was to preach at Mr. Whitefield's, he with all gravity Said Mr. Occom, Mr. Occom? Says I, yes, says he, I know nothing of it, says I again, it is So Concluded, says he—so I immediately went, and Preach'd to a Multitude of People, and the Ld gave me Some Strength."[118]

Occom was clearly bemused by his newfound celebrity and reveling in his successes, but he remained focused on his reasons for being in England and never lost sight of the fact that his family was at home, struggling in his absence. As he wrote to his wife Mary Occom, "I am Sensable of the great Burden and Care that is upon you, and I feel your Burden, Cares and Sorows. My poor Family is near and Dear to me, and you are the nearest to my Heart,—tho we are at great Distance from each other Yet you are nearer and Dearer to me than ever—But it was the Call of god and nothing but the Call of god in his Devine Providence, Cou'd have Caused me to Leave my Deare Family."[119] Wheelock had assured Occom that his wife "is, and will be, well Supplied."[120] But Mary Occom, managing eleven children on her own, was having difficulty holding things together and reported to Wheelock that her son Aaron "behaves himself so bad that I Cannt keep him."[121] She was forced to beg Wheelock for supplies, and in a 1767 letter, she writes, "I am out of Corn, and have no Money to buy any with, and am afraid we Shall suffer for want, an Sr. if you will be pleased to help me in my Distress."[122]

It remains uncertain whether or not Wheelock adequately fulfilled his obligation to Occom's family. The second of only two letters that Occom wrote to Wheelock in his two and a half years in England suggests some of the turmoil he must have been experiencing on this account, and perhaps a sense that, despite his many successes, events were slipping away from him. Occom writes,

> It has been my lot for a long time to have Sorrow of Heart, I have had Burden upon Burden, Trial upon Trial, Both without and within, far and Near, a General Concern is Riveted in my Heart, for my Poor Brethren According to the Flesh, Both for their Bodies and Souls; my Relations Causes Heavyer Sorrow; Every obstruction and Discouragement to Your School, and every Misconduct and behaviour of Your Indian scholars, Touches me to the quick; More than all these, the Consideration of my poor Family, as it ware, lets my very Hearts Blood; I am ready to Say, I am a Cruel Husband and Father, god has given me a large Family, but they have no enjoyment of me, nor I them for Some Years back, and the Whole Burden and Care of a Large Family of Children lies upon my poor Wife; What adds to my

> Sorrowful Heart is this, that Whilest I am a Teacher to others, I have Neglected [my] own Children, by my Perigrenations and now my Children are growing up, and are growing Wild, and the Devil has been Angry, yea he has & is devilish Mad with me, and if he can, he will Drag all my Children into all Manner of Sins and Down to Hell . . . If I was not fully Persuaded and Asure'd that this work was of god, and I had an undoubted Call of god to Come over into this Country, I wou'd not have come over, like a fool as I did, without any Countenance from our Board, but I am Will[ing] Still to be a fool for Christ Sake.[123]

Certainly Occom was cognizant of the fact that his family was suffering in his absence and he seems desirous of reminding Wheelock of this obligation even while he levels most of the blame on himself. The letter seems to reveal Occom at his darkest moment in England, calling into question every aspect of his years of missionary service.

Whatever his state of mind in composing this, the content also demonstrates the syncretic mode Occom had adopted, melding certain expectations of Native oratory with Christian rhetoric. He is not sad but has "sorrow of heart." He equates his personal consternation with the well-being of his people and family as a whole, but emphasizes his personal sense of a "calling" from god that has pulled him away from his people at this time. In fact, as with his original mission to Montauk, he establishes for us once again that he embarked upon this trip with no "Countenance from our Board." In other words, he had not demanded compensation and none was given. He also signals his cognizance of the fact that he is the main attraction in an untenable performance wherein his role is highly unstable and kept aloft only by the unfailing balance he brings to it. He laments he will "still be a fool for Christ Sake," because this is the only option he is allowed. His only comfort is that "I am in the way of my Duty" as God has designed it.[124]

Which begs the question, what did Occom hope to gain from his trip to England? How did he see it furthering the goals of his people? If the ties between he and Wheelock were as strained as they appear from their letters, what made Occom risk so much on the venture? It is clear from Wheelock's correspondences with the Earl of Dartmouth and others, that his intention was to build a school in the country of the Six Nations where he might raise up missionaries and send them out to "civilize" the wild heathen, as the tracts of land upon which they resided "are now become valuable and may soon be peopled."[125] It is difficult to see how Occom, even with his Christian missionary sense, would regard this as a worthwhile endeavor to the extent that he was willing to leave his large family to its own devices for a number of years. But Occom was not let in on the particulars of Wheelock's design, or if he did know of them, they were discovered in a roundabout way. One senses, in Occom's aforementioned letter, a thinly veiled critical note concerning Wheelock's efforts at Indian education. When he writes that "every Misconduct and behaviour of Your Indian scholars, Touches me to the quick," he is insinuating that Wheelock's methods of instruction are not working. They were too harsh and, as will be explored further in the next chapter, they frequently prompted his students to rebel or completely reject their schooling. One of the points Occom will make in his later autobiographical statement is how he took a less coercive approach to engaging his students and how this more openhanded method netted much greater results than the methods traditionally used by the colonists.

Meanwhile, it appears from Whitaker's letters that the ongoing Mason case was being followed closely as it came once again to argument in the London courts. He expresses the hope that, if the colonists were to win the case, the Mohegan themselves might be removed to Oneida, or some such territory, in which event, he notes, "I can't see why Mr. Occom may not join . . . in this request Since it is favorable to your Gov[ernment]; tho he does not know as yet of any Such proposal." Wheelock, himself, sent an agent to London, a Mr. Jackson of Connecticut, to propose just such a solution, and was therefore, behind Occom's back, scheming to have the Mohegan forcefully removed from their lands.[126] The backhanded nature of this scheme becomes even more insidious when one recalls the repeated remonstrations to Occom to steer clear of the Mason case. Occom presumably scaled back his vocal involvement in these proceedings believing that such a course of action would help, through the education afforded by the hoped for Indian college, secure an opportunity for the Mohegan to enter into the colonial economy and secure their rights as a landholding people. But all the while Wheelock and his "agents" were lobbying the courts to rule against the Mohegan and have them relocated, thereby opening up lands for white speculation in Connecticut and Iroquoia.

Occom rightly struggled with himself over his decision to steer clear of the Mason case. Mason, who was also in England at the time, wrote to Occom in February of 1768, noting "I haven't had the pleasure of hearing from you for some time. I should be glad of a line from you or of seeing you soon."[127] Occom, however, determined to keep his distance and had it on best authority (by Robert Keen, Occom's major advocate in England), that Mason could "never succeed to carry the point he is soliciting."[128] But if Occom chose not to put his other plans at risk by meeting with Mason, he nevertheless managed to continue advocating for the Mohegan while overseas. According to an English newsletter,

> the famous Indian convert, the Rev. Samson Occum, just before his departure from England for America, had the honour of a

> conference with the secretary of state of that department; and, after answering many questions relative to Indian affairs, (having first informed his majesty's minister, that he was under a promise, artfully obtained from him by the colony of Connecticut, not to give any account of Indian-affairs, unless legally called thereto), he was informed among other things, That his Majesty was determined, to protect and defend his faithful Indian allies in their just rights and protections.[129]

The language here once again showcases Occom's diplomatic acuity. By arranging for the minister of colonial affairs to meet with him, he manages to stay within the letter of his coerced agreement with the Connecticut Board of Correspondents, while still circumventing its intentions. He is not only able to pursue his Mohegan agenda by penetrating into the highest levels of British government (being "legally called there-to"), but he makes the Board of Correspondents look foolish in the process for having their "artful" schemes foiled. Though Wheelock and Occom had originally ventured into this endeavor together ("our design," Occom had called it), they were clearly at cross purposes by the time Occom made his way home again.

Still, there is little indication in his own correspondences articulating what exactly it is Occom hoped to gain from his time in England. Another letter from Whitaker, however, offers a glimpse into Occom's thinking. He writes,

> Mr. Occom tells me that there is a large tract of Land on Long Island on ye north Sid[e] not far west of Southhold, which was formerly offered to the Montauk Indians for Montauk, & which he thinks may be procured for a Small Sum which is handy for fish oysters Clams, & so that much of the youth's living might be obtained therefrom.[130]

Apparently Occom understood that the proposed school was to remain near Mohegan. He had no thoughts of venturing off into distant lands, but rather envisioned an institution that could support both branches of his own family, Mohegan and Montauk, on the traditional lands upon which both people had lived for centuries. No doubt he envisioned a role for himself in this institution, and it is not difficult to see how such a program, under Occom's oversight, might have been greatly beneficial for his community. Leon Burr Richardson, the Dartmouth historian who edited the collection of letters from which this passage is extracted, observes in a footnote, without any trace of irony, that "this important asset of Long Island was evidently *lost sight of* when the site of the college was fixed [italics mine]."[131] Another case of what might be thought of as "colonial eyestrain" or unwitnessing.

Whitaker finished his letter with the assurance that "Mr. Occom does not meddle in Masons affair." But this did not prevent Wheelock and Whitaker, himself, from "meddling."[132]

"The Doctor is turn'd Heretical": The Declaration of Independence in Occom's 1768 "A Short Narrative of My Life"

Occom came home sometime in the spring of 1768 after spending well over two years in England, delivering some three to four hundred sermons. His mission raised approximately £12,000 and earned Occom a reputation on both sides of the Atlantic, not necessarily as spokesman or diplomat (which he was), but as a curiosity in the evangelical community.[133] He was in demand by both Native and colonial congregations now, and throughout his life he would continue to support himself as an itinerant preacher, always invited to speak wherever he turned up. He would write to Wheelock, "I have work enough. I might preach every Day I have so many calls."[134] It was not simply that he was *an* Indian preacher, but that he was *the* Indian preacher, despite the existence of a handful of others such as Samuel Ashpo in Mohegan and Samuel Niles, the Native preacher in nearby Narragansett. But Occom was both the representative man and the exception, curiously unrepresentative of the presumed shortcomings of his race for many who flocked to see him.

Occom had so successfully dismantled the cultural barriers placed between Indian and colonist that he seems to have alarmed his original benefactors to a degree, forcing them to employ the tools of manifest manners to reconstruct an imaginary, backsliding Occom for the archives. Whereas critics previous to his trip to England were invested in denying Occom's heathen credentials, professing that he had been born and bred to a Christian education, thus explaining his advanced refinement and learning, now Wheelock and other old benefactors saw Occom's essential *Indianess* as the inevitable cause of his manufactured "fall" from grace. "I fear his Tour to England and the Great respect Shewn him there will have the Sad Effect to make him aspire after Grandure & ease, and prevent his future usefulness," Wheelock wrote to John Thornton, a benefactor in England, in the summer of 1768.[135] Occom was frequently reminded by his white missionary colleagues to mind his place, to practice humility, and guard against "that Indian distemper, *Pride*," which was thought to be the downfall of the "tawny races."[136] Wheelock further pursued this agenda, writing to another English benefactor, Robert Keen, that Occom's "sails were too high." One of Occom's former supporters and neighbors berated that, "The Doctor is turn'd Heretical—abominably erroneous—Occum is become vile indeed—a base fellow."[137] By 1771 Wheelock had concluded in a letter to Occom that "unless ye manifestation of your Repentance has been very Public, Clear, Strong & evident to every body your usefulness is near at an End where you are."[138] Not only was it "that Indian distemper, pride" that was stirring up so much trouble, but according to Wheelock, Occom had fallen repeatedly into "the Sin of Drunkenss in a public & very aggravated Manner."[139] Not content that such rumors die a natural death, Wheelock wrote to George Whitefield in England that God had allowed Occom "to fall into intemperance."[140] This flurry of accusations was hurled out in an apparent effort to distract the community of benefactors in England from Occom's dissatisfaction that the money he had raised for the Indian Charity School was now being funneled into the founding of Dartmouth College instead. As David McClure noted in a letter to Wheelock, Occom "complained, but in a friendly manner, that the Indian was converted into an English School & that the English had crouded out the Indian Youths."[141] (See figure 4.2.)

It is easy to imagine that Occom was bitter about this development and that he rankled under Wheelock's repeated defamations of character. That Occom was able to complain, "but in a friendly manner," as David McClure characterized it, demonstrates Occom's admirable composure and

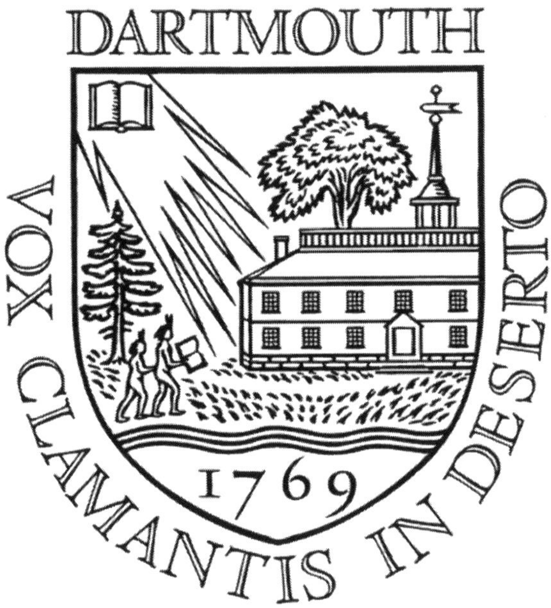

Figure 4.2. Dartmouth College seal. Courtesy of Rauner Special Collections at Dartmouth College.

politic nature, his apprehension that if he openly demonstrated the extent of his hurt, it would play directly into the hands of his detractors. In a much quoted letter to Wheelock, however, Occom expertly expressed his sense of betrayal, stating,

> I am very Jealous that instead of your Semenary Becoming alma Mater, she will be too alba mater to Suckle the Tawnees . . . In So Saying I Speak the general Sentiment of Indians and English too in these parts; So many of your Missionaries and School masters and Indian Scholars leaving You and Your Service Confirms me in this opinion—your having So many White Scholars and So few or no Indian Scholars, gives me great Discouragement—I verily thought once that your Institution was Intended Purely for the poor Indians—with this thought I Cheerfully Ventured my Body & Soul, left my Country, my poor young Family all my friends and Relations, to sail over the Boisterous Seas to England, to help forward your School, Hoping, that it may be a lasting Benefet to my poor Tawnee Brethren, With this View I went a Volunteer—I was quite Willing to become a Gazing Stock, Yea Even a Laughing Stock, in Strange Countries to Promote your Cause . . . I am going to Say Something further, Which is very Disagreeable Modisty would forbid me, but I am Constrain'd So to Write,—Many gentlemen in England and in this Country too, Say if you had not this Indian Buck you would not Collected a quarter of the Money you did.[142]

Occom was all too aware of the central role he'd played in raising funds for the college. The bitter irony of that bounty now being directed toward the benefit of white instead of Indian students is perfectly realized in his wordplay transforming "alma Mater" into "alba mater." Such an image delineated not only the racialized hierarchy by which the Natives had once again been cheated out of their possessions, but invoked in stark visual terms what were prevalent white anxieties regarding miscegenation. Should a white mother nurture "tawny" offspring? Even Occom's reference to himself as "this Indian Buck" suggests the double nature of this anxiety, the sexual allure of the Indian other who has put himself on display, prostituted himself on the colonial stage making of himself a "gazing stock" and a "laughing stock," whose progeny will not then be entitled to their share of the estate. He concluded his letter by noting, "this one consideration gives me great Quietness. I think I went to England with Honest Heart, I think I have done that which I think was my Duty to Do."[143] Occom, as always, positioned his actions firmly in the context of "duty," of advocacy for his people, reminding Wheelock of the ties of ethnicity, kinship, and nationality that he served. Wheelock, by channeling the funds elsewhere, was risking his own reputation. Occom warns him in the letter that "the opinion of many white People about here is that you have been Scheeming altogether." And in truth, he had.

Nevertheless, Occom was inclined to respond to all this with a sense of "great Quietness." This was both an inward and outward quietness, as Occom's ability to speak, to contest the power structures of colonial America, and resist within the open discursive channels of the day, were, as ever, "constrain'd." Occom's use of this word "constrained," which we will pursue further, is interesting in that he seems to regard such constraints as both the limitation and license of speech. Whereas, in the earlier letter from England, Occom had merely intimated the idea that Wheelock was not performing his duties as an instructor to the Natives as well as he might, now, in this "constrain'd" mode, Occom states outright that "So many of your . . . Indian Scholars leaving You and Your Service Confirms me in this opinion." What enabled Occom to confront Wheelock openly, and ward off coercive appeals for humble apologies and public confessions with "great Quietness," was the fact that, in Occom's mind, the break had already been made from his former school teacher. Occom's benefactors in England had donated their money not only to help the Indians or Wheelock's schemes, but because Occom, himself, had made such a positive impression upon them. And Occom correctly guessed that any further support for his endeavors would come from England and not Wheelock.[144] Upon his return from England, Occom reported directly to Robert Keen that he had traveled around visiting the Indians of the region since his return and that they were "very glad to hear the benevolent dispositions of Christians, over the mighty waters." He voiced hopes that, by such means, "their poor children's eyes may be opened, that they may see with their own eyes."[145] By appealing directly to English philanthropists like Keen and John Thornton, rather than Wheelock, and keeping them informed of his missionary efforts, Occom was effectively cutting out the middleman in the line of funds appropriated for Indian causes.

Occom also remarked to Keen at this time that "I am now writing a short narrative of my life."[146] This narrative, which he had begun prior to leaving for England, was likely meant to go into circulation around missionary circles in both England and the colonies. Perhaps it was originally meant to be an addendum to one of Wheelock's many promotional narratives concerning the state of the Indian Charity School. Apparently Keen wrote Wheelock sometime in 1768 or 1769 enquiring as to why there was no word of Occom in Wheelock's annual missionary "narrative" for that year. Keen scolds, "what is become of Mr. Occom—if he had wrote a letter acknowledging the kindness and civility he met with in England it would have looked well in the narrative we are now printing—instead of that not a word from him or about him."[147] Keen, who had been in correspondence with Occom all along, must have sensed that Wheelock was attempting to silence Occom and erase his contribution to his fundraising efforts. Quite possibly, Occom had submitted his revised version of the autobiographical narrative to Wheelock at this time, intending it to be his contribution to the missionary narrative. If Wheelock did receive the autobiographical sketch, however, he chose not to print it. Whatever its original intent when begun in 1765, the narrative as it now stood had become too radical a document to find a home in the American print venues of the day. If it began as an attempt by Occom to establish his heathen credentials to a skeptical community, it ended as nothing less than a declaration of independence from Wheelock and the Connecticut Board of Correspondents with whom he had associated in the past.

I have briefly commented upon Occom's narrative in various portions of this chapter, but it might be helpful at this point to focus on the properties of the "Short Narrative" that appear to speak toward both a public and a hidden transcript. Critics who have turned their focus upon this text have concentrated mostly on the opaque declaration at its end, in which Occom seemed to test the limits of resistant textualized speech for Indians in the late eighteenth century. Although the text lodges an open complaint in which Occom suggests he has been undercompensated and underappreciated as a missionary worker amongst the "poor Indians," his notice of this inequity does not strike one as necessarily subversive. There is a real danger that the text might be read as simply an appeal for higher wages, thereby allowing audiences to dismiss it as self-serving "whining" and not in keeping with presumed values of Christian self-sacrifice (as students in my early American literature classes often interpret it at first glance). It is doubtful, however, that Occom started or finished this piece with financial considerations in mind. If that were all that was at stake, the "Short Narrative" would fail to serve any larger rhetorical purpose or, as Jace Weaver claims, form a "communitist vindication of Natives in general."[148] We need only to have a fuller understanding of Occom's objectives, his apparent motivations as formed in Native space and entirely apart from the missionary establishment, to arrive at a more coherent interpretation of this narrative.

Part of the confusion surrounding Occom's narrative stems from the divided nature of its composition. While it begins safely enough by citing his conversion experience and his efforts as a missionary, it switches gears about three-quarters of the way through and becomes something else entirely. It is only at this later point, when Occom strays from the discursive constraints imposed by the polities of the dominant culture in general and of missionary culture in particular, that the text forces an irreconcilable rupture in the colonial narrative. Noting that white missionaries he knew of were being compensated more generously than himself, he writes, "Now you see what difference they made between me and other Missionaries; they gave me 180 Pounds over my 12 years Service, which they gave for one years Service in another Mission."[149] Perhaps, Occom muses, as a "poor Indian" he did not merit the same pay as white missionaries. Perhaps he could not be expected to have the same inherent cultural advantages that enabled white missionaries to better perform their duties. Occom's response is measured and walks a fine line between colonial and Native perspectives. By suggesting that his racial identity lies at the heart of the existing pay inequity, however, he transforms what began as a constrained discourse of colonial beneficence into an open transcript of racial discrimination. This rupture begins to reveal itself as Occom asserts, "I am now fully convinced, that it was not Ignorance" that led to his being undervalued, but rather, "I must Say, 'I believe it is because I am a poor Indian.' I can't help that God has made me So; I did not make myself so."[150]As with his wry comment referring to Dartmouth as "alba" rather than "alma mater," Occom has singled out race as the sole reason for his being misused.

The previous statement has given many readers pause. Its semi-contorted wording, with the central claim, "I believe it is because I am a poor Indian," situated within quotation marks, suggests in some manner how, as Henry Louis Gates has famously observed, "colonialism inscribes itself on the colonized."[151] Occom might be understood here to be saying that God has "made" him a "poor Indian" and by implication, a lesser creature. He may be expressing helplessness in the face of this god-made condition. But his phrasing can also be seen consciously deploying the racialized paradigms of the day in order to invert them in a veiled and convoluted articulation. Dana Nelson, in her article "I Speak Like A Fool . . . ," notes the careful couching of Occom's phrasing. He is repeatedly "constrain'd" into saying things he would rather not. He "must say" that if he is treated poorly, it is because he is " 'a poor Indian.' " In these cases, agency for Occom's speech is clouded and, according to Nelson, argues for the "structural hegemony of colonization that undercuts Occom's attempt to argue his own worth." Nelson concludes that Occom, as Christian missionary, finds himself caught in the double bind of being at once colonizer and colonized and this leads to the "sense of entrapment and division" that one apprehends in his word choice.[152] Occom's position in both worlds inhibits his ability to level a straightforward critique, and so instead it becomes bracketed and misdirected. David Murray, on the other hand, argues that Occom "actually exploits the ambiguities of his position as civilized Indian in his writing," employing his state of liminality to render a critique that otherwise could not be expressed by a "poor Indian." But still Murray cautions that it would be "a mistake to assume that in moving to a work authored . . . by an Indian we are necessarily moving further towards or away from an autonomous expression or an authentic voice."[153] Both authors see Occom's narrative as stretching the boundaries of discourse, reaching "toward a different understanding of his own agency," to quote Nelson, but still confined by the hegemonic forces that allow for such texts to speak from within the archive.[154]

The idea that any voice can be regarded as "authentic" is, of course, extremely problematic in and of itself, and brings into play concerns of what exactly informs an "authentic" speech act anyway, and how can authenticity ever really be determined in any culture. Such concerns should not distract us from the possibility, however, of a speaker's asserting *agency* from within a particular cultural moment, even if that agency has been obscured by the narrative framework through which we have habitually regarded it. What I would like to suggest is that, as long as Occom's narrative continues to be viewed from within the colonial archive, from within the narrative framework of Western hegemony in which it was housed, it will continue to read as a problematic expression of identity in which Occom argues for his place in the white missionary structure even while being marginalized from within that structure. Occom's "Short Narrative" was never more than a doorstop in this vestibule, however, and deserves to be read from within a narrative of Native continuity to be fully appreciated. When repositioned from colonial space and considered from another angle of vision, the text becomes one of liberation rather than vindication, one of independence rather than indenture.

One first has to imagine why Occom wrote this narrative at all, and for whom it was written. In all likelihood, the idea was suggested to him by Wheelock. As noted earlier, Occom wrote the first draft of this narrative on the eve of his departure for England. That Wheelock supported, and perhaps requested, this narrative is indicated by the fact that he subsequently published Occom's nascent autobiographical comments as part of a letter distributed to the New England newspapers at the time. Wheelock prefaced the letter by stating, "I do now certify the publick truth of that Matter, by giving his own Account of it, which he sent me from Boston on hearing false and injurious Reports made of that Matter before his Embarkation to Europe."[155] This was, in fact, Occom's first foray into public print. As has been already stated, at that particular moment it was important for Occom to introduce himself to the world stage he was about to enter upon, and to reinforce the notion that he was, in fact, a former "heathen" who had fully crossed over to Christian refinement, therefore modeling the efficacy of Wheelock's program. When Occom wrote to Robert Keen that he was reworking the narrative upon his return to Mohegan in 1768, he still believed that the money he had raised in England would be used to fund a true Indian school, and felt a more detailed narrative of his life would contribute to that endeavor. Occom was not yet aware while writing Keen that Moor's Charity School would be relocating to New Hampshire and he concludes the letter by noting "Doctor Wheelock's School prospers as heretofore, and the Indians are still willing to send their children."[156] But he must have soon learned otherwise, perhaps in mid-composition, and the narrative reflects this switch. As such, the finished version of the narrative, does not seem to have found a home in print, and did not appear in its entirety until Bernd Peyer retrieved it from the archives at Dartmouth and published it in 1982. Leon Burr Richardson seems not to have known of its existence when he compiled the letters surrounding the England Mission in 1933. He writes of Occom's declared intentions to narrate his life story in a footnote, claiming that "apparently this project was never carried out."[157] Neither Love nor Blodgett, Occom's biographers, speak of the "Short Narrative" (Blodgett refers to "a fragment of the autobiography which he so unfortunately never completed") and while excerpts of the narrative appear in a retrospective about the Mohegan nation published by the *Norwich Courier* in 1830, I have yet to locate an earlier version of the 1768 narrative in print.[158]

To begin to apprehend something of Occom's agenda in writing this piece, it is useful to look at the "Short Narrative" with an eye toward what speech falls under the category of "constrained" and what under the category of "unconstrained." As noted earlier, the narrative begins one way, and then finishes another. The tone is congenial enough up until the last section, given the title "From the Time I left Mr. Wheelock till I went to Europe." Up until this point, the focus is on his conversion and, in some manner, the ineffectiveness of white missionary efforts in Native space, as opposed to Occom's own successes. Occom claims of the early missions to Mohegan in his youth that "there was a Sort of School kept, when I was quite young, but I believe there never was one that ever Learnt to read anything." The white missionaries would apparently have to chase down their Indian students, and Occom notes that "he [the white missionary] used to Catch me Some times and make me Say over my letters." He describes similar conditions at Montauk when he first arrived on the scene, and how it wasn't until the departure of the white missionary there, a Mr. Horton, that there "was a remarkable revival of religion among these Indians." By way of contrast to the white missionary practices, Occom notes how he "took a mild way to reclaim them [the Native students]. I opposed them not openly but let them go on their way, and whenever I had an opportunity, I would read Such pages of the Scriptures, as I thought would confound their Notions." In this manner, he assures his audience, "the Lord was pleased to Bless my poor Endeavors, and they were reclaimed, and Brought to hear almost any of the ministers."[159]

In relating his usefulness, Occom was almost certainly hoping to achieve some measure of agency over how the Indian Charity School he hoped to run would be operated. Wheelock was known to whip his Indian students when they misbehaved. His techniques were rigid, the routines of Moors Charity School tightly regulated.[160] Wheelock locked his students into patterns of dependency and subordination in which they looked to him for all assistance, both spiritual and practical, and he apportioned out only as little of each as he deemed sufficient.[161] Occom, on the other hand, designed routines as a teacher that were "a Pleasure to them; and they soon learn their Letters this way." One method he speaks of was to glue individual letters onto chips of cedar and place them on a bench in order. Then he would ask his Indian students to fetch him the letter he required, thus having improvised the common feature of many an American childhood today known as alphabet blocks.[162] (See figure 4.3.)

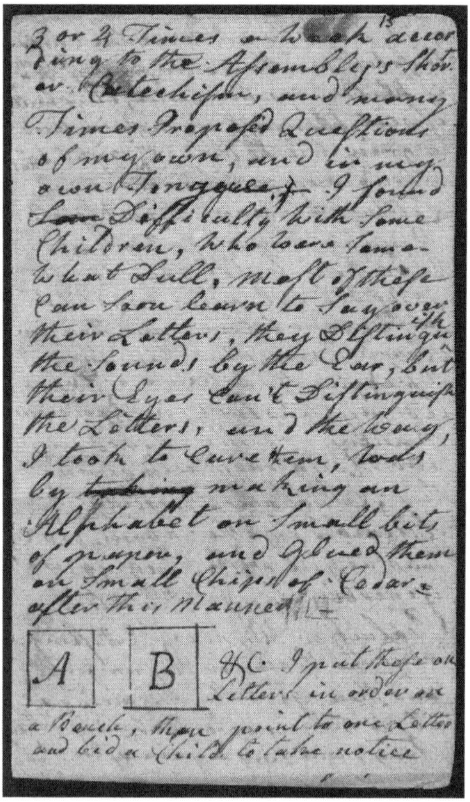
15
3 or 4 Times a Week according to the Assembly's Shor. Catechism, and many Times Proposed Questions of my own, and in my own Tongue. I found Difficulty with Some Children, who were Somewhat Dull, most of these can Soon learn to Say over their Letters, they Distinguish the Sounds by the Ear, but their Eyes can't Distinguish the Letters, and the way I took to cure them, was by making an Alphabet on Small bits of paper, and glued them on Small Chips of Cedar after this manner

A B &c. I put these on Letters in order on a Bench, then point to one Letter and bid a Child to take notice

Figure 4.3. Occom's sketch of alphabet blocks from his unpublished 1768 autobiographical narrative. Courtesy of Rauner Special Collections at Dartmouth College.

Occom's narrative seems to stray from its original purpose, however, when he begins to discuss the matter of how he made ends meet at Montauk. As stated earlier, his many occupations, aside from being preacher and teacher for the local Native communities, included bookbinding, farming, hunting, fishing, and the making of wares such as wooden spoons, ladles, and gunstocks. He worked cedar into "Pails, Piggins and Churns." He also notes that he attended the sick, performed funeral services, acted as judge, counselor, and scribe. As a local newspaper noted of him, he seems to have served as "a kind of legal adviser and magistrate among the Montauks."[163] But what begins as a Franklinesque testament to his industry, frugality, and usefulness suddenly devolves into a discourse on the pay inequities between himself and white missionaries until he is no longer referring back to past events, but exclaims in some frustration, "I Can't Conceive how these gentlemen would have me Live."[164]

As a result of Occom's public falling out with Wheelock upon his return from England, the only imaginable audience for Occom's narrative at this point was the commissioners in England who continued to support him. And it is likely that, once the prospect of the Indian school at Montauk fizzled out, the reasons for constructing such a narrative account dried up altogether. At which point Occom's speech became, in his own words, "constrained." He is forced to speak in a way that he would rather not, and yet this constraint, or outside force, is what, in effect, liberates him to speak. He writes,

> In my Service (I speak like a fool, but I am Constrained) I was my own Interpreter. I was both a School master and Minister to the Indians, yea I was their Ear, Eye & Hand, as well as Mouth. I leave it with the World, as wicked as it is, to Judge, whether I ought not to have had half as much, they gave a young man Just mentioned which would have been but £50 a year; and if they ought to have given me that, I am not under any obligations to them, I owe them nothing at all.[165]

Occom's deployment of the word "constraint" works paradoxically. He has learned to perform in a world in which his speech and textual expressions are carefully modulated bits of *orature*, and are always, in fact, constrained. Only in the moments that he acknowledges the existence of these constraints, however, does he allow himself to gesture toward the hidden transcript, or the threads of Mohegan advocacy and resistance which have informed Occom's actions from the very start. He uses the notion of constraint to actually untether the constraints of speech, and to, in fact, wipe away the tears and clear the obstructions from the "Ear, Eye & Hand as well as Mouth," that have prevented him from speaking fully for his people. Essentially, what has been overlooked by the critical reception of this text is Occom's blunt assertion to the missionary community of New England (and to "the World"), that "I am not under any obligations to them, I owe them nothing at all." He is not asking for more pay, but making a clean break. The fact of the unequal pay he has received over his many years of service is what frees him to do this.

He punctuates his narrative with an anecdote about a "Poor Indian Boy" who is called by his master to account for the beatings and whippings he has received at the hand of the man to whom he has been indentured. Occom writes that the boy was asked

> what it was he did, that he was So Complained of and beat almost every Day. He Said, he did not know, but Supposed it was because he could not drive [a plow] any better, but says he, I Drive as well as I know how; and at other Times he Beats me, because he is of a mind to beat me; but says he believes he Beats me for the most of the Time 'because I am an Indian.'[166]

The boy offers up the only explanation that has been made available to him, even though it fails to in any way address the matter at hand. He must speak as though the explanation "because I am an Indian" were sufficient in and of itself, when in reality, the two components of the verbal equation in no way connect. It is not the boy's behavior that merits his violent treatment, but the arbitrary matter of his race. Nevertheless, he *must* speak as though the two were the same. The fact that he is "whipt and Beat" as a result of his identity unveils the paper-thin layer of rhetoric that separates the cultural status of the Native from that of the African slave in eighteenth-century New England.

Occom, extending the parable of the Indian boy to his own situation, concludes his autobiographical narrative with the following explanation for his pay inequities: "I am ready to Say, they have used me thus, because I Cant Instruct the Indians as well as other Missionaries, but I Can assure them I have endeavored to teach them as well as I know how—but I must Say, 'I believe it is because I am a poor Indian.' I Can't help that God has made me So; I did not make myself So."[167] Occom understood that his methods were the more practicable and effective when it came to teaching and preaching to Native communities. Regardless of his proven effectiveness, however, he *must* say he receives lesser pay than the white missionaries for the seemingly arbitrary reason of his race. Such an utterance is forced upon the Native speaker, who is constrained to echo the justification of the colonial master. *Must* he use this excuse because it is the only possible justification available, or *must* he use it because the oppressive culture from within which he inscribes this protest allows him no other discursive recourse? Despite the wide-ranging accomplishments that had distinguished him not only amongst his fellow Natives, but in a competitive colonial world with all the advantages in favor of the colonist, Occom was readily dismissed by his peers as "a poor Indian," as "haughty," as "intemperate," and prone to what were regarded as the inevitable "failings of his race," and his "Indian mind." He was forced into numerous, humiliating public apologies throughout his career, humbled himself to those whose abilities and intellect paled in comparison to his own, and saw his many successes undermined as a result of his overall political powerlessness. At every stage of Occom's career, attempts were made to define him according to colonial agendas, whether as a "heathen," a "drunk," a "heretic," or a born Christian who knew nothing of Native language and tradition. Unlike King Philip and other Natives of an earlier generation, however, Occom was capable of countering these attacks in his own written works, leaving a standing record of his own sense of self. In his autobiographical narrative Occom suggests the tautology by which even the assimilated preacher, whose actions have gained him an international reputation, is constrained to refer to himself as a "poor Indian." But he is also, in effect, defusing this discursive containment in the same instant that he deploys it, bringing into the open the racialized underpinnings of a term that was most often invoked out of a sense of misguided altruistic pity.

Occom's "Short Narrative" languished amongst Wheelock's letters at Dartmouth until the late twentieth century. Nevertheless it articulates his point of departure from the New England missionary establishment. From this moment on, Occom would begin to carve out a path that, while still very much constrained by the limits imposed by colonial hegemony, was not beholden to the financial or ideological imprimatur of the gospelizing societies. Quite possibly he initiated an Indian church at Mohegan at this time that, while adhering to the tenants of Christianity, was built around the more sympathetic and supportive strains of evangelical philosophy that characterized Occom's style of preaching. It was ever Wheelock's assumption that his Indian pupil could not successfully function without his support and guidance. But, in fact, Occom had led a fulfilling life at Montauk without Wheelock's support, and his most productive years were still ahead of him. The publications by which his fame and historical significance were sealed had yet to be published in 1768. And the exodus of New England Natives to Brothertown had probably yet to appear on Occom's radar screen. But Occom had made the first significant step toward self-determination in an era of daunting constraints.

The devastating wave of colonialism had yet to settle, however, and Occom's narrative would, over time, be folded into colonial paradigms that remain difficult to untangle even today. By 1830 the *Norwich Courier* would publish an article entitled "The Mohegan Indians" that aptly demonstrated the machinations of unwitnessing capable of erasing the violence and tensions of colonialism and placing the blame for the diminished aspect of the Mohegan squarely back in the hands of the Mohegan themselves. The article states how "a large debt of gratitude is due from the people of Norwich and of other towns bordering on the Thames [the Thames River in Connecticut, formerly the Pequot River], to the remaining fragment of the Mohegan tribe, once a powerful Indian nation, the original owners of the soil." The reason offered for this "debt of gratitude" was the kindness shown by Uncas, the former Mohegan sachem, in "granting many of his lands to the governor, and magistrates of the Colony." Gone from this otherwise historically informed retelling is any mention of the prolonged battle of the Mason land case or the bitter racial tensions that led to political upheavals in Mohegan and accompanied the loss of Mohegan lands. In this revised version of events the "diminution of the once powerful Mohegans" is to be ascribed not to the loss of land and political autonomy through colonial legal pressure, but "to the Indians well known love of *occapee* or *strong-water*." It is suggested without irony that only a Christian "spirit of benevolence," accompanied with "temperance and industry would save the remnant of this tribe."[168]

Occom's "Short Narrative" made its first and perhaps only truncated appearance within this newspaper article, wherein Occom is presented as the great hope of the Indian, an example of what might have been had not the natural defects of the race taken over. The first sections of Occom's narrative involving his conversion and teaching at Montauk are either fully presented or faithfully paraphrased. But the last part of the narrative, "the unconstrained" part detailing Occom's split with Wheelock for making off with the monies he raised and his resentment toward the missionary societies, is left out entirely. Occom's presumed fall from grace is hinted at, but it is attributed to racial weakness. "It would be very surprising," the reporter congenially tells us, "if the flattering attention which Mr. Occum received in England should not have some effect on his *Indian mind* [italics mine] to awaken the emotions of pride and to render him discontented with his previous mode of living." While no mention is made of pay inequities or land appropriations, this article, and nearly every other future reference to Occom in the press, did not fail to repeat Wheelock's unfounded accusations concerning Occom's intemperance. Nor did it fail to suggest with a hint of pity that this defect was the downfall of the race in general.[169] Once again, the evils of colonialism are elided, and the Indian is made responsible for his own disenfranchisement and vanishing.

Interestingly enough, the impetus for this glance back at Mohegan history seems to have been occasioned by the death of Lucy Tantaquidgeon, Samson Occom's sister, who passed away in June of that year, 1830, at the age of ninety-seven, and whose death notice came under the headline "The Last of the Mohicans."[170] From this point on, a paradigm was established in which every Mohegan death worth publically noting was destined to be the "last," and Natives as a group were considered to be either compromised by assimilation or dying off as a result of their inability to assimilate. An honest appraisal of Occom's life, however, can only conclude that he could never be placed within such a binary. Only under the bitterly ironic machinations of colonial unwitnessing could the telling be retooled so that contested lands became "gifts," Wheelock's perfidy became a case study in "benevolence," and Occom's energetic advocacy for the Mohegan people became the entropic efforts of a wasted race of "poor Indians."

When we concentrate on Native lives of the eighteenth and nineteenth centuries, their devotion to a European faith often seems somehow paradoxical or a kind of betrayal that exists within an either/or binary. But Natives in New England had been conversant with some form of Christianity for over a century by time Occom came to it. The Christian faith was not seen by all Natives as existing in opposition to their own prior belief systems, but rather as something that might be incorporated into, or worked in tandem with, existing cosmologies. In many cases, as we have seen, embracing Christianity was the only discernable path toward insuring political and cultural viability. To move with the flow of Christianity became the path of least resistance, and many, rather than fight this power, chose to move with it, taking as many articles of traditional belief that they could carry along with them.

Occom's negotiation with Christianity seems to have been heartfelt and sincere, and yet failed to result in the perfectly assimilated modes that his colonial handlers expected. In the longest of his existing written sermons (other than the published sermon at the hanging of Moses Paul, which we will examine in the following chapter), Occom quoted from Luke 10:26–27, citing the maxim "thou shalt love thy neighbor as thyself." He writes,

> tho it is very natural for every Nation to have a National Love, and I believe it is not forbid in our Text, but then we Should have the Same Love to other Nations as we have to our Nation; and if this took place, there would be an End of Wicked Wars and Blood Shed Among the Nations, O How happy the Nations of the World live if they were all Neighbourly to one another but alas it is not so, Nations are pulling down one another, and Distroying each other,—but let us apply What we heard Closely to ourselves in our Daily Concerns with each other, in our Commerce.—Do we deal with one another as Neighbour, are we willing that our Neighbour should live as well as we?[171]

Occom's thought is political as well as spiritual here, taking into account the progress and concerns of nations alongside Native traditions of exchange, the principals of Christianity and the brotherhood of man as he understood it. Occom's sermons were not reliably dated, and so it is difficult to know exactly when these words were composed, although he seems to have delivered the sermon in May of 1787. In all likelihood it was written in response to events of the Revolutionary War to which many Mohegan gave their lives fighting on the side of the Americans. Occom had counseled neutrality during the war, but forces were such that young Mohegan men were drawn into the conflict, including Occom's son-in-law Joseph Johnson. In the aftermath, Occom was left to reflect upon the dark motives of men and nations. He saw no reason for nations not to profess a self-love or national pride, and undoubtedly he emphasized such convictions to his Native audiences, but he also seems to have reflected on the perceived contradictions between colonial words and actions. Christians exhorted one another to "love thy neighbor," but seemed not to extend that love beyond their own national or ethnic boundaries.

When, in the same sermon, Occom referred to the practices of "Oppressors, over-reachers, Defrauders, Extortioners with holders of Corn and other necessities," his Native audiences, at least, knew he was speaking of the practices by which colonists had culturally and economically disenfranchised Native nations over the last two centuries.[172] Occom seems to have determined that the systems by which white Europeans governed themselves were predatory in Nature and stood as the very antithesis to the spiritual teachings of both Western and Native civilizations. To be a "with holder of Corn" was to stand in opposition to the political and spiritual necessities of the "common pot," or the coexistence of many peoples and nations upon the land. It disrupted the ideal principles of reciprocity and engagement that lay at the core of Native belief systems. Occom is not explicit in laying blame to any particular nation or people. He does not assign racial characteristics to such actions of men. Yet he offers an implied critique of colonial power when he identifies "A Covetous People" who desire

> every thing that their Neighbors have, Yea This sort of People I think are Monopolizers; don't you think so? For these gen[tle] Men will Buy up evry Necessary of Life in Town or State, even of the Whole World, were it in their Power especially in the Time of great Want and Distress, and When they have Horded up What they can then they will set an Extravagant Price upon their Commodoties at once . . . and if the Times like to grow harder and Distresses increase in the Land, these People will Shut up their Stores, and will tell you a thousand Genteel Lies.[173]

Occom's Native audiences were sure to configure in these words nothing less than the strategies by which they had lost lands, power, and influence until they had, in fact, become distressed and in a situation of great want. The complex network of relations between people, animals, and the land had been violently disrupted, reorganized, cast in a terrible new die. Over the course of some two hundred years there had been a great, unthinkable loss of lives from war, poverty, and disease; territory had been ceded; traditions disrupted; the land itself was being altered, cordoned off; woodlands become depleted of game; and even the relation of man to man had undergone a vital shift. The sermon goes on to exhort against the evils of slavery and finds, in the traditional practices of Natives, an antidote to the self-destructive tendencies of Western civilization. He writes,

> this is very Remarkable among the Indian Heathen in this great Continent They discover this Noble Human Self Love, they are very Compassionate one to another, very Liberal among themselves, and also to Strangers, When there is Scarsity of Food amongst them, they will yet Divide what little they have if there is but a mouth full a Piece, and When any of [them] kills any Creature, they will equally divide it amongst them all and when they have Plenty especially what they got in Hunting & Fishing—and when anyone is destitude of a Blanket, he that has two, will freely give him one, and they are very kind to one another in Sickness, and they Weep with them that Weep—this I take to be a Human Love or Being Neighborly, according to our Text.[174]

Occom's meditations on neighborliness lead him to conclude that "I find among those who are called Christians, [people] void of natural affection according to their conduct in the world—and what shall we of you, or think of you, or what do you think of yourselves, you that are slave keepers?" Occom exhorted his audience that "there are many who are all for liberty—they will take all liberty but will give none . . . If the ministers are true liberty men, let them preach liberty for the negroes fervently and with great zeal, and them ministers who have negroes—set an example before their people by Freeing their Negroes, let them show their face by their works."[175]

Occom not only begins here to invoke a discourse of liberty so indicative of the post-Revolutionary period, but he directly contrasts American slavery with Native customs of hospitality. I would suggest, however, that the literary community of the late eighteenth century would not have tolerated from an American Indian—even a converted Christianized one—the publication of a jeremiad that directed its ire upon New England's slavery, particularly when the major forces behind Indian education, like Occom's early teacher Eleazar Wheelock, were slaveowners themselves, and the thinly veiled object of his critique.[176] Nevertheless, we might surmise that "being Born a Heathen and Brought up in Heathenism" was an education of great moral value to Occom. He seems to have understood Christian doctrine to be best exemplified in the behaviors and customs of his own people and not the other way around.

Such convictions have continued beyond Occom's time and remain important to Mohegan identity and religious practice. As tribal historian Melissa Fawcett recounts, it was Mohegan medicine woman Emma Baker who revitalized the traditional Green Corn ceremony amongst the Mohegan in the nineteenth century by attaching it to the agenda of the Church Ladies' Sewing Society. Fawcett notes that "by physically linking this festival to the Mohegan Church in the year before the Mohegan Reservation began to break up, Emma focused tribal solidarity around the only post-reservation tribally owned land parcels," which found their epicenter on Occom's former homestead, the church on Mohegan Hill.[177] (See figure 4.4.)

Figure 4.4. Mohegan Church, Uncasville, Connecticut. Photograph by author.

Which suggests that it was, and is, possible to be Christian and traditional all at once and that the two systems of belief could exist side by side. Perhaps this is best evidenced in the case of Occom's wife, Mary, who appears to have held on to many, if not all, of her traditional beliefs. She was noted by the missionary David McClure, when he visited the Occom household in 1768, to still dress in Native garb, speak her traditional language even when guests were over, and to have "retained a fondness for her Indian customs."[178] Mary's brother, Jacob Fowler, playfully concluded a letter to Occom with the lines, "I direct my love to you / Which is but your due / And to my sister dear / Which I hope him fear (I mean, in God's time will him fear)."[179] The verse seems to imply that, despite having been married to the famous Indian preacher for over a decade, Mary Occom had not quite found her way to fully embracing Christian beliefs and practices herself. But if this concerned Occom, he does not mention it in his writings.

Seneca historian and ethnographer Arthur Parker, writing in 1954, advised,

> as for the 'last of the Mohicans,' let no man mourn. Mohegans may still be found, even in colleges. One was an informant of the late Frank G. Speck at his anthropological laboratory at the University of Pennsylvania and another was a flyer in World War 1 . . . plenty of them will be found in Wisconsin, where on Green Bay, they are mingled with the migrant Oneidas . . . some are, or have been, lawyers, clergymen, teachers, physicians, farmers and skilled mechanics . . . They are among those who have refused 'to go to sleep.'[180]

When Parker speaks of Mohicans in Wisconsin, he is eluding to the Brothertown Natives, with roots in both Mohegan and Mohican culture, whom Occom would lead into Oneida territory in Upstate New York in the coming decade and who would later push westward to Green Bay. The Mohegan "informant" to whom Parker refers was none other than Gladys Tantaquidgeon, a Mohegan medicine women and culture bearer for the tribe. She was tutored not only under the eye of famed anthropologist Speck, but under the aforementioned Emma Baker. She was also the great-granddaughter of Lucy Tantaquidgeon, Samson Occom's sister, listed in the *Norwich Courier* as "the Last of the Mohican."[181] In 1998 she was still active in the restoration of the church on Mohegan Hill, once the site of Occom's home. As Melissa Jayne Fawcett reminds us, "ni ya yo mo. It is ever so."[182]

5

A Tale of Two Settlements

Mohican, Mohegan, and the Road to Brothertown (1724–1785)

In this late War we have suffered much, our Blood has been spilled with yours and many of our young men have fallen by the side of your Warriors, almost all those Places where your Warriors have left their Bones, there our Bones are seen also—now we who remain are become very poor. Now Brothers, we will let you know we have been invited by our Brothers the Oneidas to go and live with them. We have accepted their invitation.

—Hendrick Aupaumut, 1783 Indian Petition

My friends, look around and consider the goodness of the Lord. Behold this was once a wilderness wide. Now it blossoms like a rose.

—Joseph Johnson, *To Do Good to My Indian Brethren*

Mount Vision: Selectively Surveying the Terrain in Cooper's *The Pioneers*

Larzer Ziff has noted of Jeffersonian republicanism that it "required tracts of vacant space as the site for its actualization."[1] But to vacate this space demanded of the Native inhabitants that they either conveniently vanish, or become assimilated into white culture. Such a feat could not be accomplished quickly, conveniently, or without bloodshed. But one could lay the ideological groundwork as easily as one could imagine a vast continent already divided up into convenient checkerboard portions, as was already being done following the 1785 Land Ordinance, which parceled out the North American landscape along the principle meridians, extending "throughout the whole territory; provided that nothing herein shall be construed, as fixing the western boundary."[2] Intrinsic to the ideology of western expansionism was an ingrained disavowal of the fact that Natives had previously inhabited the land in any meaningful way. As the Pequot minister William Apess would write in his impassioned 1836 oratory "Eulogy on King Philip,"

> Look at the deep-rooted plans laid, when a territory becomes a state, that after so many years the laws shall be extended over the Indians that live within their boundaries. Yea, every charter that has been given was given with the view of driving the Indians out of the states, or dooming them to become chained under desperate laws, that would make them drag out a miserable life as one chained to the galley; and this is the course that has been pursued for nearly two hundred years.[3]

Apess was merely committing to paper what many Native communities had already taken to heart—the fact that there was no place for them in the dream of American expansionism.

In his well-beloved 1823 novel, *The Pioneers*, James Fenimore Cooper rendered with an elegiac eye the gradual, and what he considered to be inevitable, domestication of frontier space, his Natty Bumppo/Leatherstocking/Hawkeye and John Mohegan/Chingachgook/Serpent representing what Richard White has described as a "middle ground" where ideas of Western order come to inhabit the presumably more libertine structures of Native life.[4] Both are hybrid characters, Natty Bumppo the white man in animal skins whose habits were "so nearly assimilated to those of the savages," and John Mohegan, the Indian who has at least nominally embraced Christianity.[5] Cooper writes, "From his long association with the white-men, the habits of Mohegan, were a mixture of the civilized and savage states . . . In common with all his people, who dwelt within the influence of Anglo-Americans, he had acquired new wants, and his dress was a mixture of his Native and European fashions."[6] Cooper's creation of Chingachgook has been faulted, over the last half-century of criticism, as a romanticized notion of the Native as a sort of noble savage, unable or unwilling to make the transition into a rapidly modernizing world. *The Pioneers*, however, offers the other end of the paradigmatic extreme in which John Mohegan (as he is most typically referred to in *The Pioneers*) is, for the most part, a defeated figure, degraded by cultural submission and drink, only capable of summoning up his once formidable spirit in brief nostalgic flashes. Perhaps surprisingly, he is not undone by his intractability in the face of white civilization, but rather by the accommodations he has already made to it.

Alan Taylor notes that "according to local tradition, a wandering Mohican basket maker and hunter named Captain John served as the original model for Chingachgook."[7] If so, then it is tempting to speculate that the prototype for John Mohegan was actually of the Brothertown Natives, or perhaps a Stockbridge Indian, who had immigrated from Connecticut or Massachusetts in the previous century, as these were the Mohegan/Mohicans most likely to be residing in Iroquois country at the time. Economically marginalized by the encroachment of white communities, many Natives of the Northeast were forced to manufacture homemade crafts and peddle them amongst their white neighbors. As noted in the previous chapter, Occom himself eked out a living binding books, making spoons, ladles, and "piggins," or small wooden pails.[8] When Natives appeared at all before the settler community in the late eighteenth and nineteenth centuries, it was often to sell such wares.

There was some precedent, too, for Christian Indians from the Brothertown and Stockbridge families having, like Chingachgook, fought with the English in both the French and Indian War and the Revolutionary War. Joseph Johnson's father, a Mohegan, was known amongst the New England Natives as Captain Johnson and he participated in the defense of Fort William Henry, the battle that stands as the centerpiece for Cooper's 1826 novel, *The Last of the Mohicans*.[9] A member of the Stockbridge Mohican, Hendrick Aupaumut, or Captain Hendrick, also held the field rank of captain in the Revolutionary War.[10] Although there remains some confusion over the tribe to which Chingachgook/John Mohegan actually belonged, in Cooper's understanding of indigenous history the Mohegan and Mohican were one tribe, an offshoot of the Delaware or Lenape that had broken from the main and moved northeast to occupy the Hudson and Connecticut River valleys in precontact times. After King Philip's War, a branch of the eastern Mohegan again "sought a refuge around the council fire of the mother-tribe, or the Delaware."[11] It is this branch of the Mohegan to which Chingachgook, who had presumably been driven inland so that he might claim to have "never seen the sunshine but through the trees," traces his bloodline.[12]

Cooper's history is not entirely implausible. The Mohegan and Mohican both recognized the Delaware or Lenape as their "grandfathers" and some Mohegan did move west following King Philip's War to find refuge with the Mohican, Delaware, Shawanoe or Shawnee, and others.[13] But his conflation of the Mohican and Mohegan as one tribe remains one of many gross misunderstandings that are sprinkled throughout his "Indian" novels. Chingachgook's son, Uncas, is portrayed as one of these fugitive Mohegan, when, in fact, the historical line of Uncases remained in Connecticut on traditional Mohegan ground, and as we saw in chapter 4, were denounced by much of the tribe for selling off land to colonists. Seneca historian and ethnographer Arthur Caswell Parker referred to Cooper's constructs of Native identity as rooted in "hearsay traditions," and wondered "what plots and personalities Cooper might have found within a day's stage journey of Cooperstown" had he only bothered to look.[14] Parker suggests that if Cooper had simply spent a month or so amongst his neighbors and "studied their rich heritage of myth; legend, ceremony, social relations, government and ideals, he might have scooped the saga of Hiawatha, written one of the world's greatest classics, and got it right before J.V. H. Clark of Onondaga Valley passed along the story to Henry R. Schoolcraft, who gave it to Longfellow, who got it all wrong." He might have learned of the *Red Score* or the *Walam Olum* of the Lenape, Parker insists, and come to understand the historical intricacies of the League of the Iroquois.[15] But instead, Parker notes,

> he placed a Connecticut Uncas in King George's New York 'court yard,' mixed the Indians of the Thames with those of the Hudson and Lake George, and put the Delawares of New Jersey on Lake Champlain. He had Mohawks aiding the French instead of standing at the side of England's William Johnson and his successors, and he made the Hurons a still effective fighting force, as if they had not been thoroughly scattered in 1650 by the despised Magwas.

But, as Parker acknowledges (anticipating a great deal of contemporary scholarship by some fifty years), Cooper was not interested in writing history. He was a "fiction writer who only used the mingled aromas of fact . . . he stamped legend, synthetic though it may be, into the soil and cultivated it with his imagination so that neither criticism nor time have obliterated it."[16]

Cooper, ensnared by his own racialized aesthetics and confused sense of Native history, would never have associated John Mohegan/Chingachgook with a movement of Christian Indians who lived in framed houses, farmed the land, and even more implausibly, could read and write. But it would be a mistake to think that Cooper was completely ignorant that such beings existed, or had turned a deliberate blind eye to Indian assimilation. As in the past, Native civilization had to be acknowledged before it could be effectively unwitnessed. Therefore Bumppo laments toward the end of *The Pioneers*,

> When I look about me at these hills, where I used to could count, sometimes twenty smokes, curling over the tree-tops, from the Delaware camps, it raises mournful thoughts, to think, that not a Red-skin is left of them all; unless it may be a drunken vagabound from the Oneidas, or them Yankee Indians, who, they say, be moving up from sea-shore; and who belong to none of God's critters, to my seeming; being, as it were, neither fish nor flesh; neither white-man, nor savage.[17]

"Them Yankee Indians" Bumppo espies beyond the Delaware campfires can only be of the Brothertown settlement, which had, in actuality, already been established prior to William Cooper's "first" surveying of the land in 1785.

There is, of course, very little precedent in the shaping of America's own national mythology allowing for the efforts of Native Americans emigrating westward to carve out ordered settlements in the "wild" frontier. In an era when white speculators like Cooper were buying up land in droves, most Native American communities east of the Susquehanna were, not coincidentally, experiencing a reverse phenomenon, finding their traditional, as well as legal, holdings shrinking down to virtually nothing. As such, they were all but overlooked as Cooper and his creations surveyed the literary terrain. Ironically, when Bumppo's gaze does fall upon them, he condemns the Brothertown immigrants for being, in many ways, exactly what he and John Mohegan are—liminal figures, caught between two worlds, "neither fish nor flesh; neither white man nor savage."

Cooper, however, cannot adequately articulate this paradox. His perspective, always strategically situated from a prominent height, a "Mount Vision," that takes in and encompasses both the geographical and ideological landscapes over which he endeavors to lay narrative claim, is one that still effectively erases, or unwitnesses, Native presence. According to Cooper, the "true" Indians, the "pure," "authentic," "noble" race of Bumppo's and John Mohegan's past, had vanished, their campfires permanently doused so that "not a redskin is left of them all." Of the few exceptions he allows, either drunks or "them Yankee Indians," Cooper makes it clear these are not legitimate specimens. They are, in fact, so degraded in form that they must not even be considered amongst God's creatures. They are not only consigned, but literally damned, to inhabit an interstitial space, being neither "fish nor flesh."

As seen in the previous chapter in the life of Samson Occom, even partial assimilation came with its own snares, and any Native individual attempting it was in danger of being regarded as damaged goods, insincere or lacking authenticity. To enter into the fold of white civilization was to be physically and culturally disassociated from one's tribal inheritance, while to resist the push of European culture was to face violent reprisals that often led to forced removals from the land. To both assimilate and retain the land, as witnessed most famously by the Cherokee, Creek, Choctaw (and many other indigenous nations) in the early republic, was an option antithetical to the ideological aims of this discourse. Nevertheless, the Mohegan of Brothertown, by effectively appropriating the tool of literacy and honing their ability to wield this tool in the public transcript of the colonizers, were able to deploy the discourse of Western expansionism to their own advantage. They subverted, at least for a moment in history, the paradigmatic containment that was meant to untether them from their land, using it instead to establish a new frontier settlement. Simultaneously, the Mohicans of Stockbridge, Massachusetts were undergoing similar pressures and changes that prompted them into a partnership with the Brothertown Natives. The result for both groups was neither full assimilation, nor an act of cultural extinction, but rather an illuminating and historically counterintuitive incidence of Native adaptability and survivance. The figure of John Mohegan stands as the literary embodiment of the intersecting historical paths of the Stockbridge Mohicans and Connecticut Mohegan, a creation of "manifest manners" and "hearsay traditions." But the little understood accomplishment of these two nations remains in tacit resistance to the mythological constructions of land and Native presence long in operation on colonial soil and immortalized in the fiction produced by James Fenimore Cooper.

"We pray that it might be given us in Writing": The Mohican Mission at Stockbridge

Almost invariably, indoctrination into European literacy involved at least partial transformations of identity and space. We have seen how, as it began to take root in Native New England, the adoption of alphabetic literacy was accompanied by the reorganization of many Native communities into praying towns or areas of colonial containment. Natives entered into these spaces of containment for various reasons, but they were always, to begin with, Native spaces too, and mostly what was hoped for was the opportunity to remain peaceably in place. To begin the story of the formation of Brothertown and New Stockbridge as Native spaces, we must first attend the formation of yet another "frontier" village some fifty years earlier on Mohican lands in what is known today as the town of Stockbridge on the banks of the Housatonic River in western Massachusetts.

The Mohican, or Muhheconnuk as they called themselves, knew this place as Waubtukook, or "the Great Meadow," and for centuries residents of this general area repaired to it seasonally to fish and plant, protected from potential enemies and the first waves of colonization by heavily wooded mountains on either side.[18] As Hendrick Aupaumut would write years later after his own dislocation from these lands, his Muhheconnuk ancestors had come from the Northwest, driven by famine. When they came to the valley of the Housatonic and saw "that game was very plenty in that country, they agreed to kindle fire there, and hang a kettle whereof they and their children after them may dip out their daily refreshment." They planted "shammonon, or Indian corn, beans, and little squashes, which was chiefly under the management of women and old men who were incapable of hunting." And they cleared their land by making a fire around the foot of every tree, a process by which "an industrious woman . . . could burnt off as many logs in one day as a smart man could chop in two or three days time with an axe." Aupaumut gestures toward the drastic changes to the land brought about by colonial economies when he notes that through hunting the Muhheconnuk "supplied themselves with both clothing and diet . . . and they were not to kill more than necessary, for there was none to barter with them that would have tempted them to waste their animals, as they did after the Chuh-ko-thuk [white or "knife" men] came on this Island."[19]

But those first white settlers did come to the "Island"—this land resting upon the turtle's back—first as trappers and traders, but by the 1700s looking to settle more permanently. The Muhheconnuk had maintained more or less cordial relations with the Dutch for well over half a century by this time, but the Dutch ceded their colony to England in 1664, and by 1686 the English had officially chartered Albany as a settlement. From that moment on, it was only a matter of time before the Muhheconnuk of Housatonic (the band of Mohican most closely associated with Aupaumut's region and from here on referred to as "the Housatunnuk") began to feel the constrictions pressing in from both their eastern and western borders.

Perhaps they did not, at first, see anything particularly new or unusual about sharing the bounty of what Lisa Brooks refers to as "the Common Pot" with a few scattered settlers. There was no shortage of land and the Housatunnuk had long been part of a fluid community of kinship networks and alliances that spanned a good portion of the continent. Aupaumut notes how his Mohican forefathers were "distinguished in peacableness, whereby they had allies, even the remotest nations." Those alliances were fortified with "belts and strings of wampum," and consisted of their grandfather nation, the Delaware, as well as the Shawanoe, the Miami, Uttawa, Wehipow-waw, Misiauky, Potauwautomeew, Wnautowuhtheh, Wthaukeew, Kekeppoow, Pasakeyah, Wauwyuhtonnoow, Mkhuthkotauweew, and the Kutoohwaw and Mushoow (Cherokee and Creek) nations.[20] The Haudenosaunee, he tells us, were also considered "brothers" in their chain of relations. At the same time, the Housatunnuk were not ignorant of recent historical developments in their region. They had been witnesses and sometime participants in the frontier wars that had been raging all around them for a century or more, had endured waves of disease and hardship, and knew enough of white power to be both respectful and wary of what might come next.

Hendrick Aupaumut wrote that the Muhheconnuk of old had a sachem who was "looked upon as a great tree under whose shade the whole nation is sit."[21] But as early as 1693 the Mohican were already addressing the colonial governor, Captain Benjamin Fletcher, at Albany, as "that high Tree, under whose Branches we shelter."[22] This is not to say that the traditional hierarchy had been utterly dismantled, but the Mohican were suddenly compelled to recognize new impeding power structures. They were all too aware of how the fur trade had depleted the lands about them, and almost certainly felt pressured to buy into the systems of commerce, goods, and land use by which colonial culture organized itself. Some resorted to seasonal labor for wealthy Dutch farmers and it is likely that, given the depletion of local resources, many became dependent upon European agricultural goods to supplement their own yield.[23]

In 1710 a party of Native leaders, including the Mohican sachem Etowaukaum and the Mohawk chief Hendrick, traveled to England to plead for protection in the wars being waged against the French and their allies. Like Samson Occom some fifty years later, these men became instant celebrities, with chapbooks, ballads, and engravings produced to capitalize on the exotic spectacle they provided. Reportedly, the chiefs presented wampum to the queen of England and, in the accompanying address, requested that a missionary be sent to their respective territories. But they were also seeking to carve out a space for themselves and their people in an increasingly colonized terrain in which European powers pressed from either side.[24]

A document claiming to voice the concerns of "Mahikinders" to New York governor Peter Schulyer on August 25, 1720 notes that the Natives were in such straits that they came to this particular meeting bereft of gifts to offer. Their presents are "all wore out and we are naked and bare" they announced. This statement was punctuated with a string of wampum, before the speaker continued by reminding the English,

> we were here before the Christians came, being the antient Inhabitants of these parts . . . When the Christians first Came we made a Covenant with them which was but of bark but afterwards the English coming to have the Government of these Countries we made a Covenant Chain of silver that the thunder itself could not break it and we are now come to Renew [that covenant] . . . having a Great inclination to be Christians and turn from the heathenish life we are bred up in and wish that the minister Could speak and understand [their language].[25]

Regardless of whatever protections the Mohican may have hoped to procure from such diplomatic outreaches, the end result was the loss of more land and resources. By 1724 the Housatunnuk were doling off large portions of their land to settlers, striking a deal with Colonel John Stoddard and the Massachusetts government to release "these presents" (consisting of some ninety square miles) to the colonists in exchange for £460, three barrels of cider, and thirty quarts of rum.[26] As part of this transaction, authorities set aside two tracts of land in the region between the Housatonic and Hudson rivers, now known as Berkshire County in Massachusetts, as a reservation for the Native peoples living there.

Two leaders of the Housatunnuk who appear as liaisons to the English during these transactions were Konkapot and Umpachanee whose families dwelled respectively on the two aforementioned tracts. It is likely that their emergence into the archive at this time had to do not only with the sale of lands, but with the Housatunnuk desire to strengthen alliances with the English. Perhaps not coincidentally, English colonists had also established a new covenant with the Mohawk or "Cagnawaga" in Albany in that same year.[27] The English, at this time, were once again engaged in one of their frequent border wars on the northern edges of the colony and were asking for a show of allegiance from those who had sheltered under their "tree" for protection. In an effort to draw support from western indigenous nations, the English began offering valuable bounties for Abenaki scalps: £100 for the scalp of any male over the age of twelve and £50 for any other.[28] Whether or not this served as enticement, many Mohican braves decided to enter into the fray. Their leader, known as Aupaumut (not Hendrick Aupaumut, but almost certainly a forebear), and Captain Hendrick of the Mohawk agreed to serve alongside the English and each was accompanied by a number of scouts. It is likely that both Konkapot and Umpachanee were amongst these, serving under the command of Colonel Stoddard during this conflict sometimes referred to as Gray Lock's War.[29]

Clearly it was beneficial for the English to obtain Native scouts whose wilderness skills and knowledge of the terrain and culture could provide valuable strategic advantages. For Mohican men, this was an opportunity to acquire leadership skills in both battle and diplomacy. Reputations were built between Native and colonist during these conflicts that would lead to the possible strengthening and maintenance of relationships down the road. One wonders, however, what kind of personal bonds were forged between men of different cultural backgrounds during such times, while fighting together in frontier conditions. It is tempting to believe that these men found common strains of interest and humanity in their exposure to one another around their campfires, forging the kinds of intimacies that might transcend cultural and historical differences that had been kept separated by such a wide gulf of ignorance and fear. This is in some measure one of the suppressed cultural desires that surfaces in novels like *The Pioneers* and *The Last of the Mohicans*. There is reason to believe, however, that racial and class hierarchies were militantly maintained in frontier conflicts and, for the most part, the colonial leadership expressed an extreme distaste for their Native allies. Colonists and Natives kept separate camps and most often were organized into separate units.[30] Regardless of such missed opportunities, however, an overall confluence of interests and events at this time resulted in the opening of the Housatonic Valley to English settlers and to the 1734 commissioning of Kunkapot and Umpachanee as, respectively, captain and lieutenant.[31]

Samuel Hopkins, a West Springfield minister who was influential in establishing a mission to the Housatunnuk in 1734 writes that the character of Konkapot had been related to him as "strictly temperate, a very just and upright Man in his Dealings, a Man of Prudence, and industrious in his Business; and inclined to embrace the Christian Religion." The only obstacles to Konkapot's conversion (at least as Hopkins tells it) were, first: that "if he became a Christian, his own people would discard him," and second: the problem, oft-expressed by Occom as well, of the "ill-Conversation of Christians; it being as bad, as he tho't, if not worse than that of the Heathen."[32] Such an admission seems to suggest a self-conscious awareness on the part of both the missionaries and the Natives that English settlers did not always exemplify the upright standards of Christian behavior being advertised by their missionaries. Nevertheless, if Konkapot, putting aside such reservations, was in fact "inclined to embrace the Christian Religion," we should ask ourselves what were likely to have been his motives and were they more likely to have been driven by spiritual or political concerns? We might further ask ourselves if such concerns were likely to have been so openly articulated or if such inclinations were simply placed in his mouth by Hopkins in much the same way that Eliot, prior to King Philip's War, supposed that Philip too would be an eager Indian convert, or in the way the first settlers of the Massachusetts Bay Company supposed the Natives had, in fact, implored them to "come over and help us?"

Hopkins met with Konkapot and Umpachanee in Springfield in May of 1734 and at this meeting Konkapot reportedly expressed his desire for a missionary to come amongst them so that "their Children might be taught to read."[33] Umpachanee, on the other hand, is characterized as having been not so eager for such an arrangement. Umpachanee is often portrayed in the missionary literature as being more reticent about missionary involvement at Stockbridge than his compatriot. It is worth noting, however, that Hopkins was writing this in hindsight, knowing, as he did, of the confrontations that would play out between Umpachanee and the missionary endeavor in the years to follow. Because Hopkins is the most comprehensive source for the Stockbridge settlement, his characterization of events has exacted an undue influence upon the few historians who have passed through this archive. But we will attempt to approach these events through the longhouse of the archive, taking into consideration, as much as possible, the motives of those who did not record in their own hand the events that took place, but labored to have their voices heard nonetheless. If nothing else, we see right from the start that the desire to be taught to read, as always, was up front in the concerns of both colonist and Native in these transactions.

It goes without saying, that if the River Indians were eager to acquire literacy, they would have to embrace some measure of Christianity as well. As it turned out, however, neither of the representatives of the Housatunnuk was willing to make a decision of their own accord, but expressed that "it would be needful their Brethren should be consulted in the Affair."[34] Therefore it was decided that, in July, the parties would meet again in Housatonic and, accordingly, the Reverend Nehemiah Bull and one Stephen Williams (Hopkins himself had fallen ill and couldn't make the trip) journeyed west on the 8th of July to speak further on the subject. At this meeting Williams and Bull reiterated colonial appeals to send a missionary. Williams tells us, "it would be too tedious, to give you an Account how they managed themselves in their Debates on what was offered to them; and what Arguments (we understood) were urged for or against receiving the Christian Religion."[35] We can surmise, however, that the debate was vigorous, apparently stretching over the course of four days, and that the whole community participated. That they ultimately arrived at their determination together was signaled by the fact that "all gave in their Names, and Signify'd their Desires . . . for the Ends propos'd. Upon which the Rev. Mr. Williams deliver'd to them a small Belt of Wampum, as a Confirmation of what had pass'd between them, and as a sort of Record thereof."[36]

The gift of wampum here was a significant gesture. The English had been party to the exchange of wampum going back at least as far as their first dealings with the Pequot, and they had exploited this resource in various ways, even to the point of using it as currency themselves for a time (as detailed in chapter 1). Historically, however, the English had been inclined to view wampum as a tribute inscribing wealth and power relations. As such, until about the turn of the eighteenth century it was something that they were much more inclined to receive than offer. It is doubtful the English understood or acknowledged anything of the spiritual significance of wampum exchange or that the Puritans of the original colonies themselves would have initiated such a mode of diplomatic outreach. But colonial understanding of this ritual seems to have evolved in the late seventeenth and early eighteenth centuries, so that here we see Stephen Williams presenting a belt of wampum to the Mohican, as "a sort of Record thereof." While the idea of wampum as "Indian money" was still current, it was suddenly apparent to the colonists that wampum also served as a historical signifier of diplomatic agreements and contracts. Hopkins, writing in 1753, still describes wampum as the "coin of the Indian." But he felt obliged to note that

> It is a Custom among the Indians neighboring to us, and I suppose among all others, to give Belts of Wompum for the Confirmation

> of all Treaties, and as a Remembrance of what passes between Parties; so that if one Tribe sends a Message to another without such a Belt, the Message is call'd, an empty Word, not to be regarded or remember'd: But if a Belt accompany's the Message, it is laid up as a Record of the Thing transacted; and by it, not only the present, but future Generations, keep in Remembrance what was then done. And these are all the Records they keep in such Cases.[37]

Even as the Natives of New England were realizing that they must master European forms of alphabetic literacy in order to protect their interests in colonial space, Europeans were realizing the necessity of confirming their relationships in Native space with indigenous forms of record-keeping to ensure that their agreements would not be regarded as mere "empty words." Each party apprehended a need to legitimize their transactions in the mode most familiar to the other.

The rapidly shifting political ground of the eighteenth century provides to the historian a long string of detailed accounts concerning diplomatic relationships negotiated in the language of the condolence ceremony and sealed in wampum. Lisa Brooks refers to this as "treaty literature," a literature that precedes colonization, but is adopted by the colonists in their dealings with Native power brokers.[38] In these transactions, colonial magistrates can be pictured doling out strings of wampum to visiting indigenous dignitaries and acknowledging that they were all there to "enlarge the Fire, which was almost gone out, and to make it burn clearer; and to brighten the Chain which had contracted some Rust, and to renew their Friendship . . . which it is their Desire may last so long as the Sun, the Moon and the Stars, shall give light."[39] Colonial leaders may not have apprehended the spiritual systems of thought and meaning that lay behind such indigenous treaty language, but they bowed to the necessity of it and were, perhaps, enamored to its poetics and ritual solemnity.

The wampum exchange made on that July day in Housatonic was formalized one year later at a conference in Deerfield in August of 1735, presided over by Massachusetts governor Jonathan Belcher. The meeting was between several nations who had come to conduct business with the colonizing authorities and as such, there were delegations of Mohawk, Abenaki, and Mohegan present as well. Belcher began the proceedings by greeting all the assembled, thanking God for their safe journey, and holding out a string of wampum to each, saying, "this is to wipe away all Tears from your eyes—Then holding out a second—This is to open your Throats that you may speak with all Freedom—then a third—This is to wipe away all Blood, and to comfort you under all your past Difficulties."[40] The Mohawk delegate, Auountauresaunkee, responded by delivering a belt of wampum to the governor and declaring that the way was "now clear, and the Door open for Freedom of speech."[41]

Konkapot and Umpachanee had come to the Deerfield conference with roughly forty other members of the "Housatonucc Tribe of Indians," including women and children. On the second day of the conference they had their main audience with Belcher, at which time Konkapot expressed the reasons that his people had decided to enter into this agreement. He is recorded to have said that "we are desirous to receive the Gospel of Our Lord Jesus Christ; and hope that Our Hearts are in what we say, and that we don't speak only out of our Lips."[42] It is interesting to note how similar this language is to that of Waban in a previous generation, who also split the difference between what was in the mouth and what was in the heart when speaking of conversion. That these words are a paraphrase of biblical verse suggests that Natives were either well coached to say these things, or had been exposed to enough missionary talk to incorporate it into their address. But it may also suggest a kind of syncretic value that blended elements of both indigenous and Christian discourse together. After the formal preamble, however, Konkapot again brought the focus around to writing and the core anxieties that prompted their meeting. He said, "Our children are afraid of strict Laws, and of being brought into trouble, and put in Prison for Debt." He hoped that "we be not hurt by the severity of the Laws, seeing we don't understand how to manage in such Affairs, so as that there may not be any danger at any time that Our Children be taken away from us for Debt." He concludes, "we pray that it might be given us in Writing (or established by a Law) that Our Children after us be not wronged or injured."[43]

One gets a sense from Konkapot's words of the ruptures already taken place as a result of colonial economies forcing their way into Native space, the misunderstandings already ingrained in the system, and the sense of vulnerability the Housatunnuk felt, particularly in regards to the law and their inability to parse the written codes that kept them at a disadvantage in these transactions. As Konkapot was expected to speak for the entire band here, many of whom were apparently present, one probably gets a sampling of what the Housatunnuk had discussed amongst themselves over four days of debate a year earlier. If nothing else, they had determined that their diplomatic outreaches needed to be preserved in European inscription for their own safekeeping or wampum record.

The governor's reply, given on the following day of the proceedings, was that colonial laws were already in place to protect the Natives and were sufficient as they were. This could hardly have been a satisfactory answer. But from the governor's standpoint, the main order of business was that the Housatunnuk had agreed to accept a missionary, and to that end a young man named John Sergeant had been appointed whose ordination the next day would provide the conference's closing ceremony. Belcher concluded by reinforcing the understanding that the Housatunnuk had just entered into a Christian compact. He stated, "I expect you to be very careful to morrow in observing the Lord's Day. It is God's Day, and always to be kept holy, and you must attend the publick Worship both parts of the Day: You shall have a Place by Your Selves, that you may the better see Mr. Sergeant's Ordination."[44]

The ordination in question at Deerfield must have been an unusual affair, with roughly forty Natives in attendance (assuming all the women and children were expected to be there as well), along with heads of state, interpreters, and clergymen from various districts. Presiding over the affair was the same Stephen Williams who had visited the Housatunnuk Natives the year before. One gets a sense of how small a world this all was when one realizes that Stephen Williams was the son of the Reverend John Williams who had authored one of the most famous and influential narratives of the Puritan era, *The Redeemed Captive*, two decades earlier. This captivity narrative detailed the assault on Deerfield by a confederation of Mohawk, Abenaki, and French forces in 1704. Stephen Williams, himself, had been taken hostage in the raid along with the rest of his family and spent upward of a year living amongst his Native captors, during which time he was likely to have undergone adoption rituals. While Stephen's father and three siblings endured captivity by both the Mohawk and the French in Canada, his mother and two other siblings were killed in the events surrounding the raid, and his sister Eunice remained attached to the Mohawk Nation despite repeated efforts by her father to "redeem" her in the years that ensued. Eunice Williams married into the Mohawk Nation at Caughnawagha, converted to French Catholicism, had children, and refused all efforts to bring her back into the Congregationalist fold. Her story became the most notable period account of a colonist who assimilated into Native lifeways. But her story also speaks to the syncretic mix of ideas and beliefs at work in the land. This confluence of Native and settler epistemologies touched not only the Catholic Mohawk with whom Eunice spent the rest of her days, but nearly all who attended John Sergeant's ordination on September 1, 1735. This included the Mohican of New England, colonists like Stephen Williams who experienced the overlapping of these spaces from various angles of vision, and young Sergeant himself who would spend the rest of his years living amongst the Housatunnuk in Stockbridge.[45] Directly following the ordination, Williams turned "to the Houssatonnic Indian Tribe, who were Seated in the Gallery by themselves; and asked them if they were desirous of having Mr. Sergeant for their Minister . . . Whereupon they all rose up by one Consent, and with grave as well as cheerful Countenances signified their full, and hearty Acceptance of him."[46]

Captives and Converts: The Unmaking of Native Space in Stockbridge

John Sergeant, prior to his ordination, had already spent a few preliminary months amongst the Housatunnuk as an experiment of sorts to determine whether or not a mission was viable. In his journal he writes of exposing himself "to many Fatigues and hardships, and I know not what Dangers, among a barbarous People."[47] Such hyperbole was par for the course for anyone of Christian faith considering spending time amongst the Natives in colonial New England. Hilary Wyss, in *Writing Indians*, suggests that Sergeant viewed his life in the Housatonic River Valley along the lines of the typical captivity narrative with its harsh oppositional language representing Christian and heathen lifestyles, including a whisper of the threat of assimilation that often worked to subtly undermine such binaries.[48] Certainly Sergeant plays with these motifs in his writings, but it is hard to imagine his time there as a captivity given the voluntary nature of this assignment and the fact that he boarded with an English family already settled in the area.[49] If anything, it is the Housatunnuk themselves who were about to undergo a kind of captivity in their own Native space. As we will see, it is they and not Sergeant who will be forced to assimilate to Christian norms. It is the Housatunnuk and not Sergeant who will have to make drastic accommodations to Christian forms of property ownership and land use. In short, it was the Housatunnuk world that was undergoing radical transformation, while Sergeant, despite some playful rhetoric, had the luxury of seeing his cultural values approved and validated by the prevailing power dynamic.

By a similar token, Patrick Frazier, in his *The Mohicans of Stockbridge*, perceives that the Mohican had worn out their traditional religion and were in search of something more spiritually vital by the time of Sergeant's visit in 1734. Of Konkapot, he writes, that the "seeming inadequacy of the religion of his forefathers made him uneasy. The family idols were ineffective. Their powwows produced few revelations or any magic that helped the Indians now."[50] Rather than focusing on the economic and cultural pressures being brought to bear on the Housatunnuk, and the desire to master European literacy as a means of resisting such changes, Frazier emphasizes that the Mohican had come to see their own religion as enervated and useless, unable to stand up to the demonstrably more powerful Christian faith. Such formulas for regarding the catalysts of change forcing their way into Native spaces are engrained in much of our thinking and reveal ethnocentric positions that have been hardened into form by centuries of colonial inscription. While Christianity provided some institutional shelter for Native communities, it was not generally assumed by the Natives themselves that their traditional practices and beliefs were forfeited in such relationships or need be checked at the door.

When Konkapot articulated at Deerfield that his people were desirous of having a missionary sent amongst them, he was voicing the concerns of his community in the acceptable forms available to him before an audience of colonial magistrates. On both sides such a request was undoubtedly understood to mean much more than can be inferred from its literal interpretation. Accepting a missionary was one more explicit step toward placing oneself under colonial authority. It opened the door to further colonial settlement, greater economic and spiritual subservience, and diminished tribal autonomy. But it also allowed a measure of economic and military protection and access to the tool of literacy. Certainly it was a gambit on the part of the Housatunnuk that it would ensure their survival for yet another generation in an increasingly shrinking domain. But by no means was this development the oft-told tale of missionary captives or Native converts. Nor were the Mohican in general anxious to abandon their traditional practices. The greater truth of the situation unspooled itself in the threads of cultural negotiation resulting from Sergeant's mission and the colonial encroachment it portended on both the geographical and psychological space of the indigenous inhabitants.

When Sergeant initially arrived at Housatonic, his first order of business was to preach to the Natives, which he did through an interpreter named Ebenezer Poohpoonuc. It is not known where Poohpoonuc acquired his skill as translator. Possibly he had been a scout, like Konkapot and Umpachanee, under Captain Aupaumut in the frontier wars of the previous decade. Or perhaps he had been raised in proximity to the English, either as neighbor or indentured servant. Either way, he would become the first Housatunnuk to be baptized and, in the words of the missionaries, "forsake heathenish darkness."[51] Following Sergeant's introductory sermon it was quickly decided that a school and meeting house should be established, and this was built in a place about halfway between the homes of Konkapot and Umpachanee (modern-day Great Barrington, Massachusetts), round which some small wigwams were thrown up for the families to dwell in during this season of schooling. These concessions, though disruptive to long-held patterns of land tenure and subsistence, were readily made by the Housatunnuk.

Within his first month in the region, however, Sergeant writes that he was invited to Konkapot's home in Waubtukook to see "a religious Ceremony, they had learned of their Fathers."[52] What Sergeant goes on to describe in his diary, although he has no frame of reference in which to place it, is a Mohican Longhouse ceremony. He relates how "after we had been there for some Time, two Men appointed for the Service, took a Deer down that hung up in the Wigwam which was to be offer'd, and laid the four Quarters upon a Bark in the Middle of the House (the Rest sitting around very serious)." The priest offered prayers in "a pretty loud voice" and wampum was exchanged before the deer was apportioned out to all the participants, with the skin and hooves given to a widow woman as "a Deed of Charity they always practice upon such Occasions."[53] Sergeant, questioning his interpreter, Poohpoonuc, concerning the meaning of the ceremony, was told of a man, esteemed a hero and a prophet who long ago walked down from heaven on a pair of snowshoes and taught the Muhheconnuk their religion and survival skills. This man, he was told, cleared the land of monsters, took a wife and had two sons, one of whom was left behind to continue to teach the people after the hero himself left this world (rising up through the smoke hole of the Long House). Another story related by Sergeant told of how a certain constellation was regarded as seven men dancing, preparing a hunt for the great bear (Ursa Major)—a hunt which lasted all summer and into the fall. By fall, according to the legend, the bear was wounded and its blood dripping red upon the treetops accounted for the brilliant autumn foliage that adorns the Housatonic Valley in autumn. By winter the bear had died and the snow was the manifestation of its fat, which in the summer melted and became the sap, or maple syrup, in the trees. This legend is corroborated in part by Frank Speck's research amongst the Lenape. Speck relates a number of variations on the tale, in which seven holy men, or *asiskewtayasak*, pursue this bear whose head has been separated from its body. It is believed that when the bear, in his westward journey, reunites with his head, this will signal the end of the world as we know it.[54] In Sergeant's mind, however, these stories were "childish" and "very ridiculous." Nevertheless, as he acknowledged with a first early whiff of frustration, "they believe with firm Faith."[55]

His assertion that the Natives held on to their beliefs with "firm faith" complicates the oft-repeated assumptions that Natives were voluntarily surrendering their spiritual traditions in the face of superior belief systems. In fact, Konkapot appears to have been acting in general accordance with an indigenous philosophy of engagement and reciprocity. He was open to the introduction of Christian values into his world, but he placed the values of his own people on an equal playing field and asked that they occupy that same space together, in conversation with one another. This seems to have been his vision for colonial expansion into Native space and his more immediate motive for inviting Sergeant to a Long House Ceremony in the first few weeks of his tenancy at Housatonic. Sergeant's musings in his journal that such practices were "childish" and "ridiculous" can be a surprise to no one. But perhaps Timothy Woodbridge, who was brought to Housatonic as teacher shortly after Sergeant's arrival, articulated the Christian position of absolute containment more succinctly. After witnessing a dance at the house of Umpachanee in the winter of 1735, he told the participants that such behavior was "displeasing" to God. Although the Natives replied that "they knew no harm in it," Woodbridge strictly maintained that God "was not to be worshipped in such a manner."[56]

We have no records to tell us what school was like for the twenty-two to twenty-five scholars that Sergeant taught that early winter of 1734, what difficulties he might have encountered, or what strategies he might have used in overcoming differences in language and culture. We simply know that he instructed on the week days and preached on Sabbath days. He reports that his students went truant when Dutch traders appeared in the area in early December, obviously carrying goods that the Housatunnuk were eager to obtain. Sergeant sensed the Dutch were conspiring against his efforts, and that they denigrated his religious practice to the Natives by spreading rumors of the English that they were only out to enslave Native children.[57] Such "rumors" were not unfounded. The Housatunnuk were surely aware that English settlers, including many of the missionaries themselves, kept slaves. Survivors of King Philip's War had been sold into slavery, and many dispossessed Natives of New England, beginning with the defeated Pequot, had fallen into an indentured servitude that was indistinguishable from slavery to most Native observers. Whether spread by the Dutch or simply the result of a general Native awareness of colonial practices, such knowledge almost certainly lay behind Konkapot's original fear, expressed in the Deerfield conference, about "prison for Debt" and the "danger at any time that Our Children be taken away from us."[58]

Sergeant had to labor to convince both Konkapot and Unmpachenee that these fears were unfounded, and apparently he was successful. At the end of that year, as he returned to Yale where he was completing his studies in divinity, Sergeant proposed to bring two Indian children with him, "intending thereby to lead them into some Acquaintance with the English Language and manners," and to, perhaps, learn something of the Mohican language himself.[59] In keeping with traditional practices of cultural exchange, the local leaders Konkapot and Umpachanee agreed to send their own sons, Nangkawwat and Etowaukaum, ages nine and eight, respectively, to gather some instruction in English letters. Whatever their misgivings at this point, both leaders acknowledged through this gesture that the continuation of their people as a sovereign entity would depend upon the next generation gaining mastery of alphabetic writing. Sergeant spoke highly of the two boys, noting that they "went away with very good Courage," and that they "were made much of by everybody, for indeed they were a couple of very likely Boys, especially the Lieutenant's Son."[60]

One can hear the optimism and forward-looking tone in Sergeant's writings as he praises the progress of the two boys in those early stages and comments on the goodwill and apparent promise of his soon to be flock. Sergeant returned to the Housatonic River Valley in spring of 1735, and when he first preached to an audience of twenty Indians, they "gave great Attention, and some of them were very much affected by what I said. The Lieutenant's Wife wept almost all the Time. And others of them frequently shed Tears, especially the Captain was often very much affected."[61] Such displays must have been heartwarming to the young minister, taken as evidence of his skill and passion as a preacher. But what passes for cause and effect in the missionary literature often has a great deal to do with determinations that were made communally amongst the Natives themselves prior to the events in question. The Housatunnuk had been all along maintaining their own discourse regarding the intrusion of Christianity into their space. The previous January, in Sergeant's absence, they had met with members of other Mohican clans, the head sachem Corlair amongst them, to discuss these matters further and had apparently decided to move forward with the experiment.[62] It seems the Natives of the so-called frontier were carefully weighing the pros and cons of "embracing the Christian faith," not necessarily as individuals falling like first fruits off the tree through tears and baptism, but as entire communities attempting to decide what was best for their future. Similar deliberations were being made throughout Native space in the Northeast, from the Susquehannah to the St. Lawrence Seaway, for very similar reasons.[63] In just a matter of four years, Samson Occom, in Mohegan, would also decide upon a course of Christianity so that he might "Instruct poor [Indian] Children in Reading."[64] The dramatic change wrought in the manner of Sergeant's Housatunnuk audience, therefore, had little to do with his preaching and everything to do with the politics of necessity and a determination made collectively in his absence. One way to express this determination was through ritual tears in response to a Christian address and a sudden flow of converts.

Konkapot was consistently raised up as the model convert in the literary voices surrounding the Stockbridge colony. Sergeant notes that "Capt. Konkapot is an excellent Man, and I do believe he has the true Spirit of Christianity in him."[65] Sergeant lived with Konkapot for about a week in May of 1735 and commented that "the Fondness they show for me is surprising, and considering how much a Stranger I am to them, their own barbarous Education, and how little I have done to win them, there appears something more than humane in it."[66] The implication seems to be that this had nothing to do with indigenous custom and everything to do with God showing signs of heavenly favor. In a letter to one Dr. Coleman, an interested pastor in Boston, Sergeant writes that "some of the Indians (I perceive) have a Mind to be baptiz'd. Kunkapot, especially, who appears to me well qualified for it."[67] And, in fact, Sergeant's first official act as an ordained minister was to baptize Konkapot and his wife, as John and Mary, on November 2, 1735.

If Umpachanee failed to earn the sort of praise that Konkapot garnered from the missionary establishment, nevertheless, two weeks later, the lieutenant and his wife were also baptized, under the names Aaron and Hannah, along with nine other members of his family. Following the baptism, Sergeant described the lieutenant as "a clear-headed smart Man, of a deep Reach, and pleasant Humour, and is one of the best Speakers we hear . . . and tho' he is reckon'd somewhat haughty, yet always shews himself modest and teachable enough."[68] Perhaps we should pause to marvel at the not atypical cultural arrogance of the twenty-four-year-old Sergeant, fresh out of divinity school, with so little practical experience in life, commenting upon the nature of the mature warrior, father, and leader of his people, as "teachable enough." But for Sergeant, at least, this was a moment of greatest promise. He tended toward an optimistic appraisal of people and events. As he wrote to Coleman, "they have an earnest desire to be taught," and the wider Mohican community was taking "great notice of what is doing there; none of them oppose it, they generally approve of it."[69]

Lieutenant Umpachanee's *disapproval* of Christian conversion begins to emerge gradually in Sergeant's account of the mission, even though he accepted baptism and his wife appeared to have been visibly moved by Sergeant's address. Umpachanee's wife, an important figure in her own right, was the daughter of Etowaukaum, the Mohican sachem who had traveled to England and had an audience with Queen Anne two decades earlier. Apparently she was an eager student, described by Sergeant as "greatly engaged in learning to read . . . and urges that she may read a little further, and a little further; so that Mr. Woodbridge tells me, it grieves him to the very Heart, that he is obliged almost to force her from him, that he may have time to hear the rest of the Scholars."[70] Umpachanee's marriage to her established him as a leading figure in the Muhheconnuk power structure and his first son, who traveled with Sergeant to New Haven for schooling, was named after his grandfather Etowaukaum, the former sachem. Although Umpachanee is often regarded as the lesser authority when paired up with Captain Konkapot in the colonial literature of the period, the evidence suggests that he was a figure of some, if not greater, importance. Perhaps he and his wife did not see eye to eye on the missionary agenda. Perhaps Umpachanee disagreed with the Mohican clan council's determination to go ahead with such a program, or perhaps, at this stage, he had yet to openly express any resistance at all. But the pace of events would soon force Umpachanee to voice his uncertainty in regards to how the Stockbridge settlement was progressing. This nascent opposition was succinctly articulated in a 1736 address directed at Colonel Stoddard, wherein he stated that considerations of English kindnesses, including "taking care to have [our] Children taught to read . . . had sometimes almost drawn tears from [my] eyes." Whereas Konkapot, Umpachanee's wife, and many others made their acceptance of Christianity manifest in a display of tears, Umpachanee used a variation of condolence language to show he remained steadfastly on the fence. Colonial benevolence had "almost" drawn tears from his eyes, but something was wanting, and there were other things, he added, that "appear'd dark in his eyes."[71]

Umpachanee remained determined to assert the cultural identity of his people, and just as Konkapot had invited Sergeant to attend a Long House Ceremony on his first visit, Umpachanee, following his baptism, invited Sergeant to a ceremony he referred to as a Keutikaw, or dance. Again, the idea of shared spiritual space presents itself here, although Sergeant was not likely to see it as such. He writes of preaching a sermon at "the Lieutenant's House, to an Auditory of 80 or 90, about one Half being Strangers."[72] Sergeant doesn't explicitly say that his sermon was followed by the dance, but his description of the sermon moves seamlessly into a description of the Native ceremony, which was likely the reason that so many "strangers" were in attendance that day. The fact that Umpachanee's lodge was large enough to host upward of ninety souls and drew such a crowd is another testament to his importance in the community. The dance in question, which might have been the midwinter ceremony or a condolence ceremony, is described by Sergeant as "finishing the mourning for the Dead . . . when the Guests invited make Presents to the Relations of the Deceas'd, to make up their loss, and to end their Mourning." During the ceremony a "Speaker, appointed for the Purpose," offered "some Words of Consolation . . . desiring them to forget their Sorrow, and accept of those presents [perhaps wampum] to make up their Loss. After this, they eat together, and make Merry."[73]

Ethnographer Frank Speck tells us that the term "kantika" or "kant'kaa : he is dancing" in the Algonquian, is a "composite term with the meaning of persons dancing in a line and pushing something forward," that is used in relation to the Big House Ceremony of the Delaware. Sergeant, however, was pleased to regard this as a civil ceremony and not a religious one, which is why he remained tolerant of the proceedings. He was particularly impressed that the ceremony did not resolve in strong drink as was usual, "there being a very obvious reformation in their manners."[74] Hopkins suggests that the absence of drinking demonstrated the great respect the Natives had for Sergeant and how they were inclined to submit to him in "every Thing, their own ancient Customs not excepted."[75] It doesn't occur to either Hopkins or Sergeant that drinking was not part of any "ancient custom" at all, but a recent corruption to indigenous ritual brought on by colonization. Nevertheless, we can see in this moment the hopes of Umpachanee and the Housatunnuk band that they might forge a syncretic practice, with the sermon and the Keutikaw occupying the same ritual space rather than serving as two events in natural opposition to one another.

If this was, in fact, the wish of the Housatunnuk, such an arrangement was intolerable to the colonists. The idea, as always, was to corral the Natives in a space of spiritual and geographical containment. Hopkins tells us that there was "from the Beginning, a Design to accommodate them with Land, that they might all settle in one Place."[76] Umpachenee's band and Konkapot's band were situated roughly twenty miles apart from one another in what had been considered separate holdings by both the Natives and the colonials. The colonists desired to consolidate the two holdings into one, whereby, it was thought, the Housatunnuk could live together and be able with greater "convenience to attend the publick Worship, and have a School at their Doors." As had happened with the Massachusett Natives living in Cohannet, no sooner had they entered into an agreement with the colonists in order to preserve their space, then they were asked to remove to another place. In case the inherent generosity of this design went unnoticed, however, Colonel Stoddard, in a letter to the Indians added, "These things are great Tokens of Kindness towards the Indians, and they should be very careful how they put a Slight upon them."[77] The sight of this consolidated settlement was to be Waubtukook (meaning the Great Meadow), which was traditionally inhabited by Konkapot and his family. Umpachanee and his band would have to remove from their home in Skatekook (meaning Fork in the River), and were to be compensated with additional lands in Waubtukook.[78] Stoddard also decreed in his letter that some English families should be interspersed and settled amongst the Natives, as a kind of example to help them along the path to civilization. This was thought the "readiest way to Christianize them."[79]

The Stockbridge settlement is often referred to as an "experiment" in which Natives and colonists would occupy the same space for their mutual benefit, with this cross-cultural arrangement leading to the full assimilation of Natives into Christian lifeways.[80] Unlike the conventional praying towns of New England, which were also experiments, but failed experiments in the eyes of the colonists, Stockbridge would have Natives and settlers live side by side, attending the same schools and houses of worship, and sharing governance. And if such a thing had actually occurred, then it truly would have been a bold experiment in cultural exchange. But the actions and

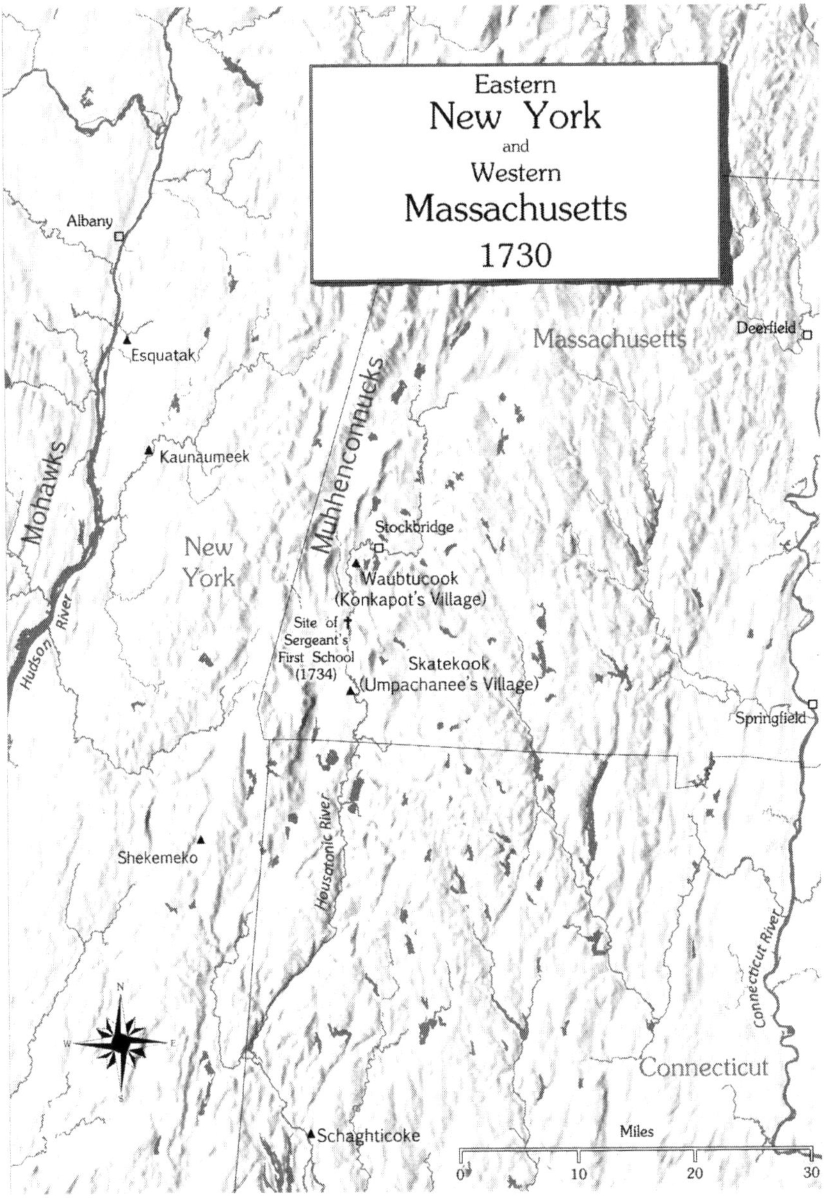

Figure 5.1. Map of New Stockbridge and Mohican Territory, 1730s. Map design by Terry Stigers.

language of the colonists made it clear that, if this was an experiment, it was one with a predetermined outcome. It began with the forced removal from Skatekook to Waubtukook and led to the methodical disenfranchisement of the Natives from positions of authority and as possessors of the land. Umpachanee, who was perhaps suspicious of English intent from the start, had to be all the more bitter about having to leave his home grounds and move the twenty miles north to Stockbridge. Not only did it force him from his traditional residence, but it tacitly undermined his authority, placing him, again, in a secondary position to Konkapot. He failed to see this as an inherent act of generosity, but correctly saw it as an act of coercion, and in a conference with colonial authorities in April 1736, he speaks of "a secret spring" of motives harbored by the colonists.[81]

Umpachanee was apprehending the hidden transcript of power, which spoke in terms of benevolence, but ground inexorably toward subjugation. He was rightly skeptical of the notion that he had been "given" lands in Waubtukook, and wondered if lands "gifted" might just as easily be taken away. The agreement to settle in Stockbridge had not been reached by treaty nor had it been sealed in wampum. "He desir'd therefore to know, how their Titles would be ascertained; and what Security they could have, that their Children would be free."[82] What he seems to have realized is that his tenure on the land was now the result of a special legal arrangement that had more in common with our modern-day reservation systems than any individually owned title, mutual agreement, or "Native right."[83] Nevertheless, the move was made in April of 1736 and the town came to be known as Stockbridge, even though it was not incorporated as such until 1739. Hopkins tells us that all "settled in their new Town [and] were greatly pleas'd with it," but this was almost certainly another act of unwitnessing.[84] The colonial record and much of the scholarship drawn from it seems to posit a harmonious beginning to Stockbridge followed by a slow collapse of Native involvement brought about by the enervating factors of sloth, disease, and alcoholism. In reality, however, the seeds of resentment had been sown at the onset.[85]

By 1739 the Williams family had established itself as the leader of the four families that were commissioned to settle in Stockbridge. Ephriam Williams was appointed justice of the peace in anticipation of his sojourn to the newly formed township and it was not long before Sergeant deepened his affiliation with the emerging power structure by marrying into this family.[86] Stockbridge was officially made a town in May of 1739 and the first town meeting was called on June 11. Although Sergeant's journal tells us that Captain Williams, Captain Konkapot, and Lieutenant Umpachanee were the ones authorized to call the meeting to order, it must have quickly been made apparent that the Native leaders were there as figureheads only. They were made selectmen along with Judge Williams, but the other important posts were given to the white settlers, with the job of town clerk going to the teacher, Timothy Woodbridge, and the job of constable given to Williams' brother-in-law, newcomer Josiah Jones.[87] It is unclear who exactly was present at this meeting or who exactly voted for these positions, if in fact there was a vote. It seems reasonable to assume that the Natives held the majority, but they were largely cut out of the governing process. More than likely, they were not even made aware of the implications of the town's incorporation or that a new governing body was being formulated. Sergeant's journal takes only the faintest notice of this, stating "this affair made some talk & difficulty, as every new thing does, among the Indians."[88]

Not long after this meeting, on August 5, Umpachanee refused communion, apparently on the grounds that he had been drinking. This must have been a highly visible challenge to Sergeant's presumed authority, and likely unfolded in the presence of his new colonial neighbors and future father-in-law. Sergeant writes in his journal that "this was the beginning of his [Umpachanee's] defective [defection] from his steadfastness, which he has since carried to a great & unhappy length."[89] Clearly it is not just the August 16th marriage that is the catalyst for Umpachanee's protest, as suggested by Hilary Wyss in *Writing Indians*, but the prior town meeting and the continuing diminishment of Umpachanee's authority in what is suddenly and irrevocably a colonial space.[90] Sergeant dates this journal passage for August 5, but his indication that "this was the beginning" of Umpachanee's dissent suggests that he was recording this retrospectively and, in a sense, reconstructing events to suit his own narrative demands. From here on in Sergeant's 1739–1740 journal becomes a record of Umpachanee's "apostasy" and Sergeant's battle with him for cultural dominance. Drinking is posited as the main cause of Umpachanee's dissatisfaction, for, as Sergeant assures us, it is "when in liquor" that his "*natural haughtiness* then breaks forth without any restraint [italics mine]."[91] But what Sergeant dismisses as "natural haughtiness" is the legitimate resentment of a proud man who has been consistently undermined by colonial mechanizations to the point of breaking.

Sergeant's journal leads us to consider what Wyss calls the "protest Umpachanee waged through alcohol," as though his individual descent into drinking was his most significant form of dissent.[92] But whether or not Umpachanee resorted to drinking in his despondency over the fate of his homeland is not what should be at issue when discussing developments at Stockbridge. One imagines that many a prominent Dutch and Englishman were given to strong drink as well, but their issues with the bottle remain of no consequence to the overall legitimacy of colonial agendas and are largely unwitnessed by the historical record. Of Umpachanee's drinking, however, we are constantly reminded. At one point Sergeant notes that "the Lieutenant had occasion to humble himself for the sin of Drunkenness," which he did with "a due appearance of Seriousness, Gravity and Resolution of better Obedience for Time to come."[93] Like Occom, Umpachanee is made to publicly grovel before colonial power and confess his intemperance. But if the case of Occom (who privately admitted to taking a small medicinal drought) is any example, one wonders if it is the very fact of resistance to colonial agendas that exacerbates such claims of drunken misbehavior.

We should be extremely wary of taking Sergeant's word on Umpachanee's drinking, as his objectivity is highly in question. For Sergeant, "intemperance" becomes a workable metaphor for any kind of objection to his missionary and colonial designs. It seems that any Indian who doesn't go along with the program is accused of taking "strong drink" as a means of undermining that individual's credibility in the archival record. Resistance to colonial hegemony is obscured by a reconstituting of the narrative, placing all focus and blame upon what is perceived as a natural weakness in the character of Indians in general. When, within two months of the town's incorporation, it is suddenly decided that the lands provided to the Natives there should be divided into individual lots, we are again reminded of the Lieutenant's "disposition to drunkenness."[94]

The decision to subdivide the lands came directly from the Massachusetts General Court, once again circumnavigating the authority of Umpachanee and Konkapot to partake in the decision-making process. Sergeant records that "thro the Lieutenant's example (whose influence is very great among the Indians) drunkenness prevailed to an unusual degree. A number were drunk while Col. Stoddard was here dividing their Lands. Several honest & well-disposed persons were led into the Snare."[95] There is great, unintended irony in Sergeant's words here, which of course, is not unusual in the contorted annals of colonial unwitnessing. No doubt several honest and well-disposed persons were led into a snare, but not by Umpachanee. The problem here is not that Natives were drinking, but that they were clearly in opposition to the subdividing of their lands and the tacit erasure of their traditional lifestyle. The "snare" in question is not alcohol but colonial appropriation. It is interesting, however, that for the first time Sergeant nods to the "great" influence Umpachanee has over the Housatunnuk, an influence that is only acknowledged in this negative context. Sergeant seems to have realized that it is Umpachanee and not Konkapot that must either be won over or delegitimized in the struggle to win the hearts and minds of the Stockbridge Indians.

In Sergeant's journal passages from October 27 and 28 of that year, he noted once again how the general failure of the Housatunnuk to embrace new developments in the settlement was a direct result of their fondness for liquor. He asserts that, under the power of alcohol, "it was easy to influence the minds of the Indians, who are not more fond of Drinking, than of their

Liberty." Sergeant interpreted Native "liberty" to mean "an unbounded Licence to do whatever their Inclinations lead them to without any restraint at all. By these means the state of religion appear'd with the most discouraging aspect that it ever had done."[96] Sergeant seemlessly equates Native drinking with Native liberty here, a concept that presumably licensed Native peoples to do whatever they pleased "without any restraint at all." In a sense he is trotting out the old chestnut that Native culture has no laws, no history, no religion of its own, in effect, no civilization. Without the harness of Christian authority to secure it in place, a Native liberty, equated with complete anarchy, takes over. And no small wonder that this also appears to Sergeant as a kind of intoxication.

This equation leads Sergeant to offer repeated sermons on the subject of temperance in the late autumn of 1739, but as he notes, "The Lieutenant, who was in a temper to cavel at every thing, found great fault in what I said."[97] In all likelihood, Umpachanee "caviled" with Sergeant's assessment that a Native weakness for strong drink lay at the root of their disagreements. In Umpachanee's understanding, the discord arose from a string of orchestrated political incidents, beginning with his removal from Skatekook, to the forming of a town government that disregarded Native input or governing hierarchies, to the dividing of land into individually owned lots ignoring Native customs of land use and distribution, and the subsequent acquisition of Native properties which were bought up cheaply by the missionary leadership and sold at a profit to eager colonists looking to expand westward. According to Hopkins, the town had been incorporated to promote the "civil and religious interests" of the Natives.[98] But the Natives could only see the dissolution of these values taking place. The split between Sergeant and Umapachanee became more and more untenable until Sergeant's only recourse appeared to be "to proceed against him with the utmost rigour of ecclesiastical authority,"[99] which presumably meant excommunicating him from the church.

To make things worse for Sergeant, word had spread abroad that his mission was in trouble, with which "the enemies to our design were not a little pleased."[100] The effort to control the narrative emerging out of the Stockbridge settlement was, at least for the time being, slipping out of the control of the missionary chroniclers. But if Umpachanee seemed to the Stockbridge settlers to have strayed from the path of righteousness, at the nearby mission to the Mohican in Shekomeko some fifty miles south, Umpachanee was considered a sober model prospect.[101] Umpachanee, it seems, was not reliant upon Sergeant alone for the dissemination of Christian beliefs, and even began to challenge Sergeant on the finer points of doctrine, claiming amongst other things that the religious fasts promoted by Congregationalist practice "were things merely of human institution," and had no authority in scripture.[102] When Umapchanee quizzed Sergeant on the practice of celibacy amongst Roman clergymen, and on their "severe" methods of doing penance, Sergeant said he was "a little surpriz'd to hear him ask such a Question; for I did not suppose our Indians knew anything of the matter."[103] As a result of such "outside" influences, Sergeant complained that the Moravians in the Mohican mission of Shekomeko had become a mighty example for Umpachanee and were purposefully corrupting him from the true path.[104]

By the winter of 1740 Sergeant's mission to the Natives seemed to be unraveling, even as the town of Stockbridge was expanding as a colonial space. Sergeant concluded in the final entry of his 1739–1740 journal that he supposed the lieutenant "must be excommunicated."[105] The lieutenant's wife was said to be sick, and in fact she would die of consumption only a few months later. The following summer Konkapot's wife also passed away of sickness. Both were said to have died on the path to salvation.[106] The program to educate the Natives in Christian discourse continued with Sergeant perpetually promoting plans for a boarding school through the 1740s, but in an effort to solicit funds from benefactors in Scotland, Sergeant noted to a patron, "you will easily perceive, in the Perusal of this Journal, that the Indians are a very difficult People to deal with . . . Opposition I always expected, but met with it in instances where I dreamt not of it, and least expected it."[107] Sergeant's missionary career was following a pattern that mirrored the overall colonial effort up until that point. Although he entered into it with a sense of unbounded optimism over the surprising willingness of the Natives to convert, and spoke in breathless tones of their tears of repentance and their general character and intelligence, he closed with an ingrained sense of Native intractability, and an unspoken awareness of how little affect his personal efforts had on the collective beliefs of his flock. When a Moravian missionary, visiting the town in 1751, passed by the schoolhouse he found the students had all returned to their homes. When he asked why, a local Native told him, "they did not have enough to eat and they were not provided with sufficient clothing to keep them warm."[108]

Some observers have noted that Umpachanee, along with his fellow dissenters, came back into the Congregationalist fold in the year after his wife's death, implying in some measure that he had been chastened by her passing and lived out his days a penitent believer, thereby redeeming Sergeant and his efforts. Sergeant wrote that "many notorious drunkards seem entirely to have broken off from their beloved strong drink," and he noted that the lieutenant too "is again reconciled to our conversion." Frazier supposes that "fate and more charity may have sobered some of the wayward Indians," suggesting that the loss of loved ones to disease and the continuing disenfranchisement of the Mohican people from their original sources of power and identity encouraged them toward Christianity.[109] Other Muhheconnuk were journeying to Stockbridge at this time, and the leadership of the tribe may have centered itself in the settlement. Frazier notes that one Benjamin Kokhewenaunaunt, head sachem of the nation and otherwise known as King Ben, became a resident of the town around this period.[110] But the inherent tensions that had been there from the beginning did not fade away so much as slip the attention of our missionary observers as the Native population became more and more disenfranchised from a position of Native space and power. It is probable that there were still Keutikaws held and Long House ceremonies, but Sergeant was no longer invited to attend and we hear nothing of them as they become part of the hidden transcript.

By 1749, in the wake of Sergeant's death, the discontentment of the Stockbridge Natives had only increased. A petition in December of that year to the General Court complains that Natives were being forced to clear lands for white farmers and do other menial chores not in their interest. They protested that, although only four white families had originally been agreed upon to settle in the area, there "now were many families settled in place." The court concluded that the Natives "should be brought to submit to the laws of the Government upon which we endeavored to show them what benefits they would receive by conforming to the law. Many of them appeared willing to be governed by the English, but their chief leader Umprichena [Umpachanee] appeared very averse."[111] Almost a quarter of a century after signing the first land agreement with the English in 1724, Umpachanee still found himself resisting colonial hegemony and lobbying for Native sovereignty in the land of his origins.

Umpachanee went into his final decline in the summer of 1751. Rachel Wheeler, whose readings of the Moravian mission transcripts of the time provide valuable insights into the mindset of the Christian Mohican, notes that during Umpachanee's final days "there was a steady stream of visitors from surrounding communities visiting . . . to pay their last regards." Such was the Native custom of the region, that when an important leader appeared to be fatally ill, well-wishers would come from hundreds of miles around to pay their respects.[112] Umpachanee died on August 10, 1751, having been in the constant presence of friends and family, a great tree, still able to offer a place of shelter for his people after all the battles lost and won on that fertile stretch of land along the Housatonic River.[113]

The Stockbridge experiment produced a generation of young Natives who had been brought up with the Christian church and could read and write in the English as well as Native languages.[114] These Mohican obviously bore little relation to Cooper's romanticized denizens of the forest. While it is true they did ultimately serve with the English in the next round of colonial frontier wars, their engagement was of a much more complex nature than Cooper imagined in his works of fiction. Chingachgook seems to follow his companion Hawkeye through these novels in unquestioning devotion, like a dog follows his master. He has no noticeable connection to a larger body of people he identifies as his own, and he has no political or cultural agendas beyond what are perceived as ancient animosities between rival tribes. The real reason for the Mohican becoming swept up in the French and Indian War, however, had to do with their position as a people held captive in a colonial containment. With the threat of war already on the horizon, a group of Natives from Shekomeko and elsewhere had come to Stockbridge in 1740 bearing three wampum belts and were anxious to consult about the possibility of war. The first belt told how all the Natives present had been "wont from time to time to consult and advise with one another upon affairs of importance, and to communicate our determinations to eachother." The second belt indicated that the Chohkoosuk, or white people, whom they lived amongst, were preparing to go to war. "We only destroy ourselves by meddling in their wars. They are great and strong and so tall as to reach the Clouds. Let us only sit and look on while they engage in war. Don't let any of your people assist your allies in their wars. But while they fight, let us sit and smoke together." Sergeant noted afterward that the Housatunnuk "seem'd to approve of the thing; but said, they must first consult their Elder men, who were at home, before they came to a final determination."[115]

The Muhhecunnuck elders counseled peace. "Let us sit and smoke together, & see who will be the Conquerors," they said.[116] But like many young men faced with the prospect of war, the new generation of Mohicans had little to sustain their interest and livelihood where they were. Without promise of advancement or cultural validation, they probably regarded the new round of frontier wars as a means of earning income for themselves and their kin while advancing individual status. They were largely educated and baptized in the Christian faith and, over the course of a generation, had seen their land and power base shrink away. As one Jacob Cheeksaunkun allegedly wrote to Sir William Johnson in the summer of 1757,

> Last year you proposed to us that we might possibly be wanted this year to go against the Enemy. I have heard nothing from you whether we are needed or no, but some of our Young Men being very desirous to go on the Scalping Design wait on You . . . for your Advice & Direction in that matter . . . I should be glad Sir if you would let them know if they take any Scalps or Prisoners what reward they shall have for it.[117]

The earliest extant example of Native writing from Stockbridge that I have been able to locate, however, comes from the report of a young Mohican scout named Lieutenant Jacob Nena Nantphtonk to his commanders during the French and Indian War dated August 13, 1756. This young man provides an interesting counterweight to our impression of Mohicans derived from Cooper's accounts of the same war. Ordered to bring in enemy scalps from the vicinity of Fort William Henry, he writes:

> Monday Evening Left Fort William Henry with 16 Stockbridge Inds 5 Cont [Connecticut?] 42 white men and the First Day went Down Opisite to the Great Mountain by the narrows There Stoopt & Refreshed our Selves on an Island then put of & Continued the whole night[.] the Second Day got Down to a Cove on the East Side of the Lake & Lay all Night by a Greate Mountain[.] in the Morning March'd up an Emenence that over Looks Ticonderoga[.] there Left our proveshions with two Indians and one white man[.] we March'd Down and Discover'd two french paithes [paths] About Half a mile South of the Advance Guard[.] Sent two of my party forward to Discover where the parth [path] Leid to[.] Some Time after heard a horse of a number of French men in the Greate path[.] I Retreated with my people & Let them pass after[.] Saw three more French men passing upon which I fired with my people[.] two of them Fell Immeditly[.] Orderd to burn and Scalp them[.] my Self was the First that Came up[.] found that one of them was yet alive & one Escap'd[.] I Immeditly Struck my Tomhawk into the side of his head & there Left it.[118]

The unpleasant business of scalping the enemy, which could bring in "five pounds sterling," is often depicted as a consequence of the Indian passion for cruelty and bloodshed. But it was required, rather, by the colonists to ensure the loyalty of Native scouts, and as a "receipt" demonstrating that their claims of enemy conquests were not fabricated.[119] The fact that Nena Nantphtonk (listed on the muster rolls as Jacob Naunaumpaataunk) left his tomahawk where it was embedded in the skull of his enemy may indicate that such work was distasteful even for some Natives. Nevertheless, his party would arrive "at Fort William Henry This Morning Aboute 10 Oclock with my party and Scalps[.]"[120]

Amongst this generation of young Natives at war was Hendrick Aupaumut's father, who, along with his grandfather, served with the English during these conflicts. Aupaumut, who would earn the title of captain during his own engagements in the American Revolution, never knew a time when his people weren't caught within a ring of colonial containment. For reasons stated here and in the remainder of this chapter, he would determine that the best chance for Mohican survival lay in a removal to Upstate New York, where he would help found a new settlement in league with the Brothertown movement, called New Stockbridge.

Coming Home: Joseph Johnson's Mohegan Diary

John Sergeant's designs for an Indian boarding school in the 1740s never truly got off the ground. But by 1754 Eleazar Wheelock, building on his success with Samson Occom, was able to open the doors to Moor's Indian Charity School, where he hoped, in the words of W. Deloss Love, "to gather the most promising youth of all the tribes out of their heathen environment, under a master who would instruct them in civilized life, where they could have mutual acquaintance, and after years of seasoning in Christian truth be fitted to return as examples and leaders to their own people."[121] Unlike the praying towns of the past, where it was concluded that exposure to the corrupting influences of traditional Native lifeways had impeded upon Christian progress, Wheelock saw potential in cultivating a cadre of young Native Christians at a distance from their own communities. Wheelock was of the opinion that he had *made* Occom what he was, and therefore would easily be able to suit up an entire legion of Indian missionaries to enter back out into the wilderness and perform as effectively as had his first student. "The influence of their own Sons among them will likely be much greater than of any Englishman whatsoever," he wrote, in the first of many narratives advertising his newly formed charity school. He asserted that "Indian Missionaries may be supposed to better understand the Tempers and Customs of Indians, and more readily conform to them in a thousand things . . . They will look upon such an one as one of them, his Interest the same with theirs . . . And will be more likely to submit patiently to his Instructions and Reproofs."[122]

This proved incorrect for a number of reasons. Wheelock wrongly assumed that a Native of one nation of peoples would naturally be able to acclimate himself to the customs of another nation and meet with little cultural resistance. But, in fact, the young, ill-prepared Native missionaries that Wheelock sent off to live with people of different nations were very much like fish out of water, unable to speak the languages of those to whom they ministered, and often unfamiliar with the diet and customs they encountered. Also they were a long way from home with little or no social, emotional, or institutional support. Eighteen-year-old Hezekiah Calvin, a young Delaware sent by Wheelock to teach to the Mohawk, wrote in 1766,

> I am ready to give out with these Indians & with the Pains I have, I have a hard head ache certain time in the afternoon

> which sometimes is so hard that I hardly know what I am about &cc The Indians say I shall not come home these three Years they think that I am their Servant & are obliged to keep school for Yem & yet they wont send their Children . . . These things make me faint hearted together my wanting to see my father Mother & relations.[123]

Calvin, frustrated by his inability to speak the language, referred to himself as a "dumb stump that has no tongue to use" amongst the Mohawk.[124] In another letter he would confess to Wheelock, "I have foolishly spent my time to no purpose I have no peace of Conscience when I come to recollect back It seems to me to be in vain to tarry here any longer, there is great many things I might relate But my Conscience forbids."[125] These matters that Calvin's "conscience" forbade him to relate remain part of the hidden transcript of his missionary effort. He gestures strongly toward a complete breakdown in the goals and methods he has been asked to represent, but has no license to fully air his misgivings in public. As such, the failure becomes his own.

Other missionaries met with similar problems and anxieties. David Fowler, Occom's brother-in-law, while staying with the Oneida would complain, "I eat like a dog here, my folks are poor and Nasty. I eat with Dogs, for they eat and drink out of the same as I do."[126] Apparently for Fowler, the idea of the Common Pot was to be metaphorically and not literally applied. As for Joseph Johnson, Occom's eventual son-in-law and one of Wheelock's more promising scholars, he would ultimately abandon his post, engaging in ritual dances and other activities with the Oneida. Johnson was probably not the only young Indian missionary to break ranks with the colonial endeavor, however briefly, and allow himself to participate in the daily structure of indigenous life rather than stand in rigid opposition to it. But he was the only one who was willing to intimate as much in writing (Hezekiah Calvin's "conscience" forbade him to speak of such matters) and it led to Johnson's falling out with Wheelock and being cast adrift in the world as a sailor on whaling expeditions for the next two and a half years.

The problems faced by these young missionaries, alone in a foreign culture, with little support and few resources at their disposal, are most poignantly expressed in yet another letter from Calvin to Wheelock. He wrote,

> there is something that makes me want to go Home, what I can't tell, Home is in my Mind all the time I want to go Home soon & see my Relations & it seems to me to tarry home awhile or all the Time & and let me see if that I am able to support myself. I have tarryed upon Charity long enough, when I have

> had no more Gratitude to my Benefactors than I have done, but all prove to the Contrary instead of being grateful, I am as ungrateful as a Beast.[127]

The extremely difficult circumstances under which Calvin and his peers labored probably contributed greatly to Sir William Johnson's judgment of 1766 that the Indian missionaries had "become a Gloomy race & lose their Abilities for hunting &co spend their time in Idleness & hang upon the Inhabit[ant]s for a Wretched subsistence hav[ing] lost those Qualities which render them usefull to us."[128] In other words, the very qualities of "savagery" that Wheelock labored to breed out of his students were the qualities found to be lacking in making them useful as missionaries. In statements like these we begin to further apprehend the double bind of becoming a "civilized" Indian in the eighteenth century. Only by distancing themselves from the colonial gaze and its contradictory paradigms meant to ground out the very existence of Native life and culture could these Christian Indians forge out a meaningful existence for themselves without having to question their own identity as indigenous peoples.

Wheelock had assumed that other young Natives would meet with the same successes that Occom had encountered amongst the Montauk. But Occom had been friendly with the Montauk even before his appointment there, already sharing culture, language, and kinship ties with them. Also, while Occom should not necessarily be held up as an exceptional example, he felt he had a personal calling and it was primarily his own decision to follow such a path. While this path, as I have maintained, is consistently communitist, he nevertheless blazes it himself, using elements of tradition, wit, and innovation as his brush. When Occom first went to the Oneida in 1761 it was as a mature adult, secure in his position as a representative and leader of his people. He seems to have understood that he was making diplomatic inroads for the Mohegan and Montauk as much as representing a coercive foreign power. He forged alliances, exchanged wampum, and brought a representative from the Oneida home with him so that they might learn one another's languages and nurture a diplomatic relationship. These practices, the patience and insight that Occom brought to his endeavors in Native space, facilitated future negotiations with the Six Nations of the Iroquois that led to the ultimate granting of lands that would become the Brothertown settlement.

It was Joseph Johnson, however, who probably did more than anyone to make the move to Brothertown a reality. Johnson is an interesting and little-known figure in Native American, and consequently, American history—perhaps not surprisingly, a conflicted and tragic youth who came of age just as the United States was inscribing itself into being. Johnson did not necessarily go unnoticed by turn-of-the-century historians like Love and Blodgett who more or less credited Occom with the sole leadership role in establishing the Brothertown community. But the invaluable contribution that his letters provide to the study of Native American literature in colonial New England is hardly hinted at in these works. Love noted of Johnson that he wandered the seven Christian towns of the Connecticut and Massachusetts colonies "preaching the emigration as one might a crusade."[129] But Love suggests that "surely the design was a development in the mind of Samson Occom."[130] Critical work on Johnson has been scarce and one must credit Laura J. Murray for her excellent commentary on his writings and for bringing him to the attention of the greater scholarly community. Murray notes how Johnson's rhetoric over the course of his career gradually shifts "from the religious to the political plane," and how "as Johnson's cause and the revolutionary cause came into competition, Johnson did on occasion champion what he calls 'Native liberty,'" which Murray interprets to mean "some kind of basic indigenous right or custom."[131]

As mentioned earlier, Johnson's father was a captain in the French and Indian War who also had apparently been instructed in reading and writing at some point in his life. The elder Johnson would have been stationed alongside Stockbridge scouts such as Jacob Naunaumpaataunk in the vicinity of Fort William Henry in the mid-1750s, and was likewise authorized to "chuse out the Indians now in our Camp, to the number of Six and Twenty; whom he is to command, and who are to obey him, not only upon the present scout, but upon any other he may be employed during the Course of this Campaign."[132] As a result of his "fidelity" and "courage," the elder Johnson was given a great deal of autonomy to conduct the war in the manner he saw fit.[133] In August of 1757 he wrote to his wife from Fort Edwards, apparently in response to a letter she had written him, commenting upon the fall of Fort William Henry and how the French had "killed and carried captive a great many Indians." He also expressed concern for a fellow Native who had fallen sick with camp fever.[134] These few appearances of Captain Johnson in the archive offer a sense of Native community and perspective that differs greatly from anything generally attributed to the involvement of Natives in this conflict.

Joseph Johnson the younger was born in 1751 and entered Wheelock's school in 1758 at seven years of age, following his father's death in combat.[135] His classmates would have included Samson Occom's brother-in-law, David Fowler, who entered the school in 1759 (though sixteen years Johnson's elder), and Occom's son, Aaron, who also entered that year. His sister, Amie Johnson, attended Wheelock's for at least a season in 1761. It was Joseph Johnson, however, who could claim the longest tenure at the school by the time Joseph Brant, David McClure, Hezekiah Calvin, and William Major, or great William, all entered through Wheelock's doors six years later in 1764.

Johnson's time at Moor's Charity School was probably as tumultuous as the rest of his life. He comes into the archive swinging as David McClure notes in a letter to Wheelock dated September 25, 1765. McClure, a white student at the school, writes,

> On Tuesday last, Sun about two hours high, Johnson, & John Wheelock, were standing near the woodpile, great William by the gait, William and John Wheelock were chatting together calling one a nother Names. At last John challenges William to fite Johnson, calling him spekkle face white Eye &c which Johnson repeated. William being run upon by Johnson's threats, advances up to Johnson & offers to fite him. Whereupon they both strip their waistcoats, & prepare for an incounter, and in the mean time the most of the School Boys were gather'd around.

As the fight progressed Johnson called Great William, who was the mixed-blood Mohawk son of the superintendent for Indian affairs of the colonies, Sir William Johnson, a "Son of a Bitch" and an "Indian Devil," and according to McClure, they remained at blows, continuing "domineering over each other till Sun down." The fight continued when the boys went inside and they tore the shirts from one another's backs. McClure wryly noted how "one Nation seem'd to be at variance with each other."[136] Interestingly, the fight appears to have been provoked by Wheelock's son, John, who, through the epithet "speckle face white eye" seems to have been calling Great William a half-breed. Rather than fight his own battles, however, the younger Wheelock called Joseph Johnson to go into combat for him. This, in some measure, would serve as an analogy for much of Joseph Johnson's early years.

Though we have no portraits and only hints to go on, Johnson appears to have been a strapping, passionate, compulsive young man, fierce in his loyalties and quick to defend those whom he felt had been done an injustice. In September of 1764 he wrote to Wheelock, by way of apology, of his involvement in yet another altercation. When an acquaintance of his threw a rock at an unsuspecting dog, Johnson offered that "I would do the Same to him, As he would do to the dog." He then proceeded to "threw him down not Violantly & there held him down About A quarter of An-hour."[137] If Johnson was given to compulsive outbursts, however, he also seemed to dwell in the thrall of strong father figures whose influence he at once courted and strained against in his short life. That he sides with the young Wheelcock rather than the Mohawk "half-breed" in the aforementioned fight encapsulates his sense of loyalty to the Wheelock family at this time. As with so many Native youths of the era, his family network had been broken apart by colonial violence. Living in the shadow of his own dynamic father (a man by all reports highly respected in the Mohegan community), but denied his father's presence, Johnson found himself caught between the bookends of a paternalistic colonial system and the fragmented Mohegan power structure. His writings not only delineate for us the process by which Brothertown was established, but they offer us rare insights into the self-conscious struggles of a charismatic young man fighting to find his own footing in a time of unprecedented personal and historic upheaval.

In his eight years with Wheelock, Johnson received a more than adequate English education. Undoubtedly Wheelock saw great promise in Johnson and entertained high hopes that he might one day rise to the level of utility that Occom had before him, without giving half the trouble. Johnson became a missionary on the Oneida reservation at the age of fifteen, serving as one of Wheelock's corps of Indian representatives, training under Samuel Kirkland and David Fowler to be a teacher. Johnson writes, "I tarry here this winter to git knowledge of Davids Art in teaching the Natives and to know how to keep a School in every Article, and the next Spring to have a School by my-self at Old Oneida."[138] But, from the start, one senses a side of Johnson that cannot but resist the paternalistic restraints being placed upon him by Wheelock's missionary designs. Like most healthy, intelligent, robust young men, Johnson had a tendency to want to assert his own individuality and independence, and unlike many of his contemporaries, he possessed the skills to subtly hint at such inclinations in his writings.

It begins, perhaps, with small literary flourishes. It was a convention of the time to sign one's letters with humble indications of one's sense of gratitude and hierarchical position of servitude to the addressee. Laura Murray has noted how it was engrained in Wheelock's Native correspondents to strictly adhere to such rituals of subordination which inclined them to belittle not only their own accomplishments but their very identity as they dutifully reported back to their mentor. Even Occom was inclined to sign off on his letters to Wheelock as "your most unworthy servant" or some variation thereof.[139] But as Murray notes, Johnson seems to have been hyper-conscious of the "formulaic" and degrading nature of these "letter closures."[140]As such, he lays it on rather thick, referring to himself at the close of the letter quoted previously to Wheelock as "your most Obedient though unworthy Servent Poor good for nothing Indian Joseph Johnson."[141] Whether intentionally or not, Johnson's awareness of the degrading nature of these phrasings (which included the derogatory epithets commonly assigned to Native identity), injected a level of irony into his closing refrains. More often than not, the rhetorical hyperbole of his closings seems to reflect his current state of personal agitation. While his most innocuous letters end with standard refrains, his more tumultuous ones pile on the adjectives so we see him refer to himself on various occasions as "your faithfull and Obedient pupil, and good for nothing not quite Old Indian," and "your ignorant Pupil, and good for nothing Black Indian." He finally asks Wheelock to allow him to "now suffer me the honour of subscribing myself your once humble servant tho more the devils."[142]

Johnson was under enormous pressure at Oneida as a young man, far from home, expected to be the standard bearer for a system of faith he was uncertain about himself. In his letters he seems to take pride in his work as teacher at Oneida over a period of nearly two years, and he watched his number of pupils rise, with even some adults attending his classes curious to see what the young Indian missionary had to offer.[143] But Johnson was also easily distracted by the crush and swirl of events around him. One gathers that he drank on occasion and had dalliances with some of the young Oneida girls. He confesses to Wheelock of having indulged himself "in Brutish ease whilst in the wilderness." Whatever his crime, it seems he also confessed it to the Oneida "as is their Custom, where they promised to Bury [it] in Oblivion and let things be as if it never happened so." Johnson must have felt torn between two systems of belief, and perhaps at times the notion of entering "the longhouse which they call Heaven" must have appealed greatly to him.[144] "O how in the Maze of fate I have blindly run and Backward trod these paths I sought to Shun," he wrote Wheelock in lyrical contortions of boastfulness and remorse.[145] One wonders where Johnson came by this snippet from Dryden's reconstruction of *Oedipus*, or if Wheelock ever bothered to call up the rest of the verse wherein it states: "Impute my errors to your own decree / My hands are guilty but my heart is free."[146]

By November of 1768 the strains of being a missionary in a strange land were wearing on Johnson. He began at this time to contemplate running off on a whaling expedition with Aaron Occom, wayward son of Samson Occom. Johnson must have queried the younger Occom concerning the prospects and the people in the whaling industry, as Occom wrote back, "Some are good Neatend and Som are not but in hool it is a pretty good bisness."[147] Living with only the sickly and demanding white missionary Samuel Kirkland for institutional support, the young Johnson seems to have chafed at the restraints and finally broke free from his situation. As Kirkland summed it up to Wheelock, Johnson "turn'd pagan for about a week-painted, sung-danc'd-drank & whor'd it, with some of the savage Indians he cou'd find."[148]

Johnson, as a restless and charismatic youth, was drawn to the company of a people in his proximity who were probably more accepting of him and likely more hospitable than the flaccid missionary who seems to have considered Johnson something of a personal manservant rather than an assistant in Christ. But the event also establishes the possibility that

Johnson, rather than "whoring," "drinking," and "dancing," had actually made intimate connections with the Oneida himself—connections that transcended the often limited role one could play as a missionary *outsider* trying to make inroads within a resistant culture. Although Kirkland seemed to view Johnson's participation in Oneida rituals as a sudden rupture or apostasy, it was probably more in keeping with a gradual inclination on Johnson's part to involve himself in the daily routines of the community. As he had written to Wheelock some seven months earlier, "I have nothing strange to Acquaint you at present. I shall go with the Indians next week to their hunt (as all my Scholars will go)."[149] Johnson, in reaching out to his Oneida students, was immersing himself in their lives and customs. Not content to be a bystander, he participated in their hunts, dances, and courtships. Such connections, though routinely downplayed by Johnson in his letters to Wheelock, may have helped facilitate the eventual Mohegan exodus to Oneida in the next decade. But his having crossed over the line by engaging in pagan ceremonies was also the event, naturally, that led to Johnson's falling out with Wheelock.

Johnson's letters to Wheelock while he was at Oneida detailed his unhappiness and his sense of rootlesness, a theme that would remain with Johnson throughout his life. Having lost his father, and seemingly ambivalent concerning his remaining family attachments, he would consistently portray himself as in search of a home and an identity. At one point, in one of his many gestures of remorse to Wheelock, he writes, "Methinks I feel in Some Measure the down Cast Spirits of Cain when He received his curse; but no equal to his; tho my Crimes are more than Equal."[150] Whether his remorse was real or simply calculated to keep the lines of communication open for further need, it is difficult to say. But his identification with the cursed biblical brother who bears the mark of a separate race and is driven away from his family and people just this side of Eden is telling both in regards to Johnson's view of himself and the discursive construction from which he was fleeing.[151]

After leaving Oneida, and having broken from Wheelock "intirely," Johnson would spend a number of years adrift, "wandering up, and down, in this Delusive World," as he later characterized it.[152] He would teach for a time in Providence and see the world from a whaling boat before returning home to Mohegan and reestablishing himself with Samson Occom and the rest of the Christian community there. That Johnson is a man very much in search of spiritual and temporal grounding is made especially clear in his journals, begun after his wayward years as a whaler. Throughout his young adult life Johnson articulates a sense of fugitive self. In one letter to Wheelock he writes that "it is as if there was no solidness in my mind; Sometimes Encouraged, & at other Time Dishearted; So yt I cant be Resolute in what I do."[153] In his journals he calls out repeatedly for a "new heart," whether through the salvation of Christ or by some other means. He asks for knowledge "of my self as I really am by Nature."[154] His private writings are loaded with a poignant and melancholy questing that settles restlessly on Christianity and teaching, but ultimately finds a more perfect fit for his energies in the endeavor to gain new lands for the Mohegan and to break new ground in Brothertown.

Johnson returned from his whaling expedition in the autumn of 1771. We have no explicit reflection from him concerning what this experience offered or if he found such a life pleasing or oppressive. In one backward glance, he notes, "I have been whire dangers were and great dangers too the year Past, I have been Preserved on the mighty Waters, and have been kept safe from the rage of the great whales who obey his Voice, and many other dangers."[155] Even here amongst such Melvillean musings, however, it is evident that spirituality is on Johnson's mind more than the rigors of whaling. Returning to Mohegan seems to have signified the turning over of a new leaf for Johnson. He began keeping a private journal upon his arrival, and as Laura Murray notes, after his first setting foot again on Mohegan land, "every week thereafter, he marks the anniversary of his return."[156] Being finally situated on home turf after years of wandering in the world seems to have provided at least some sense of comfort and stability for Johnson, the prodigal son, from which vantage he could begin reassessing his life and his ways.

He begins haltingly. Some initial dalliances upon making landfall with one "Sally Hazzard" left him with a sexually transmitted disease which he fretted over anxiously in the ensuing weeks. But it also appears to have sharpened his mind on the subject of his soul, as his private reflections quickly turned from Sally, whom he refers to as "the girl I love" in one early passage, to his new-formed resolution to "live as in the Sight of God, and wait for the Second coming of my Judge."[157] It is true that Johnson was largely reared in a Christian environment, and so this quality of thought was not new to him. But while prior to Johnson there are only spare hints concerning the private ruminations of Natives undergoing Christian conversion (Occom's journals offer a good example of this), in Johnson's journals we are privy to an exacting account of his shifting doubts and convictions, revealing the psychological strains that, for many, must have accompanied this process. A month and a half back from his whaling expedition, still taking medicines for "reasons I dare not commit to paper," Johnson berates himself, "Oh! When shall it once be thought of me, that I am Converted, and call Christ Jesus my Saviour, and God my father, and the holy Ghost my Comforter, Or when shall I have real knowledge of myself, my State and Condition whilst out of Christ, Stranger to God, and my Self."[158] The earnestness of such pleas did not, however, stop Johnson from confiding one month later, "No one knows what Troubles my mind, what doubtings, what desires there is in my mind."[159] He speaks of secret lusts and longings, a hidden transcript of the human heart, and asks Christ Jesus to "Assist me with groanings that Cannot be lettered."[160]

The desire to know not only God, but to gain real knowledge of himself, to know his own mind and to express troubles and doubts that none other can see, are all in keeping with the cultivation of a private self that is encouraged by the processes of reading and writing in alphabetic literacy. Whereas, in earlier times, entire communities of Natives adopted Christianity as a kind of outer garment to take shelter under, there was always pressure from the missionaries to internalize the process and for each individual to embrace Christianity with their hearts as well as with their mouths. While, perhaps, there were a few successes along these lines, for the most part an earlier generation of Natives had difficulty reconciling themselves to this level of acculturation. Wequash, having survived the ravages of the Pequot War but not his own grief, told us "me heart all one stone." Waban echoed this sentiment, saying, "I do not truly pray to God in my heart; no matter for good words." Umpachanee, too, could not bring the necessary tears to his eyes to demonstrate his full conversion to Christian doctrine. But Johnson, in the midst of an extended kinship community at Mohegan, commits to a very private struggle. Certainly he was impressed by the prayerful community of Christians that surrounded him, and the preachings of Occom and Samuel Ashpo touched him deeply, but his internal conflict was expressed in terms of alienation from all these factors. He exhorted himself to "live indeed as if you had in reality sat out for another Country Even a heavenly Country, and live as a Stranger, and a Pilgrim here in this world."[161] He continued to implore in his journals, "O Lord Jesus be pleased to create within me a New heart."[162]

Of course the community around him exerted its own brand of soft power and Johnson appears to have readily immersed himself in the routines of daily life at Mohegan. Not only did he partake in the assemblies and worships, and receive frequent visits from Samson Occom, the Fowlers and others, but he was constantly employed in a dizzying variety of tasks: hunting, shelling corn, making quail traps, boiling pumpkins for the hogs, ferrying a pair of white women over the Thames, making "pudden spoons," mending shoes, caning chairs, and helping his aunt in the "hewing of her broom handles."[163] He began attending council meetings and speaks of how "the Chiefs of our Nation met at the house of Mr. Occom to consult" on one matter or another.[164] Mohegan was still in turmoil in the early 1770s, with the issue of succession in the sachemship still unresolved and factions having formed that had already split the reservation's populace in half. Johnson stood in the thick of these struggles, with his uncle Zachary Johnson, who had been a counselor to Ben Uncas, apparently remaining loyal to that faction after Uncas' death in 1769. Occom and the Ashpos stood at the forefront of the opposition.

Loyalty to Uncas suggested, to a certain extent, an accommodationist relationship with the colonial overseers of Mohegan. These were the same overseers who had pursued the Mason land case against Mohegan since the seventeenth century and continued in the 1770s to encroach upon Mohegan lands, harvest Mohegan lumber for personal profit, and to stand in opposition to Occom's, Mohegan based, spiritual leadership. As such, Zachary Johnson most likely allied himself with David Jewett, the white appointed minister at Mohegan, who had been in open conflict with Occom ever since Occom's initial return from Montauk in the 1760s.[165]

It is difficult to determine how these strains played on Joseph Johnson's overall sense of place in the community, although the trajectory of his life makes clear that he felt drawn away from his allegiances to his uncle and pulled in some measure toward Occom. Perhaps in deference to his uncle, Johnson had gone to see a sermon by Jewett shortly after his return to Mohegan. In his journal he writes somewhat ambivalently that Jewett was "considerable short in his Discourse it being considerable cold, and So Dismissed the Assembly which was few Indeed."[166] More and more he found that Occom's "way of Discourse gave me a great Incouragement," and we might assume that at least some of Johnson's doubts and secret troubles were wrapped up in his divided loyalties at Mohegan.[167] Whereas Jewett's sermon left him cold, he began to feel a growing sense of personal and communal empowerment and warmth in the movement that Occom was fostering at Mohegan.

But Johnson also indulged in private activities at this time, speaking of how the "after part of the day, I spent chiefly in writing," and on another occasion, "nothing have I done but write this day and read a Little."[168] He speaks of one afternoon spent "reading of the Proverbs of Solomon, and looking over the old writings of my father."[169] Johnson expresses a level of intimacy with alphabetic literacy that informs his habits and, significantly, places him in contact with his dead father whose letters and "pocketbook" he must have still had on hand.[170] Johnson also spent many an evening "pricking out" hymns for the Mohegan congregation, a task that he would busy himself with for years to come, as hymn books were hard to come by and much in demand. His skill at penmanship was a needed asset to the community and his level of engagement with a textualized worldview was virtually unprecedented for a Native American of his times, in many ways shaping the outcome of his life.

Was it a "calling" for Johnson, as his struggle to honestly commit himself to the Christian faith came to overwhelm his thoughts and activities in the weeks to come? Or was Johnson enamored to other, less apparent elements about Occom's ministry and the level of autonomy and empowerment that it held out to Native peoples? Johnson had grown up in the shadow of Eleazar Wheelock, who had impressed upon him at an early age his worthlessness as a member of the indigenous race. In his communications with Wheelock, Johnson's very name was constantly attached to a string of epithets that reiterated and reinforced his worthless condition. But in the new church that Occom was forming at Mohegan, outside of the white missionary establishment, there was a sense of growing self-worth and entitlement. Although it is difficult to see it through the archival clouds that gather around this unrecognized institution, something was stirring at Mohegan, and from Occom's humble church, it seemed to Johnson a glorious sound was rising.

Johnson's journal entries at this time begin to read like fledgling sermons, and he speaks, as mentioned earlier, of applying himself to other extraneous writings that do not appear in his journals. While we can only speculate on what it might have been that Johnson was writing, we can assume that he was practicing his craft, improving his knowledge of the Bible, exposing himself to other Christian tracts like Bunyan's *The Pilgrim's Progress* and Baxter's *The Saints Everlasting Rest*, and, perhaps under the tutelage of Occom, aspiring to be a preacher himself. The final passage of his 1771–1772 journal begins, "There is still a great body of Snow on the face of the Earth. What may a reasonable soul learn from all things. May not every thoughtfull Soul be taught the wisdom, and the goodness of God from Every Object he cast his Eyes, whether it be Animate, or Inanimate."[171] Johnson had begun to turn from his anguished and alienated self-searching to a more wizened transcendent voice. He is also rehearsing for what will prove his first textualized appearance in the public eye as he begins to craft an open letter to one Moses Paul, a New England Native being held in the nearby New London prison for the murder of a white man.[172] And perhaps it was this letter that he labored over in his private hours as well. Paul's execution would be, of course, more famously the subject for Samson Occom's first publication, the 1772 *Sermon Preached at the Execution of Moses Paul*. But Johnson, too, was determined to put in a good written word for his doomed kinsman.

A Lesson before Dying: Moses Paul and the First Published Writings in Native North America

While a good deal of scholarship has recently emerged around Occom's sermon, particularly since its appearance in the *Heath Anthology of American*

Literature, there has been very little discussion concerning Joseph Johnson's letter, which not only stands alone as a text of interest to Native studies and the historical period in general, but adds another layer of contextualization to Occom's better-known piece. The occasion for the sermon was the execution of a fellow Native, Moses Paul, who killed a white man in a drunken encounter outside a tavern in Bethany, Connecticut. According to the press releases at the time, Paul had been refused service at the tavern and so waited outside the door and bludgeoned over the head the first person to exit the premises. The true details of the case were more complicated than this. In Paul's own petition for an appeal, he insists that it was Cook, in fact, who brutally assaulted him. When Paul tried to reenter the tavern, Cook was heard to say to another patron, "give me your cane and I'll still the dog."[173] The murder of a white man by an Indian, however, was unlikely to be considered an act of self-defense at this time. Paul's appeal petition asserts that, at the time of the trial, "the Voice of the Populace was; Hang the Indian! Hang him! Hang him!"[174] And so Paul's appeals went unheard, not only by the courts and the press, but by the later historians who chronicled the event. Nevertheless, if we hope that Occom will use the unfortunate bully pulpit of the execution sermon to exhort his audience about an unequal justice system, or the systemic pressures that led to poverty and substance abuse amongst his "poor miserable and wretched" Native "brethren," what we find instead is a somewhat studied temperance lecture in which Occom asks Paul to consider the "wages of sins" as he prepares to meet his maker.[175] This is not to say that a locus of resistance fails to reveal itself in Occom's text, but before we can identify that locus it would be helpful to know more about the specific cultural conditions that brought about this peculiar performance which in its printed form went through at least nineteen separate editions.[176]

In *Forked Tongues*, David Murray sees Occom's execution sermon of Moses Paul as an event "stage-managed by whites," and in fact, it appears that way from our distant remove, as the spectacle of the world's most famous Indian preacher delivering the exhortation at the hanging of one of his own "despised" race, was bound to sell tickets. Murray finds the event to be framed by colonial constructions such as the contrived dialogue between Occom and Paul appearing in many later editions of the sermon, and a broadside that condensed the themes of the sermon into pithy quatrains that warned against the perils of drink.[177] The introductory dialogue, authored anonymously, invites the reader to eavesdrop on the imagined conversation between Occom and Moses Paul, in Paul's cell chamber the night before his execution. It places words into the mouths of its characters, reminiscent in every way of Eliot's *Indian Dialogues*, who perform a fantasy of assimilated discourse. At one point in the dialogue Moses is made to cry out, "I deserve a thousand deaths," thereby voicing the secret wish of many a colonist.[178]

Whether or not the event was "stage-managed" as Murray claims, we should acknowledge that Occom did not choose to speak at this event simply because he relished the opportunity to appear before what would be one of the largest audiences ever assembled in Connecticut prior to the Revolution. In fact, Occom might not have felt terribly invested in the publishing of the execution sermon at all, as he notes in its preface,

> the world is already full of books; and the people of God are abundantly furnished with excellent books upon divers subjects; and it seems that every subject has been written upon over and over again: and the people in very deed have had precept upon precept, line upon line, here a little and there a little; and so in the whole, they have much, yea very much, they have enough and more than enough.[179]

There is more than a simple hint of reluctance and disgust as Occom enters once more onto the colonial stage, to play the "Gazing Stocke." Nevertheless, we might remember that Occom had been haunted by the hanging of a young girl named Elizabeth in his youth, which may have prompted him to offer what succor he could on this occasion. Twenty-nine years had passed in the interim, but Moses Paul's execution marked the first execution to take place in the state of Connecticut since the hanging of Elizabeth Shaw, and it is interesting to note that Occom was present at both events. And if we take him at his word, he was also highly motivated to appear at this otherwise lamentable production because Moses Paul, in a letter, had personally asked Occom to preside over his execution. As Occom insists, "it is an unwelcome task to me to speak upon such an occasion; but since it is the desire of the poor man himself, who is to die a shameful death this day, in conscience I cannot deny him; I must endeavor to do the great work the dying man requests."[180] Murray suggests that Paul could not have written the letter to Occom that requested his services, and this was, in fact, just one more piece of the colonial stage-managing.[181] The cultural assumption that Paul, and by extension all Natives of the period, must have been illiterate is embedded into our thinking about Native identity to the extent that even literary critics writing about literate Natives take the bait. But even within the sermon itself, Occom speaks directly to Paul, noting "you have had a good education; you can read and write well; and God has given you a good natural understanding."[182] If the event was meant to orchestrate a kind of "moral tableau," as Murray suggests, in which an Indian affinity for drink and its attendant degradations were put on public display, it also was a way for Occom to perform his role as elder counselor of his community, providing a point of mediation between the colonial spectacle and a knowledge of the institutional conditions that provoked it.

Although the sermon itself makes some interesting moves in terms of Occom's separating "his audience into different groups," of white, red, and condemned man, and addressing them in turn, the importance of this sermon from a Native perspective probably occurs off-stage.[183] The public transcript has Occom refer to Paul as "bone of my bone, flesh of my flesh," but it reveals little of how such ties of kinship and nationality between Occom and Paul transcend the staging of the public event. One might imagine, however, that Paul was comforted by Occom's presence at this moment—comforted by the knowledge that someone he knew and trusted would be near his side at his death. The local press reported that as Occom attended Paul to the gallows, "the criminal behaved with Decency and Steadiness, and appeared to be in the exercise of fervent secret Prayer all the way from the Goal [jail] to the Gallows." It is noted that, before his execution, Paul took "most affectionate leave of his countrymen the Indians (many of whom were present) and exhorted them to shun those vices to which they are so much addicted."[184]

There is a hint of solidarity in these gleanings, as perhaps the Native community of New London was performing some stage-managing of its own. This sense of unspoken empathy is enhanced by the knowledge that, in later years, Paul's grandchildren would be amongst the first baptized by Occom when the Brothertown settlement was established in Upstate New York. In fact, Occom's daughter would marry Moses Paul's son, making Paul's grandchildren Occom's grandchildren as well.[185] In other words, there is a hidden archive, or threads of intervention and interrelatedness that do not readily reveal themselves in the actual text of Occom's sermon. The dominant clergy was likely to have regarded Paul's act as the inevitable outcome of a life of savage debauchery. Indians were presumed to be creatures of little moral fortitude, with diminished intellectual capacities, and given to strong drink and impetuous, if not savage, behavior. By agreeing to preach the sermon, Occom offered Paul a promise of dignity at his death that we can safely assume had rarely been accorded him by the white community while he lived. It was incidental, perhaps, that the sermon would become much in demand by both white and Native audiences and go through so many printings in the following decades.

For anyone interested in the particulars of Paul's execution, Ava Chamberlain's "The Execution of Moses Paul: A Story of Crime and Contact in Eighteenth-Century Connecticut" should be required reading. Chamberlain's article skillfully lays out the colonial biases that adhere to the circumstances of Paul's arrest and subsequent conviction. The fact that Paul, in his defense, declared that "he was born in a Christian Land and Educated in a Christian Manner" offers a remarkable contrast to Occom's own autobiographical claim that he was born a heathen and brought up in heathenism. Such claims speak to the contorted and paradoxical nature of the performances demanded of Natives in this period when staking out their identities to a white audience. Clearly it was in Paul's interest to separate himself as much as possible from notions of Indian "savagery." It should surprise no one, however, that this strategy failed. The justice system, then as now, was heavily weighted against people of color prevailing in court. But if the institutional racism of the courts was invisible to the colonial power structure, it was only too well understood by the Native communities that had historically strained against it, and we can sense this in Johnson's letter, perhaps better than in Occom's sermon.[186]

The issue remained, however: what could precisely be stated by a Native in such an intensely public forum? Natives entering upon the house of the archive have always been involved in a performative routine, but they also regularly sought to insert their own agendas into the highly formulated speech acts required of them. Joseph Johnson's letter preceded Occom's sermon by some five months, and demonstrates not only Johnson's desire to become a leading voice in his community, but the sense of solidarity that local Natives felt regarding Paul's arrest. Johnson submitted his letter on March 29, 1772, entitled "Letter from J____h J____n, one of the Mohegan Tribe of Indians, to his Countryman, Moses Paul, under Sentence of Death, in New Haven Goal," and apparently the letter was made available for purchase at the Printing Office in New Haven.[187] There is little reason to believe that Johnson's letter was "managed" by the local power brokers. It seems to reflect, more than anything, upon the concerns and wishes of the local Native community. Like Occom's sermon, the letter adheres to the typical pieties and formalities of a discourse meant to exhort an individual to make peace with their God before dying. But the language is slightly ambiguous when it comes to addressing Paul's actual sentencing in the murder of Moses Cook. Johnson first sympathizes with Paul by identifying himself as a fellow "native of this land," and noting, "I am one who am truly sorry for your misfortune."[188] He then addresses Paul in the plural, seeming to speak on behalf of his community in general when he writes, "We hear that you are condemned by the Judges of this Colony, and that your life must be taken away by the execution of justice. Justice must, or ought to be done; and all that men can do is to kill the body: for our blessed Saviour said in the days of his flesh, Mat. x. 28. And fear not them which will kill the body, but are not able to kill the soul."[189] Johnson is careful to not openly dispute Paul's sentence in these lines, but he constructs a binary between the "we" who hear of Paul's condemnation and the "them" who carry out the sentencing, who will "kill the body" but not the soul. It is this "them," or the "judges of the colony," who have assigned Paul's guilt, and while Johnson agrees that justice must be done, he offers a slight nod toward the frequent miscarriages of colonial justice in Native space when he clarifies that justice, at least "ought to be done." Whether or not it will be done remains in question.

As with his closing refrains in his letters to Wheelock, Johnson cannot help but display his self-conscious awareness of the self-denigrating role that Natives were expected to play on the colonial stage. He cautions Paul,

> be assured, if you fall short of heaven, into hell you must be turned: and I doubt not, but this is the earnest prayer and desire of many, who have a prejudice against the Indian nations, and wish no better of your soul, than to endure God's eternal wrath, and even rejoice that one of the devilish Indians (as many express themselves) are suffered to act such a part; and wish that all were as nigh their end.[190]

As Johnson asserts, it is the colonial wish not to see Paul's soul redeemed (despite a century and a half of missionary outreach to the contrary), but rather to have their earnest desires affirmed that Paul will submit to the devilish fate assigned to his race. In fact, race has been at the center of Paul's case from beginning to end. Johnson's appeal to Moses Paul is to not gratify these colonial ambitions for the Native, but to act a different part by taking his soul's redemption into his own hands. Johnson's expressed thoughts here are likely to conform in most ways to the sentiments of the Mohegan community, or those Natives who attended Paul's execution and of whom Paul took "most affectionate leave." It is most fitting, therefore, that Occom rhetorically divided the audience into separate groups in his sermon, for they had come for separate reasons, to affirm separate truths and partake in the formation of separate archives.

Johnson, the little-known acolyte, is, perhaps, more explicit than Occom in expressing the concerns of his Native community. But he is still aware that the medium constrains his voice, and he hopes to suggest to Moses Paul the strains of hidden transcript in his open letter. "I desire you would take notice of what I have in so broken a manner hinted unto you," Johnson writes. "I mean to be sincere.—But I am uncapable of expressing myself, or writing as some may who have been favoured with great learning."[191] In other words, there are things that cannot be said openly, but must be understood all the same. Johnson's versatility with written forms allows him to insinuate this hidden or "Native" transcript through "broken hints" and through manipulations of the text and the intertext. Some of this can be apprehended when Johnson quotes scripture to Moses Paul in his letter, hinting at the protest his Native community sounded against Paul's sentencing by the colonial judges. Johnson quotes only a fragment of Luke 6:36, citing the presence of "a merciful God," but eliding the actual context of this passage. The extended verse cautions: "judge not and ye shall not be judged: condemn not and ye shall not be condemned." The elided message seems directed more at the colonial judges than at Paul himself.

As with many a Native convert to Christianity, Johnson's private perusals of the Bible must have opened up to him intriguing parallels between Native and Christian belief systems. Just as Konkapot and Umpachanee held out to John Sergeant the possibility of a syncretic religious practice where the Keutikaw and the sermon might be held under one roof, the Christian Mohegan of Connecticut remained invested in their own culture and traditions. The raw materials of this syncretic spiritual view are suggested by Johnson's quoting of Amos 5:7: "seek him that maketh the seven stars and Orion, and turneth the shadow of death into morning." Might such a passage have suggested to Moses the legend of the seven holy men who became stars in the Delaware Big House tradition and stood at the threshold between earth and heaven, illuminating the path to the afterlife? Johnson seeks out a similar reference when he asks Moses Paul to keep in mind the words of Revelation 21, which speak not only of regeneration and of a "New Jerusalum," high atop a mountain, but also of the seven angels once again, who will lead the way to this place, and how, once there, in the presence of the tree of life, God will "wipe away all tears from their eyes" (Revelation 21:4). Such intercultural overlapping of spiritual narratives could not be openly expressed by Johnson within a Christian discourse, but might easily have been understood by Moses and other Mohegan as part of Johnson's hidden transcript. Johnson, when looking at Moses Paul, probably saw some faint delineation of the path his own life might easily have run. As such he signed his letter not as an "unworthy, humble, black, Indian servant," but simply as "your soul's well-wisher, J____h J____n, a native of the Mohegan tribe."[192]

O Mohegan: The Writing of Brothertown into Being

Joseph Johnson may have begun to find his voice in the spring of 1772, but still compelled by his restless nature, the path before him was far from clear. As such, November of that year found Johnson standing at a personal crossroads as he set out to visit the "Farmington Indians" in Farmington, Connecticut some forty miles north of Mohegan. He notes how, from Hartford, "I went 3 Miles. There I was much at a stand whether to call at Farmington or no, as my design was to go to the Mohawk Country. There I stood at a Stand some time."[193] It is difficult to say what Johnson thought he might do in Mohawk country, had he decided on such a path. Was this yet another crisis of faith? Was he considering abandoning both Mohegan and his Christian convictions for something he felt he had left behind in his youthful rebellion in the country of the Six Nations? Or was it simply more restlessness? The previous six months at Mohegan had been characterized by his public dedication to the church, which was formally submitted in a written statement in May of 1772, shortly after the publication of his letter to Moses Paul. This declaration was almost immediately followed, however, by a public apology to David Jewett the very next month, in which Johnson admitted to "getting intoxicated very much," while assisting in raising the new meetinghouse, no less.[194] Such public apologies and abject displays of humility seemed almost a rite of passage for any Native aspiring to a position of spiritual authority within a colonial paradigm. But this six-month period in Johnson's life was also certainly colored by the actual event of the execution of Moses Paul in September of that year, a sorry spectacle that Johnson was sure to have witnessed. These incidents, and the general state of conflict at Mohegan, may have set a new pattern of thoughts to swirling in Johnson's young mind.

For whatever reasons, Johnson was once again untethered. As he had written in his apology to Jewett, "after I got in my right mind again, I determined within myself to go away into some far Country whire I never was heard of or might ever be heard of by you again."[195] Although in his statement he ultimately resolved against such a course of action, in his heart Johnson was still uncertain and he stood now at that very crossroads. To go to Farmington meant to reunite with Christian Natives who were in need of a teacher and would offer him community and shelter. To continue on to Mohawk would appeal to Johnson's restless longings and the part of his soul that remained unsettled in the Christian/Native discourse within which he had made so many tentative starts. Whether for good or ill, Johnson's "stand" came at an end when, like out of a fable, three strangers appeared on the road before him and led him to Farmington, thus resolving his indecision.

Once there, Johnson called a gathering of the Christian Natives and read to them Occom's execution sermon. News of this curious oration had traveled far and apparently the assembly was anxious to hear the words of their revered preacher for themselves. Johnson seems to have offered a few words of inspiration of his own, perhaps drawing from his "letter," and this was followed by some hymnody. Afterward Johnson made known to those assembled a proposal from Occom that Johnson begin keeping school there. This proposal was warmly received and, in the blink of an eye, Johnson was anchored to a job as teacher at Farmington for at least the duration of the winter.

From Johnson's journal of this period we learn that he not only taught school, but wrote letters for the Farmington Natives, established regular meetings for prayer and singing, and as he had in the past, "prick't out tunes" in his gamut for the congregation to use. He seems to have taken a great deal of pride in his work as a teacher and in the progress of his students. As he writes in one passage, "I never Saw Indians so much desireous of Learning. I have been Different Parts of this Continent, among different Tribes of the natives, Scattered up and Down but . . . My Challenge is this, that they Excel this School in Manners & Proficiency Considering the time, as well as the age of the Schollars, that they have been under my Care."[196] One still senses, however, the embattled state of Johnson's mind, and his quest for an identity that escaped the constrictive formations of Eleazar Wheelock's training and the conflicted affairs of his Mohegan elders. Johnson longed for home while in Farmington, and yet the homeland Johnson yearned for had, in his mind at least, been psychologically reduced, so that, as it stood, there was no *Mohegan* for him to go home to. As he so wistfully laments in his journal,

> Mohegan is a lonsome place, oft have I sighed—but sighed in vain—desired, but desired in vain—Cast down—but no one to Comfort me—in destress—no one to relieve me—no friend to open my heart and vent my Sorrows—I opened my mouth to the open air—and told the Stones my Sorrow. Thus o Mohegan have you treated me—and thinkest thou—I can forget thee—or thy inhabitants—thinkest thou—or thine inhabiters that I am desireing to be on thee or with them—far far from me be such a thought—but still there is a precious few in thee, which Causes my mind often to Meditate of thee—Perhaps in due time I may once more Come on thy borders—but first I have to go, to distant Lands; and far Country—and Differant Nations I have to walk through—before I see thee. Thus O Mohegan I must bid you farewell, and Shut the door of my Heart against thee.[197]

In *American Lazarus*, Joanna Brooks notes how portions of Johnson's mournful rhapsody resemble Psalm 137 "substituting 'Mohegan' for 'Jerusalem.'"[198] But really what is at work here is a sort of reverse typology. For while the biblical Psalm pines for the promised homeland that has been lost as a result of captivity, Johnson's verse seeks a homeland of the heart and mind, rejecting the geographical Mohegan which is yet within his reach. Mohegan itself is "a lonsome place" that he has been "Cast down" from, as in his earlier letter to Wheelock when he compared himself to Cain. Who exactly cast him out, and to what does he owe this fugitive condition of the heart, remains a minor mystery. But this is partly the natural lament of an energetic young man searching for his place in the world, and it is also a very real assessment of how the conditions of his life had forced him into the peripatetic wanderings that would define his remaining days. As a Christian Indian in Revolutionary America, he is as Natty Bumppo would claim, "neither fish nor flesh." If he is captive, it is not in the physical sense, but rather, to a racialized identity. He has been schooled away from the traditions of his homeland, sent to far-off lands to preach the works of an alien culture to yet another culture, and when the stress became too great, he was driven to flee from all of it and wander abroad. No wonder all he could see in front of him was further wandering to the "distant lands and far countries—and Differant Nations I have to walk through."

The mood and sensibility Johnson evokes in this passage is a far cry from the pseudo-nomadic "Wandering Life up and down in the Wilderness" that Occom described in his first personal narrative.[199] Rather than depicting the "benighted" cultural condition of an entire people, he is expressing an existential angst that has its roots in political realities. For Johnson, it seems (and perhaps for the other eventual Brothertown emigrants as well), the quest for new land was essentially a quest for spiritual reinvention or regeneration, and an opportunity to create a sense of home, a *Mohegan*, that the sociopolitical and individual circumstances of his life had all conspired to deny him. A New Mohegan, akin to the "New Jerusalem" he dangled before Moses Paul. As much as to be "indigenous" means being of a specific place, it wasn't the first time in history that the Mohegan were forced to consider uprooting their homes and building a life elsewhere. Johnson's rendering of this knowledge into a kind of sorrow song, however, demonstrates how Christian spiritual narratives were being interwoven with Mohegan sensibilities.

The singing of hymns was an important expression of the faith of not only Johnson, but the Christian Natives of New England in general. While in Farmington, it was related to Johnson that many "valued such meetings more than the other, that is the singing meetings."[200] Johnson would reflect upon his students at Farmington that, despite only a few weeks of training, none other could "Excell this Tribe in Singing, the Musical Art."[201] Occom's famous book of hymns published only a year later would showcase at least six of Occom's own compositions that similarly expressed the sense of questing and uprootedness found in Johnson's half-formed compositions. In "A Son's Farewell," or "I Hear the Gospel's Joyous Sound," Occom writes, "My due affections I'll forsake, / My parents and their house, / And to the Wilderness betake, / To pay the Lord my Vows."[202] Such versification not only invokes Johnson's wanderlust, but speaks to the condition of many Natives of New England who by 1774 were committing themselves to the notion of uprooting their lives on colonially infiltrated traditional lands and moving themselves to Brothertown. It is in Johnson's private lamentations, however, that we are offered the richest and most poignant expression of such looming events.

Laura Murray notes that "those who did move west at the end of the 18th century, in the movement to Brothertown . . . did not so in solitary flight, like Cooper's Chingachgook and Uncas, but with a determined community vision."[203] While this is certainly so, it is difficult to pinpoint the moment in letters when that community vision came into being. There are letters as early as 1767 detailing that Wheelock had been planning an Indian missionary community in the Oneida territory for quite some time. Such a community would be the fruition of his plan to educate a small portion of Natives and then remove them to a wilderness location where they might educate their so-called savage brethren through direct missionary work as well as by example. In one letter Wheelock writes, "I have been trying to collect a town of Christianized Indians, from ye New England Colonies, and settle them in some suitable place, in ye heart of ye Indian Country . . . This would furnish an Asylum for our Missionaries, set ye Savages a pattern, and exhibit to them ye advantages of a Civilized life."[204] Wheelock also mentions in a letter, written upon Occom's return from England, that he had advised Occom "to dispose of his Family and Affairs agreeably to make himself a Settlement in the Wilderness, Where he may have an Advantage which no Englishman can have, viz, as much of their best lands as he could reasonably desire."[205] Wheelock also apparently suggested that Occom start a school there, but as Occom "seemed disinclined to hear it," Wheelock lamented that "I fear his tour to England and the great Respect Shewn him there will have the Sad Effect to make him aspire after Grandeur and ease and prevent his future usefulness."[206]

Whether or not either Occom or Johnson were aware of Wheelock's designs for an Indian settlement, they took the initiative upon themselves and effectively cut Wheelock's missionary schemes out of the picture.[207] Johnson had only been in Farmington for roughly a month when he records in his journal that he attended a "Very Serious" conference.[208] Johnson appears to receive a clearer picture at this point of the mission with which he has been tasked by his Native community. No longer a lone seeker, hashing out his trail in solitude, Johnson places himself in the service of a collective vision. In February of 1773 Johnson, though still at Farmington, wrote to Occom that "When Ever I shall be losed from here, I purpose to go to Onoida."[209] Although he does not state the reason for his proposed visit, his efforts to launch a colony in New York State take off from this moment. He begins a tireless campaign to try to raise funds, ostensibly for himself and his teaching efforts, but it becomes apparent that what Johnson really seeks is the funding to get himself to Oneida so that he can negotiate for land. In this plan he seems to have found the perfect confluence for his own restless heart, his spiritual strivings, and the communitist impulses that kept him from wandering off in an aimless and solitary condition.

There was a sticking point however. Money for such an endeavor was not easy for an Indian to come by in colonial America, particularly with the thirteen colonies on the verge of revolting from their mother country. After pursuing a number of alternative opportunities, Johnson finally turned to his former mentor, Wheelock, for financial assistance. This could not have been a desirable turn of events for Johnson, and his letter of August 30, 1773 is loaded with a number of pained rhetorical contortions that were soon to become a ready staple in Johnson's bag of discursive tricks. He writes, "If I were an Englishman, and was thus respected by you, I should be very thankful, but much more doth it now, become me being an Indian, to be humble, and very thankful in very deed."[210] The forced obsequiousness here is almost blatantly ironic. In one breath he foregrounds Wheelock's inherent lack of respect for the Indian race, and yet in the next, signals that he will play the part demanded of him regardless. Johnson makes very little effort to conceal that he is merely going through the motions of a formalized deference, and finishes his preamble to the letter by saying, "But to Conclude this my Indian Introduction let me assure you, that a law of Gratitude is wrote as it were upon the table of my Once Savage heart."[211] He seems to signal here, to us and to Wheelock, that the so-called "Indian Introduction" in question is an unattractive but necessary phase of the transaction, a required ritual that has been ingrained in his heart. The real business, however, as Johnson states it is "that I, and the rest of the Chosen men, Should go into the Wilderness, to vizit our Savage Brethren, and to Converse with them Concerning our Proposals." He also adds that, "I find I am Obliged to Solicit your favor this once more, for which I am very Sorry."[212]

It is doubtful that Johnson was able to squeeze funds out of Wheelock, who preferred his Indians to go "a begging" elsewhere for resources. But by October of that year Johnson had put up a public notice on Mohegan lands addressed from the "Farmington Indians to 'All our Indian Brethren,'" calling for the Natives of Mohegan, Niantick, Pequot, Stonington, Narragansett, and Montauk to each send a man so that "they may go with us, and Seek a Country for our Brethren." That the women of the community had also weighed in on the matter was indicated by the acknowledgment that "our kind Women sends a word of Engouragement, and says that they will make little yoke hegg to give to the travelers."[213] This demonstrates that, as in the past, both the men and the women had reached this accord together.

In the series of communications that ensue, Johnson would write to Occom, the Oneida, Wheelock, the Connecticut Assembly, Connecticut governor Jonathan Trumble, and other missionary societies, attempting to raise the funds needed for a mass removal to Oneida. In these letters he repeatedly represents himself as a "poor ignorant lad," "a despised Indian," or as "fatherless, motherless and almost friendless."[214] But he was equally capable, when necessity demanded, of adopting the high tones of American liberation discourse, writing in one letter to the citizens of New Haven: "Gentlemen, let me with humility tell you, that I have exerted myself, used my uttermost endeavors to help my poor Indian Brethren in New England; to bring them out of Bondage, as it were: and to lead them into a land of Liberty, where they, and their Children might Live in peace."[215] With the Revolutionary War drawing ever nearer, such talk was bound to appeal to a colonial assembly.

The multiplicity of voices, of self-presentations, that Johnson inscribes become almost dizzying from here on in, as he travels from Mohegan to Hartford, New York City, Boston, Dartmouth, and on again to Oneida territory. He moves from being a self-described object of pity, to an example of America's burgeoning republican spirit. To the New Haven assembly he spoke of a "Native Liberty . . . admired by all noble spirits," and to the New York Congress he writes, "my love to the country in which I was born and educated . . . animate me to step forward, though at expense to my very life."[216] And the attention his scheme was garnering from the overall colonial community, not to mention the primary role he was playing, is noted in an address to the Connecticut assembly wherein he asserts,

> Gentleman, I would just enform your Honors, that I was the very first mover of this Design, the fame of which, Methinks, is now Spread almost all over the Continent, and most in leading on the affair, as all the Writings that I have can testify—and it is very probable that I shall still be the foremost, so long as there be hopes of being Serviceable . . . or so long as there shall be prospects of being usefull to my poor Indian Brethren.[217]

Johnson had managed to articulate the movement to Brothertown within a discourse of Christian benevolence that was in keeping with the rhetorical traditions of the American colonies from their very inception.

Johnson also presented himself as the respectful "younger brother" of the Oneida, whom he addresses in January of 1774, intoning "we pray you to consider seriously of our Words, ye old men who are wise, also ye warriors, and stout hearted young men. Listen unto us, yea let Children hearken, that what we say may not soon be forgotten."[218] Johnson, a quick study by anyone's standards, not only mastered the form of what he calls his "Indian Epistle," but he evidently tutored himself in the diplomatic rituals of the covenant chain, standing shoulder to shoulder with the leaders of the Six Nations of the Iroquois, exchanging calumets, tobacco, and wampum.[219] It should be noted, however, that Johnson, in his personal writings and letters to other Natives, never resorts to the obsequious tones adopted in his letters to whites. Before white audiences his fellow Natives are referred to as "poor Indians" and "savages." But when addressing the Natives themselves they become "kindred," "brethren," and "warriors." Clearly this is a controlled discourse that he is capable of stepping in and out of, and, as he writes to Occom, "I have been constantly improving my talents that God hath graciously bestowed upon me, chiefly among the English."[220] Or, in other words, he was beginning to recognize his own powers of using literacy coupled with rhetorical genius to effect political action.

Johnson also began to redefine his notion of his own identity in this period. As with many of Johnson's endeavors, he seems to have followed Occom's lead in drafting an autobiographical statement sometime in the fall of 1773. He writes, "Would you know kind Sir, who the composer of this Discourse is, Be pleased to read the following." Unfortunately, this intriguing introduction, begun upon an empty space in a draft of a different letter, was never fully realized. Johnson got far enough to note some particulars of his ethnicity and education and spoke of his "wandering up and down in this Delusive World." He noted his time amongst far Indian Nations and how he had sailed

> upon the Ocean wide. I have been down Eastward, as far as to the Western Islands twice. Curvo, & Florus, I have Seen, and to the Southward I have been as far, to the West Indies, Seen also the Islands between Antigua and Grenades, and again from Antigua I have sailed down the leeward sailed by the Virgin islands, also by Sandy Cruize, Portireco, down as far as to Mona. And after so long time Even in my 21st year I Safely arrived to my Native place.[221]

In this rearticulation of his life, Johnson was no longer the outcast bearing the mark of Cain as he had so often appeared to himself in the past. As Laura Murray notes, he now "represents his return to Mohegan as the resolution of a heroic journey," and the boons rewarded him upon his hero's return would not only be honor and prestige, but a leading role in Mohegan affairs and ultimately admission into its leading family with his marriage to Tabitha Occom, daughter of Samson.[222] Johnson achieved a new professional status when he was awarded a license to preach in August of 1774.[223] And he also renewed his childhood relationship with the Mohawk leader Joseph Brant who in turn recommended Johnson as teacher to the Onondaga.[224] In other words, Johnson seemed to be moving at a furious pace, working deals, raising funds, and establishing connections on every side of the Revolutionary divide. And with all this newfound influence and self-worth came a kind of rebirth, though not only of the Christian variety. This is hinted at during an address to Colonel Guy Johnson in 1775, when Johnson would appear before the English dignitaries as "Joseph Johnson, alias Aweriaderigha."[225] This is the only mention of an "Indian name" in all of his writings and suggests that in some ways, even as Johnson was becoming more and more implicated in colonial discourses, he was turning as well to his traditional identity as a Native to express his will in the world.

The Oneida lands were deeded over to the New England Indians on October 4, 1774. Occom and David Fowler had been to the region in July of that year and surveyed the lands to their approval. Johnson now had until the spring of the following year to try to round up willing recruits. He gloats to Wheelock that he expects "upwards of Sixty young Indian men from the Seven Tribes that will . . . be distinguished as *noble Spirited Indians*, who will do their uttermost to get good and do good [italics mine]."[226] It is doubtful whether Wheelock had ever heard any of his students refer to their own people as "noble" and "spirited" before, and in this letter Johnson conveys the spark of optimism and national pride that was engendered by the coming emigration.

Which brings us round once again to the unusual event of a group of Native Americans ordering their own westward migration at the dawn of both rampant American expansionism and Indian removal. In the spring of 1775 a small constituency of New England Natives who went up to Oneida, including Johnson and David Fowler, were able to build some crude "huts" (or more likely wigwams), to break ground, and "got some cornfields planted and gardens made."[227] That may have been the happiest time of Johnson's adult life. He had inscribed a new home into being for himself and his people. He had a new family, a new sense of identity and personal agency, and he had seen the first fruits of his dream ripened into a reality. But the settlement was begun on the eve of the American Revolution, and Johnson, whose negotiating skills had apparently earned him a reputation as a reliable and energetic Native intermediary, was soon enlisted by local powers to seek a truce of neutrality between the Iroquois and the colonial rebels. Somewhere en route between Mohegan and Oneida, while carrying a message from General George Washington to the Six Nations, Johnson disappears from view, a casualty of war, race hatred, or simply of being caught in that liminal space between contested worlds.

The letter from Washington that Johnson carried spoke highly of Johnson's "recommendations" and asked him to communicate to the Six Nations that Washington (who refers to himself here as the "Chief Warrior" of the United Colonies) did "not want them to take up the hatchet for us except they chuse it . . . we want that the chain of friendship should always remain bright between our friends of the Six Nations and us."[228] There is a surreal irony in Washington's voice here, participating in the language of the covenant chain, brightening that chain for all time on the eve of American Independence, while directing his words to Johnson, a Christian Native, mastering the discourse of alphabetic literacy on the verge of Mohegan emigration. Johnson may or may not have been a willing participant in such diplomatic endeavors, but likely he had little choice, even as the mission diverted him from his plans of building a new home and settlement. He was twenty-four years old when he, at least presumably, met his death. The only notice of his passing came in the form of a letter from Johnson's old schoolmate David McClure to Wheelock, to whom McClure wrote, "the churches this way who had a taste of Mr. Johnson's ministerial Gifts feel for the public in the loss of that zealous, pious and very promising Indian Preacher."[229] Soon after his death the fledgling Brothertown settlement was broken up by the war and would not reconstitute itself for yet another decade, after the American Revolution had finally ended.[230]

Plans for the establishment of the Brothertown community were put into motion once more by the end of the war, led by David Fowler, Occom's brother-in-law. Fowler, along with others of the original Brothertown organizers who had sold their lands in New England, took temporary refuge in the town of Stockbridge, Massachusetts when the war broke out, accepting the hospitality of their Housatunnuk brethren. Despite efforts to remain neutral, members of both nations were drawn into the colonial war raging around them and at least eighteen Mohegan men were killed fighting alongside the Americans. A census taken in 1799 reported only eighty-four residents at Mohegan, meaning something in the area of 20 percent of the Mohegan population, were forfeited fighting for American independence.[231] Fighting also took a heavy toll on the Stockbridge Mohican who reportedly lost seventeen men in combat.[232] In each case, the death toll was probably a good deal higher and included women and children as well as men. Johnson, for instance, is not counted as a casualty of combat, and yet the circumstances of the war had brought his life to an end.

In response to their service, following the war, the newly independent government in Massachusetts forged a constitution granting everyone the right to vote accepting "Negroes, Indians, and molattoes." According to Patrick Frazier, the town of Stockbridge voted thirty-nine to thirty-one in favor of ratifying this constitution.[233] This would lead Hendrick Aupaumut, a veteran of the war and now a young chief of the Stockbridge Indians, to write on behalf of his people,

> To the Senators and men of the Commonwealth of Massahcusetts who are about to smoke their Pipes together in doing the Great Business of the State—We the Chiefs of the Moheakonnuk

Tribe of Indians residing in Stockbridge this day met together to beg you to listen to us a few words. Brothers—we remember we were once Great, and you were Small when you first came on this island, but afterwards We became Small as you became Great, and now we are very small and you are very great. We also remember that our Forefathers have often looked to you for Protection, Advise and Assistance. We with pleasure look back and consider you have always heard us, when we have Spoken to you. Now Brothers since we are small we look to you as Children to their Fathers. We wish you would always remember as Parents do their Children. Brothers, we will put you in mind that ever since we first see you, we were always true Friends to you in all the Wars, until this present Day. In this late War we have suffered much, our Blood has been spilled with yours and many of our young men have fallen by the side of your Warriors, almost all those Places where your Warriors have left their Bones, there our Bones are seen also—now we who remain are become very poor. Now Brothers, we will let you know we have been invited by our Brothers the Oneidas to go and live with them. We have accepted their invitation.

Brothers. We will now tell you what we desire of you. We wish you in your wisdom to make some Laws that will protect and gard us while we may remain or hereafter have occation to come into your Government. We wish you to appoint a few of our Neighbors, whom we believe to be our Friends, to have Power to take care of the little interest of Land We have in this Town, that have been appropriated to a public or private use, either to sell or lease it out for us as they and we shall think best, directing them also to confirm all such Lands as we have honestly sold. We wish to have them described carefully to examine into all our bargains for land that the White People have made with us and see that we hant been cheated and endeavor to do justly by us and by those who have bought of us and have not as yet had their Lands confirmed to them, that when we are ready to remove, We may feel well towards all our Neighbors. We wish only to reserve Power to ourselves to do a little Business as Proprietors with regard to some unappropriated Lands. We wish that the Purchasers of our Lands might pay these our Friends for their Trouble.

Brothers We will only ask one Thing more, that we might not be sued in the law for any future Debts We may hereafter contract.[234]

Aupaumut's letter aptly demonstrates the depth to which Native relationships were in flux at this moment in history. The Mohican saw themselves turning from "Brethren" to "Children" in their relations with the colonist (even though the address retains the relationship of "Brethren" or "Brother" through the end). The bones of their war dead were intermingled with the bones of colonists. But their original hopes for joint community in Stockbridge were now being invested in a plan for Native emigration to New Stockbridge, to be established alongside the town of Brothertown, and to be gathered into and incorporated exclusively by Natives. They had gone from unlettered supplicants asking the English for instruction in reading and writing, to literate brokers plying the legal assurances of alphabetic literacy to protect what lands had yet to be extorted from them. The careful, sad, almost careworn wording of Aupaumut's letter at the close of America's colonial period suggests the long road Natives had traveled in their engagement with European literacy. But it also demonstrates the extent to which the discursive practices of Native space were being kept alive even alongside all the spiritual, economic, and educational incursions of the colonist. At every point of contact, it seems, Natives of the colonial period were being rhetorically driven off the page, and at every point they pushed back, asserting again their own cultural identities and desires. Until most recently, such assertions remained such a fragmented, diffuse, and unwitnessed portion of the colonial archive that a sustainable narrative had difficulty cohering around Native agency in this period. As Hilary Wyss noted of the writing Indians of New England, "we long to place them, to find the moment in their texts where they unmask themselves, but their positions defy easy interpretation."[235]

Still, the Natives of New England refused to become ethereal victims to the violence of colonial unwitnessing. As more scholars engage with these works and seek to understand them from a perspective informed in Native cultures and epistemologies, more and more the isolated fragments seem to fit together as pieces of a narrative whole. As Hopi poet Wendy Rose says in the epigraph with which I began this work, "the stories begin to build a new house." We stand here at the eastern door. The Brothertown and New Stockbridge settlements constituted neither the end nor the beginning of that long history of Native tracks laid down in red ink on the colonized landscape. But when Joseph Johnson, writing in 1774, spoke of "a land of Liberty," he implied a space separate from the "land of the free" being forged for colonists at the time. He longed for a "Native Liberty," a space that he fought and struggled and wrote toward that located its sphere of power and influence outside the dream of American independence and hegemony. It was a place where Natives might escape "the wretched bonds of slavery," a land "of Liberty, where they [Natives] and their children might Live in peace."[236] It was not a new idea. The movement to Brothertown and New Stockbridge opened up yet one more chapter in the hope for self-governance, peace, and the survivance of a people, leading Hendrick Aupaumut to write a few years later,

> Fathers our fire begins to burn again; our hearts rejoice to hear it; we hope it will burn brighter than ever; and that it will enlighten the nations around. Our brothers of the Stockbridge and Mohegan tribes, and many others from the eastward have already agreed to come and sit with us around it, who all hope to see the light of God's holy word.[237] (See Figure 5.2.)

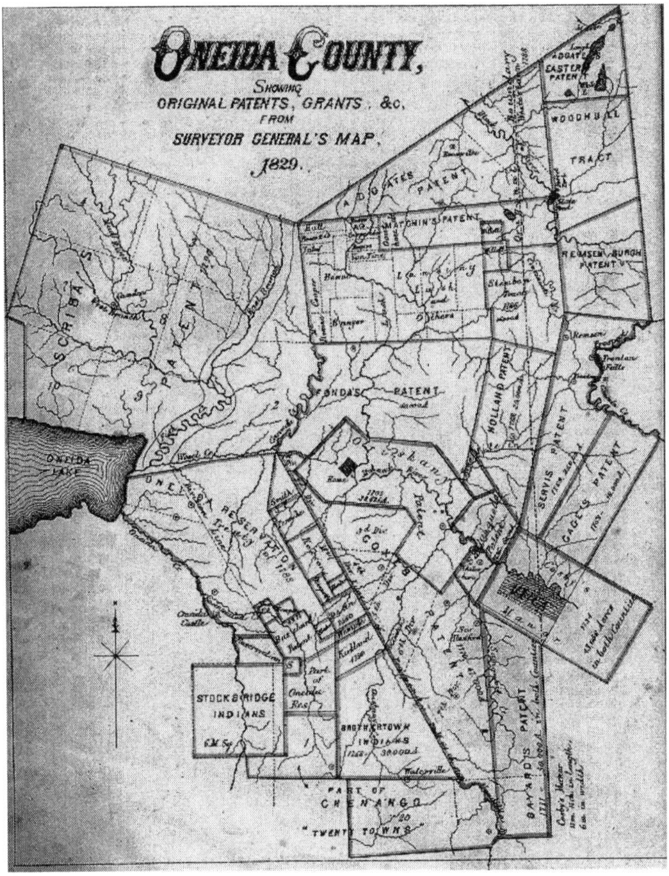

Figure 5.2. 1829 Surveyor's map of Oneida County, New York with Brothertown and New Stockbridge in lower left-hand corner.

Afterword

O' Brothertown, Where Art Thou?

> Silence a people's stories and you erase a culture. To have graphic evidence of this phenomenon, all we have to do is look at a map. Mapping is, of course, an intensely political enterprise, an essential step toward appropriation and possession. Maps write the conquerors' stories over the stories of the conquered.
>
> —Louis Owens

It is tempting at this point to want to achieve some kind of closure, or to suggest that the achievement of establishing a new home ground for Mohegan and Mohican survivance somehow culminated in the coming together of the Brothertown settlement in Upstate New York at the close of the colonial period. Certainly this was the dream of Samson Occom, Joseph Johnson, Hendrick Aupaumut, and others, but a dream deferred. Occom would travel back and forth in the years after the Revolutionary War from his house in Mohegan to the newly established village. On the first of these trips in 1785, he wrote in his journal of the welcome he received as he rode up to the fringes of the settlement after weeks of travel. Coming upon David Fowler's house in the rain, he relates how, "I heard a Melodious Singing, a number were together Singing Psalms hymns and Spiritual Songs. We went in amongst them and they all took hold of my Hand one by one with Joy and Gladness from the greatest to the least, and we sot down awhile, and then they began to sing again."[1] The words to one of his own hymns might have certainly struck home on this joyous reunion, "For I will come as fast I can, / A long that way I stear / Lord give me Strength, I shall at length / Be one amongst You there."[2]

In the following weeks Occom would recount the drawing up of the plan for the town. On Monday, November 7, 1785 he wrote,

> we proceeded to form into a Body Politick—we Named our Town by the Name of Brothertown, in Indian Eeyamquittoowaucon-

> nuck. J. Fowler was chosen clarke for the Town. Ralph Waupieh, David Fowler, Elijah Wympy, John Tuhy, and Abraham Simon were chosen a Committee or Trustees for the Town, for a year and for the future, the committee is to be chosen Annually.—and Andrew Accorrocomb and Thomas Putchauker were chosen to be Fence Viewers to continue a year. Concluded to have a Centre near David Fowlers House, the main Street is to run North & South & East and West, to cross at the centre. Concluded to live in Peace, and in Friendship and to go on in all their Public Concerns in Harmony both in their Religious and Temporal Concerns, and everyone to bear his part of Public Charges in the Town.[3]

Unlike the original Stockbridge mission where the traditional Native leadership hierarchy was undermined in the creation of a new colonial town government, Brothertown was fully Native owned and operated. The plan bespeaks a dream of permanence, order, hope. And at least in its early days there was a sense of communal effort with "everyone to bear his part of Public Charges in the Town." Some critics have argued that the very name of the town reflected the patriarchal order of Western epistemologies that had crept into this fashioning of Native space. But the relationship of "brethren" between various Native bands had been long established in Native tradition and Brothertown was, in fact, the coming together of many Native brethren in a new shared identity.[4] If the scheme and organization of the town was based somewhat upon the European notion of the grid, it is important to keep in mind that Native villages were always carefully oriented to the cardinal points as well. Occom spent the next few days surveying the territory, much as William Cooper, James Fenimore Cooper's father, would do later in that same fateful year, but whereas Cooper saw a primeval wilderness stretching out before him in want of European improvements, Occom relates joyfully in his journal, "Thirsday Fryday and Saturday, look about a little to see the land and it is the best land I ever did see in all my Travils."[5]

Occom did not immediately resettle in Brothertown, but he returned yearly to the community he had promised to make his "Home and Center."[6] He preached for both the Brothertown and the neighboring New Stockbridge settlements in Oneida in the years that followed, becoming a close associate with Hendrick Aupaumut, more generally known as Captain Hendrick, following the war. The two must have immediately felt some kind of common bond or sense of purpose, for within a short time of meeting one another, Aupaumut was attending services with Occom and playing a role in the sermons. As Occom records in his journal, "after I had done speaking Capt. Hendrick rehearsed what he could remember in his own tongue."[7] This became a feature of Occom's preaching at Brothertown and New Stockbridge, helping him to forge a bridge between traditional and Westernized lifeways.

Occom would recount preaching to assemblies of both whites and Indians, using whatever shelter was available as there was no formal church built as of yet. In certain instances he seems almost startled by the multiplicity of frontier identities gathered before him. As he relates of one Sunday service,

> four young Onoyda men were there, and were drest Compleat in Indian way they shind with Silver, they had large Clasps about their arms, one had two Jewels in his Nose, and had a large Silver half moon on his Breast; and Belts about their Legs and their heads were powdered up quite stiff with red paint, and one was White as any white man and gray Eyes, his appearance made me think of the old Britains in their heathenism.[8]

At such times, the complications of Occom's own battles with the presentation of Native identity must have appeared before him in a new light. He was no stranger to the customs and manners of other nations, had presumably been "born in heathenism" himself as he claimed, and yet on this new home ground his own rhetorics of self-identification were once again in flux, his subject position offset, perhaps, by the confluences of borderland realities coming together and the conflicted stances he, himself, had taken over the long remarkable journey of his life. The surreal paradox that in a land with white-skinned heathen, he was a Christian Native must have appeared before him as a kind of hall of mirrors distortion. But still, Occom continued in his attempts to preserve Mohegan community as he understood it, having Aupaumut translate his sermons, as he labored to spread the Christian word to his "congregation in the wilderness."[9] And for a number of decades after Occom's death in 1792 the settlement persisted as a Native incorporated space.

In fact, while the town of Brothertown bore the stamp of assimilation to colonial norms in much of its rhetorical and material design, there is reason enough to consider Brothertown and its neighbor New Stockbridge as vital examples of how elements of both indigenous and colonial tradition might be syncretically situated within a template of survivance in Native space. The fact that Occom and Aupaumut took turns before their congregations, speaking in both English and Algonquian, points to a determination to keep Christianity and Native tradition together, but distinct, similar in some ways to Umpachanee's earlier attempts to bring Sergeant's sermon into the longhouse. In fact, when John Sergeant Jr. arrived in New Stockbridge in 1786 to take over the mission, he found a great deal of resistance to his outreach. The Native settlement was apparently desirous of maintaining its spiritual as well as legal autonomy, and the church split into two entities at this time, one presided over by Sergeant, and the other by Occom.[10] In a public letter inviting Occom to be their preacher, the New Stockbridgers stated their belief that "god has raised you up, and have kept you alive until this Time, and that he has Sent You up as an Ambasador into this Wilderness upon this porpose, that you might be the Instrument or means to Stir Up Your own Nation, to try to embrace the Whole Religion."[11] It was of great significance to the newly settled Natives that they maintain their own way of worship, the practice of a "whole religion," which may have incorporated elements of Native tradition (certainly Native language) in its striving for completeness.

When the first waves of a traditional Native revitalization movement began to spread through the Six Nations in the 1790s, Aupaumut, in a manner that might be considered somewhat unchristian, perfectly articulated the advantages of maintaining a syncretic approach to spirituality. He said,

> we give our young men and women liberty to go and hear the Ministers of the Gospel anywhere—also to come here [to the Onondaga village] to hear and see the ancient way of worship of your forefathers; and if any one should find in their minds to be their duty to join this or that society, we will not forbid them; because if you and we both use these means, when one fails the other may stand; but if you, and we depend only upon one instrument; and neglect all the rest, when this fails, you and I must come to ruin.[12]

Occom, in his function as scribe for the newly formed Brothertown community, would express something similar in a 1785 petition to the also newly formed governing body of the United States Congress. He wrote,

> the good, and the Great govr of the Worlds,—Saw fit in his good pleasure, to Divide this World by the Great Waters, and he fenced this great Continent by the Mighty Waters, all around, and it pleased him, to Plant our fore Fathers here first, and he gave them this Boundless Continent, and it was well furnished, and Stored with all the Necessaries of Life.

Occom posits a world framed, not by binaries of savagery and civilization, clothed and naked, literate and illiterate, but by a God who allowed different models of spiritual practice and belief to function independently of one another. But when that same supreme being saw fit to allow the Europeans to cross over the ocean and encounter the indigenous peoples of America, the colonists rose "up against them for their maintaining the pure Religion of Jesus Christ." Only then, Occom tells us, did the Natives come to be seen as "poor, wild, and ignorant."[13] The idea that Occom saw the precontact Natives as practicing the "pure religion of Jesus Christ" is revealing in terms of how the famous Indian preacher wove Christianity and Native tradition together in his worldview.

One might conclude, after all this, that the disappearance of Brothertown and New Stockbridge as Native spaces on our contemporary maps is just one more example of colonial unwitnessing. And it is. But unwitnessing is, in essence, a retroactive phenomenon that gains force and power through repeated representation. The actual processes that ultimately undermined the dream of "Native Liberty" in Brothertown and New Stockbridge had to do with the usual forces of greed, nationalism, and fear that are always in operation both internally and externally in every good scheme. The community vision with which Brothertown was initiated gave way to the self-interest of a few, which, alongside the forces of colonization always waiting in the wings, was enough to eventually erode the power base that had hoped to keep the land under a common Native title. Where Brothertown once established itself, concluding "to live in Peace, and in Friendship and to go on in all their Public Concerns in Harmony," we now find the town of Deansboro, named after its white settler and founder, James Dean. The silence that maintains itself around such erasures is, as Louis Owens asserts in the epigraph to this afterword, intensely political. By erasing the name on the map, in all certainty, one erases a Native narrative and unwitnesses the hopes, dreams, and ambitions by which a people staked their claims on this earth.

It may seem at times that by appropriating alphabetic literacy and entangling themselves in the cultural aspirations of the colonists, the Natives of New England simply dug their own unmarked grave. But the truth is a great deal more complicated. Some Native peoples remained on their lands and today the Wampanoag, Mohegan, Narragansett, and Pequot all maintain their own reservations on or near the southern shores of New England. The Nipmuc also maintain a small portion of their ancestral lands in Grafton, Massachusetts, although the state and federal governments have yet to grant them the honor of tribal recognition there. Many of the Brothertown and New Stockbridge Natives continued on their trail to White River, Ohio and then Bowler, Wisconsin near Green Bay, under the guidance of Hendrick Aupaumut, David Fowler, and others. Their descendants are there still as members of the Stockbridge Munsee band. None of these nations has preserved itself without struggle, grief, and loss of cultural ground. But they have endured and many grow in strength and number, taking pains to keep language and tradition alive. Check their websites. Read what they have to say about themselves. Their focus is largely on the future, even if a portion of that future necessarily lies in an open engagement with the past.

Taken out of context, the writings of Christian Natives of the colonial period may still strike us as compromised, obsequious, subjugated, in short, a surrender of authentic Native identities and beliefs. Faced, however, with cultural and political imperatives that have rarely been adequately interpreted in the house of the archive, Occom and others assembled the tools for survival in a changing world and inscribed that survival for later generations to encounter. Until Joanna Brooks collected all of Occom's writings together in 2006, curious researchers like me had to travel to scattered archives around New England to grasp the full range of his accomplishment, straining to read the fading handwritten scrawl in the small pocket-sized notebooks wherein he kept his journals, sermons, and other notes. One had to dig in unexpected places for the correspondences maintained with family and acquaintances, to locate the warmth and the laughter he occasionally expressed with close associates like David and Jacob Fowler or the worry and care that manifested itself in letters to his wife and children. And even then, bold new interpretive strategies forged by the likes of Gerald Vizenor, Robert Warrior, Lisa Brooks, Jace Weaver, Craig Womack, Hilary Wyss, Laura Murray, and others had to be set in motion before such expressions and accomplishments could be fully appreciated for what they were.

And yet the discourse was never entirely opaque. Much simply went unnoticed as there were, as always, tears in the eyes, dirt in the ears, obstructions in the throat, making it difficult for Native concerns to be apprehended through colonial containments. As Occom unambiguously wrote in a complaint against the state of New York in 1788, "is there no redress for the Indians, by the Rulers, if there is none, I do declare it, I had rather be amongst the most Wild and uncultivated Indians, in the Western Wilderness." He seems to have already felt the pressure, continuously exerted by Western powers, to force Native civilization ever westward. The cry of white men toward the Indian, Occom wrote, was "Kill kill 'em, Damn em kill" (how reminiscent of Moses Paul's trial where it was argued, "the Voice of the Populace was; Hang the Indian! Hang him! Hang him!").[14] But despite having to face up to such "vulgar" prejudices, he still held to his conviction that literacy would be the saving grace of the Native. He wrote, "we are trying to keep a School to instruct our poor Children in Letters, and the Children learn beyond all expectation." He insisted that Indians needed people of their own color and Nation to instruct them. In spite of poverty, disease and other degradations that the ills of colonialism had forced upon his people, salvation would have to come from within.[15]

Samson Occom left behind textual notes and transcripts for a good many of his sermons, but he was also in the habit of speaking extemporaneously. According to his biographer Love, "especially in his later years, he made use of more similes and stories, interrupting his discourse by such illustrations."[16] A Dr. Buell of East Hampton observed that Occom, "when he preaches to the Indians, is vastly more natural, free, clear and eloquent, quick and powerful, than when he preaches to others."[17] In short, when amongst his own people, Occom's delivery was unconstrained. In 1853 Reverend Daniel Waldo, who had attended a sermon by Occom when just a boy of fourteen, was asked to recall some of the particulars of Occom's address, though some sixty years later. He writes,

> His voice was pleasant, but not very loud . . . but I recollect that his subject led him to speak somewhat at length of what he called a traditionary religion; and he told an anecdote by way of illustration. An old Indian, he said, had a knife which he kept till he wore the blade out; and then his son took it and put a new blade to the handle, and kept it till he had worn the handle out; and this process went on till the knife had had half a dozen blades, and as many handles; but still it was all the time the same knife.[18]

The Reverend Waldo went on to say that "I cannot be very particular as to the application he made of it, but the story I remember very well, and it seemed to me, at the time to be very pertinent to the object for which it was told."[19] But, if Waldo could not remember nor comprehend the context, we might be able to read into this parable a striking tale of Native transformation, syncretism, and survivance. Nothing of the sort ever appeared in Occom's published works, nor could it. And yet, Occom's Indian knife is, perhaps, something passed down to him by a line of writers, singers, storytellers who also put the knife to use, found ways to repair it and keep it sharp, using whatever materials were at hand. And it continues to pass from hand to hand. Its narrative value belongs to a longhouse of power, or a Native space where narrative occurrences have a separate weight, a separate valence that is not fully apprehended by any single discursive hegemon.

When William Apess lamented in 1829 that the Natives had "no press to record their sufferings or to make known their grievances," he was acknowledging the "manifest manners" by which the colonial archive labored to construct and constrict knowledge of Native identity and presence on American soil.[20] The violently fragmented pieces that constitute the longhouse of the archive could not be readily reassembled by Apess, and he may not have been conscious of the centuries of Native engagements with European literacy, or red ink, preceding him in his efforts to reenvision history from a Native perspective. He noted how "many a tale of blood and woe has never been known to the public." But that knowledge, that tragic wisdom, hadn't simply vanished. It was being kept in the memories, stories, songs, and perhaps sermons that passed from generation to generation, under the wave, into the hands of those like Apess, who, having read Occom or not, knew what to make of an old tool with a new handle.

Notes

Introduction. Survival Writing: Contesting the Pen and Ink Work of Colonialism

1. William Apess, "A Son of the Forest," *On Our Own Ground: The Complete Writings of William Apess, A Pequot*, ed. Barry O'Connell (Amherst: University of Massachusetts Press, [1829] 1992), 60. Undoubtedly Apess became aware of the *Cherokee Phoenix*, as he toured on the lecture circuit with Elias Boudinot in 1832 as part of an effort to fortify public opinion against the impending Cherokee removal. But at the time of his writing his autobiography (1829), Apess may not yet have known of the Cherokee press and syllabary. The *Phoenix*, founded in 1828, had only been in existence for about a year at this time. See also Elias Boudinot, *Cherokee Editor: The Writings of Elias Boudinot*, ed. Theda Perdue (Athens: University of Georgia Press, 1983).

2. In his autobiography Apess writes of being abused by his Pequot grandmother who had fallen prey to alcoholism. After having several of his bones broken when he was roughly four years old, Apess was bound out to white families in the area of Colchester, Connecticut until he ran away at the age of fifteen and ended up enlisting in the army to fight the War of 1812. See Apess, "Son of the Forest."

3. Samson Occom, *The Collected Writings of Samson Occom, Mohegan: Leadership and Literature in Eighteenth-Century Native America*, ed. Joanna Brooks (New York: Oxford University Press, 2006), 52.

4. Anonymous, "New England's First Fruits," *ET*, 58.

5. News, Opinion, "The Barnstable Patriot Says that Mr. Apes Was Arrested at Marshpee Plantation on the 4th," *Portsmouth Journal of Literature and Politics*, July 7, 1833, Issue 28.

6. Vizenor's "Manifest Manners" are the historical and rhetorical strategies adopted by a dominant colonial culture through which the indigenous population is misrepresented and delegitimized as a civilization. See Gerald Vizenor, *Manifest Manners: Postindian Warriors of Survivance* (Hanover, NH: University Press of New England, 1994).

7. William Apess, "Eulogy on King Philip," *On Our Own Ground: The Complete Writings of William Apess, A Pequot*, ed. Barry O'Connell (Amherst: University of Massachusetts Press, [1836] 1992), 278.

8. Such was the projected fate of Apess' fellow Pequot who were brutally massacred in the 1636–1637 engagement known as the Pequot War. See Alfred A. Cave, *The Pequot War* (Amherst: University of Massachusetts Press, 1996).

9. Vizenor, *Manifest Manners*, 11–12.

10. Ibid., 18.

11. Ibid., 45.

12. Douglas Edward Leach, *Flintlock and Tomahawk: New England in King Philip's War* (Hyannis, MA: Parnassus Imprints, 1958), 6.

13. Ibid., 4.

14. Christopher Columbus, *The Four Voyages*, ed. and trans. J. M. Cohen (New York: Penguin Books, 1969), 56.

15. Amerigo Vespucci, "Letter to Pier Soerini, Confalonier of the Republic of Florence," *The English Literatures of America 1500–1800*, ed. Myra Jehlen and Michael Warner (New York: Routledge, 1997), 22.

16. Edward Winslow, *A Relation or Journall of the Beginning and Proceeding of the English Plantation Setled at Plimoth* (London: John Bellamie, 1622), 68. This text is often referred to as *Mourt's Relation*.

17. See Columbus, *The Four Voyages*, 192–193. *Cemies* were described by Columbus as "wooden images carved in relief" (192).

18. Ibid., 192.

19. Fray Ramone Pané, *An Account of the Antiquities of the Indians*, ed. Jose Juan Arrom, trans. Susan C. Griswold (Durham: Duke University Press, 1999), 20.

20. Edward Winslow, *Good Newes from New England: A True Relation of Things Very Remarkable at the Plantation of Plimoth in New England* (Bedford, MA: Applewood Books, 1624), 22–23.

21. Bartolomé de las Casas, *In Defense of the Indians*, trans. Stafford Poole (DeKalb: Northern Illinois University Press, 1992), 30.

22. As Winslow notes in *A Relation*, the presumed failure of Natives to improve upon the land made it not only imperative, but legal, for Europeans to take ownership. He writes, "As the ancient Patriarkes therefore removed from straiter places into more roomthy, where the Land lay idle and waste, and none used it, though there dwelt inhabitants by them . . . So it is lawful now to take a land which none useth, and make use of it" (*Relation*, 68).

23. Winslow, *Good Newes*, 3.

24. Cathy Caruth, *Unclaimed Experience: Trauma, Narrative and History* (Baltimore: Johns Hopkins University Press, 1996).

25. Thomas King, *The Truth About Stories: A Native Narrative* (Minneapolis: University of Minnesota Press, 2003), 2.

26. Judith Herman, *Trauma and Recovery: The Aftermath of Violence—from Domestic Abuse to Political Terror* (New York: Basic Books, 1992), 37.

27. Robert Allen Warrior, *Tribal Secrets: Recovering American Indian Intellectual Traditions* (Minneapolis: University of Minnesota Press, 1995), 2.

28. Herman, *Trauma and Recovery*, 9.

29. Gerald Vizenor, *Fugitive Poses: Native American Indian Scenes of Absence and Presence* (Lincoln: University of Nebraska Press, 1998), 19.

30. Vizenor, *Manifest Manners*, 12.

31. Jace Weaver, *That the People Might Live: Native American Literatures and Native American Community* (New York: Oxford University Press, 1997), xiii.

32. "Alphabetic writing" is distinguished from other forms of inscription by its adherence to phonetic indicators. It is a distinction that comes into play when one

begins to recognize that other forms of writing exist but are often denigrated as a result of cultural biases. Peter L. van der Loo, from whom I take the term, notes that writing should not be perceived as an evolutionary process from pictures to alphabetic literacy. Hieroglyphic systems in the Americas were flexible, informative, and could be understood by different peoples regardless of language groups. Peter L. van der Loo, "Voicing the Painted Image: A Suggestion for Reading the Reverse of the Codex Cospi," *Writing Without Words: Alternative Literacies in Mesoamerica and the Andes*, ed. Elizabeth Hill Boone and Walter D. Mignolo (Durham, NC: Duke University Press, 1994), 84.

33. Quoted in Joseph Johnson, *To Do Good to My Indian Brethren: The Writings of Joseph Johnson, 1751–1776*, ed. Laura J. Murray (Amherst: University of Massachusetts Press, 1998), 231.

34. Leslie Marmon Silko, "Language and Literature from a Pueblo Indian Perspective," *Nothing but the Truth: An Anthology of Native American Literature*, ed. John L. Purdy and James Ruppert (Upper Saddle River, NJ: Prentice Hall, 2001), 159.

35. "A Treaty Held at the Town of Lancaster in Pennsylvania," *Benjamin Franklin, Pennsylvania, and the First Nations: The Treaties of 1732–62*, ed. Susan Kalter (Urbana: University of Illinois Press, 2006), 95. Canassatego was most specifically referring to the infamous Walking Purchase of 1737 by which the Penn family of Pennsylvania defrauded the Delaware out of large tracts of land by misinterpreting former treaties. See James H. Merrell, "Introduction: Indians and Colonists in Early America," *The Lancaster Treaty of 1744 with Related Documents*, ed. James H. Merrell (Boston: Bedford/ St. Martin's, 2008), 21–22.

36. Some of the more famous primary texts from the nineteenth- and early twentieth-century boarding school era were Charles Eastman, *From the Deep Woods to Civilization* (Boston: Little Brown, 1916); Zitkala-Sa, *American Indian Stories* (Lincoln: University of Nebraska Press, 1985); Luther Standing Bear, *My People the Sioux* (Lincoln: University of Nebraska Press, 1928).

37. Peter Nabokov, *A Forest of Time: American Indian Ways of History* (Cambridge, UK: Cambridge University Press, 2002), 249.

38. Jacques Derrida, *Archive Fever: A Freudian Impression*, trans. Eric Prenowitz (Chicago: University of Chicago Press, 1996), 2.

39. Ibid., 23.

40. Ibid., 31.

41. James C. Scott, *Domination and the Arts of Resistance: Hidden Transcripts* (New Haven: Yale University Press, 1990).

42. Ibid., xii.

43. Ibid., 87, 90.

44. Ibid., 160.

45. Frank G. Speck, *A Study of the Delaware Indian Big House* (Harrisburg: Publications of the Pennsylvania Historical Commission, 1931), 22.

46. Luther Standing Bear, *Land of the Spotted Eagle* (Lincoln: University of Nebraska Press, [1933] 1978), 249.

47. Ibid., 249.

48. Craig Womack, *Red on Red: Native American Literary Separatism* (Minneapolis: University of Minnesota Press, 1999), 11.

49. Lisa Brooks, *The Common Pot: The Recovery of Native Space in the Northeast* (Minneapolis: University of Minnesota Press, 2008), 13.

50. Ibid., 3.

51. Ibid., 5.

52. Mary Louise Pratt, *Imperial Eyes: Travel Writing and Transculturation* (New York: Routledge Press, 1992), 7.

53. Thomas Morton, *New English Canaan* (New York: Da Capo Press, [1637] 1969), 10.

54. See Winslow, *A Relation*, 68.

55. This pre-Columbian population estimate of the North American mainland is taken from Jack Utter, *American Indians: Answers to Today's Questions* (Lake Anne, MI: National Woodlands Publishing Co., 1993), 23.

56. Brooks, *The Common Pot*, 158–159.

57. Henry Wadsworth Longfellow, "The Song of Hiawatha," *Longfellow: Poems and Other Writings* (New York: Library of America, 2000), 278. "The Song of Hiawatha" became the most famous poem of its time, eclipsing sales for any work of poetry prior to its publication. It popularly sealed the position of Longfellow as America's Poet Laureate.

58. Anthony Wallace, in his examination of Iroquois revitalization, *The Death and Rebirth of the Seneca*, describes *Gaiwiio* as a kind of gospel "transmitted by word of mouth from preacher to preacher" so that it might be chanted in the longhouse ceremonies at midwinter and again at the green corn ceremony in the fall. Anthony F. C. Wallace, *The Death and Rebirth of the Seneca* (New York: Knopf, 1970), 95. Other Haudenosaunee scholars translate *Gaiwiio* as meaning "smooth mind." See Barbara A. Mann, "The Lynx in Time: Haudenosaunee Women's Tradition and History," *American Indian Quarterly* 21, no. 3 (Summer 1997): 423–449.

59. Arthur Parker, "The Constitution of the Five Nations," *Parker on the Iroquois*, ed. William N. Fenton (Syracuse: Syracuse University Press, 1968), 20. See also Paul A. W. Wallace, *White Roots of Peace: The Iroquois Book of Life* (Santa Fe: Clear Light Publishers, 1994), 52.

60. Horatio Hale, ed., *The Iroquois Book of Rites* (Toronto: University of Toronto Press, 1963), 117.

61. Frederick Matthew Wiseman, *Voice of the Dawn: An Autohistory of the Abenaki Nation* (Hanover, NH: University Press of New England, 2001), 81.

62. Herman, *Trauma and Recovery*, 2.

63. Apess, "Eulogy," 280.

64. Ibid., 282.

65. Ibid., 310.

66. Ibid., 277.

Chapter 1. Wussuckwheke, or the Painted Letter: Glimpses of Native Signification Acknowledged and Unwitnessed (1492–1643)

1. A form of the earth-diver narrative exists amongst a number of indigenous nations of the Northeast. In most versions it is the muskrat who finally succeeds in scoring a piece of the ocean floor and bearing it to the surface, but in others it is the mink or the beaver. In some versions of the story Sky-Woman is pushed through

the hole in the sky by her husband in response to a suspected act of infidelity. In another she is asked to uproot the tree and falls in through the hole in the world that she has made. Some sources for these versions are *The Oneida Creation Story*, ed. Demus Elm and Harvey Antone (Lincoln: University of Nebraska Press, 2000); David Cusack, *Sketches of Ancient History of the Six Nations* (Lockport, NY: Turner & McCollum, 1848); Paul A. W. Wallace, *White Roots of Peace: The Iroquois Book of Life* (Santa Fe, NM: Clear Light Publishers, 1946); and Basil Johnston, *The Manitous: The Supernatural World of the Ojibway* (New York: HarperCollins, 1995), 10–13.

2. Arthur Parker, *Seneca Myths and Folk Tales* (Buffalo: Buffalo Historical Society, 1923), 59–73.

3. *JR* V, 155.

4. *JR* XI, 153.

5. *JR* X, 125.

6. Ibid., 117.

7. The myth concept of "The American Adam" has proven fruitful in the twentieth-century critical exploration of American literary motifs and is crystallized in the works of midcentury critical giants (to borrow a mythic term) such as F. O. Matthiessen, R.W. B. Lewis. and Henry Nash Smith.

8. *Jesuit Relations and Allied Documents: Travels and Explorations of the Jesuit Missionaries in North America (1610–1791)*, ed. Edna Kenton (New York: Albert & Charles Boni, 1925), 287.

9. Gerald Vizenor, *The People Named the Chippewa: Narrative Histories* (Minneapolis: University of Minnesota Press, 1984), 7.

10. Barbara Mann offers an excellent corrective for understanding the Haudenosaunee creation narrative in the face of so many colonial corruptions of the tale, particularly offering commentary on the elided importance of Jigonsaseh, Sky-Woman, or the head clan mother of the Iroquois. See Barbara Mann, "The Lynx in Time: Haudenosaunee Women's Traditions and History," *American Indian Quarterly* 21, no. 3 (Summer 1997): 423–449.

11. Thomas Morton, *New English Canaan* (New York: Da Capo Press, [1637] 1969), 19.

12. John Josselyn, *John Josselyn, Colonial Traveler: A Critical Edition of Two Voyages to New-England*, ed. Paul J. Lindholt (Hanover, NH: University of New England Press, [1674] 1988), 96–97.

13. Johnston, *The Manitous*, 12–13.

14. Ibid., 5.

15. Vizenor, *Chippewa*, 7.

16. Gerald Vizenor, *Manifest Manners: Postindian Warriors of Survivance* (Hanover, NH: University Press of New England, 1994), 15.

17. One of the more notable instances of this is Henry Rowe Schoolcraft's misattributing the Deganawidah legend of the Six Nations of the Iroquois to Anishinaabe belief systems. Schoolcraft's mistake became immortalized in Henry Wadsworth Longfellow's famous 1855 poem "The Song of Hiawatha." For further discussion of this see Helen Carr, *Inventing the American Primitive: Politics, Gender and the Representation of Native American Literary Traditions, 1789–1936* (New York: New York University Press, 1996).

18. Parker, *Seneca Myths*, 64–65.

19. Barbara Mann discusses how Christian concepts of good and evil worked their way into the Haudenosaunee origin stories. She denies the cosmic dichotomy of "good mind / evil mind" offered by Parker and others and offers the translation "Smooth Mind / Wrinkled Mind" in its place. Mann, "The Lynx in Time," 427.

20. By John Smith's estimation Pocahontas was "a child of tenne yeares old" at the time of their first encounter. Subsequent retellings have unwitnessed both her age and her eventual captivity to make of her story a romance. See John Smith, "A True Relation," *Capt. John Smith: Writings with Other Narratives of Roanoke, Jamestown, and the First English Settlements of America* (New York: Library of America, 2007), 34.

21. John Heckewelder, *History, Manners, and Customs of the Indian Nations Who Once Inhabited Pennsylvania and the Neighboring States* (Philadelphia: Publication Fund of the Historical Society of Pennsylvania, 1876), 254.

22. Ojibwe author David Treuer has recently offered a provocative argument against the idea that Native civilization was predicated on a balanced relationship with the local environment. He writes, "our (Native) perceived virtues are closely tied to white guilt—virtues only because they speak to that guilt and point out the failings of Western cultures. We are, according to many, near the earth, natural born conservationists, non-materialistic (which is a great benefit when you're too poor to own very much), egalitarian and unpretentious." He rebuts that in Native cultures, "cruelty was praised, revenge was elevated to the level of art," and hunters "regularly set large forest fires to increase the buffalo range, or nearly trapped the beaver to extinction, or massacred buffalo by the thousands (long before the white man showed up) just for their tongues and humps," and so forth. Treuer argues that Western culture is enamored to an "idea" of Native identity that, in fact, absolves them of actually having to understand Native culture in any kind of in-depth manner (*Native American Fiction*, 112–113). While I agree with this assessment, I also find his argument against a balanced natural aesthetic somewhat reactionary. To assault Western romanticism, he tears down a cherished notion, ignoring the current of actuality that resides beneath it. Robert Warrior and Vine Deloria Jr. both speak of being indigenous as "being of a place." From long experience with a particular geography arises the intellectual traditions of how best to occupy that land, including a "recognition that the world had a moral being and that disruptions amongst human societies created disharmonies" in the world. From this system of knowledge, Warrior argues, arose the clan and kinship systems (*Tribal Secrets*, 110–111). Notions of "balance" that are generally attributed to traditional Native culture need not be seen as fetishization, essentialism, or romanticism in the service of exorcising white guilt. There are pragmatic cultural distinctions that can be drawn between the manners in which Western and Native American cultures understood their relationship to the land. See David Treuer, *Native American Fiction: A User's Manual* (St. Paul: Graywolf Press, 2006). Robert Allen Warrior, *Tribal Secrets: Recovering American Indian Intellectual Traditions* (Minneapolis: University of Minnesota Press, 1995). Vine Deloria Jr. and Daniel R. Wildcat, *Power and Place: Indian Education in America* (Golden, CO: Fulcrum Resources, 2001). Vine Deloria Jr., "Traditional Technology," *Winds of Change* 5, no. 2 (Spring 1990): 20–23. Wil-

liam Cronon, *Changes in the Land: Indians, Colonists, and the Ecology of New England* (New York: Hill and Wang, 1983).

23. Vine Deloria Jr., *God Is Red: A Native View of Religion* (Golden, CO: Fulcrum Publishing, 1992), 153–154.

24. Slotkin is referring specifically here to a Delaware creation myth recounted originally in Heckewelder, in which humans live underwater, at the bottom of a great lake, and the first man to come to the surface world does so by chasing a deer through a log. Richard Slotkin, *Regeneration through Violence: The Mythology of the American Frontier, 1600–1860* (Norman: University of Oklahoma Press, 1973), 46.

25. *JR* X, 111–113.

26. Elaine Pagels, *Adam, Eve, and the Serpent* (New York: Vintage Books, 1988), xix.

27. The French philosopher Jean-Jacques Rousseau, in his 1754 *Discourse on Inequality*, posited that man, in his original "state of nature," enjoyed an uncorrupted morality. His ideas are generally thought to have birthed the notion of the noble savage. Lest we think this a flattering characterization, note that Rousseau says of his "savage man," that "he is so far from the degree of knowledge, that he can have neither foresight nor curiosity . . . he lacks the wit to wonder at the greatest marvels; and it is not to him that one would turn for the Philosophy man needs in order to be able to observe what he has seen everyday. His soul, which nothing stirs, yields itself wholly to the sentiment of its present existence, with no idea of the future." Nor should we imagine that Rousseau speaks of some hypothetical "savage" of the past. He directly equates the previous description with the mindset of "the Carib" who "sells his Cotton bed in the morning and comes weeping to buy it back in the evening, having failed to foresee that he would need it for the coming night." Jean-Jacques Rousseau, "Discourse on the Origin and the Foundations of Inequality Among Men," *The First and Second Discourses Together with the Replies to Critics and Essays on the Origin of Languages*, ed. and trans. Victor Gourevitch (New York: Harper and Row, 1986), 150–151.

28. Thomas King, *The Truth About Stories: A Native Narrative* (Minneapolis: University of Minnesota Press, 2003), 24.

29. The idea that Genesis is in fact two or more separate narratives stitched together by the authors of the Old Testament is a generally accepted notion amongst biblical scholars. The differing accounts of creation have been separated into two distinct accounts that are, by scholarly tradition, attributed to "P," representing the priestly cast who regard the creator as a more distant, all-powerful force, and "J," representing the continuance of an older, sustained oral tradition that includes the Garden of Eden and a more interactive God who is known by his name, Yahweh. For more see Armstrong, *In the Beginning: A New Interpretation of Genesis* (New York: Ballentine Books, 1996), 9–21, and Pagels, *Adam, Eve, and the Serpent*, xxii.

30. According to Pagels, Saint Augustine regarded the human condition as diseased after the fall of Adam and Eve. Adam's sinful act "changed the structure of the universe itself, bringing death and other ills into the world." Quoted in Pagels, *Adam, Eve, and the Serpent*, 144–145.

31. Mary Louise Pratt, *Imperial Eyes: Travel Writing and Transculturation* (New York: Routledge, 1992), 31.

32. Ibid., 31.

33. Walter D. Mignolo, "Signs and Their Transmission: The Question of the Book in the New World," *Writing Without Words: Alternative Literacies in Mesoamerica and the Andes*, ed. Elizabeth Hill Boone and Walter D. Mignolo (Durham, NC: Duke University Press, 1994), 220.

34. Vizenor, *Chippewa*, 7–8.

35. "A Treaty Held at the Town of Lancaster in Pennsylvania," *Benjamin Franklin, Pennsylvania, and the First Nations: The Treaties of 1736-62*, ed. Susan Kalter (Urbana: University of Illinois Press, 2006), 106.

36. William Deloss Love, *Samson Occom and the Christian Indians of New England* (Syracuse: Syracuse University Press, [1899] 2000), 3. See also *The Federal and State Constitutions, Colonial Charters and Other Organic Laws of the United States, Vol. II*, compiled by Ben Perley Poore (Washington: Government Printing Office, [1878] 1888).

37. Christopher Columbus, *The Four Voyages*, ed. and trans. J. M. Cohen (New York: Penguin, 1969), 66.

38. Howard Zinn, *On History* (New York: Seven Stories Press, 2001), 100.

39. Columbus, *Four Voyages*, 66–67.

40. Ibid., 67.

41. Ibid., 56.

42. Bernal Diaz, *The Conquest of New Spain*, trans. J. M. Cohen (New York: Penguin, 1963), 21, 214. *Amadis de Gaule* was a popular prose romance dating back to the thirteenth or fourteenth century, its hero suggesting a knightly code of honor idealized by the Spanish soldier.

43. Diaz, *Conquest of New Spain*, 237. See also Fray Toribio Motolinia, *Motolinia's History of the Indians of New Spain*, trans. Elizabeth Andross Foster (Westport, CT: Greenwood Press, 1950).

44. Jose de Costa, *A Natural and Moral History of the Indes*, ed. Jane E. Mangan and trans. Frances M. Lopez-Morillas (Durham, NC: Duke University Press, [1590] 2002), 339. Mangan's footnote here explains that the Franciscan Diego de Landa ordered all the Mayan books that could be found burned in 1562. Landa wrote that "these people also used certain characters or letters, with which they wrote in their books about the antiquities of their sciences; with these, and with figures and certain signs in the figures, they understood their matters, made them known, and taught them. We found a great number of books . . . and since they contained nothing but superstitions and falsehoods of the devil we burned them all, which they took most grievously and gave them great pain."

45. King, *Truth About Stories*, 98.

46. Walter Mignolo, "Afterword: Writing and Recorded Knowledge in Colonial and Postcolonial Situations," *Writing Without Words: Alternative Literacies in Mesoamerica and the Andes*, ed. Elizabeth Hill Boone and Walter D. Mignolo (Durham, NC: Duke University Press, 1994), 296.

47. Ibid., 293–294 (quoting Reents-Budet).

48. Elizabeth Hill Boone, "Introduction: Writing and Recorded Knowledge," *Writing Without Words: Alternative Literacies in Mesoamerica and the Andes*, ed. Elizabeth Hill Boone and Walter D. Mignolo (Durham, NC: Duke University Press, 1994), 3.

49. The *Chilam Balam*, or the "Jaguar Translator," is the sacred book of the Yucatan, which has also survived in alphabetic form.

50. *Popul Vuh: The Definitive Edition of the Mayan Book of the Dawn of Life and the Glories of Gods and Kings*, trans. Dennis Tedlock (New York: Simon and Schuster, 1985), 65.

51. Ibid., 63.

52 Dennis Tedlock, "Introduction," *Popul Vuh: The Definitive Edition of the Mayan Book of the Dawn of Life and the Glories of Gods and Kings*, trans. Dennis Tedlock (New York: Simon and Schuster, 1985), 29.

53. Mignolo, "Signs and Their Transmissions," 247.

54. Elizabeth Hill Boone, "Aztec Pictorial Histories," *Writing Without Words: Alternative Literacies in Mesoamerica and the Andes*, ed. Elizabeth Hill Boone and Walter D. Mignolo (Durham, NC: Duke University Press, 1994),71.

55. Motolinia, *History of the Indians*, 42. See also Diego Duran who speaks of the branding of slaves writing that "justly or unjustly, men women and children were taken, branded on their faces, and sold as slaves for the mines or as servants. In those times they even loaded ships with slaves to be carried away from New Spain. I myself met some of them in the homes of my relatives, and they were marked in the face with the name of the man who had sold them." Diego Duran, *The History of the Indes of New Spain*, trans. Doris Heyden (Norman: University of Oklahoma Press, 1994), 561. Bernal Diaz, in fact, was the custodian of the branding iron in Guazacualco, Honduras, but apparently objected to the practice and petitioned the government to end it. See Motolinia, *History of the Indians*, 42.

56. Charles Dibble, "Sahagun's Historia," *Florentine Codex: General History of the Things of New Spain*, ed. Arthur J. O. Anderson and Charles Dibble (Santa Fe, NM: School of American Research and the University of Utah, 1982), 9.

57. Bernardino De Sahagun, *Florentine Codex: General History of the Things of New Spain*, ed. Arthur J. O. Anderson and Charles Dibble (Santa Fe, NM: School of American Research and the University of Utah, 1982), 46.

58. Ibid., 75, 47.

59. Dibble, "Sahagun's Historia," 9.

60. Miguel Leon-Portilla, "Introduction," *The Broken Spears: The Aztec Account of the Conquest of Mexico*, ed. Miguel Leon-Portilla (Boston: Beacon Press, 1962), xliv–xlv.

61. Tedlock, *Popul Vuh*, 25, 63, 65.

62. Sahagun, *Florentine Codex*, 84.

63. Arthur J. O. Anderson, "Sahagun: Career and Character," *The Florentine Codex: General History of the Things of New Spain, Introductory Volume*, ed. Arthur J. O. Anderson and Charles E. Dibble (Santa Fe, NM: School of American Research and the University of Utah, 1982), 36–37.

64. Sahagun, *Florentine Codex*, 94.

65. Motolinia, *History of the Indians*, 189.

66. Sahagun, *Florentine Codex*, 94.

67. *JR* VIII, 113.

68. James Axtell, *After Columbus: Essays in the Ethnohistory of Colonial North America* (New York: Oxford University Press, 1988), 93.

69. Ibid., 91–92.

70. Captain John Smith wrote of his capture by the Powhatans and his subsequent release, which was partly procured by his ability to impress the Natives with the magical properties of writing as if "he could either divine or the paper could speake." John Smith, "The Generall Historie of Virginia, New-England and the Summer Isles," *Capt. John Smith: Writings with Other Narratives of Roanoke, Jamestown, and the First English Settlements of America* (New York: Library of America, 2007), 319.

71. 122. Williams, *Key*, 126.

72. The 1991 movie *Black Robe* directed by Bruce Beresford presents a more recent staging of this discursive phenomenon, suggesting that, despite the movie's worthwhile attempts at historical accuracy and breaking down of the subject position of the colonist to accommodate the Huron point of view, the stereotypical reaction itself remains quite persuasive. While it is clear that the writers of this film paid close attention to the source material, native writing once again remains invisible.

73. Daniel Richter, *Facing East from Indian Country: A Native History of Early America* (Cambridge: Harvard University Press, 2001), 26. Jesuit historian Joseph Jouvency notes that Canada is the name the Natives give for the St. Lawrence River, "a name thence extended to the whole country." See *JR* I, 245.

74. *JR* X, 225.

75. Richard White, *The Middle Ground: Indians, Empires, and Republics in the Great Lakes Region, 1650–1815* (New York: Cambridge University Press, 1991), 16.

76. *JR* I, 207.

77. Ibid., 161.

78. Ibid., 163–165.

79. *JR* II, 231–233.

80. Richard White aptly describes the Jesuit missions in New France when he notes that in Canada, "missions did not attract Indians; Indians attracted missionaries who usually came to existing settlements." White, *Middle Ground*, 23.

81. *JR* XI, 209.

82. Ibid., 209–211.

83. *JR* X, 91.

84. *JR* XI, 153.

85. Ibid., 157.

86. Navajo chanter Frank Mitchell describes the nature of oral narrative and song as "like a trail . . . You see a trail runs in certain ways, and if you have gone that way more than once, you know every little thing that is on that trail." Quoted in Peter Nabokov, *A Forest of Time: American Indian Ways of History* (Cambridge, UK: Cambridge University Press, 2002), 32.

87. *JR* XI, 159.

88. Ibid., 41.

89. Selwyn Dewdney, *The Sacred Scrolls of the Southern Ojibway* (Toronto: University of Toronto Press, 1975), 32.

90. William Warren, *History of the Ojibwe People* (St. Paul: Minnesota Historical Society Press, [1885] 1984), 55.

91. *JR* X, 293.

92. The unwitnessing of Native writing is perhaps complicated by the *Walam Olum* or Red Score, which survives as a transcript of Lenapi belief systems as interpreted

by an eccentric nineteenth-century European immigrant to the United States, Constantine Samuel Rafinesque. The *Walam Olum* purports to be a record of the Lenape creation narrative and the details of their migration to the Delaware River Valley. Written in hieroglyphic symbols that were originally said to have been carved out on sticks or wooden tablets, the *Walam Olum* begins at the dawn of time and concludes with the arrival of white men. Often presented as the only pre-Columbian text of North American origin, the *Walam Olum* stands in defiance of those who insist that Native civilization was prehistoric and therefore lacking in the key ingredients that make up a civilization. As such, the veracity of this document has been strenuously disputed. A central problem to the interpretation of the *Walam Olum* is that critics of the text, as transcribed by Rafinesque in 1836, tend to consider it a definitive version, set in stone, just as the Old and New Testaments of Judeo-Christian traditions are presumed to be. Most treatments of the text have regarded it in just such a manner, with the, perhaps, counterintuitive effect of making it easier to discredit. Rafinesque, who mysteriously acquired and then lost the original wooden tablets, claims to have been given a translation of the hieroglyphs, in the "Linapi" language which he then studiously transcribed into English at his own leisure. Inherent in this process are all the usual problems of translation. How much was the presumed Delaware informant willing to reveal to Rafinesque of sacred songs and traditions? How much of the narrative is misinterpreted or garbled by conflicting cultural codes and desires? How much was the translation whittled down by time restraints of both the informant and the editor? And how much of the narrative, as told to Rafinesque, was deliberately cast to meet the demands of European audiences and culture? As David McCutchen, who has written the most comprehensive contemporary examination of the *Walam Olum*, notes, "it was not until well into the twentieth century that the Delawares were allowed to practice their ancient religion legally and openly." This would have created compelling reasons to suppress various aspects of the narrative. The scope, the richness, the potentialities for narrative expression suggested by the hieroglyphic markings can only be guessed at by contemporary readers, and it is doubtful that Rafinesque offers anything like a complete translation of the ceremony that would have accompanied any ritual reading of the *Walam Olum*. But to simply discredit the viability of such a document based on Rafinesque's interpretations is to ignore or unwitness the documented evidence of native systems of communication. See David McCutchen, *Walam Olum or Red Score: The Migration Record of the Lenni Lenape or Delaware Indians* (Indianapolis: Indiana Historical Society, 1954), 8. Also see, David McCutchen, *The Red Record, the Wallam Olum: The Oldest Native North American History* (Garden City Park, NY: Avery Publishing Group, 1993); and David Oestricher, "Unraveling the *Walam Olum*," *Natural History* 105, no. 10 (October 1996): 2.

93. *JR* XII, 215.

94. Heckewelder, History, *Manners, and Customs*, 130.

95. Gordon Sayre regards the acknowledgment and subsequent denial of Native civilization by the French as a trope of what he labels "negation and substitution." In Sayre's estimation, before declaring that Natives lacked the basic "elements of civilized life," European travelers would first create a context by which to understand such categories. Natives were like Edenic children of the forest. As such, these "noble savages" in their perceived purity were ripe for the substitution of the finer elements of Christian belief. This belief allowed French explorers to alleviate their anxieties

over cultural superiority, by ascribing difference to Natives while still acknowledging a common humanity. Gordon M. Sayre, *Les Sauvages Americains: Representations of Native Americans in French and English Colonial Literature* (Chapel Hill: University of North Carolina Press, 1997), 138–143.

96. *JR* XII, 215.

97. Ibid., 215.

98. Ibid., 215.

99. These were also known as *wikhegans* and were described by Gideon Lincecum in 1818 as "a set of hieroglyphs, that any other set of hunters or travelers who might pass that way could read, telling what *iksa* they belonged to, how long they had remained at that camp, how many there were in the company, if any were sick or dead, and if they had been successful or otherwise in the hunt." He describes how *wikhegans* could be found "drawn very neatly on a peeled tree near the camp." See Garrick Mallory, *Picture Writing of the American Indians* (New York: Dover Publications, 1972), 347.

100. The shaking tent ritual used to consult certain manitous regarding the whereabouts of game is still part of Innu, Naskapi, Cree tradition. See Le Jeune's thorough description in *JR* XII, 17–23. For more on genii of light, see *JR* VI, 163–173.

101. *JR* VI, 183.

102. Adrian Tanner, "Foreword," Dorothy Burnham, *To Please the Caribou: Painted Caribou-Skin Coats Worn by the Naskapi, Montagnais, and Cree Hunters of the Quebec-Labrador Peninsula* (Seattle: University of Washington Press, 1992), ix.

103. Dorothy Burnham, *To Please the Caribou: Painted Caribou-Skin Coats Worn by the Naskapi, Montagnais, and Cree Hunters of the Quebec-Labrador Peninsula* (Seattle: University of Washington Press, 1992), 1.

104. Ibid., 59.

105. *JR* XIV, 265–267.

106. Dorothy Burnham, *To Please the Caribou*, 3. Hans M. Carlson, *Home Is the Hunter: The James Bay Cree and Their Land* (Vancouver: UBC Press, 2008), 48.

107. Carlson, *Home Is the Hunter*, 48–49.

108. *JR* VIII, 121.

109. Ibid., 41.

110. In his *Key*, Roger Williams notes that God or Kautantowwit "made one man and woman of a stone, which disliking, he broke them in pieces, and made another man and woman of a Tree, which were the Fountaines of all mankind." Roger Williams, *A Key into the Language of America* (Bedford, MA: Applewood Books, [1643] 1936), 135.

111. *JR* VII, 265; *JR* XII, 67.

112. *JR* XI, 97, 101.

113. *JR* XII, 237–239.

114. Ibid., 183.

115. *JR* VIII, 261.

116. Ibid., 261.

117. *JR* VIII, 131–133.

118. Ibid.

119. According to David L. Schmidt and Murdena Marshall who have edited a recent translation of the hieroglyphs, this symbology, originally used "for maps and tribal records, constituted a system that could be deciphered by anyone literate in the discipline rather than a series of mnemonic devices that were inseparable from the ritualized context in which they were traditionally used." David L. Schmidt and Murdena Marshall, eds., *Mi'kmaq Hieroglyphic Prayers: Reading in North America's First Indigenous Script* (Halifax, NS: Nimbus Publications, 1995), 4–6.

120. *JR* VII, 7–9.

121. *JR* LIX, 357. The painting Father Marquette describes bears relation to Misshiepeshu, the Great Lion, or underwater panther manitou of Anishinaabe legend. The underwater lion plays a part in the Montagnais creation cycle recounted by Le Jeune as well.

122. Thomas Hariot, "A Briefe and True Report of the New Found Land of Virginia," *The English Literatures of America, 1500–1800*, ed. Myra Jehlen and Michael Warner (New York: Routledge, [1588] 1987), 85–86.

123. Williams, *Key* 126.

124. Ibid., 137.

125. Ibid., 61.

126. Ibid., 61, 136.

127. Ibid., 121.

128. Ibid., 192.

129. Ibid., 192.

130. Ibid., 128.

131. William Wood, *New England Prospect*, ed. Alden T. Vaughan (Amherst: University of Massachusetts Press, [1634] 1977), 108.

132. Josselyn, *Two Voyages*, 92.

133. Ibid., 101–103.

134. Edward Winslow, *Good Newes from New England: A True Relation of Things Very Remarkable at the Plantation of Plimoth in New England* (Bedford, MA: Applewood Books, 1624), 63.

135. Cotton Mather, *Magnalia Christi Americana or the Ecclesiaticle History of New England, Vol. I* (Hartford: Silus Andrus, [1702] 1820), 505.

136. Henry Rowe Schoolcraft, *Indian Legends*, ed. Mentor L. Williams (East Lansing: Michigan State University Press, 1991), 15. He writes, "in the long period in which these tribes have been subjects of observation, we are not aware that powers of this kind [lore-keeping] have been attributed to them."

137. W. Deloss Love, *Samson Occom and the Christian Indians of New England* (Syracuse: Syracuse University Press, [1899] 2000), 4.

138. John Rolfe, *A True Relation of the State of Virginia Lefte by Sir Thomas Dale Knight in May Last 1616* (Charlottleville: University Press of Virginia, [1616] 1951), 12.

139. Karen Ordhal Kupperman, *The Jamestown Project* (Harvard: Belknap Press at Harvard University Press, 2007), 236.

140. Ibid., 57. Sir Thomas Gates, governor of the Virginia Colony, requested in 1609 that the colonists "procure from them [the Natives] some convenient number

of their children to be brought up in your language and your manners." Quoted in Margaret Connell Szasz, *Indian Education in the American Colonies, 1607–1783* (Albuquerque: University of New Mexico Press, 1988), 53.

141. Love, *Samson Occom*, 7.

142. Quoted in William Kellaway, *The New England Company, 1649–1776, Missionary Society to the American Indians* (Westport, CT: Greenwood Press, 1961), 3.

143. "New England's First Fruits," *ET*, 59.

144. William Bradford, *Of Plymouth Plantation: The Pilgrims in America*, ed. Harvey Wish (New York: Capricorn Books, 1962), 184.

145. "New England's First Fruits," *ET*, 60.

146. William Hubbard, *The History of the Indian Wars in New England from the First Settlement to the Termination of the War with King Philip, in 1677* (Roxbury, MA: W. Elliot Woodward, 1865), 60.

147. Maria Yellow Horse Brave Heart and Lymera DeBruyn, "The American Indian Holocaust: Healing Historical Unresolved Grief," *American Indian and Alaska Native Mental Health Research* 8, no. 2 (1998): 60–82.

148. Deborah L. Madsen, "On Subjectivity and Survivance: Rereading Trauma through *The Heirs of Columbus* and *The Crown of Columbus*," *Survivance: Narratives of Native Presence*, ed. Gerald Vizenor (Lincoln: University of Nebraska Press, 2008), 66.

149. John Winthrop, *History of New England from 1630 to 1649*, Vol. I (Baltimore: Clearfield, [1853] 2003), 148.

150. John Eliot, "The Glorious Progress of the Gospel Amongst the Indians of New England Manifested by Three Letters, Under the Hand of That Famous Instrument of the Lord Mr. John Eliot," *ET*, 160.

151. Cockenoe was identified by William Wallace Tooker in his short book *Cockenoe de Long Island: John Eliot's First Indian Teacher and the Story of His Career from the Early Records* (New York: Francis Harper, 1896).

152. Winthrop, *History*, 279.

153. Ibid., 278.

154. "New Englands First Fruits," *ET*, 59.

155. Winthrop, *History*, 305.

156. Alfred A. Cave, *The Pequot War* (Amherst: University of Massachusetts Press, 1996), 3.

157. John Winthrop, *Winthrop's Journal: History of New England, 1630–1649* (New York: Elibron Media Corporations, 2005), 109.

158. Winthrop, *History*, 238.

159. Ibid., 260.

160. John Underhill, *Newes from America* (New York: Da Capo Press, [1638] 1971), title page.

161. Williams, *Key*, 157.

162. Ibid., 152.

163. Evan T. Pritchard, *Native New Yorkers: The Legacy of the Algonquian People of New York* (San Francisco: Council Oak Books, 2002), 148.

164. Frank G. Speck, *A Study of the Delaware Indian Big House Ceremony* (Harrisburg: Pennsylvania Historical Commission, 1931), 63.

165. Bradford, *Plymouth Plantation*, 139.

166. See Lynn Ceci, "Wampum as a Peripheral Resource in the Seventeenth-Century World System," *The Pequots in Southern New England: The Fall and Rise of an American Indian Nation*, ed. Laurence M. Hauptman and James D. Wherry (Norman: University of Oklahoma Press, 1990), 60.

167. Hubbard, *Indian Wars in New England*, 10–11. See also Winthrop's journal.

168. For contemporaneous accounts of the Pequot War see *History of the Pequot War*, ed. Charles Orr (Cleveland: Helman-Taylor Co., [1862] 1980).

169. Philip Vincent, "A True Relation of the Late Battell Fought in New England, between the English and the Pequet Salvages," *History of the Pequot War*, ed. Charles Orr (Cleveland: Helman-Taylor Co., [1862] 1980), 137.

170. Ibid., 104.

171. Ibid., 105.

172. John Mason, "A Brief History of the Pequot War: Especially of the Memorable Taking of Their Fort at Mistick in Connecticut in 1637," *History of the Pequot War*, ed. Charles Orr (Cleveland: Helman-Taylor Co., [1862] 1980), 35.

173. Ibid., 40.

174. Underhill, *Newes from America*, 39–40.

175. Ibid., 43.

176. Ibid., 40.

177. Ibid., 40.

178. Ibid., 40.

179. Wood, *New England's Prospect*, 80.

180. "New England's First Fruits," *ET*, 74.

181. Ibid., 74.

182. Richard Cogley, *John Eliot's Mission to the Indians Before King Philip's War* (Cambridge: Harvard University Press, 1999), 25, and Williams, *Key*, A6.

183. Roger Williams, *The Complete Writings of Roger Williams*, vol. 6 (New York: Russell & Russell, 1963), 22.

184. Williams' *Key* states that "Wequash-shauog" means "swan." Williams, *Key*, 90.

185. Williams, *The Complete Writings*, vol. VI, 47–57. See also Samuel Drake, *Biography and History of the Indians of North America, from Its First Discovery* (Boston: Benjamin B. Mussey & Co., 1841), 149–174. (Wequash meaning "swan," 166).

186. "First Fruits," *ET*, 61.

187. Ibid., 61–62.

188. Ibid., 62.

189. Ibid., 62.

190. Ibid., 62.

191. Williams, *Key*, 25.

192. Ibid., 26.

193. Ibid., 27.

194. Vizenor, *Manifest Manners*, 8.

195. "First Fruits," *ET*, 62.

196. "Lust" is offered up alongside "revenge" as one of the two sticking points that Wequash hopes to purge from his system in *First Fruits*. My feeling, however, is that this "lust" refers to the Native custom of keeping more than one wife,

which to Puritan recorders did not seem a cultural practice so much as a personal failing.

197. Catherine Maria Sedgwick, *Hope Leslie*, ed. Mary Kelley (New Brunswick, NJ: Rutgers University Press, [1827] 1987), 48.

198. Samuel Drake, *Biography and History of the Indians of North America from Its First Discovery* (Boston: Benjamn B. Mussey & Co., 1841), 160.

199. Timothy Dwight, "Greenfield Hill," *The Heath Anthology of American Literature*, vol. A, ed. Paul Lauter (Boston: Houghton Mifflin Co., 2006), 1236.

200. Ola Winslow, *Master Roger Williams: A Biography* (New York: Macmillan, 1957), 150.

201. Underhill, *Newes from America*, 43.

202. Walter Ong, *Orality and Literacy: The Technologizing of the Word* (London: Routledge, 1982), 132.

203. John Eliot, "The Light Appearing More and More Towards the Perfect Day or a Farther Discovery of the Present State of the Indians in New England," *ET*, 206.

Chapter 2. Praying Indians, Printing Devils: Centers of Indigeneity within Colonial Containments (1643–1665)

1. Daniel Gookin, "Historical Collections of the Indians of New England," *Collections of the Massachusetts Historical Society* (*CMHS*) I (Boston: Munroe & Francis, [1674] 1806), 176.

2. See "First Fruits" title page. "First Fruits," *ET*, 57.

3. Ibid., 58.

4. According to Morison an Eleazar "Indus Senior Sophista" of the Harvard Class of 1679 wrote an elegy in Greek to Thomas Thatcher, his teacher, that reads, "Dust holds your body, but your name will never parish on earth, famous in our and in future ties; and the soul, flying from your limbs, ascends steep heaven, mingling, immortal, with the immortal spirits." Samuel Eliot Morison, *Harvard College in the Seventeenth Century* (Cambridge: Harvard University Press, 1936), 196–197. While nothing seems to be known of this Eleazar, Daniel Gookin briefly mentions an Eleazar who fought alongside the colonists in King Philip's War and who distinguished himself by rescuing a British soldier from Philip's armies. See Daniel Gookin, *An Historical Account of the Doings and Sufferings of the Christian Indians of New England in the years 1675–1677*(Cambridge: Cambridge University Press, 1836), 477–478. The last praying Indian to attend Harvard was Benjamin Larnell from 1712–1714. See *The Diary of Samuel Sewall*, vol. II, 1709–1729 (New York: Farrar, Straus and Giroux, 1973), 651. Harvard president Leverett described Larnell as "An acute Grammarian, an Extraordinary Latin poet, and a Good Greek one. Larnell also died while attending." Morison, *Harvard College in the Seventeenth Century*, 196 and 357. According to Ruth Walker, writing for the *Harvard Gazette*, Harvard would not graduate another declared Native American student until well into the twentieth century. Ruth Walker, "350th Anniversary of Indian College Commemorated," April 14, 2005, Native Americans at Harvard, http://www.hcs.harvard.edu/nahc/.

5. Hugh Amory, *Bibliography and the Book Trades: Studies in the Print Culture of Early New England*, ed. David Hall (Philadelphia: University of Pennsylvania Press, 2005), 35.

6. "First Fruits," *ET*, 58.

7. This quote originated in Neal's *History of New England* (1720), and can be found in John W. Ford, *Some Correspondence Between the Governors and Treasurers of the New England Company in London and the Commissioners of the United Colonies in America: The Missionaries of the Company and Others Between the Years 1657 and 1712*, ed. John W. Ford (New York: Burt Franklin, 1970), xx.

8. Amory calls it "a tool of the government and of John Eliot's mission to the Indians." Amory, *Bibliography and the Book Trades*, 111.

9. Morison, *Harvard College in the Seventeenth Century*, 349.

10. See Hugh Amory, *First Impressions: Printing in Cambridge, 1639–1989* (Cambridge: President and Fellows of Harvard College, 1989), 5.

11. William Kellaway, *The New England Company 1649–1776: Missionary Society to the American Indians* (Westport, CT: Greenwood Press, 1961), 127, 152.

12. Larzer Ziff, *Writing in the New Nation: Prose, Print, and Politics in the Early United States* (New Haven: Yale University Press, 1991), x. According to Ziff the "immanent" self was in constant negotiation and competition with the represented self that flourished with the blossoming of print discourse in the United States. Although Ziff focuses on the era leading up to, and overtaking the creation of the United States, he points out early on that this phenomenon was at its most virulent in relation to Native Americans, noting "the imperial scale" by which representations of Indians were forged to replace and annihilate real Indians (x).

13. Gerald Vizenor, *Manifest Manners: Postindian Warriors of Survivance* (Hanover, NH: University Press of New England, 1994), 65.

14. Ibid., 23.

15. For Eliot's contributions to the prosecution of Anne Hutchinson see *The Antinomian Controversy, 1636–1638: A Documentary History*, ed. David D. Hall (Durham, NC: Duke University Press, 1990), 311–388 (see p. 346 in particular for Eliot's strong censure of Hutchinson). In Winthrop's journal for November 27, 1634 it is noted that the governing council deemed it necessary to censor Eliot for speaking out too strongly against an initial peace negotiated with the Pequots. Eliot was asked to apologize and publicly reconsider his position. John Winthrop, *History of New England from 1630–1649*, vol. 1., ed. John Savage (Baltimore: Clearfield Company, [1853] 1996),179.

16. Clark, *ET*, 9. See also Morison, *Harvard College in the Seventeenth Century*, 340–341.

17. Clark, *ET*, 3.

18. Cotton Mather, *Magnalia Christi Americana or the Ecclesiastical History of New England from Its First Planting in the Year 1620, Unto the Year of Our Lord, 1698*, vol. 1 (Hartford: Silas Andrus, 1820), 510.

19. Ibid., 491.

20. Ibid., 514.

21. W. Deloss Love, *Samson Occom and the Christian Indians of New England* (Syracuse: Syracuse University Press, [1899] 2000), 19.

22. See Francis Jennings, *The Invasion of America: Indians, Colonialism, and the Cant of Conquest* (Chapel Hill: University of North Carolina Press, 2010), 233 and more generally 228–253.

23. Ibid., 241.

24. Richard W. Cogley, *John Eliot's Mission to the Indians Before King Philip's War* (Cambridge: Harvard University Press, 1999), 4 and 52.

25. James Axtell, *After Columbus: Essays in the Ethnohistory of Colonial North America* (New York: Oxford University Press, 1988), 49–54. Specific quote on 54.

26. George E. Tinker, *Missionary Conquest: The Gospel and Native American Cultural Genocide* (Minneapolis: Fortress Press, 1993), 16.

27. "The shadows of remembrance" is a term Gerald Vizenor uses, suggesting the intangibility of the past. It speaks to the overall inability of historical processes to accurately pierce through the veil of unwitnessing or faithfully reconstruct an authentic sense of Native identity. All we have are traces of stories and remembrances that we apply as best we can to our own contemporary narrative agendas. Vizenor, *Manifest Manners*, 65.

28. John Eliot, *Indian Dialogues: A Study in Cultural Interaction*, ed. Henry W. Bowden and James P. Ronda (Westport, CT: Greenwood Press, 1980, 1671), 60.

29. *RMBC* III, 56–57.

30. Kathleen Bragdon calls this *nokake*, a flattened corn bread, and notes that it probably resembled the tortilla. Kathleen J. Bragdon, *Native People of Southern New England 1500–1650* (Norman: University of Oklahoma Press, 1996), 104.

31. Roger Williams, *A Key into the Language of America* (Bedford, MA: Applewood Books, 1936), 38.

32. William Bradford wrote that they found the people near where they settled being "dead & abundantly wasted in the late great mortalitie which fell in these parts about three years before the coming of the English, wherein thousands of them dyed, they not being able to burie one another; their sculs and bones were found in many places lying still above ground, where their houses and dwellings had been; a very sad spectacle to behold." William Bradford, *Of Plymouth Plantation: The Pilgrims in America*, ed. Harvey Wish (New York: Capricorn Books, 1962), 78. See also John Josselyn, "An Account of the Two Voyages to New England," *CMHS* III, series 3, 294; Winthrop, *History of New England*, 137–138, and Thomas Morton, *New English Canaan* (New York: Da Capo Press, [1637] 1969), 22.

33. See Samuel G. Drake, *Biography and History of the Indians of North America, from Its First Discovery* (Boston: Benjamin B. Mussy & Co., 1841), 118.

34. Thomas Shepherd, "The Day Breaking, if not The Sun Rising of the Gospell with the Indians in New England," *ET*, 83. According to Daniel Mandell, Thomas Waban's Indian name was Weegramomenit and he would occasionally use this name in court records throughout his life. Daniel Mandell, " 'Standing by His Father': Thomas Waban of Natick, circa 1630–1722," *Northeastern Indian Lives 1632–1816*, ed. Robert S. Grumet (Amherst: University of Massachusetts Press, 1996), 171.

35. Thomas Shepherd, "The Day Breaking," *ET*, 83.

36. Ibid., 84–86.

37. Ibid., 87.

38. Ibid., 82.

39. From "First Fruits," *ET*, 74.

40. Cogley, *John Eliot's Mission to the Indians*, 57. Cogley takes this to mean that the lands of the Massachusett had been greatly diminished already, perhaps to the size of a town. Waban does not make this distinction however. When he speaks of possessing the lands where their wigwams have always stood, he is referring to more than just the plot of land before them. As for needing this land allotment in writing, the tract entitled "The Clear Sunshine of the Gospel" suggests that the Natives desired "an able faithful man in Concord to record and keep in writing what they had generally agreed upon." Thomas Shepherd, "The Clear Sunshine of the Gospel Breaking Forth Upon the Indians in New England," *ET*, 114.

41. Thomas Shepherd, "The Clear Sunshine," *ET*, 114. The sachem of the Nonantum Natives is asked, "why hee desired a towne so neare, when as there was more room for them up in the country." The sachem seems to have replied that if they moved up-country the people would not be so inclined to hear the word of God.

42. For details on the life of Cockenoe see William Wallace Tooker, *John Eliot's First Indian Teacher and Interpreter, Cokenoe de Long Island, and the Story of His Career* (New York: Francis Harper, 1896).

43. Shepherd, "The Day Breaking," *ET*, 91.

44. See Josselyn, "An Account of the Two Voyages to New England," *CMHS*, 301.

45. This version of the Wampanoag legend was taken from a series of articles published in the *Independent*, May 16, 1928 as told by Red Shell, and located in New England Indians, Site Index, Cape Cod Indians 2, chapter 5, "Legend of the Flood," http://freepages.genealogy.rootsweb.ancestry.com/~massasoit/ccod02.htm.

46. Shepherd, "The Day Breaking," *ET*, 90.

47. Ibid., 94.

48. Thomas Shepherd, "The Clear Sunshine of the Gospel Breaking Forth Upon the Indians in New England," *ET*, 135.

49. Red Shell, "Legend of the Flood."

50. James Mooney, *Myths of the Cherokee* (Washington, DC: Government Printing Office, 1900), 232–233. Although Mooney's book is clearly about the Cherokee, he is speaking specifically to Algonquian beliefs and practices here.

51.Williams, *Key*, A4.

52. Ibid., 104.

53. Mooney, *Cherokee*, 233.

54. Shepherd, "The Day Breaking," *ET*, 95.

55. Ibid., 97.

56. The Massachusetts Court Records for November 4, 1646 state that certain individuals were authorized to seek out "such parcels of land which they judge meete to purchase for the incouragement of ye Indians, to live in an orderly way amongst us." *RMBC* III, 85.

57. Ibid., 97.

58. Stated in a letter from Eliot to Shepherd, September 24, 1647. See George Emery Littlefield, *The Early Massachusetts Press 1638–1711* (New York: Burt Franklin, 1907), 172.

59. Shepherd, "The Day Breaking," *ET*, 97.

60. Ibid., 98.

61. This Wampas would later be publicly reprimanded for beating his wife. In his dying speech, recounted by Eliot, he remembered that he brought four children to Eliot, one of them his own son, and prayed that they would remain in their English homes and learn the ways of the Christian God. *ET*, 127 and 222–223.

62. Shepherd, "The Day Breaking," *ET*, 96.

63. See Thomas Lechford's "Plain Dealing" in which he asserts that Dunster "deserves commendations above many; he hath the plat-forme and way of conversion of the Natives indifferent right, and much studies the same, wherein yet he wants not opposition, as some others have also met with . . . He will make it good, that the way to instruct the Indians, must be in their owne language, not English; and that their language may be perfected." Thomas Lechford, "Plain Dealing: Or Newes from New-England," *CMHS* III, series 3 (1642), 105–106.

64. Samuel Eliot Morison, *The Founding of Harvard College* (Cambridge: Harvard University Press, 1935), 313–314. The Massachusetts Court Records show that Dunster was allowed £100 on November 4, 1646, presumably for the care of these children. *RMBC*, 87.

65. Morison, *The Founding of Harvard College*, 344–347. Also Littlefield, *The Early Massachusetts Press*, and George Parker Winship, *The Cambridge Press 1638–1692* (Freeport, NY: Books for Libraries Press, 1946).

66. Morison, *The Founding of Harvard College*, 346.

67. Kellaway, *The New England Company*, 14–15. See also Morison, *The Founding of Harvard College*, 320–322.

68. Cogley, *John Eliot's Mission to the Indians*, 69.

69. Morison, *The Founding of Harvard College*, 348.

70. Quoted in Winship, *The Cambridge Press*, 113.

71. Gookin, "Historical Collections," *CMHS*, 185.

72. Eliot made an accounting of the funds he had received to Winslow in 1649, stating that "five pounds I gave to a grave women in Cambridge who taught the Indian Children last year. It is not clear precisely when Elijah Corlett's grammar school first opened to Indian students. Littlefield, *The Early Massachusetts Press*, 178.

73. Franklin is apprenticed to his brother James in 1717 at the age of twelve. Benjamin Franklin, "The Autobiography of Ben Franklin," *The Heath Anthology of American Literature*, vol A, ed. Paul Lauter (Boston: Houghton Mifflin Company, [1791] 2006), 835.

74. Margaret Connell Szasz, *Indian Education Education in the American Colonies, 1607–1783* (Albuquerque: University of New Mexico Press, 1988), 117.

75. Morison, *The Founding of Harvard College*, 348.

76. Morison notes that "almost every printing and publishing house in New England can trace its ancestry to the little college 'printery' operated by the Days and Greens." Morison, *Harvard College in the Seventeenth Century*, 352.

77. Ibid., 5–6.

78. Gookin, "Historical Collections," *CMHS*, 176.

79. Morison, *Harvard College in the Seventeenth Century*, 309–320.

80. For details see Morison, *Harvard College in the Seventeenth Century*, 298–319. Dunster had also run afoul of the Puritan magistrates as a result of his refusal to

baptize his children. It was determined by the court that those of unsound faith were prohibited from preaching at Harvard. Philip F. Gura, *A Glimpse of Sion's Glory: Puritan Radicalism in New England, 1620–1660* (Middleton, CT: Wesleyan University Press, 1984), 121.

81. Morison, *Harvard College in the Seventeenth Century*, 46. Morrison posits that the press may have been kept in a separate printing house until 1659 when a new press was brought over to assist in the making of the Eliot Bibles. Either way it seems likely to me that James remained with the press at all times.

82. The dimensions of the building offered in Morison, *Harvard College in the Seventeenth Century*, 342.

83. Quoted in Szasz, *Indian Education*, 116.

84. Drake, *Biography and History of the Indians*, 114.

85. Eliot, "The Light Appearing More and More Towards the Perfect Day or a Farther Discovery of the Present State of the Indians in New-England," *ET*, 206.

86. Ibid., 187.

87. Neal Salisbury, "Red Puritans: The 'Praying Indians' of Massachusetts Bay and John Eliot," *The William and Mary Quarterly* 3rd series 31, no. 1 (January 1974): 42. This suggestion occurs in a footnote of Salisbury's article in which he says, "I am indebted to Frank Seibert for pointing out to me that the Indian assistants, rather than Eliot himself, did the actual translating."

88. Szasz, *Indian Education*, 115.

89. Cogley, *John Eliot's Mission to the Indians*, 119.

90. Ibid., 121.

91. Gookin, "Historical Collections," 218.

92. Gookin, "Historical Account," 444. On Nesuton's death, Gookin writes, "the loss of such a useful and trusty man was great in the forementioned respects."

93. See Drake, *Biography and History of the Indians*, 115.

94. Shepherd, "The Clear Sunshine," *ET*, 136.

95. Eliot, "Tears of Repentance," *ET*, 271.

96. Littlefield, *The Early Massachusetts Press*, 176.

97. Winfield Scott, "Excerpt from *The Memoirs of Lieut. General Scott, LL.D.: Written by Himself*," *Voices from the Trail of Tears*, ed. Vicki Rozema (Winston-Salem, NC: John F. Blair Publishers, 2003), 186.

98. Cogley, *John Eliot's Mission to the Indians*, 105.

99. Eliot, "Tears of Repentance," *ET*, 269.

100. Broadside entitled "Christians Oonoowae Sampoowaonk" or "A Christian Covenanting Confession," see L. G. Starkey Bibliography of Cambridge Press, unpublished University of Virginia Dissertation, 1949, 240–244. Found on *Early American Imprints*, series 1: Evans Digital Library. http://infoweb.newsbank.

101. Salisbury, "Red Puritans," 47.

102. Eliot, "Tears of Repentance," *ET*, 271–272.

103. Salisbury, "Red Puritans," 48.

104. Cogley, *John Eliot's Mission to the Indians*, 128.

105. Eliot, "Tears of Repentance," 272.

106. Ibid., 278–279.

107. Ibid., 277.

108. Ibid., 277.

109. Monequassun's testimony appears in Eliot, "Tears of Repentance," *ET*, 274–279. Eliot's postscript is on p. 279.

110. Ibid., 294.

111. Ibid., 274.

112. Ibid., 251.

113. See Eliot, "A Further Accompt of the Progress of the Gospel Amongst the Indians in New England," *ET*, 379.

114. Nishokou's oration appears in Eliot, "A Further Account," *ET*, 377–381.

115. Eliot, "A Late and Further Manifestation," *ET*, 303–304.

116. Eliot, "Tears of Repentance," *ET*, 283.

117. Ibid., 282.

118. Eliot, "A Late and Further Manifestation," *ET*, 306.

119. Quoted in Eliot, "A Further Accompt," *ET*, 333. Waban exhorts upon this theme again in "A Further Account," *ET*, 374-376.

120. See Shepherd, "The Clear Sunshine," *ET*, 132, and Daniel Gookin, "Historical Collections," 178.

121. Bernd Peyer, *The Tutor'd Mind: Indian Missionary Writers in Antebellum America* (Amherst: University of Massachusetts Press, 1997), 42. Also Experience Mayhew, *Indian Converts: or Some Account of the Lives and Dying Speeches of a Considerable Number of the Christianized Indians of Martha's Vineyard in New England* (Ann Arbor, MI: University Microfilms International, 1992) and Henry Whitfield, *A Further Discovery of the Present State of the Indians in New England* (New York: Sabin's Reprints, [1651] 1865).

122. Quoted in Henry Whitfield, "The Light Appearing," *ET*, 187.

123. Quoted in Henry Whitfield, "Strength Out of Weaknesse; or a Glorious Manifestation of the Further Progresse of the Gospel among the Indians in New-England," *ET*, 241.

124. Gookin, "Historical Collections," *CMHS*, 172.

125. "First Fruits," *ET*, 72–74.

126. Eliot, "A Further Accompt," *ET*, 353.

127. It is uncertain how many Natives actually attended at this time, but only Joel, Caleb, and John Wampas appear on the records.

128. William Wood, *New England's Prospect*, ed. Alden T. Vaughan (Amherst: University of Massachusetts Press, 1977), 104.

129. William S. Simmons, *Spirit of the New England Tribes: Indian History and Folklore, 1620–1984* (Hanover, NH: University Press of New England, 1986), 38–45.

130. Williams, *Key*, A5.

131. See chapter 3.

132. Littlefied, *The Cambridge Press*, 192.

133. Gookin, "Historical Collections," *CMHS*, 173.

134. Bragdon, *Native People of Southern New England*, 191–193 and 219–220.

135. See note 4 in this chapter.

136. Wolfgang Hochbruck and Beatrix Dudensing-Reichel, "'Honoratissimi Benefactores': Native American Students and Two Seventeenth-Century Texts in the University Tradition," *Early Native American Writing: New Critical Essays*, ed. Helen Jaskoski (New York: Cambridge University Press, 1996), 5.

137. This translation from the Latin was is from Hochbruck and Dudensing-Reichel, "'Honoratissimi Benefactores,'" 5.

138. Hochbruck and Dudensing-Reichel, "'Honoratissimi Benefactores,'" 5.

139. Simmons, *Spirit of the New England Tribes*, 67.

140. Wood, *New England's Prospect*, 100–101.

141. Jarold Ramsey, "From 'Mythic' to 'Fictive' in a Nez Perce Orpheus Myth," *Traditional Literatures of the American Indian: Texts and Interpretations*, ed. Karl Kroeber (Lincoln: University of Nebraska Press, 1981), 25.

142. Ake Hultkrantz, *The North American Indian Orpheus Tradition: A Contribution to Comparative Religion* (Stockholm: Ethnographical Museum of Sweden, 1957), 208.

143. Quoted in Hultkrantz, *The North American Indian Orpheus Tradition*, 249. The source cited is an 1893 report on Dakota grammar by S. R. Riggs.

144. Simmons, *Spirit of the New England Tribes*, 141–142.

145. Gookin, "Historical Collections," CMHS, 73.

146. See Jill Lepore, *The Name of War: King Philip's War and the Origins of American Identity* (New York: Vintage Books, 1998), 27.

147. See David J. Silverman, *Faith and Boundaries: Colonists, Christianity, and Community among the Wampanoag Indians of Martha's Vineyard, 1600–1871* (New York: Cambridge University Press, 2005), 92–93.

148. Gookin, "Historical Accounts," CMHS, 517–518.

149. Ibid., 518.

150. Samuel Seawall, *The Diary of Samuel Sewall*, vol. 1, 1674–1708, ed. M. Halsey Thomas (New York: Farrar, Straus and Giroux, 1973), 394.

Chapter 3. King Philip's Signature: Ascribing Philip's Name to Land, War, and History in Native New England (1600–1709)

1. Cotton Mather, *Diary of Cotton Mather*, vol. 1, 1681–1709 (New York: Frederick Ungar Publishing Co., 1911), 408–409.

2. Quoted in Russell Bourne, *The Red King's Rebellion: Racial Politics in New England 1675–1678* (New York: Oxford University Press, 1990), 107.

3. Upon entering into the Dighton Rock Museum today, one finds oneself within a colonial containment surrounded by colonial trappings. The forty-ton rock was removed from its original Native space in the river in 1963 and placed within a small enclosed pagoda in what is now called Dighton Rock State Park just outside the town of Berkley, Massachusetts. The museum was erected with the discordant objectives of "displaying objects associated with Dighton Rock and with the History of the Portuguese and other landings, explorations and settlements." As such, the small museum has the Portuguese flag displayed along with glass-encased models of the ships Vasco de Gama and Magellan both used in their various explorations of the globe (neither of whom ever came anywhere near New England, it should be noted). Although it is said that the relocation of the rock was carefully performed in such a manner as to retain its "original orientation," the fact remains that the museum's orientation is toward the European continent, and Portugal, in keeping with Edmund Burke Delabarre's theory that the writings on Dighton Rock were made

by the sixteenth-century explorer Corte Real (see Edmund Burke Delabarre, *Dighton Rock: A Study of the Written Rocks of New England* [New York: Walter Neale, 1928]).

4. Edward J. Lenik, *Picture Rocks: American Indian Rock Art in the Northeast Woodlands* (Hanover, NH: University Press of New England, 2002), 133–134.

5. Captain Benjamin Church offers an account of a Wampanoag Summer Festival that he stumbled onto in June of 1676. He writes of cresting a small dune on the beach near the Sippicin River, looking for hostiles and beholding instead "Indians of all Ages and Sexs, some on Horse-back running races, some at Foot-ball, some catching Eels & Flat-fish in the water, some Clamming, &c." It is a rare description of Native life in the colonial annals, in that it seems to depict Natives in a benign community gathering without concern for qualifying it as either a pagan or militaristic ritual. Benjamin Church, "Entertaining Passages Relating to Philip's War," *So Dreadful a Judgment: Puritan Responses to King Philip's War, 1676–1677*, ed. Richard Slotkin and James K. Folsom (Hanover, NH: Wesleyan University Press, 1978), 431.

6. Chadwick Allen, *Blood Narrative: Indigenous Identity in American Indian and Maori Literary and Activist Texts* (Durham, NC: Duke University Press, 2002), 16.

7. Cotton Mather, "The Wonderful Works of God Commemorated," *Early American Imprints*, series 1: Evans Digital Display (2006): 4, http://infoweb.newsbank.com.

8. Although Danforth, too, assumes the rock to be from a lost antiquity and wonders if the marks are "hieroglyphical," the tradition he relates of settlers arriving on these shores and slaying the local sachem differs in no way from the particulars of the Pilgrims and King Philip's War. In fact, it is difficult to imagine what event in Wampanoag history other than King Philip's War would conform so perfectly to the narrative details Danforth offered. Perhaps it could refer to Samuel de Champlain's early voyage to the area under the command of Sieur de Poutrincourt in 1606, in which the French expedition slaughtered a band of Nausets in the same region of Cape Cod where the Mayflower Pilgrims would first make land. Thomas Hunt had come to the area as well in 1614 and took Native captives to sell into slavery including the famous Patuxet survivor Squanto. Traders, explorers, and fishermen stretching back all the way to the Vikings, according to Wampanoag tradition, had been coming to this place and sowing the seeds of conflict. Whichever story you choose, the legend on the rock serves as the basis for an indigenous recounting of local history that has no purchase in the colonial archive, and so finds itself continuously up for grabs in the frenzy of cultural appropriation let loose by the processes of colonization.

9. Robert Gray, *A Good Speed to Virginia* (New York: Da Capo Press, [1609] 1970), 19.

10. As to the unruliness of the Jamestown colony in its early years, much has been written, but John Smith's words perhaps sum it up best when he assert that it was only the help of the Natives and particularly the agency of Pocahontas that preserved "this Colonie from death, famine and utter confusion; which if in those times, [it] had once beene dissolved, Virginia might have line as it was at our first arrival to this day." John Smith, *The Travels and Works of Captain John Smith, President of Virginia and Admiral of New England, 1580–1631* (Edinburgh: John Grant, 1910), 532.

11. Edward W. Said, *Orientalism* (New York: Vintage Books, 1978), 39.

12. Gray, *Good Speed*, 20.

13. We see a certain atavistic reliance on this foundation to Judeo-Christian law in the modern-day insistence of certain Christian fundamentalist judges who wish to place stone facsimiles of the Ten Commandments in their courtrooms. The Supreme Court recently ruled that a six-foot granite monument of the Ten Commandments can remain outside the Texas Capitol under the justification that such an edifice hearkens to legal rather than religious traditions. See Charles Lane, "Court Split over Commandments," *Washington Post*, Tuesday, June 28, 2005, p. 1.

14. Walter Ong, Orality *and Literacy: The Technologizing of the Word* (New York: Routledge, 1982), 85.

15. As Derrida points out in "Plato's Pharmacy," it has long been understood that writing was a gift given from the Gods. According to Nicholas Hudson, "writing was thought to have been created by God at the beginning of the world, and to have a close relation with the natural universe." Nicholas Hudson, *Writing and European Thought 1600–1830* (Cambridge: Cambridge University Press, 1994), 9. See also Jacques Derrida, *Dissemination*, trans. Barbara Johnson (Chicago: University of Chicago Press, 1981), 75.

16. Quoted in Hudson, *Writing and European Thought*, 77.

17. Jill Lepore, *The Name of War: King Philip's War and the Origins of American Identity* (New York: Vintage Books, 1998), xvi.

18. *RCNP* V, 64.

19. William Kellaway, *The New England Company, 1649–1776: Missionary Society to the American Indians* (Westport, CT: Greenwood Press, 1961), 41–51.

20. William Hubbard, *The History of the Indian Wars in New England from the First Settlement to the Termination of the War with King Philip, in 1677*, ed. Samuel G. Drake (Roxbury, MA: W. Elliot Woodward, 1865), 46–47. (This work was originally published under the title *A Narrative of the Troubles with the Indians in New England*.)

21. Hubbard, *History of the Indian Wars*, 15.

22. Ibid., 47. The so-called insolence of the Narragansett was to a great extent manufactured by the colonists. While it is true that there had been historical tensions between the Massachusett and the Narragansett, the involvement of the colonists in these conflicts was initiated by the Mohegan sachem Uncas, who circulated rumors concerning Narragansett hostility. The colonists were all too ready to believe these rumors in their bid for control of the region and threw their support behind Uncas in the capture and execution of the Narragansett leader Miantonomo.

23. Douglas Edward Leach, *Flintlock and Tomahawk: New England in King Philip's War* (Hyannis, MA: Parnassus Imprints, 1958), 23–24.

24. Kathleen J. Bragdon, *Native People of Southern New England, 1500–1650* (Norman: University of Oklahoma Press, 1996), 140.

25. Roger Williams, *A Key into the Langauge of America* (Bedford, MA: Applewood Books, 1936), 142.

26. In June 13, 1660 it is recorded amongst the deeds of Plymouth Colony that "at the earnest request of Wamsitta, desiring that in regard his father is lately deceased, and hee being desirous, according to the custome of the natives, to change his name, that the Court would confer an English name upon him, which accordingly

they did, and therefore ordered, that for the future hee shalbee called by the name of Allexander Pokanokett; and desiring the same in the behalf of his brother, they have named him Philip. See Jeremy Dupertuis Bangs, *Indian Deeds: Land Transactions in Plymouth County* (Boston: New England Historic Genealogical Society, 2002), 297. See also Leach, *Flintlock and Tomahawk*, 23–24. William Hubbard maintained that King Philip was so called for his "ambitious and haughty spirit." This is the interpretation that has stuck ever since. Hubbard, *A Narrative*, 52.

27. Eliot, "Glorious Progress," *ET*, 152.

28. Details of Wamsutta's arrest and subsequent death can be found in Hubbard's *A Narrative*, 50–51.

29. Bragdon, *Native Peoples*, 138.

30. *RCNP* XII, 229.

31. Ibid., 237.

32. For example, in 1646 the Massachusett sachem Cutshumoquin had, on the behalf of all his people, ceded all "rights, interest and priviledg" to a six-mile tract of land along the Merrimack River to John Woodbridge. In the language of this clause, the Massachusett still had liberty to "take alewives . . . for their oune eating" so long as they didn't spoil or steal corn growing there. Should the new owners determine that the clause was in any way violated, however, "this liberty of taking fish would for ever cease." One imagines that such a clause could be activated at the slightest complaint, however unjustified, and upon such arbitrary and difficult to prove stipulations were ancestral practices forfeited. *RCMB* III, 74.

33. *Native Writings in Massachusett*, ed. Kathleen Bragdon and Ive Goddard (Philadelphia: American Philosophical Society, 1988), 365.

34. Bangs, *Indian Deeds*, 444.

35. See in particular, Bangs' introductory arguments in *Indian Deeds* where he claims that "the history of colonial acquisition of land rights in Plymouth colony has for many years been obscured by cant." Bangs, *Indian Deeds*, 1. Bangs feels that revisionist scholars have constructed a sense of grievance surrounding the colonial record of land transactions that is not justified by the colonial archive. He uses the official deeds as evidence of the legality of these acquisitions, but the deeds themselves are an omission of the verbal contracts as understood by the Natives involved in these deals and serve to mask the pressure being placed upon Native communities, forcing them to either comply or resist and risk losing everything in their already precarious positions as a people weakened by disease and other ills.

36. Bangs, *Indian Deeds*, 474. The editor of *Indian Deeds* speculates that the letter was written sometime in the summer of 1674 in response to a dispute between Philip and Peter Talmon of Rhode Island.

37. Morison offers the tantalizing suggestion, which he traces back to Hutchinson's *Narratives of the Indian Wars*, that Philip's brother and "privy counselor" may also have been one of the students at Cambridge. My suspicion is that there has been some confusion here and the "brother" in question has been mixed up with Sassamon. See Morison, *Harvard College in the Seventeenth Century* (Cambridge: Harvard University Press, 1936), 373.

38. John Easton, "A Relacion of the Indyan Warre, By Mr. Easton, of Roade Isld., 1675," *Narratives of the Indian Wars, 1675–1699*, ed. C. H. Lincoln (New York: Barnes and Noble, 1913), 11.

39. Ibid., 10.

40. *RMBC* IV, 102–103.

41. Ibid., 102.

42. Gookin breaks down the number of villages, converts, and readers and writers in Daniel Gookin, "Historical Collections of the Indians of New England," *Collections of the Massachusetts Historical Society* (CMHS) I (Boston: Munroe & Francis, 1806, 1674), 195–198.

43. Quoted in David J. Silverman, *Faith and Boundaries: Colonists, Christianity and Community Among the Wampanoag Indians of Martha's Vineyard, 1600–1871* (New York: Cambridge University Press, 2005), 93.

44. George E. Tinker, *Missionary Conquest: The Gospel and Native American Cultural Genocide* (Minneapolis: Fortress Press, 1993), 35.

45. Gookin, "Historical Collections," 182.

46. *RMBC* V, 216.

47. The most detailed biography of Gookin is from the 1836 reprint of his *Historical Account*, put together by the American Antiquarian Society and compiled by Jared Sparks. Daniel Gookin, *An Historical Account of the Doings and Sufferings of the Christian Indians in New England in the Years 1675–1677* (Cambridge, MA: Society of the University Press, [1674] 1836), 426.

48. These details to be found in Gookin, "Historical Collections," 181.

49. Ibid., 140. The notion that amongst the fourteen praying towns only Natick had a frame house has recently been challenged by the findings of an archeological dig at Magunkaquog (today Ashland, Massachusetts), about fifteen miles west of Natick. The team of archeologists who began investigating the site in 1997 note that "the real surprise" was "the remains of a fairly substantial, stone foundation." In no way however, as the authors of the study relate, does this contradict the assertion that the praying villages were sites of syncretic culture and organization. Stephen A. Mrozowski, Holly Herbster, David Brown, and Katherine L. Priddy, "Magunkaquog Materiality, Federal Recognition, and the Search for Deeper History," *International Journal of Historical Archeology* 13 (2009):430–463.

50. Gookin, "Historical Collections," 186.

51. Ibid., 183.

52. Ibid., 181.

53. Morison, *Builders of the Bay Colony* (Boston: Houghton Mifflin Co., 1930), 300.

54. Gookin, "Historical Collections," 184.

55. Mrozowski, Herbster, Brown, and Priddy, "Magunkaquog Materiality," 430–463.

56. Gookin, *Historical Account*, 436.

57. John Eliot, *John Eliot's Indian Dialogues: A Study in Cultural Interaction*, ed. Henry W. Bowden and James P. Ronda (Westport, CT: Greenwood Press, [1671] 1980), 123.

58. Neal Salisbury makes a strong case for the antipathy toward praying Indians throughout King Philip's War in his edition of Rowlandson's captivity narrative. See Neal Salisbury, *The Sovereignty and Goodness of God, Together with the Faithfulness of His Promises Displayed, Being a Narrative of the Captivity and Restoration of Mary Rowlandson and Related Documents*, ed. Neal Salisbury (Boston: St. Martin's Press, 1997), 23.

59. Eliot, *Indian Dialogues*, 96.

60. Ibid., 96.

61. Ibid., 109.

62. Ibid., 134.

63. Ibid., 130. Eliot is anticipating what seemed to have been an actual concern of some of the principal sachems of New England, although the root cause of that concern was deeply misunderstood, having nothing to do with greed and everything to do with tradition. While it is true that the sachems collected tribute of strings of wampum from neighboring sachems and petit-sachems, the misunderstanding is grounded in the European notion of wampum as currency when in fact it was a component of ritual exchange with strong ties to the condolence ritual practiced by the Iroquois.

64. Cotton Mather, *Magnalia Christi Americana*, 514.

65. Quoted in Hubbard, *A Narrative*, 54–55.

66. Quoted in George Parker Winship, *The Cambridge Press, 1638–1692* (Freeport, NY: Books for Libraries Press, 1946), 65.

67. Roger Williams, "Letter from Roger Williams, President of Providence Colony, 8 Oct. 1654," *RCNP* I, 438.

68. Rowlandson's narrative is seen as a defining text of King Philip's War, in many ways instructing her Puritan community on how to see the war as a chastisement from God for Puritan backsliding. But she maintains that, by reaffirming one's faith even in the darkest wilderness removes from Christian light, God will redeem the promise of his covenant with his chosen people and bring the sinners back into a place of favor. Nevertheless, critics have pointed out the many ways in which her narrative also strains against such a neat rhetorical containment. At times it seems Rowlandson can't help but recognize the humanity of her captors and see their struggle in ways that complicate the beliefs of her Puritan community. Michelle Burnham, in particular, pays attention to the layers of acculturation that work within Rowlandson's text and in many ways define her related experience. See Michelle Burnham, *Captivity and Sentiment: Cultural Exchange in American Literature, 1682–1861* (Hanover, NH: University Press of New England, 1997). Neal Salisbury, "Introduction: Mary Rowlandson and Her Removes," *The Sovereignty and Goodness of God, Together with the Faithfulness of His Promises Displayed, Being a Narrative of the Captivity and Restoration of Mary Rowlandson and Related Documents*, ed. Neal Salisbury (Boston: St. Martin's Press, 1997); Richard Slotkin, *Regeneration Through Violence: The Mythology of the Frontier, 1600–1860* (Norman: University of Oklahoma Press, 1973); Lepore, *The Name of War*.

69. See Mary Rowlandson, *The Sovereignty and Goodness of God, Together with the Faithfulness of His Promises Displayed, Being a Narrative of the Captivity and Restoration of Mary Rowlandson and Related Documents*, ed. Neal Salisbury (Boston: St. Martin's Press, 1997), and particularly the preface by Increase Mather in which the master narrative for King Philip's War is best articulated.

70. Gookin, *Historical Account*, 437.

71. Easton, "A Relacion," 9.

72. Ibid., 11.

73. Ibid., 9, 11.

74. Hubbard, *A Narrative*, 60.

75. See *RCNP* XII, 230.

76. Sassamon's role in the Pequot War is reported in Lepore, *The Name of War*, 31. His service as messenger for Roger Williams is detailed in Roger Williams, "The Letters of Roger Williams," *The Complete Writings of Roger Williams*, vol. VI (New York: Russell and Russell, 1963), 57. Sassamon's presence at Harvard College is affirmed in a 1675 letter written by Nathaniel Saltonstall, a Boston merchant during King Philip's War. He states that Sassamon "was brought up (amongst others) an Indian in the Colleg at Cambridg." This would place him at Harvard with Joel Hiacoomes, Caleb Cheeshateaumauk, and others. Nathaniel Saltonstall, "The Present State of New-England with Respect to the Indian War," *Narratives of the Indian Wars, 1675–1699*, ed. C. H. Lincoln (New York: Barnes and Noble, 1913), 24.

77. Ibid., 24–25.

78. Increase Mather, "A Brief History of the Warr with the INDIANS in NEW-ENGLAND," *So Dreadful a Judgment: Puritan Responses to King Philip's War 1677–1677*, ed. Richard Slotkin and James K. Folsom (Hanover, NH: Wesleyan University Press, 1978), 87.

79. Leach, *Flintlock and Tomahawk*, 31.

80. Ibid., 31.

81. James D. Drake, *King Philip's War: Civil War in New England, 1675–1676* (Amherst: University of Massachusetts Press, 1999), 68–69.

82. Ibid., 58–59.

83. Lepore, *The Name of War*, 27.

84. Ibid., 25.

85. Hubbard, *A Narrative*, 52.

86. Saltonstall, "The Present State," 24.

87. Hubbard, *A Narrative*, 52.

88. See Easton, "A Relacion of the Indyan Warre," 7.

89. John Eliot, "Letter to the Commissioners of the United Colonies, 25 Sept. 1664," *RCNP* I, 383–384.

90. Drake, *King Philip's War*, 69. See also Lepore, *The Name of War*, 43.

91. Gookin, *Historical Account*, 440–441.

92. *RCNP* V, 66 and 71.

93. Hilary E. Wyss, *Writing Indians: Literacy, Christianity, and Native Community in Early America* (Amherst: University of Massachusetts Press, 2000), 30.

94. Easton, "A Relacion," 7.

95. Ibid., 8.

96. A telling string of invectives in the introduction to Mary Rowlandson's captivity narrative captures the overall sentiment of the colonists concerning Native identity at this time. The author, presumably Increase Mather, writes, "none can imagine what it is to be captivated, and enslaved to such atheistical, proud, wild, cruel, barbarous, brutish (in one word) diabolicall creatures as these, the worst of the heathen . . . but those that have tried it." Rowlandson, *Sovereignty and Goodness*, 67.

97. Gookin, *Historical Account*, 449.

98. Ibid., 470.

99. Ibid., 450.

100. Gookin, Historical Account, 453.
101. Saltonstall, "The Present State," 40–41.
102. Gookin, *Historical Account*, 430.
103. Easton, "A Relacion," 11.
104. Gookin, *Historical Account*, 473–474.
105. See Lepore, *The Name of War*, 136.
106. Quoted in Kellaway, *The New England Company*, 118.
107. Ibid., 118.
108. John W. Ford, *Some Correspondences Between the Governors and Treasurers of the New England Company in London and the Commissioners of the United Colonies in America: The Missionaries of the Company, and Others Between the Years 1657 and 1712*, ed. John W. Ford (New York: Burt Franklin, 1970), 53.
109. Gookin, *Historical Account*, 517.
110. Ibid., 451. Gookin quotes the council held at Boston August 30, 1675, "it shall be lawful for any person, whether English or Indian, that shall find any Indian traveling in any of our towns or woods, contrary to the limits above named, to command them under guard and examination, or to kill and destroy them as they best may or can." An extension of this law, referred to as the 1675 Indian Imprisonment Act, remained on the Massachusetts law books until May of 2005.
111. Morison writes that, as early as 1656, Chauncy had begun to hint that a better use might be found for the Indian College building "than to house Indians, and the Commissioners for the United Colonies cheerfully accorded him permission to 'improve the said building to accomodate some English students,'" which Morison says was accomplished in 1665. Morison, *Harvard College in the Seventeenth Century*, 359.
112. Gookin, "Historical Collections," 176.
113. Quoted in Thomas Doughton, "Notes on the Nipmuc Indian Reservation at Hassanamesit or Hassanamisco and the Nipmuc People of Hassanamesit, later Grafton, Massachusetts," http://freepages.genealogy.rootsweb.com/com/~massasoit/grafton1.htm, 5. Originally appearing in MA microfilm: 30:169.
114. Gookin's characterization. Gookin, *Historical Account*, 483.
115. Quoted in Gookin, *Historical Account*, 483.
116. Fred B. Brown, "The Broken Treaty," *Narragansett Dawn*, May 1935, no. 1, 9.
117. Ibid., 10.
118. Ibid., 10.
119. Ibid., 11.
120. Neal Salisbury, "The Examination and Relation of James Quannapaquait," *The Sovereignty and Goodness of God, Together with the Faithfulness of His Promises Displayed, Being a Narrative of the Captivity and Restoration of Mary Rowlandson and Related Documents*, ed. Neal Salisbury (Boston: St. Martin's Press, 1997), 121.
121. Ibid., 122.
122. Quoted in Dennis A. Connole, *The Indians of the Nipmuck Country in Southern New England, 1630–1750: An Historical Geography* (Jefferson, NC: McFarland Company, 2001). 208. Originally in the anonymous "A True Account of the Most Considerable Occurrences That Have Happened in the Warre Between the English and the Indians in New England."

123. Gookin, *Historical Account*, 494. Samuel Drake, who edits Hubbard's account of this event is the first to suggest, in a footnote, that it was James Printer who left this note. The assertion is reasonable since James will later be revealed to be amongst this crew in the negotiations for Mary Rowlandson's release. See Hubbard, *A Narrative*, 171.

124. Lepore, *The Name of War*, 95.

125. Gookin, *Historical Account*, 494.

126. Wyss, *Writing Indians*, 44.

127. Hubbard, *A Narrative*, 249.

128. Increase Mather, "A Brief History of the Warr with the Indians in New England," 130.

129. Hubbard, *A Narrative*, 249.

130. MA, microfilm 30:207.

131. MA, microfilm, 30:216.

132. "Petition to the Governor and Council of Massachusetts," quoted in *The Sovereignty and Goodness of God, Together with the Faithfulness of His Promises Displayed, Being a Narrative of the Captivity and Restoration of Mary Rowlandson and Related Documents*, ed. Neal Salisbury (Boston: St. Martin's Press, 1997), 138.

133. Ibid., 138.

134. Mattamuck et al.: "Letter to John Leverett et al.," quoted in *The Sovereignty and Goodness of God, Together with the Faithfulness of His Promises Displayed, Being a Narrative of the Captivity and Restoration of Mary Rowlandson and Related Documents*, ed. Neal Salisbury (Boston: St. Martin's Press, 1997), 140–141.

135. Ibid., 141.

136. Benjamin Church, "Entertaining Passages," 451.

137. Leach, *Flintlock and Tomahawk*, 234.

138. Milton A. Travers, *The Wampanoag Indian Federation of the Algonquian Nation: Indian Neighbors of the Pilgrims* (Boston: Christopher Publishing House, 1957), 117.

139. I take Benjamin Church's account for my source here, although the anecdote about Philip's hair being cut is from Hubbard. See Church, "Entertaining Passages," 442–443 and Hubbard, *A Narrative*, 261.

140. Chingwauk, also known as Shingwaukonse (Little Pine), was a noted Ojibwe leader and a "high-ranking Medig" or prophet. He was the keeper of a number of sacred birch bark scrolls which he apparently had destroyed or concealed just before his death. Schoolcraft also reported that he would keep private scrolls of his personal visions which were sometimes used as evidence of having foretold certain events. See Michael Angel, *Preserving the Sacred: Historical Perspectives on the Ojibwa Midewiwin* (Winnipeg: University of Manitoba Press), 28–29.

141. Quoting Schoolcraft in Delabarre, *Dighton Rock*, 114–115.

142. Ibid., 115

143. For a full reading of Chingwauk's translation, see Delabarre, *Dighton Rock*, 114–116.

144. Ibid., 119.

145. That the origins of the rock fall under question at all is a direct result of the ongoing unwitnessing of Native writing in American culture. Edmund Burke

Delabarre, in his 1924 publication on Dighton Rock, dismisses Chingwauk's reading out of hand and offers that the initial marks on the rock were made by the Portuguese sailor Miguel Cortereal in 1511—this despite the fact that Cortereal was thought to have been shipwrecked off the coast of Newfoundland some nine years earlier. In Delabarre's reading Cortereal survived (and made his way southward), leaving his name and the date on this rock so rescue crews might discover him. In the interim Delabarre posits that Cortereal somehow managed to become chief of the local indigenous peoples who were later inclined to ape his efforts by making their own crude palimpsestic markings over his own on the rock. Delabarre even entertains the notion that, as a result of Cortereal's inevitable rise to indigenous royalty, he was likely to have been a forebear to Metacom or King Philip who leads the 1676–1677 insurrection against the English. Once again, despite all available evidence, Indian writing is regarded as an offshoot, mere mimicry, of European writing. It remains a popular researcher's obsession to offer new, complex, and bizarre interpretations of who might have left the markings on Dighton Rock. Interestingly enough, though, if you ask the Wampanoag themselves, the story is one of contact.

146. William Apess, "Eulogy on King Philip," *On Our Own Ground: The Complete Writings of William Apess, A Pequot*, ed. Barry O'Connell (Amherst: University of Massachusetts Press, 1992), 302.

147. Church, "Entertaining Passages," 452.

148. See Travers, *The Wampanoag Indian Federation*, 207.

149. Richard Slotkin, "Benjamin Church: King of the Wild Frontier," *So Dreadful a Judgment: Puritan Responses to King Philip's War, 16760–1677*, ed. Richard Slotkin and James K. Folsom (Hanover, NH: Wesleyan University Press, 1978), 383.

150. Church, "Entertaining Passages," 456.

151. Ibid., 455–456.

152. According to Williams' *Key*, under the chapter heading "Of Fowle," the word *anawhone* means "wing-shot." Williams, *Key*, 91.

153. R. A. Douglas Lithgow, *Native American Place Names in Massachusetts* (Bedford, MA: Applewood Books, 1909), 3.

154. See William S. Simmons, *Spirit of the New England Tribes: Indian History and Folklore, 1620–1984* (Hanover, NH: University Press of New England, 1986), 38–41.

155. Church, "Entertaining Passages," 460.

156. Slotkin, "Benjamin Church: King of the Wild Frontier," 385.

157. Church, "Entertaining Passages," 460.

158. John Josselyn, *John Josselyn, Colonial Traveler: A Critical Edition of Two Voyages to New-England*, ed. Paul J. Lindholt (Hanover, NH: University of New England Press, 1988), 101.

159. Slotkin, "Benjamin Church: King of the Wild Frontier," 460.

160. Henry Wadsworth Longfellow, "The Song of Hiawatha," *Longfellow: Poems and Other Writings* (New York: Library of America, 2000), 278. The implication is clearly that Native myths must give way to Christian truths, and in the poem Hiawatha becomes a collaborator in this paradigm.

161. Frank G. Speck, *A Study of the Delaware Indian Big House Ceremony* (Harrisburg: Publications of the Pennsylvania Historical Commission, 1931), 63.

162. Church, "Entertaining Passages," 460.

163. These letters are quoted from Travers, *The Wampanoag Indian Federation*, 214–215, whose little book on the Wampanoag holds a wealth of small regional details.

164. See Bourne, *The Red King's Rebellion*, 205. Bourne notes that Church gave "Philip's royalties, according to form," to Plymouth's Governor Winslow, "And he, in turn, gave them to Charles II of England—though it is doubtful that they ever reached him. So they were thrown away and lost, these unique evidences of a once rich culture."

165. Quoted in Simmons, *Spirit of the New England Tribes*, 70.

166. Doughton, "Notes on the Hassanamesit Indian Reservation," http://freepages.genealogy.rootsweb.ancestry.com/~massasoit/grafton1.htm.

167. MA, microfilm. 30:265

168. See Doughton, "Notes on the Hassanamesit Indian Reservation."

169. Hugh Amory, *First Impressions: Printing in Cambridge 1639–1989* (Cambridge: President and Fellows of Harvard College, 1989), 41.

170. See Connole, *Indians of the Nipmuck Country*, 247–249.

171. Quoted in Rowlandson, "Sovereignty and Goodness," 98.

172. Quoted in Kellaway, *The New England Company*, 153.

Chapter 4. Beneath the Wave: The Maintenance of Native Tradition in Hidden Transcripts (1709–1768)

1. Melissa Jayne Fawcett, *The Lasting of the Mohegans* (Uncasville, CT: Mohegan Tribe, 1995), 6.

2. Craig Womack, *Red on Red: Native American Literary Separatism* (Minneapolis: University of Minnesota Press, 1999), 57.

3. Ibid., 87.

4. *RMBC* V, 130.

5. Fawcett, *The Lasting of the Mohegans*, 6.

6. Ibid., 6.

7. Robert Warrior, *Tribal Secrets: Recovering American Indian Intellectual Traditions* (Minneapolis: University of Minnesota Press, 1995), 2.

8. Ibid., 3, 91.

9. Found in Ives Goddard and Kathleen Bragdon, *Native Writings in Massachusett* (Philadelphia: American Philosophical Society, 1988), 447, 457.

10. W. Deloss Love, *Samson Occom and the Christian Indians of New England*, ed. Margaret Connell Szasz (Syracuse: Syracuse University Press, [1899] 2000), 19.

11. Jean O'Brien, *Dispossession By Degrees: Indian Land and Identity in Natick, Massachusetts, 1650–1790* (New York: Cambridge University Press, 1997), 127.

12. Ibid., 127. O'Brien describes her project here as one of listening for "Indian voices in documents that had been produced for other purposes."

13. James Drake, *King Philip's War: Civil War in New England 1675–1676* (Amherst: University of Massachusetts Press, 1999), 4–5.

14. Kathleen J. Bragdon, "Crime and Punishment among the Indians of Massachusetts, 1675–1750," *EthnoHistory* 28, no.1 (Winter 1981): 23.

15. Harold W. Van Lonkhuyzen, "A Reappraisal of the Praying Indian: Acculturation, Conversion and Identity at Natick, Massachusetts, 1646," *New England Encounters: Indians and Euroamericans ca 1600–1850: Essays Drawn from New England Quarterly*, ed. Alden T. Vaughan (Boston: Northeastern University Press, 1999), 222, 224.

16. Goddard and Bragdon, *Native Writings in Massachusett*, 11.

17. I assume the "Waban" who was town clerk throughout this period is, in fact, Thomas Waban, who was amongst the first cultural intermediaries to train with Eliot in the 1640s. By the 1720s he would have been in his seventies, assuming he was about ten when Eliot undertook his scholastic training. He is succeeded by yet another Thomas Waban who becomes influential in town politics in the second decade of the eighteenth century. The first Waban of colonial record passed away sometime in the decade following King Philip's War. See Samuel G. Drake, *Biography and History of the Indians of North America, from Its First Discovery* (Boston: Benjamin B. Mussey & Co., 1841), 180.

18. Ibid., 179–180.

19. Goddard and Bragdon, *Native Writings in Massachusett*, 277 and 301.

20. Bragdon, "Crime and Punishment," 25.

21. Ibid., 27.

22. Ibid., 25.

23. Goddard and Bragdon, *Native Writings in Massachusett*, 273.

24. Laurel Thatcher Ulrich notes that in colonial New England the law dictated that "land and livelihood . . . were normally transmitted from father to son" save under extraordinary circumstances. Laurel Thatcher Ulrich, *Goodwives: Image and Reality in the Lives of Women in Northern New England, 1650–1750* (New York: Vintage Books, 1980), 36.

25. Goddard and Bragdon, *Native Writings in Massachusett*, 321.

26. Van Lonkhuyzen, "The Praying Indian," 221.

27. Goddard and Bragdon, *Native Writings in Massachusett*, 14.

28. Samuel Sewall, *The Diary of Samuel Sewall, vol. II 1709–1729* (New York: Farrar, Straus and Giroux, 1979), 751.

29. Goddard and Bragdon, *Native Writings in Massachusett*, 19.

30. See John W. Ford, *Some Correspondence Between the Governors and Treasurers of the New England Company* (New York: Burt Franklin, [1896] 1970), 64.

31. Bernd Peyer, *The Tutor'd Mind: Indian Missionary Writers in Antebellum America* (Amherst: University of Massachusetts Press, 1997), 14.

32. Goddard and Bragdon, *Native Writings in Massachusett*, 33.

33. Ibid., 33.

34. Ibid., 373.

35. This phrase is coined by Charles Edward Banks who wrote a history of Martha's Vineyard in the first decade of the twentieth century. He refers to the natives as "a people without record or civilization, but to whom it [Martha's Vineyard or Noe-pe as the indigenous inhabitants called it, meaning "middle of the water"] was a home." Charles Edward Banks, *History of Martha's Vineyard Mass*, vol. 1 (Edgartown: Dukes County Historical Society, [1911] 1966), 32.

36. Goddard and Bragdon, *Native Writings in Massachusett*, 373.

37. Ibid., 373.

38. David J. Silverman, *Faith and Boundaries: Colonists, Christianity, and Community Among the Wampanoag Indians of Martha's Vineyard, 1600–1871* (New York: Cambridge University Press, 2005), 50.

39. Goddard and Bragdon, *Native Writings in Massachusett*, 6.

40. Banks, *History of Martha's Vineyard*, 53.

41. Goddard and Bragdon claim that the Massachusett language became "extinct" in the nineteenth century and they have reassembled the language from archival sources. Goddard and Bragdon, *Native Writings in Massachusett*, xix.

42. Goddard and Bragdon, *Native Writings in Massachusett*, 97.

43. For more on how the Martha's Vineyard Wampanoag attempted to combat colonial land acquisitions see Silverman, *Faith and Boundaries*.

44. Love, *Samson Occom*, 298. When Love refers to Occom as the "Indian Moses" it appears evident that he is echoing a common sentiment understood amongst the evangelical communities of the time that remembered Occom and attempted to place his acts within a Christian paradigm.

45. An early draft of Occom's autobiographical sketch appeared in the newspapers on March 13, 1766 as part of a letter written by Wheelock to "certify the Public as to the truth of that matter" that Occom was, as he had claimed, a true Mohegan, brought up in "heathenism." The point of this letter was to dispel doubts concerning Occom's heritage and upbringing. In service to this agenda Occom offered "his own account of it, which he sent to me from Boston on hearing the false and injurious reports made of that matter before his embarkation for Europe. See "Lebanon Feb 20 1766," *Boston News Letter and New England Chronicle*, March 13, 1766, p. 3.

46. Love, *Samson Occom*, 152.

47. Ibid., 153.

48. Bernd Peyer, *The Elders Wrote: An Anthology of Early Prose by North American Indians, 1768–1931* (Berlin: Dietrich Reimer Verlag, 1982) and Bernd Peyer, "Samson Occom: Mohegan Missionary and Writer of the 18th Century," *American Indian Quarterly* 6, nos. 3–4 (1982): 215.

49. David Murray, *Forked Tongues: Speech, Writing and Representation in North American Indian Texts* (Bloomington: Indiana University Press, 1991), 57. Also Dana D. Nelson, "'(I Speak Like A Fool But I Am Constrained)' Samson Occom's Short Narrative and the Economies of the Racial Self," in *Early American Native Writing: New Critical Essays*, ed. Helen Jaskoski (Cambridge: Cambridge University Press, 1996).

50. Jace Weaver, *That the People Might Live: Native American Literatures and Native American Communities* (New York: Oxford University Press, 1997), 49–53.

51. Love, *Samson Occom*, 21.

52. Samson Occom, "Autobiographical Narrative, Second Draft" Sept. 17, 1768, which will from here on be referred to as *AN*. The original draft is located with the Occom Papers in the archives at Dartmouth College's Rauner Library, Vault 4, Journals and Sermons: Occom's Journal, Occom's Early Life, written Sept. 17, 1768.

53. David McClure and Elijah Parish, *Memoirs of the Reverend Eleazar Wheelock, D. D.* (New York: Arno Press, [1811] 1972), 16.

54. Margaret Connell Szasz, *Indian Education in the American Colonies, 1607–1783* (Albuquerque: University of New Mexico Press, 1988), 196–197.

55. See Laura Murray, introduction to *To Do Good to My Indian Brethren: The Writings of Joseph Johnson 1751–1776*, ed. Laura J. Murray (Amherst: University of Massachusetts Press, 1998), 37.

56. See Fawcett, *The Lasting of the Mohegans*, 17–18.

57. Lisa Brooks, *The Common Pot: The Recovery of Native Space in the Northeast* (Minneapolis: University of Minnesota Press, 2008), 80.

58. Fawcett, *The Lasting of the Mohegans*, 17–18.

59. The first anecdote is related in Laura Murray, *To Do Good*, 38. The second anecdote comes from John W. De Forest, *History of the Indians of Connecticut from the Earliest Known Period to 1850* (Hamden, CT: Archon Books, [1851]1964), 461. De Forest, writing in the 1850s, collected a number of local anecdotes that had their origins in the local community at Mohegan.

60. Silverman, *Faith and Boundaries*, 183.

61. Lisa Brooks, *The Common Pot*, 3–8, 69, 70.

62. Kevin Bruyneel, *The Third Place of Sovereignty: The Postcolonial Politics of US-Indigenous Relations* (Minneapolis: University of Minnesota Press, 2007).

63. John Bulkley, "An Inquiry into the Right of the Aboriginal Natives to the Lands in America, and the Titles Derived from Them," 1724, *CMHS* IV, 159.

64. Ibid., 163, 165, 166.

65. Ibid., 174.

66. Ibid., 166, 181.

67. For the Mason quote see Major John Mason, "A Brief History of the Pequot War," *The History of the Pequot War*, ed. Charles Orr (Cleveland: Helman-Taylor Co., 1897), 35. The Masons probably saw their title to the land bound up with that of the Mohegan in a state of protectorship. Therefore it was in their interest to argue against the idea that the Mohegan had actually ceded their land rights over to the state. See Laura Murray's arguments in *To Do Good*, 34–36.

68. See Murray, *To Do Good*, 35.

69. Brooks, *The Common Pot*, 84.

70. Samson Occom, "Journal 1, 1743–1748," *The Collected Writings of Samson Occom, Mohegan: Leadership and Literature in Eighteenth-Century Native America*, ed. Joanna Brooks (New York: Oxford University Press, 2006), 248. Original journals to be found at Dartmouth College, Rauner Special Collections and the Connecticut Historical Society.

71. Ibid., 249.

72. A broadside published in 1772 looks back in poetic verse on the execution of one Elizabeth Shaw who murdered her newborn child and, according to this text, was hung on November 18, 1744 in Windham, Connecticut. It reads, "Parental pity she had none / unto her infants cry, / On the cool ground she laid it down / and left it there to die.// It is not known how long alone / it languish'd in the grove. / Its mournful cries that did arise, / was heard by God above." Possibly the passage of years between the actual hanging and the printing of this broadside allowed for a misrepresentation of the dates and this is, in fact, the same hanging Occom witnessed. If so, there is no mention of Elizabeth Shaw's being a Native American. In all likelihood, such a detail, if known, would have been readily exploited. It is curious, however, that someone would choose to publish a poem on this event in

the year 1772, some twenty-six years after the fact. One wonders if the popular reception of Occom's "A Sermon Preached at the Execution of Moses Paul," which was published the same year, had anything to do with the production of this poem. If so, then we come back to the possibility that there was a cultural connection between Paul and Shaw. Occom's sermon was also paraphrased in verse and circulated as a broadside. Another execution sermon was printed in New London in 1738, for Katherine Garret, a Pequot, who also was charged with murdering her newborn child. Her family had been one of the leading families of the Pequot, descended from the sachem Hermon Garet who was also known as Wequash Cook (not the same Wequash from *New England's First Fruits* fame). Her descendant, Hannah Garret, would become the wife of David Fowler, Occom's brother-in-law.

73. Joanna Brooks, *The Collected Writings of Samson Occom, Mohegan: Leadership and Literature in Eighteenth-Century Native America*, ed. Joanna Brooks (New York: Oxford University Press, 2006), 14. See also George Whitfield, *The Religious Intelligencer . . . Containing the Principal Transactions of the Various Bible and Missionary Societies, with Particular Accounts of Revivals of Religion* (New Haven) November 9, 1822; 7:24, p. 378. American Periodicals Series Online.

74. Love, *Samson Occom*, 38.

75. Occom, "Journal 1," *Collected Writings*, 249.

76. Love, *Samson Occom*, 42.

77. Ibid., 39.

78. Ibid., 44.

79. Occom, AN.

80. Occom, "An Account of the Montauk Indians, of Long Island," *Collected Writings*, 47–51.

81. Ibid., 47. For a list of all the roots and their cures see OP at Dartmouth College, Rauner Special Collections, Vault 4, Journals and Sermons: "Occom's Journal, Herbal Remedies, 1754."

82. Love, *Samson Occom*, 48.

83. Occom, AN.

84. From the diary of David McClure, May 8, 1764. Quoted in Love, *Samson Occom*, 101. This collection of books was apparently purchased in England with the intent to create a library for the Indian school that Wheelock had proposed. The books remained in Occom's possession, however, as Wheelock never opened the school that he had proposed to Occom. See Harold Blodgett, *Samson Occom* (Hanover: Dartmouth College Publications, 1935), 107.

85. In his journal for 1786 he recounts meeting a young woman near Brothertown who fondly recalls to him the book he had given her years ago when she was a child, bringing the very book out for his inspection. See Occom, *Collected Writings*, 336–337. For Occom's possession of an Indian Bible, see Joanna Brooks, *Collected Writings of Samson Occom*, 15.

86. See the subscribers list to the 1792 edition of *The Writings of Thomas Paine* in Early American Imprints, 1st series, no. 46536.

87. Love, *Samson Occom*, 50.

88. Occom, "Journal 3, 1757–1760," *Collected Writings*, 255.

89. Occom, "Journal 4, 1761," *Collected Writings*, 260.

90. Ibid., 260.

91. Quoted in Love, *Samson Occom*, 98.

92. Occom, "Journal 4, 1761," *Collected Writings*, 260.

93. Love, *Samson Occom*, 93.

94. George Whitfield, "Samson Occom," *The Religious Intelligencer*, November 9, 1822; 7, 24, p. 380. This article offers numerous quotes from Occom's missing journal of 1761. There is reason to believe that the heretofore missing journal fragments transcribed are slightly embellished, but, wherever possible, they have been compared with the originals and prove to be faithful to the overall content of Occom's writings, if moderately expanded upon in places. There is every reason to believe that, in the passages in question, the authors had the original journals and letters on hand, which they claim were placed in their possession by a George Spalding of New York.

95. *An Indian Preacher in England*, ed. Leon Burr Richardson (Hanover, NH: Dartmouth College Manuscript Series, 1933), 74.

96. Occom, "An Account of the Montauk," *Collected Writings*, 49.

97. Ibid., 50. Both descriptions of a deity and the description of heaven bear a fairly remarkable resemblance to Roger Williams' account of Narragansett spirituality in *A Key to the Language of America*. This either implies that Occom had read Williams and is echoing a certain brand of colonial rhetoric, or, given his intimate knowledge of Montauk custom, he is unintentionally reaffirming the veracity of Williams' observations.

98. Ibid., 49.

99. *The Letters of Eleazar Wheelock's Indians*, ed. James Dow McCallum (Hanover, NH: Dartmouth College Manuscript Series, 1932), 39.

100. *An Indian Preacher in England*, Eleazar Wheelock to George Whitefield, May 4, 1765, 30.

101. Ibid., 30.

102. *An Indian Preacher in England*, Charles Smith to Eleazar Wheelock, March 30 1764, 20.

103. *An Indian Preacher in England*, Wheelock to Brainerd, January 14, 1765, 26.

104. *An Indian Preacher in England*, from the minutes of the Connecticut Correspondents, March 12, 1765, 28.

105. Love writes, "Samson Occom, who was morbidly sensitive, loaded this sin upon this honest soul and did humbly ask forgiveness." Love, *Samson Occom*, 128. The "firm hand" quote belongs to Leon Burr Richardson, who edits the compilation of letters surrounding Occom's trip to England in *An Indian Preacher in England* (see fn p. 29).

106. Brooks, *The Common Pot*, 97.

107. Ibid., 97.

108. Dana D. Nelson argues that the confusion in Occom's self-presentation is a gesture "toward a self-affirming articulation of identity that later would be evidenced more explicitly in Occom's actions toward Wheelock and the Christian missionary project." Nelson, "'(I Speak Like A Fool But I Am Constrained),'" 43. I agree with this assessment, but I think it fails to acknowledge that Occom was consciously participating in a performance to establish his "Indian" credentials for the naysayers who sought to sabotage his mission to England.

109. See *An Indian Preacher in England*, ed. Leon Burr Richardson.

110. Occom, "Autobiographical Narrative, First Draft, Nov 28, 1765," *Collected Writings*, 51.

111. *An Indian Preacher in England*, Occom to Wheelock, December 6, 1765, 75.

112. Ibid., 75.

113. Mahomet was finally given a commemorative stone in November 2006 when tribal members came to England and met with Queen Elizabeth. According to Two Dogs Bozsum of Uncasville, Mahomet had never received "a proper funeral in our tribal tradition [and] this is what we want to give him now." Katie Fretland, "Queen Joins Homage to Chief," *Houston Chronicle*, Thursday, November 23, 2006, A22.

114. Occom, "Journal 6, 1765–1766," *Collected Writings*, 267.

115. Ibid., 268.

116. *An Indian Preacher in England*, Jillard to Wheelock, March 2, 1767, 27.

117. Love, *Samson Occom*, 137.

118. Occom, "Journal 6, 1765–1766," *Collected Writings*, 273–274.

119. "1792 Letter to Mary Fowler Occom, Collected Writings, 80–81.

120. *An Indian Preacher in England*, Wheelock to Occom, April 9, 1766, 118.

121. *An Indian Preacher in England*, Mary Occom to Wheelock, November 8, 1766, 182.

122. *An Indian Preacher in England*, Mary Occom to Wheelock, July 15, 1767, 279.

123. *An Indian Preacher in England*, Occom to Wheelock, February 12, 1767, 220.

124. Ibid., 220.

125. Ibid., 162.

126. This is all somewhat obliquely laid out in Whitaker's lengthy January 20, 1767 letter to Wheelock. He refers to Mr. Jackson as Wheelock's "agent" and suggests that the solution of a removal would "be best for the Indians" regardless of the fact that the Mohegan are assuredly not advised of such an option, and it begs the question, how were they to be removed? And what would be done if they refused this invitation? The implication here is that the policy of Indian removal, already practiced in some small measure by the Puritans, has direct ties to Wheelock and the missionary endeavor. See *An Indian Preacher in England*, 203–209.

127. CHS, John Mason to Samson Occom, February 18, 1768.

128. CHS, Robert Keen to Samson Occom, September 8, 1767.

129. "To the Hon. Jame Otis, and Thomas Chushing, Esqs. Mr. Samuel Adams and John Hancock Esq," *Scotts Magazine* 30, no. 7 (Edinburgh: Sands, Brymer, Murray & Cochran, July 1768): 370–374.

130. *An Indian Preacher in England*, Whitaker to Wheelock, February 12, 1767, 219.

131. Ibid., 221.

132. Occom may have met with Mason while he was in England, although the details of this are unclear. It appears that Mason, who had fallen into abject poverty while pleading his case in England, hoped to acquire funds from Occom to return home. The reporting on this is all secondhand, however, made in imputations from Robert Keen to Nathaniel Whitaker. Occom remained silent on the issue, and Mason died from impoverished circumstances in England. See *An Indian Preacher in England*, 295–296.

133. Brooks, *Collected Writings of Samson Occom*, 161; Love, *Samson Occom*, 147.

134. Harold Blodgett, *Samson Occom* (Hanover, NH: Dartmouth College Publications, 1935), 133.

135. *An Indian Preacher in England*, Wheelock to John Thornton, August 25, 1768, 351.

136. The "Indian distemper" quote is from a letter by Wheelock to Nathaniel Whittaker, November 28, 1767, and can be found in *An Indian Preacher in England*, 321. Occom himself frequently uses the term "tawny races" to refer to indigenous peoples, as will be seen in further letters, and it is much in practice at the time.

137. Blodgett, *Samson Occom*, 116.

138. *An Indian Preacher in England*, Wheelock to Occom, January 22, 1771, 352–353.

139. Ibid., 321, 357.

140. Blodgett, *Samson Occom*, 110.

141. *An Indian Preacher in England*, David McClure to Wheelock, May 21, 1770, 354.

142. Occom, July 24, 1771 "Letter to Eleazar Wheelock," *Collected Writings*, 98–99.

143. Ibid., 100.

144. Occom would in fact receive an annual £50 stipend from Thornton, who concluded that "Occom was the Instrument under God that was the means of collecting all the Money & had the Doctor (Nathaniel Whitaker) come without him the disgrace would have all fell to his share, whereas poor Occom proved the Scape Goat." Blodgett, *Samson Occom*. 127.

145. *An Indian Preacher in England*, Occom to Robert Keen, September 27, 1768, 348.

146. Ibid., 348. Also in Occom, *Collected Writings*, 84.

147. CHS, quoted in a letter from Woodward to Occom, August 24, 1769.

148. Weaver, *That the People Might Live*, 52. I do not feel as though Weaver backs up this claim with enough substantial evidence, but I believe he reads it correctly nonetheless, having taken the care to regard Occom's career from a perspective that has deconstructed the colonial framework that has constrained it. I hope my reading offers concrete details to back up Weaver's assertion.

149. Occom, AN.

150. Ibid.

151. Henry Louis Gates, quoted in Nelson, "'(I Speak Like A Fool),'" 42.

152. Ibid., 60.

153. Murray, *Forked Tongues*, 57.

154. Nelson, "'(I Speak Like A Fool),'" 61.

155. See "Lebanon Feb 20 1766," *Boston News Letter and New England Chronicle*, March 13, 1766, 3.

156. *An Indian Preacher in England*, Occom to Robert Keen, September 27, 1768, 348.

157. Richardson, *An Indian Preacher in England*, 348.

158. Blodgett, *Samson Occom*, 108.

159. Occom, AN.

160. See McClure and Parish, *Memoirs of the Reverend Eleazar Wheelock*.

161. Dana Nelson does an excellent job of describing this dynamic in her article. Nelson, "'(I Speak Like A Fool).'"

162. Occom, AN.

163. "The Mohegan Indians," *Norwich Courier*, December 8, 1830, 1.

164. Occom, AN.

165. Occom, AN.

166. Ibid.

167. Ibid.

168. "The Mohegan Indians," *Norwich Courier*, December 8, 1830, 1.

169. Ibid., 1.

170. News, "The Last of the Mohicans," *Norwich Courier*, June 22, 1830, 3.

171. Occom, "Thou Shalt Love Thy Neighbor as Thyself," *Collected Writings*, 201.

172. Ibid., 202.

173. Ibid., 202–203.

174. Ibid., 203–204.

175. Ibid., 206.

176. Occom's biographer Love points out that Wheelock paid £50 for a negro, "Ishmael by name," in 1757. He notes that the "ministers very commonly had one or more blacks as servants in their households." Love, *Samson Occom*, 176.

177. Fawcett, *The Lasting of the Mohegans*, 54.

178. Love, *Samson Occom*, 53.

179. CHS, Jacob Fowler to Samson Occom, March 27, 1772.

180. Arthur Caswell Parker, "Sources and Range of Cooper's Indian Lore," *New York History* 35, no. 4 (October 1954): 447–456.

181. Fawcett, *The Lasting of the Mohegan*, 12.

182. Ibid., 171.

Chapter 5. A Tale of Two Settlements: Mohican, Mohegan, and the Road to Brothertown (1724–1785)

1. Larzer Ziff, *Writing in the New Nation: Prose, Print, and Politics in the Early United States* (New Haven: Yale University Press, 1991), 130.

2. C. Albert White, *A History of the Rectangular Survey System* (Washington, DC: U.S. Department of the Interior, 1983), 2.

3. William Apess, "Eulogy on King Philip," in *On Our Own Ground: The Complete Writings of William Apess, Pequot*, ed. Barry O'Connell (Amherst: University of Massachusetts Press, 1992), 306.

4. See Richard White, *The Middle Ground: Indians, Empires, and Republics in the Great Lakes Region, 1650–1850* (Cambridge: Cambridge University Press, 1991). White demonstrates how cultural accommodations were made on both sides when Europeans and Natives came into contact with one another. These cultural accommodations were generally forged and tested on both an ideological and geographical middle ground where the rules of contact were constantly being improvised.

5. James Fenimore Cooper, *The Pioneers* (New York: Oxford University Press, 1980), 85.

6. Ibid., 85–86.

7. Alan Taylor, *William Cooper's Town: Power and Persuasion on the Frontier of the Early American Republic* (New York: Vintage, 1995), 40.

8. Occom, AN.

9. See Laura J. Murray, introduction to *To Do Good to My Indian Brethren: The Writings of Joseph Johnson, 1751–1776*, ed. Laura J. Murray (Amherst: University of Massachusetts Press, 1998), 25–26.

10. For further details on the life of Hendrick Aupaumut, see Lisa Brooks, *The Common Pot: The Recovery of Native Space in the Northeast* (Minneapolis: University of Minnesota Press, 2008) and Hilary E. Wyss, *Writing Indians: Literacy, Christianity, and Native Community in Early America* (Amherst: University of Massachusetts Press, 2000), 106–122. See also Electra F. Jones, *Stockbridge, Past and Present or, Records of an Old Mission Station* (Springfield, MA: Samuel Bowles & Co., 1854).

11. Cooper, *The Pioneers*, 84. James Fenimore Cooper, *The Last of the Mohicans* (New York: Oxford University Press, 1980), 23–26. Much of what Cooper relates as history here is in agreement with Mohegan tribal historian Melissa Jayne Fawcett's recounting of Mohegan origins. Melissa Jayne Fawcett, *The Lasting of the Mohegans*, Part 1: The Story of the Wolf People (Uncasville, CT: Mohegan Tribe, 1995), 7–22.

12. Cooper, *The Last of the Mohicans*, 25.

13. Hendrick Aupaumut's "Indian History" establishes the Delaware as grandfathers of the Mohican, "according to the ancient covenant of our grandfathers." This is quoted in Jones, *Stockbridge, Past and Present*, 16.

14. Arthur C. Parker, "Sources and Range of Cooper's Indian Lore," *New York History* 35, no. 4 (October 1954): 447–456.

15. Ibid., 451.

16. Ibid., 452, 453.

17. Cooper, *The Pioneers*, 452–453.

18. SC, Box 1, File 4, Samuel Hopkins, *Historical Memoirs Relating to the Housatunnuk Indians* (Boston: Kneeland Publishing, [1753] 1911), 3. From here on cited as *Historical Memoirs*.

19. Jones, *Stockbridge, Past and Present*, 15

20. Ibid., 16–17.

21. Ibid., 20.

22. *A journal kept by Coll. Stephen Courtland, & Coll. Nich. Beyard, of Their Majesties Council for the Province of New-York*, "The Address to the River Indians, to his Excellency Benjamin Fletcher & co. at Albany, August the 18th, 1694" (New York: Bradford, 1693), 15, *Early American Imprints*, series 1, no. 39307.

23. See Patrick Frazier, *The Mohicans of Stockbridge* (Lincoln: University of Nebraska Press, 1992), 11.

24. See Timothy J. Shannon, *Iroquois Diplomacy on the Early American Frontier* (New York: Viking Press, 2008), 1–7.

25. *Documents Relative to the Colonial History of New York*, vol. V (Albany: Weeds Parsons & Co., 1853–87), 562.

26. *Indian Deeds of Hampden County*, ed. Harry Andrews Wright (Springfield, MA: 1905), 116. Rachel Wheeler, *To Live Upon Hope: Mohicans and Missionaries in the Eighteenth-Century Northeast* (Ithaca, NY: Cornell University Press, 2008), 17. Frazier, *The Mohicans of Stockbridge*, 13.

27. In the 1735 conference at Deerfield between Governor Belcher and the Cagnawaga, a "special covenant" is mentioned that was made between "this Government and you (the Cagnawaga Indians) at Albany, eleven years ago." "At a Conference Held at Deerfield in the County of Hampshire, the Twenty Seventh Day of August," 4, *Early American Imprints*, series 1, no. 3916.

28. Colin G. Calloway, *Western Abenaki of Vermont 1600–1800: War, Migration and the Survival of an Indian People* (Norman: University of Oklahoma Press, 1990), 115.

29. For more on Gray Lock's War, see Calloway, *Western Abenaki of Vermont*.

30. This is expressed fairly comprehensively by Patrick Frazier in *The Mohicans of Stockbridge* as he describes the involvement of the Stockbridge Natives in the French and Indian War. He quotes British General Gage as saying the Indians were a great "nuisance to the army and did no manner of service." General Jeffrey Amherst, who has retained a rare level of infamy in colonial and Native relations, said of his Native scouts, "I know what a vile crew they are, and I have as vile opinion of those lazy rum-drinking scoundrels as anyone can have." Nevertheless he determined he would still use them in battle, to "keep them from doing mischief elsewhere." Frazier, *The Mohicans of Stockbridge*, 129. Frazier does little to combat these stereotypes or arrange them in another cultural perspective.

31. Hopkins, *Historical Memoirs*, 3.

32. Ibid., 2.

33. Ibid., 3–4.

34. Ibid., 3–4.

35. SC, Box 1, File 2: Mr. Appleton's Sermon at the ordination of the Reverend Mr. John Sergeant, August 31, 1735, "Preface," iv.

36. Hopkins, *Historical Memoirs*, 4.

37. Ibid., 4.

38. Brooks, *The Common Pot*, 229.

39. *The Lancaster Treaty of 1744 with Related Documents*, ed. James H. Merrell (Boston: Bedford/St. Martin's, 2008), 47.

40. "Conference at Deerfield," 2.

41. Ibid., 2–3.

42. Ibid., 10.

43. Ibid., 11.

44. Ibid., 15.

45. For more on Stephen Williams and the Deerfield raid see John Williams, "The Redeemed Captive Returning to Zion," *Puritans Among the Indians: Accounts of Captivity and Redemption 1676–1724*, ed. Alden T. Vaughan and Edward W. Clark (Cambridge: Harvard University Press, 1981), 167–226; John Demos, *The Unredeemed Captive: A Family Story from Early America* (New York: Vintage Books, 1995); Evan Haefeli and Kevin Sweeney, *Captors and Captives: The 1704 French and Indian Raid on Deerfield* (Amherst: University of Massachusetts Press, 2003).

46. "Conference at Deerfield," 18–19

47. Hopkins, *Historical Memoirs*, 6.

48. Wyss, *Writing Indians*, 86–95.

49. Hopkins writes that the school would be set up between two Native villages, "near some English families, in one of which Mr. Sergeant might live while he served them." Hopkins, *Historical Memoirs*, 9–10.

50. Frazier, *The Mohicans of Stockbridge*, 16. This is based on a paraphrase from a letter written by Stephen Williams in which he states that Konkapot was "apprehensive that the Religion of his Fore-fathers was not right." But it would be difficult to call this a direct quote from Konkapot. It is at best an interpretation, offered second hand. SC, Box 1, File 2: Sermon by Nathaniel Appleton, "Gospel Ministers Must Be Fit for the Master's Use and Prepared to Every Good Work," August 31, 1735, iii.

51. Hopkins, *Historical Memoirs*, 8. Frazier speculates that Ebenezer was a scout under Aupaumut during Gray Lock's War. Frazier, *The Mohicans of Stockbridge*, 20.

52. Hopkins, *Historical Memoirs*, 10.

53. Ibid., 11–12.

54. Frank G. Speck, *A Study of the Delaware Indian Big House Ceremony* (Harrisburg: Pennsylvania Historical Commission, 1931), 48. Mohegan medicine woman Gladys Tantaquidgeon speaks of the journey of the spirit after death on the beautiful white path. Here "stars are the advanced form taken by Indian people with extraordinary gifts of the spirit after they pass into the spirit world." Melissa Jayne Fawcett, *Medicine Trail: The Life and Lessons of Gladys Tantaquidgeon* (Tucson: University of Arizona Press, 2000), 3–5.

55. Hopkins, *Historical Memoirs*, 11–13.

56. Ibid., 23–24.

57. Ibid., 13, 15.

58. "Conference at Deerfield," 11.

59. Hopkins, *Historical Memoirs*, 16, 18

60. Ibid., 16, 17.

61. Ibid., 28.

62. Ibid., 21. SC, Box 1, File 2: Mr. Appleton's Sermon at the ordination of the Reverend Mr. John Sergeant, August 31, 1735, "Preface," vi.

63. A letter from Hopkins to Appleton, dated July 3, 1735, relates that the Mohican have gone as far westward as the Susquehanna to discuss the developments of the Stockbridge settlement. SC, Box 1, File 2: Sermon by Nathaniel Appleton, "Gospel Ministers Must Be Fit for the Master's Use and Prepared to Every Good Work," August 31, 1735, xi.

64. Occom, *Collected Works*, AN, 54.

65. Hopkins, *Historical Memoirs*, 18.

66. Ibid., 28–29.

67. SC, Box 1, File 2: Mr. Appleton's Sermon at the ordination of the Reverend Mr. John Sergeant, August 31, 1735, "Mr. Hopkins's Letter of July 3d, 1735," ix–x.

68. Hopkins, *Historical Memoirs*, 35.

69. SC, Box 1, File 2: Mr. Appleton's Sermon at the ordination of the Reverend Mr. John Sergeant, August 31, 1735, "Mr. Hopkins's Letter of July 3d, 1735," xi.

70. Ibid., xii.

71. Hopkins, *Historical Memoirs*, 48.

72. Ibid., 37.

73. Ibid., 38.

74. Ibid., 38.

75. Ibid., 38.

76. Ibid., 43.
77. Ibid., 44.
78. Skatekook was in the vicinity of present day Marlborough, Massachusetts. The word translates as "fork in the river," but this application may have referred to Umpachanee's kinship ties to the Schagticoke Mohican who were located further south in present-day Connecticut.
79. Hopkins, *Historical Memoirs*, 44. There is some suggestion in Hopkins that the Natives requested this consolidation themselves and the colonists were simply granting their wish. Frazier clarifies this, however, noting that Governor Belcher had first broached the subject in the 1735 Deerfield conference and later passed the idea along to the General Court as though it had come from the Housatunnuk themselves. Frazier, *The Mohicans of Stockbridge*, 39.
80. Hilary Wyss refers to the settlement "as an experiment in cross-cultural exchange," as an "Anglo-American-style township comprising both Christianized Natives and a small number of white settlers." Wyss, *Writing Indians*, 83.
81. Hopkins, *Historical Memoirs*, 48.
82. Ibid., 50.
83. Umpachanee's words are prophetic in this case. He is paraphrased as arguing that "because the land was in great Measure given to them, there might hereafter some Contention arise between their [Mohican] children and ours [English]; and that ours would look upon themselves to have a Superiority over theirs, because the Land was given them." See Hopkins, *Historical Memoirs*, 50.
84. Ibid., 51.
85. Perhaps a good example of this is the chapter heading Frazier uses to describe this period, "Approval on Both Sides." Frazier, *The Mohicans of Stockbridge*, 28–38.
86. Ibid., 47.
87. See SC, Box 1, File 7, Copy of Sergeant's Second Journal, April 1, 1739–March 30, 1740; Sergeant's Journal, June, 11, 1739. See also Frazier, *The Mohicans of Stockbridge*, 46.
88. SC, Sergeant's Journal, June 11, 1739.
89. SC, Sergeant's Journal, August 5, 1739.
90. Wyss, *Writing Indians*, 101–102.
91. SC, Sergeant's Journal, February 5, 1740.
92. Wyss, *Writing Indians*, 105.
93. Hopkins, *Historical Memoirs*, 65.
94. SC, Sergeant's Journal, October 21, 1739.
95. Ibid.
96. Ibid.
97. Ibid.
98. Hopkins, *Historical Memoirs*, 45
99. SC, Sergeant's Journal, March 27, 1740.
100. SC, Sergeant's Journal, October 21, 1739.
101. See Rachel Wheeler, *To Live Upon Hope: Mohicans and Missionaries in the Eighteenth-Century Northeast* (Ithaca: Cornell University Press, 2008), 175–180. Shekomeko was a Mohican village located on the Hudson River in Upstate New York

and visited by the Moravians in the 1740s. Because the records of this mission were kept in an esoteric German script, there have been few scholarly inroads made into its archive prior to Rachel Wheeler's recent work. Wheeler argues that the Mohican at Shekomeko were particularly open to the Moravian message, as it corresponded in significant ways with their own traditional belief systems. The Moravians apparently did not demand the kind of severe cultural concessions that were so important to the New England Congregationalists. And the Mohican, lacking the kind of monologic insistence in one God and one set of spiritual demands that is so central to most scriptural doctrine, were accepting of new frameworks and approaches to soliciting spiritual aid. Wheeler argues that the Mohicans of Shekomeko, while apparently finding strength in Moravian spirituality, were still able to maintain traditional epistemologies to an extent not generally acknowledged by incorporating Christian belief into their own sense of the world.

102. SC, Sergeant's Journal, March 27, 1740.

103. Hopkins, *Historical Memoirs*, 43.

104. SC, Sergeant's Journal, March 27, 1740.

105. Ibid.

106. Hopkins, *Historical Memoirs*, 83.

107. Ibid., 88.

108. Wheeler, *To Live Upon Hope*, 178.

109. Frazier, *The Mohicans of Stockbridge*, 54.

110. Ibid., 55.

111. SISC, Box 1 File 29, "Decree of General Assembly at Boston," December 30, 1749.

112. This practice is articulated by Plymouth colonist Edward Winslow who, according to their (the Natives') "laudable custom," travels to see Massasoit upon his presumed deathbed in 1623 and finds his wigwam filled with hundreds who had come to pay their respects. See Edward Winslow, *Good Newes from New England* (Bedford, MA: Applewood Press, 1624), 31–39.

113. Wheeler, *To Live Upon Hope*, 178–180.

114. In May of 1775 a letter was intercepted by the English armies that was written by Joseph Brant in the Iroquoian language and apparently translated by one of the Stockbridge Natives. In the letter Brant, a Mohawk, is appealing to the Oneida to offer support and protection to Guy Johnson, son of the powerful superintendent of Indian affairs, William Johnson. It is essentially a plea for loyalty to the British crown as the Revolutionary War gets under way. See SISC, Box 1, File 6.

115. SC, Sergeant's Journal, January 20, 1740.

116. SC, Sergeant's Journal, January 20, 1740.

117. PL, "Mohican Warriors: A Documentary History (1747–1813)," compiled by Leon G. Miles, 5.

118. SISC, Box 1, File 27. "A Journal of a Scoute of Leiut. Jacob of the Stockbridge Indians," August 13, 1756 (original copy in Louden Collection, 1480).

119. SISC, Box 1, File 27. "Instructions for Captain Jacob Chuksunkin Sept. 2, 1756." (original copy in Louden Collection, no. 1679). For thoughts on the practice of scalping, one should refer to James Axtell and William C. Sturtevant, "The Unkindest Cut, or Who Invented Scalping?" *William and Mary Quarterly* 37, no. 3

(July 1980): 451–472. The authors argue against what they term the "new wisdom," that in the 1970s began to argue against the traditional notion that scalping was the custom of primitive "savages," indigenous to America. Despite the feel-good impetus of this new revised version, the authors find that the preponderance of evidence suggests that scalping was in fact an indigenous custom. Nevertheless, they don't deny that the custom was exacerbated by bounties placed on Native scalps by the colonial governments.

120. SISC, Box 1, File 27. "A Journal of a Scoute of Leiut. Jacob of the Stockbridge Indians," August 13, 1756 (original copy in Louden Collection, 1480). Jacob Naunaumpaataunk would serve the English as a scout for at least the next four years. He rose to the rank of captain, but was taken prisoner by the St. Francis Indians in 1759. He was redeemed through a prisoner exchange in 1760.

121. W. Deloss Love, *Samson Occom and the Christian Indians of New England* (Syracuse, NY: Syracuse University Press, [1899] 2000), 57.

122. Eleazar Wheelock, "A Plain and Faithful Narrative of the Original Design, Rise, Progress and Present State of the Indian Charity-School at Lebanon, in Connecticut," (1763) *Early American Imprints*, series 1, no. 9537.

123. *The Letters of Eleazar Wheelock's Indians*, ed. James Dow McCallum (Hanover: Dartmouth College Publications, 1932), 51.

124. Ibid., 58.

125. Ibid., 54–55.

126. Ibid., 91.

127. Ibid., 63.

128. Ibid., 21.

129. Love, *Samson Occom*, 223.

130. Ibid., 207.

131. Murray, *To Do Good*, 23.

132. This coming from Lieutenant Commander John Young of the Royal American Regiment. Quoted in Love, *Samson Occom*, 65.

133. Ibid., 65.

134. Quoted in Murray, *To Do Good*, 26.

135. According to church records at Groton, Johnson was born in 1751 and baptized on June 3rd of that year. However, an enigmatic passage in Occom's first journal speaks of Occom meeting up with Joseph Johnson Sr. in April of 1745 and traveling with him to Groton. He writes, "and there I saw Joseph, was the first time that I ever saw him." Occom, *Collected Writings*, 249. Joanna Brooks supposes this to be the infant Joseph Johnson, although the event occurs five years prior to his recorded birth. This could be a discrepancy in the records, or perhaps Occom is speaking of another Joseph altogether (perhaps a first Joseph Johnson who died in infancy). Johnson himself notes that he was twenty-one years of age when he came back from his whaling trip to Mohegan in 1771, which would conform with the 1751 birth date.

136. *Letters of Eleazar Wheelock's Indians*, 76–77.

137. Joseph Johnson, *To Do Good to My Indian Brethren: The Writings of Joseph Johnson*, 1751–1776, ed. Laura J. Murray (Amherst: University of Massachusetts Press, 1998), 60. Most of Johnson's writings can be located at the Connecticut Historical

Society in Hartford, Connecticut. Some of his correspondence remains with the Wheelock papers at Dartmouth Library.

138. Ibid., 60.

139. See Occom's letters, Occom, *Collected Writings*, 64–139.

140. Murray, introduction, *To Do Good*, 15.

141. Johnson, *To Do Good*, 61.

142. In truth, as Laura Murray notes, "every one of Wheelock's Indian students who lived long enough or studied long enough to take up a post in the field did break with Wheelock." See Laura J. Murray, " 'Pray Sir, consider a little': Rituals of Subordination and Strategies of Resistance in the Letters of Hezekiah Calvin and David Fowler to Eleazar Wheelock," *Early Native American Writing, New Critical Essays*, ed. Helen Jaskoski (Cambridge: Cambridge University Press, 1996), 19. Wheelock underpaid his Indian missionaries or left them entirely to their own devices, and they often labored under great financial and physical want in endeavoring to meet Wheelock's objectives. Generally their letters to him, requesting funds, clothing, or simply acknowledgment of their work, went unanswered.

143. Johnson, *To Do Good*, 67.

144. Ibid., 76, 70.

145. Ibid., 73.

146. The quote is from John Dryden, *Oedipus: A Tragedy* (London: J. Darby, A. Bettesworth and F. Clay, 1727), 53.

147. Johnson, *To Do Good*, 73.

148. Ibid., 78.

149. Ibid., 71.

150. Ibid., 74.

151. Ibid., 61–77.

152. Ibid., 192.

153. Ibid., 65.

154. Ibid., 126.

155. Ibid., 126.

156. Murray, *To Do Good*, 85.

157. Johnson, *To Do Good*, 95, 104.

158. Ibid., 98, 110.

159. Ibid., 122.

160. Ibid., 114.

161. Ibid., 123.

162. Ibid., 127.

163. Ibid., 92–114.

164. Ibid., 108.

165. See Murray, *To Do Good*, 86–87, for her assessment of Zachary Johnson's opposition to Occom.

166. Johnson, *To Do Good*, 103.

167. Ibid., 121.

168. Ibid., 108, 138.

169. Ibid., 109.

170. Apparently Johnson lost his father's letters a few years later. He wrote to Occom in something of a panic that "my father's pocket Book is not here, neither do I know where it is. I have none of my father's writing, I think, at least I cant find any now" (Johnson, *To Do Good*, 232). It is not clear why Occom wished to refer to the letters of Johnson's father. Perhaps he simply wished to know that they were preserved for the sake of history. What a loss this must have been to Johnson, and to history in general.

171. Ibid., 139.

172. On December 7, 1771, Moses Paul waited outside of Clark's Tavern in Bethany, Connecticut where he was boarding, and struck and killed Moses Cook with a club when the latter exited the establishment. While the traditional handling of the case presented the event as a result of the Indian weakness for drink and the subsequent relapse into savage behavior, there is reason to believe that Paul was, at any rate, provoked by Cook and that the two had gotten into a more extended fight outside the tavern doors. It was not a case of a simple ambush. Paul was born in 1742 in Barnstable, Massachusetts, probably of Wampanoag or Pequot descent, and was bound out at an early age to work for local white families. His father served with the English in the Battle of Louisbourg in 1745. Paul, himself, served in the Provincial Service under Colonel Putnam's Company. See the broadside entitled, "A Short Account of the Life of Moses Paul (an Indian) Who Is This Day to Be Executed in New Haven," September 2, 1772, *Early American Imprints*, series 1, no. 42358.

173. For centuries accounts detailing Moses Paul's murder of Moses Cook have shared the biases of the overall colonial community that ascribed to the Indian qualities of low self-control and intellectual ability. Ava Chamberlain's recent article, "The Execution of Moses Paul: A Story of Crime and Contact in Eighteenth-Century Connecticut," reveals the racial undercurrents that had been elided from this narrative, showing Cook, in fact, to be the aggressor, and detailing the racial biases inherent in the colonial justice system that, while offering Paul access to all the legal procedures and rights of a white convict, nevertheless, were incapable of hearing Paul's side of the story or viewing an Indian act of violence against a white man as anything less than savage.

174. See Ava Chamberlain, "The Execution of Moses Paul: A Story of Crime and Contact in Eighteenth Century Connecticut," *New England Quarterly* 77, no. 3 (September 2004): 436.

175. OP, *A Sermon at the Execution of Moses Paul, an Indian Who Had Been Guilty of Murder* (New Haven, 1789), A-3.

176. Occom's sermon went through nineteen editions in the eighteenth and nineteenth centuries and according to Joanna Brooks, it not only places him in the forefront of the American sermon tradition but marked his public emergence as "an intertribal spiritual and political leader." Brooks, *Collected Writings*, 162, 164. I use this 1789 version of Occom's sermon here, as it contains the added dialogue and introduction from which I also quote.

177. A verse from the broadside reads: "Tis Drunkenness, this is the Sin you know, / Has been and is poor Indians overthrow;/ 'Twas Drunkeness that was the leading Cause, / That made poor Moses break God's righteous Law." See the

broadside entitled "Mr. Occom's Address to His Indian Brethren, on the Day That Moses Paul, an Indian, Was Executed at New Haven," 1773, *Early American Imprints*, series 1, no. 12911.

178. OP, *A Sermon at the Execution*, 2.

179. Ibid., 1.

180. Ibid., A-3.

181. David Murray, *Forked Tongues: Speech, Writing and Representation in North American Indian Texts* (Bloomington: Indiana University Press, 1991), 45.

182. Samson Occom, from "A Sermon Preached at the Execution of Moses Paul, an Indian," *Collected Writings*, 189.

183. David Murray notes that Occom stage-manages the stage-managing by addressing the crowd separately in regards to ethnicity and creating a moment of cultural eavesdropping, so that the white audience may listen in to an appeal by Indian to Indian. By doing this Murray concedes that Occom turns the event, "if only marginally, to his own purposes." Murray, *Forked Tongues*, 46–47.

184. "The Death of Moses Paul," *Connecticut Courant*, September 1–September 8, 1772, no. 402, 3.

185. Occom, *Collected Writings*, 376.

186. Chamberlain, "The Execution of Moses Paul."

187. Johnson, *To Do Good*, 141–146.

188. Johnson, *To Do Good*, 141.

189. Ibid., 142.

190. Ibid., 144.

191. Ibid., 145.

192. Ibid., 146.

193. Ibid., 151.

194. Ibid., 147–150.

195. Ibid., 149.

196. Ibid., 165.

197. Ibid., 160–161.

198. Joanna Brooks, *American Lazarus: Religion and the Rise of African-American and Native American Literatures* (New York: Oxford University Press, 2003), 69.

199. Occom, AN.

200. Johnson, *To Do Good*, 157.

201. Ibid., 165.

202. Occom, *Collected Works*, 236.

203. Laura J. Murray, "Introduction," *To Do Good*, 5.

204. Richardson, *An Indian Preacher*, 315.

205. Ibid., 352.

206. Ibid., 352.

207. Although it must be confessed that once Brothertown is established Wheelock manages to send two white missionaries to the settlement, who then become the source of a great deal of friction in the religious community there. See Wyss, *Writing Indians*, 123–153.

208. Johnson, *To Do Good*, 160.

209. Ibid., 181.

210. Ibid., 190.

211. Ibid., 190. In Laura Murray's article "'Pray sir, consider a little'" and Dana D. Nelson's "'(I Speak Like A Fool But I Am Constrained)': Samson Occom's Short Narrative and the Economies of the Racial Self," in *Early American Native Writing: New Critical Essays*, ed. Helen Jaskoski (Cambridge: Cambridge University Press, 1996), we see the obsequious manner that Wheelock seems to have cultivated in his Indian students.

212. Johnson, *To Do Good*, 190–191.

213. Ibid., 198–200.

214. Ibid., 194–195. I should note that "removal" is a word that Johnson himself often uses to refer to the emigration to Brothertown. Johnson, *To Do Good*, 235.

215. Ibid., 225.

216. Ibid., 225, 266.

217. Ibid., 234.

218. Ibid., 206.

219. The Covenant Chain was a term for the alliance between the Five Nations and the English, first established by Governor Andros and the Iroquois in the late seventeenth century, and ending a long period of conflict between the two powers. The rituals of this alliance were established in accordance with the rites of the condolence ceremony and the Great League of Peace, and these rituals were sealed with the exchange of wampum. See Daniel K. Richter, *The Ordeal of the Long House: The Peoples of the Iroquois League in the Era of European Colonization* (Chapel Hill: University of North Carolina Press, 1992), 133–161.

220. Johnson, *To Do Good*, 232.

221. Ibid., 192.

222. Laura J. Murray, "What Did Christianity Do for Joseph Johnson? A Mohegan Preacher and His Community," *Possible Pasts: Becoming Colonial in Early America*, ed. Robert Blair St. George (Ithaca, NY: Cornell University Press, 2000), 165.

223. Johnson married Tabitha sometime in 1773. There are a number of letters between Johnson and Samson Occom in the first two weeks of October wherein Johnson asks Occom for permission to marry his daughter (Johnson, *To Do Good*, 192–201). Johnson reveals his intentions to Tabitha in a letter dated November 5, 1773 (Johnson, *To Do Good*, 202). And by August 26th of 1774 Johnson writes to Tabitha from Dartmouth as "My dear, and well beloved wife" (Johnson, *To Do Good*, 240). Somewhere between November 1773 and August 1774 they were married. Johnson also obtained his license to preach on August 25, 1774.

224. Ibid., 224.

225. Ibid., 255.

226. Ibid., 252.

227. Ibid., 265.

228. Ibid., 281.

229. Love, *Samson Occom*, 230.

230. Love suggests that the settlement was hastily abandoned during the attack on Fort Schuyler by the British army. Love, *Samson Occom*, 231–232.

231. *CMHS* 9, "Numbers and Names of the Mohegans," 76.

232. Frazier, *The Mohicans of Stockbridge*, 224.

233. Ibid., 226.

234. SISC, Box 1, File 2. "Copy of an Indian Petition," September 2, 1783. The note is cosigned by Johoiakim Motokson, Joseph Shaugushqueat, Jehoikakim Naunnaphtonk, and Joseph Quononikaut.

235. Wyss, *Writing Indians*, 122.

236. Johnson, *To Do Good*, 225.

237. Quoted in Jones, *Stockbridge, Past and Present*, 86.

Afterword. O' Brothertown, Where Art Thou?

1. Samson Occom, "Occom's 12th Journal, October 24, 1785," *The Collected Writings of Samson Occom, Mohegan: Leadership and Literature in Eighteenth-Century Native America* (New York: Oxford University Press, 2006), 306.

2. Occom, "The Slow Traveller, or, O Happy Souls How Fast You Go," *Collected Writings*, 235.

3. Ibid., 308–309.

4. Hilary Wyss writes that the condition for equality in Brothertown is "the disempowerment of Native women, and thus the founders of Brothertown find themselves aligned with Anglo-American social model." Hilary Wyss, *Writing Indians: Literacy, Christianity, and Native Community in Early America* (Amherst: University of Massachusetts Press, 2000), 139.

5. See William Cooper, *A Guide in the Wilderness or the History of the Settlements in the Western Counties of New York with Useful Instructions for Future Settlers* (Dublin: Gilbert & Hodges, 1810). Occom, "Journal 12, November 9, 1785," *Collected Writings*, 309.

6. Ibid., 309. Occom would relocate in Brothertown for good in 1789.

7. Occom, "Journal 19, July 13, 1787," *Collected Writings*, 373.

8. Occom, "Journal 16, July 30, 1786," *Collected Writings*, 339

9. Occom, "Journal 16, Oct. 1, 1786," *Collected Writings*, 343.

10. Electra F. Jones, *Stockbridge, Past and Present or, Records of an Old Mission Station* (Springfield, MA: Samuel Bowles & Co., 1854), 87.

11. Occom, "Mahican-Stockbridge Tribe to Samson Occom, Aug. 27, 1787," *Collected Writings*, 154.

12. Jones, *Stockbridge, Past and Present*, 93.

13. Occom, "Brothertown Tribe to United States Congress [1785?]," *Collected Writings*, 149.

14. See Ava Chamberlain, "The Execution of Moses Paul: A Story of Crime and Contact in Eighteenth-Century Connecticut," *New England Quarterly* 77, no. 3 (September 2004): 436.

15. Occom, "Indians Must have teachers of their own Coular or Nation, Nov. 1791," *Collected Writings*, 134.

16. Love, *Samson Occom*, 175.

17. William Buell Sprague, *Annals of the American Presbyterian Pulpit or Commemorative Notices of Distinguished Clergymen of the Presbyterian Church in the United States*, vol. 3 (New York: Robert Carter and Bros., 1860), 195.

18. Ibid., 195.
19. Ibid., 195.
20. See Gerald Vizenor, *Manifest Manners: Postindian Warriors of Survivance* (Hanover, NH: Wesleyan University Press, 1994).

Bibliography

Allen, Chadwick. *Blood Narrative: Indigenous Identity in American Indian and Maori Literary and Activist Texts*. Durham, NC: Duke University Press, 2002.

Amory, Hugh. *Bibliography and the Book Trades: Studies in the Print Culture of Early New England*, ed. David Hall. Philadelphia: University of Pennsylvania Press, 2005.

———. *First Impressions: Printing in Cambridge, 1639–1989*. Cambridge, MA: President and Fellows of Harvard College, 1989.

Apess, William. *On Our Own Ground: The Complete Writings of William Apess, A Pequot*, ed. Barry O'Connell. Amherst: University of Massachusetts Press, 1992.

Axtell, James. *After Columbus: Essays in the Ethnohistory of Colonial North America*. New York: Oxford University Press, 1988.

Bangs, Jeremy Dupertuis. *Indian Deeds: Land Transactions in Plymouth County*. Boston: New England Historic Genealogical Society, 2002.

Banks, Charles Edward. *History of Martha's Vineyard Mass*, Vol. 1. Edgartown: Dukes County Historical Society, 1966.

Blodgett, Harold. *Samson Occom*. Hanover, NH: Dartmouth College Publications, 1935.

Boone, Elizabeth Hill, and Walter D. Mignolo. *Writing Without Words: Alternative Literacies in Mesoamerica and the Andes*, ed. Elizabeth Hill Boone and Walter D. Mignolo. Durham, NC: Duke University Press, 1994.

Boudinot, Elias. *Cherokee Editor: The Writings of Elias Boudinot*, ed. Theda Perdue. Athens: University of Georgia Press, 1983.

Bourne, Russell. *The Red King's Rebellion: Racial Politics in New England 1675–1678*. New York: Oxford University Press, 1990.

Bradford, William. *Of Plymouth Plantation: The Pilgrims in America*, ed. Harvey Wish. New York: Capricorn Books, 1962.

Bragdon, Kathleen J. "Crime and Punishment among the Indians of Massachusetts, 1675–1750." *EthnoHistory* 28, no. 1 (Winter 1981): 23–32.

———. *Native People of Southern New England 1500–1650*. Norman: University of Oklahoma Press, 1996.

Brave Heart, Maria Yellow Horse, and Lymera DeBruyn. "The American Indian Holocaust: Healing Historical Unresolved Grief." *American Indian and Alaska Native Mental Health Research* 8, no. 2 (1998): 60–82.

Brooks, Joanna. *American Lazarus: Religion and the Rise of African-American and Native American Literatures*. New York: Oxford University Press, 2003.

Brooks, Lisa. *The Common Pot: The Recovery of Native Space in the Northeast*. Minneapolis: University of Minnesota Press, 2008.

Brown, Fred B. "The Broken Treaty." *Narragansett Dawn*, May 1935, no.1.

Bruyneel, Kevin. *The Third Place of Sovereignty: The Postcolonial Politics of US-Indigenous Relations*. Minneapolis: University of Minnesota Press, 2007.

Bulkley, John. "An Inquiry into the Right of the Aboriginal Natives to the Lands in America, and the Titles Derived from Them." 1724, CMHS IV.

Burnham, Dorothy. *To Please the Caribou: Painted Caribou-Skin Coats Worn by the Naskapi, Montagnais, and Cree Hunters of the Quebec-Labrador Peninsula*. Seattle: University of Washington Press, 1992.

Calloway, Colin G. *Western Abenaki of Vermont 1600–1800: War, Migration and the Survival of an Indian People*. Norman: University of Oklahoma Press, 1990.

Carlson, Hans M. *Home Is the Hunter: The James Bay Cree and Their Land*. Vancouver: UBC Press, 2008.

Caruth, Cathy. *Unclaimed Experience: Trauma, Narrative and History*. Baltimore: Johns Hopkins University Press, 1996.

Cave, Alfred A. *The Pequot War*. Amherst: University of Massachusetts Press, 1996.

Ceci, Lynn. "Wampum as a Peripheral Resource in the Seventeenth-Century World System." *The Pequots in Southern New England: The Fall and Rise of an American Indian Nation*, ed. Laurence M. Hauptman and James D. Wherry. Norman: University of Oklahoma Press, 1990.

Chamberlain, Ava. "The Execution of Moses Paul: A Story of Crime and Contact in Eighteenth-Century Connecticut." *New England Quarterly* 77, no. 3 (September 2004): 414–450.

Clark, Michael P., ed. *The Eliot Tracts*. Westport, CT: Praeger Press, 2003.

Cogley, Richard. *John Eliot's Mission to the Indians Before King Philip's War*. Cambridge: Harvard University Press, 1999.

Columbus, Christopher. *The Four Voyages*, ed. and trans. J. M. Cohen. New York: Penguin Books, 1969.

Connole, Dennis A. *The Indians of the Nipmuck Country in Southern New England, 1630–1750: An Historical Geography*. Jefferson, NC: McFarland Company, 2001.

Cooper, James Fenimore. *The Last of the Mohicans*. New York: Oxford University Press, 1980.

———. *The Pioneers*. New York: Oxford University Press, 1980.

Cooper, William. *A Guide in the Wilderness, or a History of the Settlements in the Western Counties of New York with Useful Instructions for Future Settlers*. Dublin: Gilbert and Hodges, 1810.

Costa, Jose de. *A Natural and Moral History of the Indes*, ed. Jane E. Mangan, trans. Frances M. Lopez-Morillas. Durham, NC: Duke University Press, 2002.

Cronon, William. *Changes in the Land: Indians, Colonists, and the Ecology of New England*. New York: Hill and Wang, 1983.

De Forest, John W. *History of the Indians of Connecticut from the Earliest Known Period to 1850*. Hamden, CT: Archon Books, 1964.

Delabarre, Edmund Burke. *Dighton Rock: A Study of the Written Rocks of New England.* New York: Walter Neale, 1928.

Deloria, Vine Jr. *God Is Red: A Native View of Religion.* Golden, CO: Fulcrum Publishing, 1992.

———. "Traditional Technology." *Winds of Change* 5, no. 2 (Spring 1990): 20–23.

Deloria, Vine Jr., and Daniel R. Wildcat. *Power and Place: Indian Education in America.* Golden, CO: Fulcrum Resources, 2001.

Derrida, Jacques. *Archive Fever: A Freudian Impression*, trans. Eric Prenowitz. Chicago: University of Chicago Press, 1996.

———. *Dissemination*, trans. Barbara Johnson. Chicago: University of Chicago Press, 1981.

Dewdney, Selwyn. *The Sacred Scrolls of the Southern Ojibway.* Toronto: University of Toronto Press, 1975.

Diaz, Bernal. *The Conquest of New Spain*, trans. J. M. Cohen. New York: Penguin, 1963.

Doughton, Thomas. "Notes on the Nipmuc Indian Reservation at Hassanamesit or Hassanamisco and the Nipmuc People of Hassanamesit, later Grafton, Massachusetts." http://freepages.genealogy.rootsweb.com/com/~massasoit/grafton1.htm.

Drake, James D. *King Philip's War: Civil War in New England, 1675–1676.* Amherst: University of Massachusetts Press, 1999.

Drake, Samuel. *Biography and History of the Indians of North America, from Its First Discovery.* Boston: Benjamin B. Mussey & Co., 1841.

Dryden, John. *Oedipus: A Tragedy.* London: J. Darby, A. Bettesworth and F. Clay, 1727.

Duran, Diego. *The History of the Indes of New Spain*, trans. Doris Heyden. Norman: University of Oklahoma Press, 1994.

Dwight, Timothy. "Greenfield Hill." *The Heath Anthology of American Literature*, Vol. A, ed. Paul Lauter. Boston: Houghton Mifflin Co., 2006.

Eliot, John. *John Eliot's Indian Dialogues: A Study in Cultural Interaction*, ed. Henry W. Bowden and James P. Ronda. Westport, CT: Greenwood Press, 1980.

Fawcett, Melissa Jayne. *The Lasting of the Mohegans.* Uncasville, CT: Mohegan Tribe, 1995.

———. *Medicine Trail: The Life and Lessons of Gladys Tantaquidgeon.* Tucson: University of Arizona Press, 2000.

Ford, John W. *Some Correspondence Between the Governors and Treasurers of the New England Company in London and the Commissioners of the United Colonies in America: The Missionaries of the Company and Others Between the Years 1657 and 1712*, ed. John W. Ford. New York: Burt Franklin, 1970.

Frazier, Patrick. *The Mohicans of Stockbridge.* Lincoln: University of Nebraska Press, 1992.

Goddard, Ives, and Kathleen J. Bragdon. *Native Writings in Massachusett.* Philadelphia: American Philosophical Society, 1988.

Gookin, Daniel. *An Historical Account of the Doings and Sufferings of the Christian Indians in New England in the Years 1675, 1676, 1677.* New York: Arno Press.

———. "Historical Collections of the Indians of New England." *Collections of the Massachusetts Historical Society* (CMHS) I. Boston: Munroe & Francis, 1806, 1674.

Gray, Robert. *A Good Speed to Virginia*. New York: Da Capo Press, 1970.
Hale, Horatio, ed. *The Iroquois Book of Rites*. Toronto: University of Toronto Press, 1963.
Hall, David D. *Worlds of Wonder, Days of Judgment: Popular Religious Belief in Early New England*. Cambridge: Harvard University Press, 1989.
Hariot, Thomas. "A Briefe and True Report of the New Found Land of Virginia." *The English Literatures of America, 1500–1800*, ed. Myra Jehlen and Michael Warner. New York: Routledge, 1987.
Heckewelder, John. *History, Manners, and Customs of the Indian Nations Who Once Inhabited Pennsylvania and the Neighboring States*. Philadelphia: Publication Fund of the Historical Society of Pennsylvania, 1876.
Herman, Judith. *Trauma and Recovery: The Aftermath of Violence—from Domestic Abuse to Political Terror*. New York: Basic Books, 1992.
Hopkins, Samuel. *Historical Memoirs Relating to the Housatunnuk Indians*. Boston: Kneeland Publishing, 1911.
Hubbard, William. *The History of the Indian Wars in New England from the First Settlement to the Termination of the War with King Philip, in 1677*. Roxbury, MA: W. Elliot Woodward, 1865.
Hudson, Nicholas. *Writing and European Thought 1600–1830*. Cambridge: Cambridge University Press, 1994.
Hultkrantz, Ake. *The North American Indian Orpheus Tradition: A Contribution to Comparative Religion*. Stockholm: Ethnographical Museum of Sweden, 1957.
Jaskoski, Helen. *Early Native American Writing: New Critical Essays*, ed. Helen Jaskoski. New York: Cambridge University Press, 1996.
Jennings, Francis. *The Invasion of America: Indians, Colonialism, and the Cant of Conquest*. Chapel Hill: University of North Carolina Press, 2010.
Johnson, Joseph. *To Do Good to My Indian Brethren: The Writings of Joseph Johnson, 1751–1776*, ed. Laura J. Murray. Amherst: University of Massachusetts Press, 1998.
Johnston, Basil. *The Manitous: The Spiritual World of the Ojibwe*. St. Paul: Minnesota Historical Society Press, 1995.
Jones, Electra F. *Stockbridge, Past and Present, or Records of an Old Mission Station*. Springfield: Samuel Bowles & Co., 1854.
Josselyn, John. *John Josselyn, Colonial Traveler: A Critical Edition of Two Voyages to New-England*, ed. Paul J. Lindholt. Hanover, NH: University of New England Press, 1988.
Kalter, Susan, ed. "A Treaty Held at the Town of Lancaster in Pennsylvania." *Benjamin Franklin, Pennsylvania, and the First Nations: The Treaties of 1732–62*. Urbana: University of Illinois Press, 2006.
Kellaway, William. *The New England Company, 1649–1776*. Missionary Society to the American Indians. Westport, CT: Greenwood Press, 1961.
Kenton, Edna, ed. *The Jesuit Relations and Allied Documents: Travels and Explorations of the Jesuit Missionaries in North America 1610–1791*. New York: Albert & Charles Boni, 1925.
King, Thomas. *The Truth About Stories: A Native Narrative*. Minneapolis: University of Minnesota Press, 2003.

Kupperman, Karen Ordahl. *The Jamestown Project*. Cambridge: The Belknap Press at Harvard University Press, 2007.

Las Casas, Bartolomé de. *In Defense of the Indians*, trans. Stafford Poole. DeKalb: Northern Illinois University Press, 1992.

Leach, Douglas Edward. *Flintlock and Tomahawk: New England in King Philip's War*. Hyannis, MA: Parnassus Imprints, 1958.

Lechford, Thomas. "Plain Dealing: or Newes from New-England." *CMHS* III, series 3 (1642).

Lenik, Edward J. *Picture Rocks: American Indian Rock Art in the Northeast Woodlands*. Hanover, NH: University Press of New England, 2002.

Leon-Portilla, Miguel, ed. *The Broken Spears: The Aztec Account of the Conquest of Mexico*. Boston: Beacon Press, 1962.

Lepore, Jill. *The Name of War: King Philip's War and the Origins of American Identity*. New York: Vintage Books, 1998.

Lincoln, C. H., ed. "The Present State of New-England with Respect to the Indian War." *Narratives of the Indian Wars, 1675–1699*. New York: Barnes and Noble, 1913.

Lithgow, R. A. Douglas. *Native American Place Names in Massachusetts*. Bedford, MA: Applewood Books, 1909.

Littlefield, George Emery. *The Early Massachusetts Press 1638–1711*. New York: Burt Franklin, 1907.

Longfellow, Henry Wadsworth. "The Song of Hiawatha." *Longfellow: Poems and Other Writings*. New York: Library of America, 2000.

Love, William Deloss. *Samson Occom and the Christian Indians of New England*. Syracuse: Syracuse University Press, 2000.

Madsen, Deborah L. "On Subjectivity and Survivance: Rereading Trauma through *The Heirs of Columbus* and *The Crown of Columbus*." *Survivance: Narratives of Native Presence*, ed. Gerald Vizenor. Lincoln: University of Nebraska Press, 2008.

Mallory, Garrick. *Picture Writing of the American Indians*. New York: Dover Publications, 1972.

Mandell, Daniel. "'Standing by His Father': Thomas Waban of Natick, circa 1630–1722." *Northeastern Indian Lives 1632–1816*, ed. Robert S. Grumet. Amherst: University of Massachusetts Press, 1996.

Mann, Barbara A. "The Lynx in Time: Haudenosaunee Women's Tradition and History." *American Indian Quarterly* 21, no. 3 (Summer 1997): 423–449.

Mather, Cotton. *Diary of Cotton Mather*, Vol. 1, 1681–1709. New York: Frederick Ungar Publishing Co., 1911.

———. *Magnalia Christi Americana or the Ecclesiastical History of New England*, Vol. 1. Hartford: Silus Andrus, 1820.

———. "The Wonderful Works of God Commemorated." *Early American Imprints*, series 1: Evans Digital Display (2006): 4, http://infoweb.newsbank.com.

Mayhew, Thomas. *A Further Discovery of the Present State of the Indians*, compiled by Henry Whitfield. New York: Sabin's Reprints, 1865.

McCallum, James Dow, ed. *The Letters of Eleazar Wheelock's Indians*. Hanover: Dartmouth College Manuscript Series, 1932.

McClure, David, and Elijah Parish. *Memoirs of the Reverend Eleazar Wheelock, D. D.* New York: Arno Press, 1972.

McCutchen, David. *Wallam Olum or Red Score: The Migration Record of the Lenni Lenape or Delaware Indians*. Indianapolis: Indiana Historical Society, 1954.

Merrell, James H. "Introduction: Indians and Colonists in Early America." *The Lancaster Treaty of 1744 with Related Documents*, ed. James H. Merrell. Boston: Bedford / St. Martin's, 2008.

Meserve, Walter T. "English Works of Seventeenth-Century Indians." *American Quarterly* 8, no. 3 (Autumn 1956): 264–276.

Mooney, James. *Myths of the Cherokee*. Washington, DC: U.S. Government Printing Office, 1900.

Morison, Samuel Eliot. *Builders of the Bay Colony*. Boston: Houghton Mifflin Co., 1930.

———. *The Founding of Harvard College*. Cambridge: Harvard University Press, 1935.

———. *Harvard College in the Seventeenth Century*. Cambridge: Harvard University Press, 1936.

Morton, Thomas. *New English Canaan*. New York: Da Capo Press, 1969.

Motolinia, Fray Toribio. *Motolinia's History of the Indians of New Spain*, trans. Elizabeth Andross Foster. Westport, CT: Greenwood Press, 1950.

Murray, David. *Forked Tongues: Speech, Writing and Representation in North American Indian Texts*. Bloomington: Indiana University Press, 1991.

Murray, Laura J. "What Did Christianity Do for Joseph Johnson? A Mohegan Preacher and His Community." *Possible Pasts: Becoming Colonial in Early America*, ed. Robert Blair St. George. Ithaca, NY: Cornell University Press, 2000.

Nabokov, Peter. *A Forest of Time: American Indian Ways of History*. Cambridge, UK: Cambridge University Press, 2002.

O'Brien, Jean. *Dispossession By Degrees: Indian Land and Identity in Natick, Massachusetts, 1650–1790*. New York: Cambridge University Press, 1997.

Occom, Samson. *The Collected Writings of Samson Occom, Mohegan: Leadership and Literature in Eighteenth-Century Native America*, ed. Joanna Brooks. New York: Oxford University Press, 2006.

Ong, Walter. *Orality and Literacy: The Technologizing of the Word*. London: Routledge, 1982.

Orr, Charles, ed. *History of the Pequot War*. Cleveland: Helman-Taylor Co., 1980.

Ortiz, Simon J. *From Sand Creek*. Tucson: University of Arizona Press, 1981.

Pagels, Elaine. *Adam, Eve, and the Serpent*. New York: Vintage Books, 1988.

Pané, Fray Ramone. *An Account of the Antiquities of the Indians*, ed. Jose Juan Arrom, trans. Susan C. Griswold. Durham: Duke University Press, 1999.

Parker, Arthur C. "The Constitution of the Five Nations." *Parker on the Iroquois*, ed. William N. Fenton. Syracuse: Syracuse University Press, 1968.

———. *Seneca Myths and Folk Tales*. Buffalo: Buffalo Historical Society, 1923.

———. "Sources and Range of Cooper's Indian Lore." *New York History* 35, no. 4 (October 1954): 447–456.

Pearce, Roy Harvey. *Savagery and Civilization: A Study of the Indian and the American Mind*. Berkeley: University of California Press, 1988.

Peyer, Bernd. *The Elders Wrote: An Anthology of Early Prose by North American Indians, 1768–1931*. Berlin: Dietrich Reimer Verlag, 1982.

———. "Samson Occom: Mohegan Missionary and Writer of the 18th Century." *American Indian Quarterly* 6, no. 3–4 (1982): 208–217.

———. *The Tutor'd Mind: Indian Missionary Writers in Antebellum America*. Amherst: University of Massachusetts Press, 1997.

Pratt, Mary Louise. *Imperial Eyes: Travel Writing and Transculturation*. New York: Routledge Press, 1992.

Pritchard, Evan T. *Native New Yorkers: The Legacy of the Algonquian People of New York*. San Francisco: Council Oak Books, 2002.

Ramsey, Jerald. "From 'Mythic' to 'Fictive' in a Nez Perce Orpheus Myth." *Traditional Literatures of the American Indian: Texts and Interpretations*, ed. Karl Kroeber. Lincoln: University of Nebraska Press, 1981.

Richardson, Leon Burr, ed. *An Indian Preacher in England*. Hanover, NH: Dartmouth College Manuscript Series, 1933.

Richter, Daniel. *Facing East from Indian Country: A Native History of Early America*. Cambridge: Harvard University Press, 2001.

———. *The Ordeal of the Long House: The Peoples of the Iroquois League in the Era of European Colonization*. Chapel Hill: University of North Carolina Press, 1992.

Rolfe, John. *A True Relation of the State of Virginia Lefte by Sir Thomas Dale Knight in May Last 1616*. Charlottesville: University Press of Virginia, 1951.

Rousseau, Jean-Jacques. "Discourse on the Origin and the Foundations of Inequality Among Men." *The First and Second Discourses Together with the Replies to Critics and Essays on the Origin of Languages*, ed. and trans. Victor Gourevitch. New York: Harper & Row, 1986.

Rowlandson, Mary. *The Sovereignty and Goodness of God, Together with the Faithfulness of His Promises Displayed, Being a Narrative of the Captivity and Restoration of Mary Rowlandson and Related Documents*, ed. Neal Salisbury. Boston: St. Martin's Press, 1997.

Sahagun, Bernardino De. *Florentine Codex: General History of the Things of New Spain*, eds. Arthur J. O. Anderson and Charles Dibble. Santa Fe, NM: School of American Research and the University of Utah, 1982.

Said, Edward W. *Orientalism*. New York: Vintage Books, 1978.

Salisbury, Neal. *Manitou and Providence: Indians, Europeans, and the Making of New England, 1500–1643*. New York: Oxford University Press, 1982.

———. "Red Puritans: The 'Praying Indians' of Massachusetts Bay and John Eliot." *William and Mary Quarterly* 31, no. 1, series 3 (January 1974): 27–54.

Sayre, Gordon M. *Les Sauvages Americains: Representations of Native Americans in French and English Colonial Literature*. Chapel Hill: University of North Carolina Press, 1997.

Schmidt, David L., and Murdena Marshall, eds. *Mi'kmaq Hieroglyphic Prayers: Reading in North America's First Indigenous Script*. Halifax, NS: Nimbus Publications, 1995.

Schoolcraft, Henry Rowe. *Indian Legends*, ed. Mentor L. Williams. East Lansing: Michigan State University Press, 1991.

Scott, James C. *Domination and the Arts of Resistance: Hidden Transcripts*. New Haven: Yale University Press, 1990.

Scott, Winfield. "Excerpt from The Memoirs of Lieut. General Scott, LL.D.: Written by Himself." *Voices from the Trail of Tears*, ed. Vicki Rozema. Winston-Salem, NC: John F. Blair Publishers, 2003.

Seawall, Samuel. *The Diary of Samuel Sewall*, Vols. I and II, 1674–1708, ed. M. Halsey Thomas. New York: Farrar, Straus and Giroux, 1973.

Sedgwick, Catherine Maria. *Hope Leslie*, ed. Mary Kelley. New Brunswick, NJ: Rutgers University Press, 1987.

Shannon, Timothy J. *Iroquois Diplomacy on the Early American Frontier*. New York: Viking Press, 2008.

Silko, Leslie Marmon. "Language and Literature from a Pueblo Indian Perspective." *Nothing but the Truth: An Anthology of Native American Literature*, ed. John L. Purdy and James Ruppert. Upper Saddle River, NJ: Prentice Hall, 2001.

Silverman, David J. *Faith and Boundaries: Colonists, Christianity, and Community amongst the Wampanoag Indians of Martha's Vineyard, 1600–1871*. New York: Cambridge University Press, 2005.

Simmons, William S. *Spirit of the New England Tribes: Indian History and Folklore, 1620–1984*. Hanover, NH: University Press of New England, 1986.

Slotkin, Richard. *Regeneration through Violence: The Mythology of the American Frontier, 1600–1860*. Norman: University of Oklahoma Press, 1973.

Slotkin, Richard, and James K. Folsom, eds. *So Dreadful a Judgment: Puritan Responses to King Philip's War, 1676–1677*. Hanover, NH: Wesleyan University Press, 1978.

Smith, John. *Capt. John Smith: Writings with Other Narratives of Roanoke, Jamestown, and the First English Settlements of America*. New York: Library of America, 2007.

Speck, Frank G. *A Study of the Delaware Indian Big House Ceremony*. Harrisburg, PA: Pennsylvania Historical Commission, 1931.

Sprague, William Buell. *Annals of the American Presbyterian Pulpit or Commemorative Notices of Distinguished Clergymen of the Presbyterian Church in the United States*, Vol. 3. New York: Robert Carter and Bros., 1860.

Standing Bear, Luther. *Land of the Spotted Eagle*. Lincoln: University of Nebraska Press, 1978.

Stilgoe, John R. *Common Landscapes of America, 1580 to 1845*. New Haven: Yale University Press, 1982.

Szasz, Margaret Connell. *Indian Education in the American Colonies, 1607–1783*. Albuquerque: University of New Mexico Press, 1988.

Tanner, Adrian. "Foreword." Dorothy Burnham, *To Please the Caribou: Painted Caribou-Skin Coats Worn by the Naskapi, Montagnais, and Cree Hunters of the Quebec-Labrador Peninsula*. Seattle: University of Washington Press, 1992.

Taylor, Alan. *William Cooper's Town: Power and Persuasion on the Frontier of the Early American Republic*. New York: Vintage, 1995.

Tedlock, Dennis, trans. *Popul Vuh: The Definitive Edition of the Mayan Book of the Dawn of Life and the Glories of Gods and Kings*. New York: Simon and Schuster, 1985.

Tinker, George E. *Missionary Conquest: The Gospel and Native American Cultural Genocide*. Minneapolis: Fortress Press, 1993.

Tooker, William Wallace. *Cockenoe de Long Island: John Eliot's First Indian Teacher and the Story of His Career from the Early Records*. New York: Francis Harper, 1896.

Travers, Milton A. *The Wampanoag Indian Federation of the Algonquian Nation: Indian Neighbors of the Pilgrims*. Boston: Christopher Publishing House, 1957.

Treuer, David. *Native American Fiction: A User's Manual*. St. Paul: Graywolf Press, 2006.

Ulrich, Laurel Thatcher. *The Age of Homespun: Objects and Stories in the Creation of the American Myth*. New York: Alfred A. Knopf, 2001.

———. *Goodwives: Image and Reality in the Lives of Women in Northern New England, 1650–1750*. New York: Vintage Books, 1980.

Underhill, John. *Newes from America*. New York: Da Capo Press, [1638] 1971.

Utter, Jack. *American Indians: Answers to Today's Questions*. Lake Anne, MI: National Woodlands Publishing Co., 1993.

Van Lonkhuyzen, Harold W. "A Reappraisal of the Praying Indian: Acculturation, Conversion and Identity at Natick, Massachusetts, 1646." *New England Encounters: Indians and Euroamericans ca 1600–1850: Essays Drawn from New England Quarterly*, ed. Alden T. Vaughan. Boston: Northeastern University Press, 1999.

Vespucci, Amerigo. "Letter to Pier Soerini, Confalonier of the Republic of Florence." *The English Literatures of America 1500–1800*, ed. Myra Jehlen and Michael Warner. New York: Routledge, 1997.

Vizenor, Gerald. *Fugitive Poses: Native American Indian Scenes of Absence and Presence*. Lincoln: University of Nebraska Press, 1998.

———. *Manifest Manners: Postindian Warriors of Survivance*. Hanover, NH: University Press of New England, 1994.

———. *The People Named the Chippewa: Narrative Histories*. Minneapolis: University of Minnesota Press, 1984.

Wallace, Anthony F. C. *The Death and Rebirth of the Seneca*. New York: Knopf, 1970.

Wallace, Paul A. W. *White Roots of Peace: The Iroquois Book of Life*. Santa Fe: Clear Light Publishers, 1994.

Warrior, Robert Allen. *Tribal Secrets: Recovering American Indian Intellectual Traditions*. Minneapolis: University of Minnesota Press, 1995.

Warren, William. *History of the Ojibwe People*. St. Paul: Minnesota Historical Society Press, 1984.

Weaver, Jace. *That the People Might Live: Native American Literatures and Native American Community*. New York: Oxford University Press, 1997.

Wheeler, Rachel. *To Live Upon Hope: Mohicans and Missionaries in the Eighteenth-Century Northeast*. Ithaca, NY: Cornell University Press, 2008.

White, C. Albert. *A History of the Rectangular Survey System*. Washington, DC: U.S. Department of the Interior, 1983.

White, Richard. *The Middle Ground: Indians, Empires, and Republics in the Great Lakes Region, 1650–1815*. New York: Cambridge University Press, 1991.

Williams, Roger. *A Key into the Language of America*. Bedford, MA: Applewood Books, 1936.

———. *The Complete Writings of Roger Williams*, Vol. 6. New York: Russell & Russell, Inc., 1963.

Winship, George Parker. *The Cambridge Press, 1638–1692*. Freeport, NY: Books for Libraries Press, 1946.

Winslow, Edward. *A Relation or Journall of the Beginning and Proceeding of the English Plantation Setled at Plimoth*. London: John Bellamie, 1622.

———. *Good Newes from New England: A True Relation of Things Very Remarkable at the Plantation of Plimoth in New England*. Bedford, MA: Applewood Books, 1624.

Winslow, Ola. *Master Roger Williams: A Biography*. New York: Macmillan Company, 1957.

Winthrop, John. *History of New England from 1630 to 1649*, Vol. 1. Baltimore: Clearfield, 2003.

Wiseman, Frederick Matthew. *Voice of the Dawn: An Autohistory of the Abenaki Nation*. Hanover, NH: University Press of New England, 2001.

Wright, Harry Andrews, ed. *Indian Deeds of Hampden County*. Springfield, MA: 1905.

Womack, Craig. *Red on Red: Native American Literary Separatism*. Minneapolis: University of Minnesota Press, 1999.

Wood, William. *New England Prospect*, ed. Alden T. Vaughan. Amherst: University of Massachusetts Press, 1977.

Wyss, Hilary. *Writing Indians: Literacy, Christianity, and Native Community in Early America*. Amherst: University of Massachusetts Press, 2000.

Ziff, Larzer. *Writing in the New Nation: Prose, Print, and Politics in the Early United States*. New Haven, CT: Yale University Press, 1991.

Zinn, Howard. *On History*. New York: Seven Stories Press, 2001.

Index